Economics and Performativity

Economists do more than merely describe an external economic world. They shape it in the image of their theories and models. This idea, following the philosophy of language, proposes that economic theories are performative, and not only descriptive.

This idea has become a powerful critique of the scientificity of economics, since it removes the idea of an external world against which our description could be evaluated as truth. If any theory can become true, there are no true theories *per se* because there is no such thing as a pre-existing economy to describe. Is such a relativist stance a foregone conclusion? This is the question at stake in this book. Furthermore, the author asks whether any theory is able to "perform" social reality, or are there actually some limits to performativity? For philosophers, a performative statement is a statement that cannot fail to mean something, but can fail to do what it calls for. The state of the world may or may not be changed; the performative statement may be happy or unhappy. In economic terms, this can be interpreted as: some theories change the world while some do not. This book argues that this possibility of failure, a perspective previously missing from discussions on the subject, should be at the heart of any definition of failure.

Taking on the question of why some theories change the world while others do not, *Economics and Performativity* will be of interest to those studying advanced courses on the philosophy of economics as well as those studying and researching in the areas of the philosophy of sciences and sociology of science and economics.

Nicolas Brisset is an associate professor at the Université Côte d'Azur (GREDEG-CNRS), France, and an associate member of the Centre Walras-Pareto of the University of Lausanne, Switzerland. His areas of specialisation are the philosophy of social sciences, history of economic thought and economic sociology. More precisely, his research focuses on three issues: the interaction between economic theories and social reality, the history of economic thought under the Vichy regime, and the limits of commodification.

Routledge INEM Advances in Economic Methodology

Series Editor: Esther-Mirjam Sent
University of Nijmegen, the Netherlands

The field of economic methodology has expanded rapidly during the last few decades. This expansion has occurred in part because of changes within the discipline of economics, in part because of changes in the prevailing philosophical conception of scientific knowledge, and also because of various transformations within the wider society. Research in economic methodology now reflects not only developments in contemporary economic theory, the history of economic thought and the philosophy of science, but also developments in science studies, historical epistemology and social theorising more generally. The field of economic methodology still includes the search for rules for the proper conduct of economic science, but it also covers a vast array of other subjects and accommodates a variety of different approaches to those subjects.

The objective of this series is to provide a forum for the publication of significant works in the growing field of economic methodology. Since the series defines methodology quite broadly, it will include books on a wide range of different methodological subjects. The series is also open to a variety of different types of works: original research monographs, edited collections, as well as republication of significant earlier contributions to the methodological literature. The International Network for Economic Methodology (INEM) is proud to sponsor this important series of contributions to the methodological literature.

For more information about this series, please visit: www.routledge.com/Routledge-INEM-Advances-in-Economic-Methodology/book-series/SE0630.

Economics for Real
Aki Lehtinen, Jaako Kuorikoski and Petri Ylikoski

Philosophical Problems of Behavioural Economics
Stefan Heidl

Philosophy of Mathematics and Economics
Image, context and perspective
Thomas A. Boylan and Paschal F. O'Gorman

The Individual and the Other in Economic Thought
An introduction
Edited by Ragip Ege and Herrade Igersheim

Economics and Performativity

Exploring Limits, Theories and Cases

Nicolas Brisset
Translated by Mila Webb

Routledge
Taylor & Francis Group
LONDON AND NEW YORK

First published 2019
by Routledge
2 Park Square, Milton Park, Abingdon, Oxon OX14 4RN

and by Routledge
52 Vanderbilt Avenue, New York, NY 10017, USA

First issued in paperback 2020

Routledge is an imprint of the Taylor & Francis Group, an informa business

British Library Cataloguing in Publication Data
A catalogue record for this book is available from the British Library

Library of Congress Cataloging-in-Publication Data
Names: Brisset, Nicolas, 1986- author.
Title: Economics and performativity : exploring limits, theories and cases / Nicolas Brisset ; translated by Mila Webb. Other titles: Performativité des énoncés de la théorie économique. English
Description: Abingdon, Oxon ; New York, NY : Routledge, 2018. | Series: Routledge INEM advances in economic methodology ; 18 | Includes bibliographical references and index.
Identifiers: LCCN 2018012136 (print) | LCCN 2018013393 (ebook) | ISBN 9781315112077 (Ebook) | ISBN 9781138083790 (hardback : alk. paper)
Subjects: LCSH: Economics—Philosophy. | Performative (Philosophy)
Classification: LCC HB71 (ebook) | LCC HB71 .B7783513 2018 (print) | DDC 330.01—dc23
LC record available at https://lccn.loc.gov/2018012136

ISBN 13: 978-0-367-58819-9 (pbk)
ISBN 13: 978-1-138-08379-0 (hbk)

Typeset in Bembo
by Swales & Willis Ltd, Exeter, Devon, UK

To M. B.

Contents

Acknowledgements

This book is the result of working for many years with the members of the Centre Walras-Pareto at the University of Lausanne. All my thanks go to Roberto Baranzini, Pascal Bridel, Michele Bee, François Allisson, Francesca Dal Degan, Maxime Desmarais-Tremblay, Nicolas Eyguesier, Raphaël Fèvre, Antoine Missemer, Thomas Müller, Sophie Swaton, Amanar Akhabbar and Pelin Sekerler-Richiardi. I am very privileged to have worked in such a stimulating research centre.

In parallel, the materials of this book have been regularly presented at the *Albert O. Hirschman Seminar* of Paris 1 University, led by Jérome Lallement and Annie Cot. I received comments on early versions of chapters from Dorian Jullien, Pierrick Dechaux, Aurélien Goutsmedt, Matthieu Renault, Érich Pinzon Fuchs, Francesco Sergi, Isselmou Oud Boye, Cléo Chassonnery-Zaïgouche, Nicolas Vallois, Sophie Pellé and Judith Favereau.

I finished writing this book as an Associate Professor at the University of Nice. I deeply thank Richard Arena, Muriel Dal-Pont, Tom Juille and Dorian Jullien for encouraging me in the final stage of this project.

This book has benefited a great deal from the comments of Olivier Favereau, Harro Maas, Emmanuel Picavet, Philippe Steiner, Dominique Vinck, Bernard Walliser, Cyril Hédoin, Bruno Ambroise and Christian Walter. I am immensely grateful to them for giving me their time.

Several portions of chapters have earlier appeared in different forms in other publications. I acknowledge the various publishers' permission to reprint, with significant revisions, those materials here. Portions of Chapter 2 have been published in the *Revue de philosophie économique* under the title "Deux approches de l'influence du discours économique sur les phénomènes sociaux" (Brisset, 2012a). Chapter 6 is a translation of "D'une convention à une autre: quand la rationalité performe le réel", also published in the *Revue de philosophie économique* (Brisset, 2014b). Parts of Chapter 4 have been published in *Œconomia*: "Les limites de la performativité des énoncés en économie: les apports de John Searle" (Brisset, 2011) and "The future of performativity" (Brisset, 2017c). Chapter 7 has been published under the title "On performativity: option theory and the resistance of financial phenomena in the *Journal of the History of Economic Thought* (Brisset, 2017a). More generally, I benefited from comments from a great number of anonymous reviewers I want to deeply thank.

This work has been translated by Mila Webb, to whom I address all my gratitude.

Introduction

Since the 1970s, historians of economic thought and sociologists have largely studied the interactions between economic theories and economic practices. These studies indicate the porosity of the boundary between scientific activity (observe, measure, theorise) and participation in the social world. This is precisely the object of an important current of economic sociology, namely "performativity of economics": economists institute markets as much as they observe and theorise, they produce and shape the social world as we live it today. This sociology, which will be described as "performativist", intends to study the influence of economic theories by focusing mainly on the socio-technical devices of which it informs the elaboration. It starts from the observation that these devices frame and condition social behaviours, so that the economic reality is gradually brought to conform to the theories. This is, for example, the assumed principle of market design: economists conceive, from their theories, auction systems, matching or trading platforms in order to bring reality to behave like their models. While the heuristic originality of these reflections should certainly be emphasised, the present research intends to question the explanatory relevance of the conceptual tools they mobilise, to identify their limits and to make a theoretical contribution to the question of performativity. This relevance will be judged (and it is a choice that must be justified) in the light of the capacity of the theory of performativity to think of performative failures: when a theory fails to make the social world work according to the mechanisms it describes. We will see that the performativist theory displays a certain type of relativism, a relativism that precisely limits its capacity to apprehend the cases of failure. We will see that this limit mainly takes roots in the technological approach of performativity. Like an internal combustion engine or open source software, the social world is, in this perspective, extremely malleable. It is open to economists to shape it in the image of their own theories. The theoretical contribution will go in this direction by answering the following question: how does one explain theoretically the fact that the performativity of economic theories does not always succeed? In response, a singular approach to the economic theories' performativity will be mobilised, an approach consisting of a return to a definition of the performativity more in conformity with the original notion. We must not forget that the concept of "performative utterance" comes directly from the philosophy of language, a link often overlooked. However, this book will show that the fundamental problem of performativist sociology stems directly from a substantial distance from the Austinian conception of the performative – namely, from no longer defining it by its conditions of success and its potential failures. While Austin defines performative utterances as utterances whose mark of failure is the inability to do something and not to establish a state of affairs, performativist sociology considers only the technical modalities of economic language translation in the social world. This bias seems to make him lose the heuristic force of his first intuition, closing the door to the idea of performative failure. In this introduction, I will first discuss the specificities of the notion of performativity, before indicating its limits, thus justifying the necessity of the approach which will be developed. Finally, a few words will describe the method of analysis that will be selected.

Economics and economy: what is performativity?

Sociology has regularly criticised the economic discipline. From Durkheim to Bourdieu, from Weber to Granovetter, it intends to play the role of a credible alternative to this dismal science. The theory of performativity is from this perspective carrying a new perception: instead of considering economics as a theoretical corpus whose explanatory relevance it is appropriate to criticise, it is firstly necessary to consider it as the heart of economic activity. This is the starting point of Michel Callon, who in 1998 published the collective work marking the foundation of performativist sociology, *The Laws of the Markets*. Callon's introduction serves as a manifesto. A primary definition of performativity is provided:

> [E]conomics, in the broad sense of the term, performs, shapes and formats the economy, rather than observing how it functions.
>
> (Callon, 1998: 2)

The role of economists in the construction of the social world, had, however been largely studied well before *The Laws of the Markets*, so this first definition is not enough to elevate the originality of performativist sociology. Karl Marx, in his *Economic and Philosophic Manuscripts of 1844* (1844 [2007]), makes representations of economists one of the engines of capitalism. He writes at length about the way in which the phenomenal order of the world has been brought to take the form of the descriptions made by classical economists:

> It is therefore self-evident that only the political economy which acknowledged *labour* as its principle (Adam Smith), and which therefore no longer looked upon private property as a mere *condition* external to man – that is this political economy which has to be regarded on the

> one hand as a product of the real *energy* and the real *movement* of private property – as a product of modern *industry* – and, on the other hand, as a force which has quickened and glorified the energy and development of modern *industry* and made it a power in the realm of *consciousness*.
>
> (Marx, 1844 [2007]: 93)

This intuition would later be taken up by Karl Polanyi. A major author in the constitution of economic sociology, he asserts that the figure of "rational man", motivated solely by the desire for wealth, was an essential element in the establishment of industrial capitalism. An economics based on this anthropology has, according to him, engendered its reification: the real man attires himself little by little with the characteristics of the *Homo economicus* (Polanyi, 1977b). If performativist sociology, in its turn, seized the study of the phenomenon of economic theories' influence on the social world in the 1990s, it would be to grasp it in a new light. It draws its originality from its predecessors' perspective that no longer emphasises the influence of economic ideas on mentalities and beliefs, but essentially the constitution of a material world that supports social actors' decisions. Far from referring, as in Marx's case, to the material base of relations of production, this "material world" refers here to all the socio-technical devices made available to the actors in their daily practices. By "socio-technical", Callon means the assembly of humans and "non-humans", human beings and techniques. To confer on them a place of choice in the study of the social world represents a real innovation *vis-à-vis* traditional economic sociology. The case study in this area is the role of the Black-Scholes-Merton (BSM) equations in the constitution of the financial markets in the 1960s–1970s (MacKenzie and Millo, 2003). These equations make it possible to evaluate the "normal" price of options on the derivatives markets. From observation of some key parameters (underlying asset prices, risk-free interest rate, volatility), the model calculates a price corresponding to a standard representation of the market, fixed in the hypothesis of an informational efficient market. Not only have these equations been used by brokers, but they have been integrated to quotation systems: prices on the financial markets are calculated from them. We see here how an economic model contributes to the construction of a market that it is first supposed to describe. It can both produce a new practice within an existing marketplace (agents arbitrate on options using BSM equations) and create a new economic arena from scratch (the BSM equations integrate the very structure of the same market). This conception of the influence of economic theories on the social world, anchored in the materiality of markets, is rooted in a particular sociological corpus, which we will return to: actor-network theory (ANT). This theory, closely related to the Centre de Sociologie de l'Innovation of the École des Mines de Paris, has as its fundamental starting point considering the world as a network of humans and techniques: the life of social actors cannot be dissociated from decision-making technologies, technologies developed, in the performativist framework, by economists. Finance software, market equations, competition law, pricing methods and market architectures participate in human actions. These devices constitute the strength of economic theories in making the social world's objectivity: an equation participates in the price-fixing that market agents consider as objective data.

As previously mentioned, this book intends to interrogate the heuristic value and complete this theoretical representation. Indeed, it attempts to show that performativist sociology does not seem to consider social resistance to the performativity of economic theories. While the role of technical devices is being re-evaluated, the human component is losing (within socio-technical devices) much of its explanatory power, insofar as the sociologists of performativity refuse to approach individual human activities as set in a social world imposing itself on humans. For Callon, there is no common world made of norms, institutions and conventions; there are only humans and techniques taken in their singularities. As such, it is never considered that for a theory to shape the social world, it must be imposed within a space of collective norms and beliefs, or that it must also become one of these norms. The re-evaluation of the role of techniques on the one hand and the explicit refusal to approach human beings as if immersed in a social world imposing on them on the other are two elements which have potential to direct the theory of performativity towards a certain relativism (which it is often reproached for): any theory could perform a very malleable social world in the absence of social constraints. Now, to say that the economist performs the social reality, in the sense of the old French *parformer* (to train, to perfect), is to imply that performativity is likely to fail in the broad sense: the total failure (the theory has no impact on the real) to a situation imposing the theory of significant changes. The challenge here is clearly the explanatory value of the theory of performativity, its capacity to embrace the entirety of a performative process. It is in response to this specific point that there will be an emphasis on reintroducing the social into the theory of performativity.

Theorising both the failure and the success of performativity

The thesis defended here will follow a ternary rhythm. It will first be necessary to enter the theory of performativity, to restore internal coherence, to explore the main criticisms and show that they can be reduced to a theoretical lack related to performative failure. It will then be proposed to overcome this lack by means of a different conceptualisation of the influence of economic theories on the social world. Finally, this conceptualisation will be applied to three case studies to illustrate its relevance.

The first of the three parts, which explores in depth the theory of performativity, is rendered difficult by the heterogeneity of the performativist works that followed Michel Callon's *The Laws of the Markets*. A decade after the publication of the 1998 collective work (which already contained many contributions adopting different methodologies), a second work, *Do Economists Make Markets?*, was edited by Donald MacKenzie, Fabian Muniesa and Lucia Siu – a sign of the vitality of this theoretical corpus. The ten years between the two books have been rich in debates. In *Do Economists Make Markets?*, we find a critical contribution by Mirowski and Nik-Khah (2007), criticising performativist sociology for its allegiance to standard economic theory. If one were to consider economic science as the origin of the social world, its matrix, one would lose any critical distance: the economist does and (thus) tells the truth. A rich debate has also emerged from the work of the anthropologist Daniel Miller, who is also hampered by the critical poverty of performativist theory in relation to the mainstream economics (Miller, 2002, 2005; Callon, 2005; Holm, 2007). The critics of Miller, Mirowski and Nik-Khah point to a gap mentioned above: the easy acceptance of the construction of the social world by economists. The introduction of *Do Economists Make Markets?*, however, seems to address this point, considering that theories may be unable to perform the social world:

> Economics is at work within economies in a way that is at odds with the widespread conception of science as an activity whose sole purpose is to observe and study, that is to "know" the world. The issue of that needs to be tackled in relation to economies and economics is not just about "knowing" the world, accurately or not. It is about producing. It is not (only) about economics being "right" or "wrong" but (also, and perhaps more important) about it being "able" or "unable" to transform the world.
> (MacKenzie et al., 2007 2)

In line with the nuances of MacKenzie, Muniesa and Siu, who clearly envisage the possibility of performative failures (being "able" or "unable" to transform the world), Callon and Muniesa observe: "It is because it [economics] produces models and representations which involve proofs of truth, it can intervene, with its own efficiency, in these arrangements and learn from the experiences they organise" (Muniesa and Callon, 2009: 319; our translation). These authors thus seem to avoid the pitfall of a driven constructivism by introducing the idea of a "test of truth". The first thesis that will be defended is that the performativist conceptualisation is, despite these declarations of intention, in difficulty when it comes to thinking of performative failures. By considering the creative act of theories essentially from the angle of technical devices, performativist theory artificially renders the social world more plastic than it actually is. The counterpart of the technological thesis is, for Callon, the bracketing of the social world, defined as a set of shared beliefs imposing themselves on the social actors: it disappears in favour of an extremely malleable technical world. It is not a question of explaining behaviours by referring to the social world that precedes them, but of understanding the construction by agents of their own socio-technical world. It is precisely this lack of consideration for a social reality imposing itself on individuals that prevents the theorisation of performative failures. If performativist sociology builds its social ontology around the technical devices containing the economic theories and producing individual behaviours in conformity with them, it will be required to concentrate on a necessary precondition to this process, knowing that the uses of these devices become conventions, shared practices based on collective beliefs – that is, members of a population who coordinate on the use of particular devices. By integrating this idea, the thesis of performativity opens the door to the understanding of performative failure: a theory fails to perform the social world when it fails to become a convention. The notion of convention will be at the heart of our reasoning. Borrowed from David Lewis, in line with the French economics of conventions, it allows the determination of certain mechanisms that lead to the failure of performativity. The idea of convention refers in a first approximation to a social device of perception of the world, indicating to the actors the ways they must act when facing certain situations and circumstances. Thus, to be guided by a technical device is to accept a standard of action. The problem with performativist sociology is therefore not so much the valorisation of the role of technical objects as the evacuation of the social in the definition of the human component of socio-technical devices: considering that technical devices are the prime elements in the construction of reality, we forget the conditions under which they take their place within a social world that precedes them. Our disagreement will be, on this point, as much epistemological as ontological: not only is the convention, as social entity, a concept necessary to the understanding of the life in community, but it is also a real object which it is advisable to approach by our theories. This ontological position will be the philosophical foundation of the approach developed here. Conventions are objective elements of the social world, elements limiting the performative possibilities of a theory. This work therefore aims to establish an alternative but complementary conception to the theory of performativity. It is an elaborate design to answer the question, "How can we understand, conceptually, the failures of performativity?" To identify the possibilities of failure is to take a more complete look at the performative processes. In a way, it is a return to a conception close to that developed in the philosophy of language by John Austin. Inventor of the term "performative utterance", Austin starts from the simple observation that certain statements fail not when they do not manage to signify, but when they do not change the world. Such is the well-known case of the statement "I christen this ship *Queen Elizabeth*." In order for it to be performative – that is, for individuals to subsequently use the name "*Queen Elizabeth*" to designate that ship – certain conditions must be met at the time of the utterance. For example, the speaker must be an official character following a specific conventional procedure. One of the results will be to bring into play the idea of necessary conditions within the theory of the performativity of Callon's theoretical statements, and thus, to return to a conception of performativity close to that of Austin, a conception placing at the heart of reasoning the conditions for the success of performativity. One of the results will be to bring into play the idea of necessary conditions within the theory of the performativity of Callon's theoretical statements – to return to a conception of performativity close to that of Austin, a conception placing at the heart of reasoning the conditions for the success of performativity. To take a convention status, a theory will have to:

i provide social actors with a representation of their social world allowing them to choose among several actions;
ii indicate an option considered relevant when the agreement is generalised;
iii be compatible with all the conventions constituting the social environment.

These three conditions, emanating directly from the Lewisian definition of conventions, make it possible to identify three limits to performativity. To be able to intervene in the social world, a theory – for example, the theory of rational action – must already be able to become a focal point. That is, it must be able to serve as a cognitive framework through which agents perceive the world. This imperative is that of empiricity: a theory must be able to be at the origin of empirical statements of the type "*X* is rational in the sense of the economic theory, contrary to *y*." It is on this condition that a technical device can promote the standard theory of rationality, allowing individuals to distinguish between rationality and irrationality. This is, for example, the case with "nudges", political devices whose objective is to induce individuals to make rational decisions in the sense of economic theory. Once this imperative is posited, a theory will only retain its convention status if it allows individuals to achieve the goals they have set for themselves by taking it as a benchmark – or at least, they must believe it. We will address a criterion of self-fulfilment, namely that the diffusion of a strategy modifies the social world in accordance with the agents' expectations. If not, they will abandon the strategy proposed by economic theory. Finally, the third condition requires that a concept proposing itself as a convention be compatible with the conventions already in place within the social world. For example, the representations of the world of many societies make it difficult to establish a market for organs. These are not considered as objects that can be sold through market devices. The third part of the book will constitute the use of these concepts in an understanding of what we call "scenes of performativity", where there seems to have been a performativity of a particular economic theory. Three case studies will each serve to isolate one of the three criteria: the social impact of the theories of rationality, the role of financial models in the constitution of markets, and the establishment of markets in the context of organ trade. Each of these studies will have one of our criteria applied:

– The notion of rationality could only have been part of rationalisation policies from the moment when its definition made it possible to plausibly distinguish the rationality of irrationality. The promotion of rational behaviour is closely linked to the ability to indicate the contours of such behaviour.

- If finance is the privileged object of performative studies, theoretical models face financial phenomena that resist them, forcing theorists to adapt their tools to the world. It is not enough for market agents to adopt a theory for the world to comply with. To be performative, the theory must be self-fulfilling.
- In the context of organ markets, theorists are confronted with a set of social representations limiting the plasticity of the world. In this case, the social rejection of the organ as a commodity has led economists to move towards alternative modes of matching with the markets.

Method of analysis

Let it be said: the notion of performativity of economic theories is certainly one of the richest conceptual innovations of recent decades. Its strong diffusion, whether in economics, sociology or philosophy, is a sign of this. I do not intend to call it into question from a position of *lector*, as described by Bourdieu (1997 [2000]: 61–62):

> The *lector*'s reading strives to find sources, always imaginary [. . .] with the intention, so typical of *academica mediocritas*, of explaining the unknown in terms of the already known, the academic variant "nothing new under the sun" [. . .]. [The] lector's reading is an end in itself, [. . .] it is interested in texts, and in the theories, methods or concepts that they convey, not in order to do something with them, to bring them, as useful, perfectible instruments, into a practical use, but so as to gloss them, by relating them to other texts.

My criticism is theoretical, not scholastic. It does not intend to artificially dry a rich corpus rooted in fundamental questioning, but only to bring a different point of view based on a different concern: that of the social limits to performativity. If one will have to question certain points of Callonian performativity, and especially its removal of social categories in favour of technical devices, the ambition is absolutely not to reject the idea according to which the techniques are an important element of the performative processes, nor that this theory has objectives that are simply not mine. If we want to tackle the failures and the conditions for the success of performativity, then my theoretical framework is a possibility. If this question is not considered relevant, then the framework developed will not be either. It is necessary to insist on the fact that if the framework of analysis drawn in this book is a pure definition of performativity as a conventional process, its interest is not only to produce sanctions of the type "Theory *x* was performative or *y* was not." Between perfect performativity and its complete failure, the interest is to go further and provide an enlightened reading of a performative process in order to identify the difficulties a theory has had to impose itself as a convention in a population. In addition, the intention is to identify the way in which a theory has been modified, amended under the pressure of the economic reality, so that the performative process can continue. The choice was made to combine at the same time a theoretical work and an empirical work, taken as an application of the tools mobilised to particular cases, to particular scenes of performativity. Like the crime scene, the performativity scene is a place where there *seems* to have been performativity, but where everything remains to be proven. On this point, an assumed and important limit of our approach is the entirely bookish origin of the accounts of these scenes. One relies mainly on the works of others. This is the condition of an all-encompassing approach to the performative phenomenon.

Part I

The performativist approach

Introduction to Part I

The original expression of the performativity of economic theory was by Michel Callon (1998: 2):

> [E]conomics, in the broad sense of the term, performs, shapes and formats the economy, rather than observing how it functions.

However, the originality of the performativity thesis cannot be reduced to this simple formulation. The specificity of the performativist approach is to be found in the way in which the social influence of economic theories is considered. The latter participate in the construction of the social world insofar as they inform the development of technical devices that actors use in their daily decision-making. The term "theory" is used here for ease of language in that it is not strictly speaking that the economic theories are important in this type of approach, but any element emanating from theorisation – concepts, principles, normative and positive criteria which can also serve the construction of such devices.

The role Callon gives to what he calls "socio-technical devices" locates the originality of the performativist approach away from conceptualisations from both sociology and economics. We particularly think of Bourdieu's "theory effect" in the first case – the idea that a scientific description is always capable of contributing to its own verification by exerting an effect of theory favouring the advent of what it announces (Bourdieu, 1981: 72) – and self-fulfilling prophecies, a concept of prime importance in economics, in the second case. Understanding performativity requires grasping this conceptual distance, which we achieve by situating the performativist theory both *vis-à-vis* the works that constitute its theoretical roots and those against which it is constructed. This approach to the performativist corpus is an important methodological choice. One could have lingered only on the theory of performativity for itself. This choice is nevertheless of major interest. The idea that there is a unified theory of performativity collides with the lack of systematic theorisation of this notion. Beyond Callon's 1998 text (programmatic, and of which many notions will not find any posterity), the only summary that has been identified is the article in French by Muniesa and Callon (2009), "La performativité des sciences économiques". However, the article is essentially built around a critique of what performativity is opposed to, criticism based on taxonomy of the different types of performativity (to which we will return at the end of Chapter 1). Although extremely informative, this article does not elaborate on the theoretical framework underlying the use of the concept of performativity. This first part constitutes, from this observation, a reconstruction of the theory of performativity. It makes it possible to highlight two central elements of this theory: the role given to devices, and the refusal to consider the social world as a set of macro-entities (conventions, institutions, collective beliefs, etc.) within which markets would be embedded. For Callon, markets are singular places whose technical constitution is fuelled by economic theories.

In Chapter 1, I have chosen to identify two foundations to performativity: the philosophy of John Austin's speech acts and the actor-network theory developed by Bruno Latour and Michel Callon. Austin's linguistics is at the origin of the concept of "performative" utterance, understood then as the capacity of language to modify the world welcoming the enunciation. Two statements such as "unemployment goes up" and "I declare the session open" seem from this point of view to belong to two different registers of speech. The first states, the second performs an action. Austin goes even further in defending the idea that saying is always doing something. This is the meaning of the performative approach: economists do not just say, they produce the world they are meant to describe. The notion of description is the subject of many epistemological debates – What is describing? What is knowing? What are the methods of knowledge? – so many questions which constitute the philosophy of knowledge. Philosophy of economics has developed a rich literature about a main instrument of knowledge of economics: formal models (Morgan and Morrison, 1999; Boumans, 2005; Walliser, 2011; Morgan, 2012). If we go back to what is meant by theory further on in this work, the idea of description refers in first approximation to the reverse of the intervention on reality: to say that a theoretical discourse has a vocation to describe is to say that it is not intended to transform. To approach the performativity of economic theories is therefore to question, like Austin, this border between the declarative and the performative: to describe the economic world is in itself to have an effect on it.

The sociologists of performativity nevertheless move substantially away from Austin's linguistic approach. If the term and the general idea are repeated, it is with a view to giving them a different content. Yes, economists make the world, but according to different modalities of the acts of language: the construction of the social world is for Callon a socio-technical construction, mixing humans and non-humans. Equations, computer programs, market architectures, auction systems and accounting standards are all technical devices whose development can be informed by economists and influence the behaviour of the humans who use them. As for Callon, techniques make humans do things (*faire faire* in French); in the Austinian perspective, the mayor "makes to do" through language. It is enough for him to say (as mayor), "I call this library 'Vladimir Maiakovski' library," and so we will call this place and use it as such.

For Callon, the economist makes to do through socio-technical devices: he gives a price calculation equation to implement on the financial markets, and the assets' price will be in everybody's eyes the price that this equation will produce. The traders will make their decisions based on this price, and will arbitrate on this price too.

This way of seeing the social world as so many technical devices shaping individual choices, as well as the idea of "making to do" by technical devices are the legacy of an important sociological trend, actor-network theory. This approach intends, in effect, to repopulate the social world it describes with elements forgotten by classical sociology: technical devices understood as crutches ensuring the social actors' actions. Chapter 1 will provide an opportunity to tell the story from the philosophy of language to the theory of performativity – not as a historian of thought would do, but for the sole purpose of pointing out the fundamental originality of performativist sociology that is the idea of "making to do" by devices. Despite its prominence in the contemporary social sciences, performativist intuition is not new. Both economists (particularly through the use of the notion of self-fulfilling prophecies) and sociologists (who have examined the symbolic power of economists) have addressed the question of the social influence of economic theories. Chapter 2 will provide an opportunity to characterise the performativist corpus within the economic and sociological literature in order to underline another originality, namely the rejection of explanation by social structures: socio-technical devices acquire an important explanatory role as long as they replace social structures within the conceptual schemes of performativist sociology.

If Michel Callon, in line with ANT, focuses his attention on socio-technical devices, and thus on the entanglement of composite entities integrating techniques and the social, then the notion of "social" has a particular meaning. It refers to the human being as an individual technique user – like a monad which, by attaching itself to the technical devices and to other humans, makes society. This perspective refers to what Callon (1986) and Latour (2005) called the "principle of symmetry", namely the idea that it is heuristically more interesting to consider humans and techniques with the help of a single and same theory. Humans thus lose (epistemologically) their privilege to be social (in the sense of consubstantiality between the human and society) to become, in the same way as the technical device, what Latour calls "actants". As such, in the framework of the Callonian approach, economic theory therefore performs when it is embodied in devices capable of diverting, influencing the action of human actors. This is a twofold detachment that Callon operates with respect to the standard approaches to the social influence of economic theories – oriented towards the propagation of economic ideas, the rationalisation of the world, the symbolic power of economists leading to self-fulfilling prophecies – but also *vis-à-vis* the corpus of economic sociology as a whole. Indeed, Michel Callon's central point of sociology is the rejection of the idea of social embeddedness of markets, interpreted as explaining the economic by the social (collective beliefs, institutions, conventions). The market is not an idea, a belief or a mentality (to use Karl Polanyi's term), but a set of socio-technical devices built with the help of economists. This rejection of the social as a structuring element of economic reality is at the same time what underlies the idea of "making to do" and what opposes performativist sociology to standard sociology.

After putting into perspective both fundamental characteristics of performativist sociology (the concentration on technique, and the rejection of the social), we will show that these are at the heart of the criticisms (more or less justified) of which it could be the target. More particularly, a technicity approach would lead to an extremely malleable vision of the social world, no longer allowing us to understand why some theories have the power to perform the world and not others. Let us say that the theory of performativity does not allow us to understand performative failures. It will be understood that even if this criticism is exaggerated (as Callon and Latour call the notion of a "test of truth"), it nevertheless touches on an important point, refusing to approach performativity as a social movement order which considerably weakens the understanding of performative failures.

1 From language to device

How economics shapes the world

The notion of "performativity" originates in the theory, derived from Austinian philosophy, that speech acts are a form of social action. According to Austin, the term "performative" refers to a class of utterances having the property of failing – not when they fail to be uttered or accurately describe, but when they fail to initiate action, to do things. Thus, the statement "I close the session" precisely fails as a performative utterance when no one acts to close his binder and leave the room. The performative problematic originates from a fundamental questioning of language's traditional philosophy. Initiated by Wittgenstein, then Quine, it leads on to what is understood as the theory of ordinary language: faced with the impossibility of building language on a stable base (whether it is logical or empirical), the role of the philosopher should be to understand linguistic usages, and not to try to standardise them. Thus, whereas philosophy of language typically intended to define some rules for utterances that are both semantically truthful and syntactically correct, Austin strives to understand language's possibilities and its role within the social world.

If performativist sociology incorporates the concept of performativity, it renews the content: the economist does not influence economy through its discourse, but in the trail of the actor network, with the technologies of the decision-making which is at its origin. This chapter will recount the path from language philosophy to performativist sociology in order to emphasise what is a salient feature of the definition of performativity: the notion of "making to do". The economics discipline performs the real to the extent where, through technical devices, it is doing things to the actors of the social world. This chapter is clearly a theoretical reconstruction. It is a conceptual journey, developed by a non-specialist in the philosophy of language, rather than a history of science. It therefore has the ambition to support the view that focuses on performativist sociology, the view oriented towards the notions of "making to do" and technical devices. The focus on the critical route will come later (Chapter 3). The return to the Austinian theory will establish that the main difficulty of the performativity theory (knowing its difficulty in thinking about performative failure) comes precisely from the transformation of the concept of performativity. For Austin, the performative requires social utterance conditions, which, if not included, will lead to the failure of the statement. On the contrary, the idea of social conditions necessary to the reception of speech is rejected in the sociological performativity definition – hence an evident problem when encountering failures of performativity. Previously, the sociology of performativity has been criticised for having devalued the Austinian concept (Mäki, 2013; Ambroise, 2015). Here, conversely, the objective is to appreciate Austin, to take him seriously in order to create a new approach to performativity.

From philosophy of language to social sciences

When John Langshaw Austin proposed in *How to Do Things with Words* (1962), collated from twelve interventions made in 1955 in the William James Lectures at Harvard, that to utter is to do, he split with the dominant philosophical discourse at the time. The representationalist focuses exclusively on the constative of the statement: language is a veil over the external world. The coincidence with this external world is that through a lens one can judge the similarities of several accounts: two accounts reflecting to the same object have the same meaning.

It would be wrong to homogenise all the so-called representationalist approaches to language since there is a certain continuity between the latter and Austinian linguistics. Thus one can already distinguish the purely ostensive approach of language from a more psychological approach to meaning. In the first case, a term refers directly to a referent (referred to as a referential approach), locating the meaning in the object itself: "This is a cat" refers directly to the animal; "The cat is in the kitchen" refers to the place it occupies. To teach others what is behind the word "cat", it is enough to point at the animal while articulating the word "cat". Several terms, for example drawn from several languages (cat, cat, gatto, кошка), have the same meaning if they designate the same object. This approach immediately poses the problem of entities that cannot be designated if the object is not in front of us ("water on Mars") or it simply does not exist ("the", "this"). This difficulty imposes a refinement: a term does not designate a physical object, but the idea that one has of it. It is an idea forged through the sensitive experience of the outside world and codified within a linguistic community. Thus, language refers to the physical world through the psychic world, and the cornerstone of the meaning is the content of consciousness. This perspective can be found throughout the history of the philosophy of language, whether in Descartes or the grammar of Port-Royal. We find traces of this in Aristotle:

> Spoken words are the symbols of mental experience and written words are the symbols of spoken words. Just as all men have not the same writing, so all men have not the same speech sounds, but the mental experiences, which these directly symbolise, are the same for all, as also are those things of which our experiences are the images. This matter has, however, been discussed in my treatise about the soul, for it belongs to an investigation distinct from that which lies before us.
>
> (Aristotle, 2015, 16a: 2–8)

Anglo-Saxon empiricism, of which John Locke is an emblematic representative, constitutes the apogee of such a representation:

> Words are sensible signs, necessary for communication of ideas. Man, though he have great variety of thoughts, and such from which others as well as himself might receive profit and delight; yet they are all within his own breast, invisible and hidden from others, nor can of themselves be made to appear. The comfort and advantage of society not being to be had without communication of thoughts, it was necessary that man should find out some external sensible signs, whereof those invisible ideas, which his thoughts are made up of, might be made known to others. For this purpose nothing was so fit, either for plenty or quickness, as those articulate sounds, which with so much ease and variety he found himself able to make. Thus we may conceive how words, which were by nature so well adapted to that purpose, came to be made use of by men as the signs of their ideas; not by any natural connexion that there is between particular articulate sounds and certain ideas, for then there would be but one language amongst all men; but by a voluntary imposition, whereby such a word is made arbitrarily the mark of such an idea. The use, then, of words, is to be sensible marks of ideas; and the ideas they stand for are their proper and immediate signification.
>
> (Locke, 1689 [2015], Book II)

Such a vision is not without its problems, because the significance of the statements depends on the singularity of the psychological states of the different interlocutors. Yet how can we understand language, even reduced to a mere communication tool, when there are potentially an infinity of mental representations linked to the same utterance? This question will be at the heart of the foundation of the analytic philosophy of language, which is regularly traced (even if, with regard to what has just been said, this statement should be nuanced) to two short articles by Gottlob Frege (1948, 1956). The problem, as expressed by Frege, comes from the proximity of the following three propositions:

- Everyone has their own representation (idea) of the object *x*.
- There are an infinite number of ways of representing the object *x*.
- Yet we manage to designate to each other this object *x*.

This apparent contradiction applies only if the meaning is reduced to an individual representation (idea), which Frege disputes by introducing sense (*Sinn*) as that which, unlike idea, is capable of maintaining a relation of truth *vis-à-vis* the reference (*Bedeutung*). Frege distinguishes the outer world, ideas (psychological processes) and thoughts (Frege, 1956). The latter two, referring to sense, correspond with ideas in that they cannot be the objects of sensible perceptions. Nevertheless, they are something independent of subjectivity in that they do not need to be reduced to the content of consciousness of any particular individual:

> The idea is subjective: one man's idea is not that of another. There result, as a matter of course, a variety of differences in the ideas associated with the same sense. A painter, a horseman, and a zoologist will probably connect different ideas with the name "Bucephalus". This constitutes an essential distinction between the idea and the sign's sense, which may be the common property of many and therefore is not a part or a mode of the individual mind.
>
> (Frege, 1948: 212)

Frege therefore intends to restore his semantic objectivity to language by introducing notions of sense and truth value – namely, a correspondence between the utterance and the external world. The distinction between meaning (sense) and reference is the foundation of the analytic tradition. By separating objective (and independent) thought from the subjective act of thinking, the objectivity of semantics has as its lens the reference. The truth value of a proposition, whether based on experience (synthetic utterances) or on the laws of logic (analytic utterances), is here independent of a speaker's reservation:

> A third realm must be recognized. What belongs to this correspond with ideas, in that it cannot be perceived by the senses, but with things in that it needs no bearer to the contents of whose consciousness to belong. Thus the thought, for example, which we expressed in the Pythagorean theorem is timelessly true, true independently of whether anyone takes it to be true. It needs no bearer. It is not true for the first time when it is discovered but is like a planet which, already before anyone has seen it, has been in interaction with other planet.
>
> (Frege, 1956: 302)

Returning laws of logic to the centre of truth value opens the door to a normative epistemology which will be at the heart of the Vienna Circle. Any utterance devoid of truth value is devoid of meaning, and philosophy must discover not the way one thinks and speaks, but the manner in which it should be done. Empiricism and logic are two sides of the same coin (Laugier, 1992: 120).

The idea that language functions as a (logical) veil over reality, the latter transcending the first, would undergo a succession of attacks, leading, among other things, to Austin's theory of performativity. Willard Van Orman Quine[1] is often considered the first to challenge Frege's semantic reduction of language in a profound and indelible way. In two texts that entered into the pantheon of philosophy, "Two dogmas of empiricism" (Quine, 1951) and "Le mythe de la signification" (Quine, 1958), Quine defends the idea of an absence of a common core (the transcendence of meaning) in different languages. This thesis is supported by two subaltern theses: that of the impossibility of any radical translation, and that of the indeterminacy of meaning – that is, the impossibility of clearly identifying the object of the discourse. The essence of these two theses can be reconstructed by means of a famous thought experiment elaborated by Quine. It consists of thinking about how it would be possible for an ethnographic linguist to translate the language, unknown to himself, of a tribe into his own language. He thus starts with a blank page, no link of linguistic correspondence being given. The linguist observes that whenever a rabbit leaps into the rabbit hole, a native repeats "gavagai" and points at the animal. The first reflex of the linguist is to note in his logbook "gavagai = rabbit". Thus translating is only a form of a search for synonyms, and the translator has the possibility of relying on the behaviours of the native in order to detect the stimulus meanings (here the passing rabbit) that would transcend synonymy. But on closer inspection:

> [W]ho knows whether the objects to which the term applies are not, after all, anything other than rabbits, and, for example, simple phases, brief temporal segments of a rabbit? [. . .]. To point at a rabbit is to point the finger at a phase of a rabbit and a piece of rabbit at the same time. To point out a part of a rabbit is to show at the same time the whole rabbit and a rabbit phase.
>
> (Quine, 1958: 164)[2]

Moreover, who decides that the pointing of fingers really has the meaning of "showing what is meant by the word that is pronounced", or that the native really desires to teach us his language.

Starting the translation process always requires that a certain number of hypotheses are proposed stemming from the culture and language of the translator. These hypotheses, necessarily subjected to an empirical under-determination, may concern, for example, the way in which to cut the rabbit that is displayed, or the significance of the gesture. Quine calls these "analytical", as they are directly involved in the translation process. The latter are necessary for the transitions from the observed linguistic behaviours to the creation of a dictionary, as well as a coherent grammar for these observations. There are potentially an infinite number of analytical hypotheses compatible with the observed language behaviours, especially when one moves from the observation of a physical characteristic ("being a rabbit") to that of a non-physical characteristic (for example, "to be single"). In this way, it is only because he projects his own habits of language in the study of the indigenous language that the ethnologist discovers general terms, or, having discovered them, matches them to his own (Quine, 1958: 174). From this first thesis flows the inanity of the Fregean notion of meaning –a transcendent basis to language:

> The notion of meaning seems acceptable because it is less absurd than the notions it has replaced. Moreover, it seems acceptable because of its legitimate services, which are attributed to it, or are expected of it as a supporting element of truth and as the object of propositional and attributive attitudes. But, in fact, this notion of meaning is like a will-o'-the wisp that vanishes as soon as one wishes to grasp it: the advantages attributed to it or which one hopes for are based on errors of imputation and false hopes.
> (Quine, 1958: 194)

The radical indeterminacy of the reference fundamentally challenges the truth value of the statements: it is impossible to answer precisely the question, "What are we talking about?" This is the content of the second subordinate thesis: "Pending a satisfactory explanation of the notion of meaning, linguists in semantic fields are in the situation of not knowing what they are talking about" (Quine, 1963: 47). Quine is not arguing that words do not mean anything – quite the contrary. Only the verb "to mean" should, for Quine, be intransitive: a term, a sentence, means, point. In this way, Quine attacks the conception of language as a veil held over the world, in order to turn to non-referential linguistics, which considers language for itself. This is the starting point of ordinary language philosophy, whose main representatives are Wittgenstein, Austin and, in more contemporary fashion, Stanley Cavell (1969) and Sandra Laugier (2013). Starting from the impossibility of founding the relation of language to the world, which calls into question the normativity of classical logic, these authors restore an ontological density to language and question its functioning *in situ*.[3] According to Laugier, Quine's position leads beyond the search for meaning to a logical anthropology.[4] Contemporary to Quine, Wittgenstein, in his *Philosophical Investigations*, as well as in his *Blue and Brown Books*, also attacks Frege. He enshrines his theory of language in everyday practice and what he calls language games, in essence "the whole, consisting of language and the actions into which it is woven" (Wittgenstein, 1953: § 7). Indeed, to say that a word is connected with a thing remains insufficient, in that to denominate would be no more than a preparation for the use of a word. How can one answer the question "What is a word?" if one does not understand its use *in situ*? Wittgenstein, like Quine, comes to question the finiteness of language in general, and the role of the logician in particular. Beyond a set of formally bound terms (a dictionary and a grammar), to speak is to follow social rules that cannot be transcribed (hence the impossibility of a private language):

> 107. The more narrowly we examine actual language, the sharper becomes the conflict between it and our requirement. (For the crystalline purity of logic was, of course, not a result of investigation: it was a requirement.) The conflict becomes intolerable; the requirement is now in danger of becoming empty. We have got on to slippery ice where there is no friction and so in a certain sense the conditions are ideal, but also, just because of that, we are unable to walk. We want to walk: so we need friction.

> 108. We see that what we call "sentence" and "language" has not the formal unity that I imagined, but is the family of structures more or less related to one another. – But what becomes of logic now? Its rigour seems to be giving way here. – But in that case doesn't logic altogether disappear? – For how can it lose its rigour? Of course not by our bargaining any of its rigour out of it. – The preconceived idea of crystalline purity can only be removed by turning our whole examination round.
>
> (Wittgenstein, 1953)

The philosophy of logic does not speak of phrases and words in a different sense than the one we give them in everyday life when we say, "There is a sentence written in Chinese," or "It looks like a written sign, but it is in fact an ornament." Like Quine, Wittgenstein puts an end to the myth of systematic control or examination of language. Language is an object we have inherited which connects us to a community (a constituent element of this community) and is at the heart of social practices:

> We are talking about the spatial and temporal phenomenon of language, not about some non-spatial, non-temporal phantasm. [Note in margin: Only it is possible to be interested in a phenomenon in a variety of ways.] But we talk about it as we do about the pieces in chess when we are stating the rules of the game, not describing their physical properties. The question "What is a word really?" is analogous to "What is a piece in chess?"
>
> (Wittgenstein, 1953: § 108)

The framework is in place so that we can move on to our interest here: the theory of performativity and speech acts in general. John Austin, in his *How to Do Things with Words*, takes note of the idea that to speak is above all to follow a socially acquired language rule. As such, a statement is not only susceptible to being semantically false, but it also can fail to do something. However, depending on the conditions in which it takes place, only action directed towards an end is susceptible to failure. By underlining the semantic under-determination of language, Austin operates a pragmatic revolution in the philosophy of language: in that it is also an act, the conditions for the realisation of an utterance go beyond its semantic conditions. In his own style of "midwife" (*maïeutician*), Austin begins by taking the standard approach to language at its word while observing that many statements cannot be classified as observative, being themselves actions influencing the content and evolution of the external world. The examples of this type of utterance, known as "performative", are now well known: "I name this ship *Queen Elizabeth*"; "I bet you sixpence it will rain tomorrow" (Austin, 1962: 5). The primary characteristic of these statements is that they directly influence the world's state: an anonymous craft becomes the *Queen Elizabeth* in the eyes of all; I agree to abide by the terms of a contract in light of future weather conditions. Truth or falsity, in the sense of a correspondence between words and the things they describe, are no longer relevant criteria here, but rather the concretisation of the act invoked by the speech.

A performative utterance is then said to be happy or unhappy. This nature depends on what Austin calls felicity conditions: "Who speaks?" and "Under what circumstances?" Following this observation, Austin engages in the search for a criterion of stable distinction between the two types of enunciation. It is a quest that ultimately leads to a dead end: "Now we have failed to find a grammatical criterion for performatives" (Austin, 1962: 91). This conclusion is motivated by the idea that to say is always to do something. It is no longer a question of defining the boundaries between two worlds, that of the performative and that of the observative, but of considering from a more general point of view the question: "In what sense is to say one thing to do it?" To the syntactic conditions constituting the enunciation as such, there are added pragmatic conditions, namely social conditions of enunciation:

> Speaking generally, it is always necessary that the circumstances in which the words are uttered should be in some way, or ways, appropriate, and it is very commonly necessary that either the speaker himself or other persons should also perform certain other actions, whether "physical" or "mental" actions or even acts of uttering further words.
>
> (Austin, 1962: 8)

It will be considered hereafter that the performative character of an utterance always depends on the accompanying conditions of felicity; the performative force is not as dependent on the linguistic sphere as on the conventional sphere. The theory of performative utterances leaves room for the theory of speech acts in general. Whereas Austin's starting point was that a discourse was initially intrinsically performative, the conditions of felicity subsequently clarifying its happy or unhappy nature, it is now the performative thickness of the same discourse that is determined by the conditions of enunciation. In Austin, this density is divided into three dimensions: that of the true and the false, which defines the locutionary act (which "means"); that of happiness and misfortune, which defines the illocutionary act (which possesses a power); and that of the effects of the locutionary act not dependent on any internal procedure (which defines the perlocutionary act).[5]

In this way, following Austin, performativity, in the sense of a characteristic intrinsic to language, is stillborn. Nevertheless, many researchers have taken up this notion in order to deepen its analytical value by moving it aside from the purely linguistic field in order to exploit it in the more general domain of the social world. The concept of performativity gradually slips from purely linguistic considerations to the discussion and study of the conditions of enunciation. This transformation continues in sociology, among other fields, with the remarks of Bourdieu with regard to the Austin project:

> Austin's account of performative utterances cannot be restricted to the sphere of linguistics. The magical efficacy of these *acts of institution* is inseparable from the existence of an institution defining the conditions (regarding the agent, the time or place, etc.) which have to be fulfilled for the magic of words to operate.
>
> (Bourdieu, 1991: 73)

Thus felicity conditions, which were in the first stage of Austinian research rejected beyond language and only served to bring about the intrinsic power of words, are now at the heart of the very notion of performativity. We pass from performativity as a characteristic peculiar to language to a set of conditions necessary to render the speech act felicitous. The performative utterance requires that the discourse be in a space where it will be audible. Sociology is therefore legitimate to introduce itself into performative studies. From a perspective peculiar to himself, Bourdieu considers that every act of elocution takes place in a social field via the agent who is its transmitter: words become effective only when the receiver recognises the one who produces them as having a certain status, the status being conferred on him by the institution: "meaning to institute in an active way someone or something endowed with this or that status or property" (Bourdieu, 1991: 125). Delphes participates as much as Pythia in the credibility of the prophetic utterances. In line with Bourdieu's remarks, studies of performative acts have multiplied. For example, an investigation conducted by Béatrice Fraenkel with bailiffs shows that their signature, to take all its performative strength, requires a relationship to the particular time. The signature is not a quick act performed by a woman who is of a supreme authority, but rather a long act taking place following the mobilisation of a latent performativity (Fraenkel, 2008: 23). Three released characteristics are thus essential to any performance: the institutional structure, the rite linked to the act, and the reception of the statement (uptake).

We must not, however, misunderstand Bourdieu's rupture: Bourdieu is more of a contributor to the Austinian project than a critic of it (Ambroise, 2008: 125). Austin was, as we have seen, the first to emphasise the impossible distinction between performative and observative utterances (Austin, 1979). On the one hand, it shows that, like performatives, every statement has a strong procedural character (also subjected to conditions of felicity), and on the other hand, that the performatives themselves require a measure of correspondence (in what to do is always to do something). The Bourdieusian project must therefore be considered as an additional step rather than a rupture.

In line with Bourdieu's studies (see Chapter 2), the Callonian approach applies the idea of performativity to scientific utterances, and to those of economic science in particular. It defines the performativity of economic sciences as the idea that the sciences in general, economic in particular, are not limited to representing the world: they provoke it (Muniesa, 2014), even constitute it, at least to some extent and under certain conditions (Muniesa and Callon, 2009: 289). These works definitively seal off language as the only performative medium and move towards a reflection on socio-technical equipment assisting the agent in his decision-making. The economic discourse "performs" the economic reality via the market devices of which it informs the elaboration: accounting standards, pricing software, etc. – a bias that is rooted in actor-network theory, the subject of the next section. To disembody performativity of the Austinian theory of language also means that Callon will no longer define performativity by its failures. This, however, is the starting point of Austin: that certain utterances fail when they do not do anything. It will be important to bear this point in mind for the rest of the book, and more particularly in Chapter 4, dedicated to a critique of the theory of performativity, and Chapter 5, where I will return to Austin.

Bruno Latour on science in action

Studies of the performativity of economic sciences focus on socio-technical devices while setting aside the effects of language (Brisset, 2014a). This isolation has its roots in the theoretical foundations of performativist sociology: actor-network theory. The latter, mainly through the works of Michel Callon and Bruno Latour, will from then on establish a point of entry into the theory of performativity. ANT, which originates in studies of scientific fields of practice, originally claimed to be a take-over of the sociology of the sciences (sociology of social knowledge, or SSK) mainly carried out by the Edinburgh School. This section will provide an opportunity to review the thematic extension of ANT to social studies in general, and then to the performativity of economic theories in particular.

The 1970s constituted a turning point in reflections on the sciences: the latter became a stimulating study object for the sociological method. Where the validity of reasoning structures and modes of inference (induction, deduction, abduction, causality, etc.) were examined, with a focus on the development of relevant discovery procedures (various criteria of truth), sociologists of science begin to consider systems of thought as language games whose validity is linked to the contexts of enunciation. In this context, the social environment, in that it constitutes registers of truth linked to habits of action, is a decisive element in the resolution of the controversies between the competing theories. This approach to the sociology of science leads to a precept (Bloor, 1976): competing research programmes should not be studied in terms of their successes or failures. On the contrary, they should be approached in a "symmetrical" way in order to trace the controversies that have led to this state of affairs. This movement is obviously not peculiar to sociology as a discipline. Indeed, we are witnessing a change in the field of epistemology from a normative perspective to an explanatory perspective mobilising sociological arguments to varying degrees. The work of Popper is the seminal influence: posing falsificationism as a primary convention, it establishes the first milestone for the study of the agreements taking place in the various scientific fields. The philosophy of science integrates these elements to varying degrees, from Lakatos (1976), who still awards epistemology a decisive role, to Feyerabend (1970), for whom epistemology tends to disappear behind subjective interests. It should be noted that economic philosophy did not remain alien to this movement (Hands, 2001). If Latourian sociology takes note of the sociological turn of the study of sciences, it claims a substantial distance with respect to SSK. In particular Bruno Latour (1989) refuses to view science as an activity merely imitating an institutional background of collective conventions and interests. Thus, he rejects the adoption of Sirius' point of view, relying on macrostructures that would brim over individual decisions (Latour, 2005: 63):

> For the social sciences to regain their initial energy, it's crucial *not* to conflate all the agencies overtaking the action into some kind of agency – "society", "culture", "structure", "fields", "individuals", or whatever name they are given – that would *itself* be social.
>
> (Latour, 2005: 45)

It is no longer society that determines the outcomes of scientific controversies, but in fact researchers, engineers and their diverse and varied networks that stabilise the social world around the technical facts they produce as a consequence of controversies.[6] It is therefore necessary for him to return to practices: not to reduce the history of science to its social context – as if society was the determining framework of scientific activity – but to explain the way in which science creates facts, objects accepted by all. Such is the adage of ANT.[7]

To this view, Callon (1986a) and Latour (1991) contest the separation – which the latter qualifies as being modern – between the human and the non-human, and between nature and society. Society and techniques must be treated equally using the same theoretical tools:

> We know that the ingredients of controversies are a mixture of considerations concerning both Society and Nature. For this reason, we require the observer to use a single repertoire when they are described. The vocabulary chosen for these descriptions and explanations can be left to the discretion of the observer. He can not simply repeat the analysis suggested by the actors he is studying. However, an infinite number of repertoires is possible. It is up to the sociologist to choose the one that seems the best adapted to his task and then to convince his colleagues that he made the right choice. Having opted in this text for a vocabulary of translation, we know that our narrative is no more, but no less, valid than any other. But given the principle of generalised symmetry, the rule we must respect is not to change registers when we move from the technical to the social aspects of the problem studied. Our hope is that the translation repertoire, which is not that of the actors studied, will convince the reader.
>
> (Callon, 1986a: 176; our translation)

In reference to SSK, they speak of a principle of "generalised symmetry": the validity of a scientific fact, far from referring to an external reality or to a system of truth socially constructed and shared within a community, depends on the solidity of the links uniting the different components of a network of actants, human and non-human, of which it is the centre. The notion of *actant*, in contrast to that of an agent, does not in fact reduce the social to the human, but opens it to all who have the faculty of acting on the world. In line with the works of Gabriel Tarde, Callon, like Latour (Latour et al., 2012) rejects the conscious subject as the determining factor of the march of the world. There is no social transcendence nor naturalistic transcendence, only networks of agents: "Since the settlement of a controversy is the *cause* of Nature's representation, not its consequence, we can never use this consequence, Nature, to explain how and why a controversy has been settled" (Latour, 1987: 258). By scientific fact, Latour means an object, an equation, a reasoning, an article, whose relevance is no longer questioned. Accepted by all as a black box, it is only summoned instrumentally within other reticular processes that create other scientific facts. Acquiring factual status requires it to emerge victorious from controversies with other competing facts. In order to do so, it must prove its resistance, and place itself at the heart of a network of other accepted facts in order to establish its legitimacy. Thus, the objectification of the fact is the result of the construction of a network of allies, and the history of science is summed up in a sequence of network construction and deconstruction. In 1973, Fischer Black and Myron Scholes published the basis for an option pricing model (MacKenzie and Millo, 2003; MacKenzie, 2007). The Black-Scholes-Merton equations were still far from being accepted as a fact on the financial markets. Indeed, the two economists summon as allies many facts borrowed from their predecessors, facts enclosed as "black boxes" within their own theory: the use of variance as a marker of price volatility (Markowitz, 1952), the efficient market hypothesis (Fama, 1965c) and the idea that the prices of the underlying assets follow a Brownian motion.[8] But they also have to compete with other valuation models, such as the Capital Asset Pricing Model developed by Jack Treynor, William Sharpe and John Lintner. This controversy is actually a resistance to the advance of the Black-Scholes-Merton equations as a black box. It is a "concretisation" that will involve the expansion of the socio-technical network (human/non-human mediation) to various technical devices. In the first instance, Black provides the arbitrager with price-sheets allowing the equations to be used both quickly and on the basis of easily visible parameters. Furthermore, the equations serve as an institutional tool for pricing through financial market quotation schemes. The equations have even been taught as a scientific fact in standard finance manuals (Hull, 2011). This example is indicative of the ANT approach: a scientific fact is the knot of a network uniting allies (Markowitz, 1952; Fama, 1965c) in controversies to be won by translating the fact within devices (price-sheets, system of quotations, teaching manuals) in such a way that it is taken as a given for another. We also speak of the sociology of translation in relation to ANT: scientists produce entities, devices, enlist allies, elements of nature, and translate them into a stable network constituting the scientific fact (Callon, 1986a).[9] Within the framework of the theory of performativity, it is the economist who produces facts accepted as such by the social agents. Before approaching the notion of performativity properly, it is necessary to understand Latour's thematic extension, namely to treat the social world as we treat the scientific milieu.

From science to social

When they devoted themselves to the study of science, Callon and Latour adopted the following procedure:

- to emphasise the importance of the role of non-humans in building socio-technical networks;
- to consider that truth is never the stable base that precedes analysis;
- to study the scientific facts under construction.

As a result of his work on the sociology of science, Latour extends his concepts to the study of the social world in general: beyond the scientific evidence, he applies the notion of construction to the social world (Latour, 2005). One might also wonder whether ANT would ultimately provide a metaphorical study of the social, the latter becoming a laboratory (Dubois, 2007). This point is coherent with the Latourian rejection of the transcendence of the social with respect to individual actions: in the same way that no social background or no ideology is sufficient to understand theoretical conflicts' path, no element of the same type makes it possible to grasp the evolution of the world of the actants. Latour, on the other hand, extends to non-humans the privilege of outflanking human activities, making them do things.

The objective of ANT is therefore to understand the elaboration of the social, groups, institutions, as assemblages of heterogeneous actants integrating both humans and non-humans at the same time:

> The observer must abandon all *a priori* distinctions between natural and social events. He must reject the hypothesis of a definite boundary which separates the two. These divisions are considered to be conflictual, for they are the result of analysis rather than its point of departure. Further, the observer must consider that the repertoire of categories which he uses, the entities which are mobilized, and the relationships between these are all topics for actors' discussions. Instead of imposing a pre-established grid of analysis upon these, the observer follows the actors in order to identify the manner in which these define and associate the different elements by which they build and explain their world, whether it be social or natural.
>
> (Callon, 1986b: 200–201)

Thus, when it focuses on socio-technical devices,[10] ANT theorises a particular link between humans and non-humans: that of "making to act". The technical device (Black's price-sheets) constitutes the behaviour of its user, it makes him do things. From this perspective, an important distinction is made between science and technology. As Madeleine Akrich (2006a: 159; our translation) points out:

> Science refers to the outside of the social world and is intended to be the expression of a truth not subject to the contingencies of human life. [. . .] technical objects are given from the outset as composite, heterogeneous; half-flesh, half-fish, we do not know how to take them. They always refer to an end, a use for which they are designed.

This is a distinction of primary importance. It bases ANT's view on scientific activity as a technical activity, linked to the objective of making other actants do something. The thematic extension of ANT to the social world (Saldanha, 2003) makes it possible to generalise the three points of view previously underlined by applying them directly to the social world:

- to emphasise the importance of the role of non-humans in building socio-technical networks;
- to consider that the social world is never the stable base that precedes analysis;
- to study the social world under construction.

We can already note, like Dubois (2005), that there is no explicit justification for the passage from the first three points of view to the last three. The question of the social in the performativist approach will be the heart of the next chapter. ANT seeks to view the world as a constant process of assembling and disassembling networks of actants, both human and non-human, holding as one only because of the strength of the ties that bind them together. The Black-Scholes-Merton equations, quotation software and standard manuals form a sustainable network constitutive of the social world: beyond the debates of specialists, markets and prices are mostly considered objective realities. By studying the constitution of devices, ANT tries very precisely to probe the fabric of the objectivity of knowledge[11] using technical objects: "From the moment when the technical object is practically stabilised, it becomes, by its erasure, an instrument of knowledge" (Akrich, 2006a: 176; our translation). Technical devices therefore constitute a central point. They substitute themselves for the social facts of classical sociology: instead of considering the individual evolving in a macro-social group that precedes it, Latourian sociology conceives the social world as many micro-networks in constant reconstruction and uniting human and non-human. It is a question of avoiding the hypostasis of the social, a position Latour often attributed to Durkheim (the great theoretical enemy of Tarde) as well as Bourdieu. This motivation is a common trait of the approaches of ANT. This desire is a common feature of approaches referring to ANT: "One of the potentially insightful, enabling, and even frustrating aspects of the work [. . .] is the refusal to stop analyses at catch-all terms such as 'social', 'worldview', 'Western rationality', and 'capital'" (Hinchliffe, 1996: 662).

Latour (1996) perfectly illustrates this inversion in an example concerning setting up a technical device as a translator of a moral rule: persuading a guest to bring his hotel key back to reception at the end of his stay. For Latour, this rule cannot explain by itself its own application. It is necessary to dwell on the technical devices put in place to enforce it. For example, it is possible to write on the invoice for the hotel room the imperative "Return your keys to the reception." Experience shows that this device is ineffective, in that the injunction depends fundamentally on the goodwill of the guest, who may resist the terms. Faced with this type of failure, the idea was to make the moral rule adopt a more constraining form, for example attaching cast iron weights to the key-rings, imposing a difficulty that results in customer compliance. The technical device translates the rule to enforce it. We therefore witness the assemblage of a solid socio-technical network that positions humans, non-humans, statements and objects. Representing with the same importance objects and persons, erasing differences of scale in the constitution of networks, is the trademark of ANT:

> Instead of dividing the subject with social/technical, or with human/animal, or with the micro/macro dichotomies, we will only retain for the analysis *gradients of resistivity* and consider only the *variations in relative solidity and durability of different sorts of materials.*
>
> (Callon and Latour, 1981: 284)

Latour rejects, as we have seen, both the idea of a conscious subject (the actor) and of the common world. The social world is not an element that conscious actors actualise, but an assemblage of human and non-human actants caught up in a network dynamic. As such, there is no common world (Latour, 2011). There is only one set of heterogeneous objects taken in their reciprocal relations, and we must explain the constitution of the social world through networks of socio-technical devices. Two characteristics of ANT emerge: on the one hand, the idea of having the technical device make other actants do things, and on the other hand, the refusal to consider the macro-social entities – it is not the moral norm that brings the keys to the hotel reception desk, it is the weight as a technical device. It is precisely this foundation for the theory of performativity that will pose a problem. I will return to this in Chapter 3.

From the social to the performative: an approach through the device

In line with ANT, the sociology of performativity takes the liberty to emancipate itself from a linguistic vision of performativity in order to be part of an approach identifying the places and technologies bringing together theories and practices. While the various sociological traditions generally agree on the socially constructed aspect of markets and on the role of economists in this process, performativist sociology seizes with both hands the study of the setting up of markets as socio-technical devices. It also rejects the Great Divide between the social and the natural, the human and the non-human, refuses to focus on social facts beyond agents, and considers science as an active element in the construction of the social world. The fundamental assumption is that society is not considered as a framework within which actors evolve, but as the provisional result of a socio-technical construction. If it is human/non-human mediation (the socio-technical device) which seems to be at the heart of the analysis, it is a de-socialised human (in the Callonian sense of the social as a framework preceding the analysis). Performativist works most often approach behaviours through the prism of a technical apparatus whose elaboration has been informed by an economic theory. The core of reasoning thus concerns above all the technical device as mediation between economic theories and human behaviour. The originality of performativistic sociology *vis-à-vis* the classical sociology of economic knowledge is precisely that it has envisaged technical devices in the light of an unprecedented characteristic: once recorded in a technical device, the theory no longer needs to be known by agents in order to have an effect on their behaviour. Economic theory performs (shapes) the social world by belonging to market devices considered as black boxes by agents. Such is the intimate connection between ANT and performativist sociology. The latter differs considerably from the classical opposition between economics and sociology in that it refuses both to consider individual choice as the result of internal deliberation and the role of "social institutions" in the formation of behaviours.

Let us look specifically at markets. Callon and Muniesa (2005) define markets as socio-technical devices that can compromise on the nature of the goods to be produced, distributed and consumed, but also on the value of these. The performativist project tries, from there, to understand the way in which economic theory brings about a concept, that of the market, through the devices from which it informs the development. In the example of the BSM equations, it is indeed the technical device that translates the equation, thus helping to create a price, that of the option. The definition of Callon and Muniesa (2005) puts the idea of calculation at the centre of market devices. Faced with a set of possibilities, an economic actor proceeds in three stages:

1. Take the objects out of context in order to integrate them into a computing space.
2. Associate these abstract entities with each other, move, and rework within this same calculation space.
3. Extract the results – that is, release new entities enhancing the capacity of choice: price, information, label, etc.

This definition of calculation is very broad. It consists essentially of the establishment of a continuum between qualitative and quantitative judgements. The notion of calculation constitutes the performativistic counterpart of the notion of ANT translation. In order for a market transaction to take place, it is first of all necessary to make the goods calculable (to translate them) within calculation spaces (markets), a necessary step for negotiation between the various parties involved (Millo, 2007). MacKenzie (2006a) outlines, for example, the important role of the standardisation of commodities required for trading in forward markets. In order for a forward market for seed to be set up, seed must first be standardised, transported and mixed. Michel Callon (2013: 347) speaks of the "passivation of goods" (*passivation des biens*) to describe this process of transformation of a good into a commodity stable enough to pass from hand to hand. The second phase is that of the penetration of the good, rendered calculable, into the buyer's world: that is to say, the latter's appreciation of the value or price of the product (Muniesa and Teil, 2006). This "valuation" (Callon, 2013: 358) allows an adjustment between buyer and seller.

In addition to suppliers and demanders, this process involves evaluation bodies whose objective is precisely the adjustment between supply and demand (for example, pricing equations). The exchange can then take place. Attention is mainly focused on these spaces of calculation as technical devices, allowing the translation of the exchanged goods, but also of the agents' subjectivity, defined with respect to their activity in the socio-technical network, namely their relationship to technical devices:

> The perception of differences and their evaluation (a double operation that defines judgment) implies a consumer who is immersed in a socio-technical system whose various elements will participate, each in his own way, in the implementation of this double operation.
>
> (Callon et al., 2000: 224)

Here we reach the intimate connection between the theory of performativity and the thoughts of Michel Foucault, and more specifically his reflections on the techniques (productions) of oneself. A market operation consists in the attachment of a good to an agency (an agent) so that it enriches and maintains its identity. It is in the sales relationship that the self-constructing activity of the seller and the consumer resides. This last point comes into resonance with the very term actor-network theory: "they [the agents] do not have to open up to the world because they contain their world. Agents are actor-worlds" (Callon, 1998: 8). It is because economic theory nourishes these places of calculation and of self-construction as a market agent that it influences the social world: it nourishes the interpretative framework of the agents regarding the real market (marketplace), and allows the adjustment of individual calculations to a specific standard, that of economic theory. It participates in the construction of a network of technical devices whose characteristic is to make actors act, to impose behaviours by inserting them in certain provisions to act. The technical device, often invisible to its user, transmits to him the technical skills required to achieve a certain goal. Brought back to markets, the main conceptual point of the theory of performativity is to consider economic theory as participating in the construction of networks of actors whose result is to make things happen to individuals. As in the example of an automobile, whose users do not need to know the physical theories that it integrates to use it, economic theory imposes behaviours on human actors without their being aware of this theory. So, if the theory of performativity is concerned with the constitution of socio-technical networks (combining human and non-human), this construction is mainly addressed through the prism of technical actors. In order to underline the diversity and complexity of performative processes' form, Muniesa and Callon (2009) combine the studies of performativity around four "constituent tensions" (*tensions constitutives*), each of which sets out two approaches. These tensions will allow us to illustrate the originality of the performativistic approach when it captures "scenes of performativity", but also to discern what it refuses to be: a perspective focusing solely on the role of the academic economist in the construction of social conventions. This latter type of approach, which will be called conventionalist, will be explored in more detail in the next chapter.

Theoretical performativity and experimental performativity

As we have seen, if the notion of performativity emerges from the linguistic domain, it is not reduced to it. If it is understood that the very speech of economic theorists brings about certain social representations ("theoretical performativity"), the influence of economics on the world it describes also appears through social engineering taking root outside the strict academic field ("experimental performativity"). In this respect, Muniesa and Callon summon the figure of the engineer-economist, driven not by a desire to construct abstract systems whose vocation is the representation or stylisation of real economic systems, but by the resolution of concrete problems. This engineer spirit is characterised above all by the idea that the relevance of a theoretical construct must be evaluated in the light of its capacity to guide the action within a given empirical framework (Vatin, 2008). The French engineering economist Jules Dupuit, for example, regularly returns to this subject in performativist literature.

The economic growth of nineteenth-century France raises the problem of the need for transport networks. The Ponts et Chaussées Corps, founded in 1716, actively participated in major development programmes, notably under the aegis of its general manager, Alexis-Victor Legrand. For example, he was the originator of a project, known as "Legrand's Star", of the railway network centred on Paris. This type of project leads to two major interrelated sets of problems: first, technical problems, focusing on the establishment of construction standards (materials to be used, construction techniques, etc.), and secondly, economic issues. The latter are concentrated around two poles: the issue of expropriation, and the financing of railroad structures (construction and maintenance). These two questions led Dupuit to take an interest in the calculation of the utility of public works (Dupuit, 1844), as well as its balance with the costs they generate. This makes it possible to determine their methods of financing (Dupuit, 1849). The first phase consists of building evaluation tools. In his famous article of 1844, "De la mesure de l'utilité des travaux publics", Dupuit's ambition was to provide an instrument for assessing the economic impact of civil engineering works. Opposing Jean-Baptiste Say, who evaluated the utility of a public good in the light of what society is willing to pay for it, Dupuit pointed out that it is necessary to consider not only potential utility for people who are not ready to finance it at this cost, yet could be able to do so if it were to decrease (for example, through technical progress), but also those who would be willing to pay more. Taking the example of a civil engineering structure costing 500 million francs a year (for construction, maintenance and depreciation), he states:

> If the society pays 500 million for services brought by roads, that proves only one thing – that their utility is 500 million at least. But it may be a hundred times, a thousand times more considerable; this is what this fact lets you ignore.
>
> (Dupuit, 1844: 206; our translation)

Pushed to its limits, this reasoning defines the utility of a work as the provisions sum to be paid by the whole population – that is, the area under the demand function of a good. The second phase of the French engineer's approach is based on the tools he developed to establish what financing arrangements would be most likely to guarantee the highest social utility. Starting from his law of consumption, Dupuit initially dismissed private monopoly in favour of public monopoly. He showed that there is no automatic correspondence between the amount of money brought in by a toll and the total social utility (Dupuit, 1849). Equipped with the concept of "willingness to pay", he then advocated a differential pricing method according to the capacity to pay, in order to widen the levy base and deprive the wealthy of a rent resulting from the gap between the tax and their willingness to pay. Economic theory is used here to produce an evaluation device. These two stages reveal two fundamental aspects of what Muniesa and Callon call experimental performativity: contrary to the contemplative approach of the pure economics of Walras (Baranzini, 2006; Vatin, 2008), for whom the ideal-type of market is necessarily intended to be discovered and applied by the reformer, the concepts developed within the approach of an economist engineer like Dupuit are above all the result of empirical considerations: for each specific problem, a contingent tool. As such, one leaves the strict academic field: it is the situation that imposes the theory, and one does not hesitate to borrow modes of extra-academic reasoning. The idea of profiting from differentials of propensity to pay is, for example, directly inspired by the trader who, taking advantage of a lack of competition:

> resorts to an infinity of tricks to make each of them pay the greater part possible of the benefit that he considers to be at his expense. The same merchandise, disguised in various shops in various forms, is very often sold at very different prices to the rich, the wealthy, and the poor. There is the fine, the very fine, the superfine, the extra fine, which, though out of the same barrel and presenting no real difference except that of the superlative of the label, are sold at very different prices.
>
> (Dupuit, 1844: 212)

Furthermore, its tools are directly involved in the construction of the social world by setting up specific technical devices.[12]

Such is the first "tension": rather than a vision of purely theoretical performativity, in which the economist brings about a world conforming to pure ideas from his pulpit, the performativistic sociologist prefers to consider the construction as a process of trial and error in order to activate the construction of economic valuation schemes.

Psychogenic performativity and material performativity

Performativist sociology aims to move away from conventional approaches to the influence of economic theories – approaches in terms of collective representations, self-realisation or beliefs. The fundamental idea is that there are several possible reasons for an agent to act in accordance with a particular economic theory. If this can be the case because of his beliefs, he can also act in a particular sense simply because a specific technical device requires it. The first type of performativity, which gathers together the approaches we will call "conventionalist", is here called "psychogenic", in that economic theories influence the social world in the form of psychic experiences – that is, collective beliefs. The second type is called "material", insofar as it takes into account the material systems that shape the actions.

The works of Frédéric Lebaron (2000, 2010) are perfect illustrations of the psychogenic perception of performativity. In his text with the revealing title *La croyance économique* ("economic belief"), he produced the history of the constitution of a collective representation of the social world stemming from the dominant economic theory in France. This representation, essentially characterised by adherence to fundamental "economic laws" (for example, the law of supply and demand), a rational vision of human behaviour, and acceptance of the liberal dogma of self-regulation of markets, would be established following a true "proselytizing of economic reason" (Lebaron, 2000: 154). The author's remarks, however, are not to characterise the *ex nihilo* construction of a monolithic collective representation, but rather to identify a certain number of elective affinities between a conception of the social and the values of those who have the power to direct the social field in their favour. He asserts rightfully that neo-classical economics exerts a form of seduction on students: a taste for the theory of rational action and equilibrium presumes rationalising dispositions and a tendency to predict the economic world as the result of an adjustment of individual interests. These provisions are valued among young people of the dominant classes who are readily perceived as rational and balanced subjects (Lebaron, 2000: 118). As a result of his early work, Lebaron examines the shake-up of "economic belief" in the wake of the 2007 financial crisis (Lebaron, 2010). This shock is again addressed in terms of a transformation in the discourse of professional economists (mainly forecasters). Based on the principle that:

> an official forecast is [. . .] much more than a simple scientific proposal on the future to which a probability can be associated: it is also an action whose function is to construct an official representation of the "economic order" which is used as a marker for the actors.
>
> (Lebaron, 2010: 43; our translation)

Any predictive anomaly is likely to reverse the trust in the established cognitive order. Here we recognise the Bourdieusian vocabulary attached to the notion of the effect of theory. This type of process is clearly the opposite of the more classical performativist approaches described in the previous sections, focused on the role of devices that make people act as rational social actors.

Distributed performativity and planned performativity

Performativity can be rigorously "planned" or emerge from multiple interactions, which Muniesa and Callon call "distributed performance":

> An economic artefact happens to be in the right place and at the right time and the fact that it is put into use ensures its success firstly locally then its wider diffusion.
>
> (Muniesa and Callon, 2009: 301; our translation)

In the latter case, economic science does not perform social reality alone. On the contrary, it is the meeting of several collectives that leads to a movement to construct this reality. When the military junta took power in Argentina in 1976, the primary objective was to "discipline" a population deemed "ungovernable". The interests of dictatorship (or rather, of successive dictatorships) have nothing to do with the liberal dogma defended by a number of economists trained in the United States. This is without taking into account the fact that neo-liberalism can be considered as a particular mode of government which, by refocusing individuals on their interests as autonomous consumers, eliminates the worker as a turbulent political entity capable of growing the ranks of the Peronists. At least this is what Daniel Fridman (2010) defends when he studies the media campaign put in place by the Argentinian finance minister in 1977. This campaign, with the evocative name "A change of mentality", promoted the behaviour of responsible consumers and wise investors.

In the first case, advertising encourages price arbitrage, quality comparisons and savings, while in the second, a financial press is created to educate investors in finance. For Fridman, this process of normalisation of the population has as its primary objective to re-polarise the population around oppositions typical of standard economics – consumers/producers, investors/savers – in order to depart from a conflictual representation of the social world, between the military regime, benefiting the interests of entrepreneurs, and the parties, like the Peronists, defending the rights of the workers.

Without reducing the focus on the economist's single effort, considering the emergence of a community of interest prior to the performative effort, these are two important precepts of performativist sociology. The performative effort is not unique. It is found in a large number of actors (for example, economists, consumers and government) occupying heterogeneous places. The distributed conception of performative action is the essence of the notion of "make to act": an individual action is the result of a set of devices making actors act in a specific way.

Limited performativity and extended performativity

A final distinction relates to the place of performance. If restricted performativity consists of a direct link between the scientific world and the external social world, it is also necessary to focus on the transition from one world to another in a specific place where the reception conditions require various adjustments. From performativity confined within a university – where it is shown, for example, that economics students tend to cooperate less in the games of the prisoner's dilemma – we turn to an open-air performativity involving a large number of agents. Fabian Muniesa's work on the establishment of a continuous quotation system in the Paris Bourse from 1986 onwards, in place of the old auction system, is a perfect example of how an economic entity, price (Muniesa, 2011), is socially constructed within an open environment hindering the direct link between economic theory and the social world. Muniesa stresses in particular that such a study needs to open its eyes to a large number of extra-theoretical elements. Of course, financial theorists played an important role in making the technical system of continuous quotation by defining the efficient situation to which such a system would lead. Nevertheless, the practical implementation of continuous quotation reveals a large number of problems, as the transition from theoretical to practical is crucial. Consider two problematic examples: a technical example (Muniesa, 2000) and a sociological one (Muniesa, 2005). The transition from a price-fixing auction on the Paris stock exchange, namely an auction led by a broker and leading to the fixing of a price at which exchanges may take place, to continuous electronic quotation cannot be achieved without conflict. If one of the theoretical objectives of continuous quotation is price efficiency – that the latter should reflect the intrinsic value of the underlying assets – a phenomenon disturbed this assumption: we can observe high price volatility at 5 p.m. (linked to a strong concentration of activities just before the close of the market). It was found that this phenomenon, known as the "deadline effect", was mainly due to the special status of the closing price: it is held as the official price at the date of a derivative contract (Muniesa, 2000: 144). Consequently, its manipulation can be a particularly important issue for some market players: a trader or a portfolio manager may have an interest in supporting the stock upwards insofar as he participates in his assessment; conversely, he may have an interest in pulling the stock down on the day before a takeover bid. We therefore have to deal with cases of manipulation that the listed companies bear badly, especially since 1996, when the minimum number of securities to be traded was abolished (Muniesa, 2003). A continuous listing system implies that the transaction of a single security could be sufficient to determine the closing price. To alleviate this problem, the quotation needs to be adjusted by the introduction of a closing fixing: during the last five minutes of trading, exchanges are suspended, orders are collected, the price is calculated according to an automatic procedure, and exchanges are then realised.

The second example of adjustment Muniesa studies is stockbrokers' resistance to a technical system which diminishes their power of action. The end of the auction and the introduction of a computerised pricing system raised two issues. On the one hand, it was necessary to prevent the old practices from being able to "push back" on the new ones – that is, the brokers could work at the auction over the computer system. As a result, the trading terminals were kept as far away from the stock market as possible: "brokers had to be sent home". On the other hand, it was necessary to enlist "whizz kids" from the public prosecutor's office, who could prevent the implementation of the new system by integrating them into the implementation process. Various methods adopted to overcome these difficulties included offering training for older traders in order to restore power to colleagues, and reviewing the use of terminals. It is as a result of these new conditions that the device can gradually produce effects of univocity and spontaneity (Muniesa, 2000: 152) – that is, become a black box in the sense of ANT: the market price is considered as given.

These two examples show that the conditions of performativity are not contained in the theory. The number of stakeholders is therefore broadened: a technical device (closing fixing), a mode of enrolment, and market architecture (distance of the terminals from the stock exchange), etc.

Conclusion: two types of performativity

As a first approximation, the theory of performativity can be considered at the intersection of the philosophy of language and ANT. The sociological approach to performativity is essentially shaped by three works (Callon, 1998; Callon et al., 2007; MacKenzie et al., 2007a) that provide a heterogeneous view of the concept. Faced with such diversity, I have decided to concentrate on the more specifically Callonian approach developed by Callon, but also by

Fabian Muniesa (Callon, 1998; Callon and Muniesa, 2005; Muniesa and Teil, 2006; Muniesa and Callon, 2009). Starting from this, we will view it through the prism of ANT. The fundamental idea is that economic science, in the broad sense of the term, formats reality rather than observing how it works. According to Callon, economic theories create the objects they are supposed to describe, so much so that economic reality would be truly embedded in economic science. This is the meaning of the polemical assertion that:

> Yes, homo oeconomicus really does exist. Of course, he exists in the form of many species and his lineage is multiple and ramified. But if he exists he is obviously not be found in a natural state – this expression has little meaning. He is formatted, framed and equipped with prostheses which help him in his calculations and which are, for the most part, produced by economics.
>
> (Callon, 1998: 51)

The Callonian project is rooted in the idea that the daily decisions of economic agents are only possible because of their being embedded within socio-technical devices. The flagship idea of the sociology of performativity is that the scientist influences the world he is supposed to describe via a grip on individual and collective decision-making, economic science being embedded in the more technical apparatus:

> Economic agents are calculators because they are equipped, endowed with a heap of prostheses; some of them have very large powers of calculation and decision, others are virtually devoid of powers and are calculated by the strongest: they choose rationally, but by following algorithms defined by others, much like when a player of chess falls under the calculating hold of his opponent.
>
> (Callon and Ferrary, 2006: 44)

The influence of technology is then contrasted with a broader view of the social influence of economic science in terms of the transmission of knowledge (Steiner, 2001b; Lebaron, 2000, 2010), for example via economics by academia (Frank et al., 1993). According to this last view, the social world is formed in the image of a theory from the moment when everyone adopts the representation of its world. Dumez and Jeunemaître (2010b: 130) perfectly summarise this position by stressing that the theory of performativity is opposed to the very idea of a convention, namely an agreement on rules, standards and explicit or tacit coordinates. Callon is very clear on this point:

> Agency as a capacity to act and to give meaning to action can neither be contained in a human being nor localised in the institutions, norms, values, and discursive or symbolic systems assumed to produce effects on individuals. Action, including its reflexive dimension that produces meaning, takes place in hybrid collectives comprising human beings as well as material and technical devices, texts, etc.
>
> (Callon, 2005: 4)

Two theoretical elements must be retained as the originality of performativistic sociology:

A Economics performs through socio-technical devices making individuals carry out actions.

B There is a refusal to consider macro-social sets in favour of socio-technical devices.

These two points will be particularly emphasised in the next chapter, which will no longer situate the theory of performativity in relation to its theoretical roots, but will oppose it to social influence's standard approaches to economic theories. For the moment, the distinctions made by Muniesa and Callon clearly make it possible to bring out different traits of performativity. Firstly, it is experimental and material, in that it focuses mainly on the establishment of technical devices in the formation of socio-technical networks. *De facto*, the principle of symmetry between human and non-human leads mainly to a focus on the non-human. As real bridges between theory and practice, these devices act by causing actors to do things without their needing to be aware of the theories they translate. It is then distributed and expanded, in that the structuring of the social as a large socio-technical network is the consequence of a multitude of decentralised interventions. In the light of these characteristics, we view clearly what the performativist approach tends to reject: an approach that concentrates too narrowly on the direct influence of theories as systems of representations.

This chapter has focused on ANT by questioning its theoretical roots. Nevertheless, there emerges a positioning with regard to the standard approaches to the influence of economic theories on the social world. Chapter 2 will address the sociology of performativism through the prism of this positioning.

Notes

1 Quine simultaneously occupies a primordial and ambiguous place in the history of philosophy. His encounter with Carnap in Prague, while attending Schlick's lectures and being invited to the Vienna Circle, is considered the founding act of post-pragmatist American philosophy. In 1935, Carnap arrived in the United States with the support of Quine, and with him many thinkers of the century. Despite this rather unusual relationship – Quine dedicated *Word and Object* (1960) to Carnap – Quine is nonetheless the most important critic.

2 These reflections would lead Quine to a more radical critique of the ontological type: "It is philosophically interesting, moreover, that what is indeterminate in this artificial example is not just meaning, but extension, reference. My remarks on indeterminacy began as a challenge to likeness of meaning. I imagined 'an expression that could be translated into English equally defensibly in either of two ways, unlike in meaning in English'. Certainly, likeness of meaning is a contentious notion that is repeatedly challenged. Of two predicates which are alike in extension, it has never been clear when to say that they are alike in meaning and when not; it is the old matter of featherless bipeds and rational animals, or of equiangular and equilateral triangles. Reference, extension, has been the

firm thing; meaning, intention, the infirm. The indeterminacy of translation now confronting us, however, cuts across extension and intension alike. The terms 'rabbit', 'unattached rabbit part', and 'rabbit stage' differ not only in meaning; they are true of different things. Reference itself proves behaviorally inscrutable" (Quine, 1968: 191). This is the myth of the object that is disturbed: "Physical objects are postulated entities which round out, and simplify our account of the flux of experience, just, as the introduction of irrational numbers simplifies laws of arithmetic. From the point of view of the conceptual scheme of the elementary arithmetic of rational numbers alone, the broader arithmetic of rational and irrational numbers would have the status of a convenient myth, simpler than the literal truth (namely, the arithmetic of rationals) and yet containing that literal truth as a scattered part. Similarly, from a phenomenalistic point, of view, the conceptual scheme of physical objects is a convenient myth, simpler than the literal truth and yet containing that literal truth as a scattered part" (Quine, 1963: 18).

3 As Strawson underlines, Wittgenstein's objective is: "to get us away from our fascination with the dubious relation of naming, of meaning and to make us look at the speaking and writing of language as one human activity among others, interacting with others; and so to make us notice the different parts that words and sentences play in this activity" (Strawson, 1954: 72).

4 On Quine and Malinowski, see Bonnay and Laugier (2003).

5 An effective way to account for these three dimensions is to characterise the failures to which they are linked. Consider the following statement: "Fedor appreciates black tea." At first, we can fail to say that "Fedor appreciates black tea", that is to say, to refer to (Fedor, black tea, etc.). It is here the locutionary act that fails. One can then fail to affirm that "Fedor appreciates black tea", to create a new assertion inserted in a socially codified practice and which cannot be reduced to the locutory act. It is the illocutionary act: "Unless a certain effect is achieved, the illocutionary act will not have been happily, successfully performed. [. . .] I cannot be said to have warned an audience unless it hears what I say and takes what I say in a certain sense. [. . .] Generally the effect amounts to bringing about the understanding of the meaning and of the force of the locution. So the performance of an illocutionary act involves the securing of uptake" (Austin, 1962: 115–116). Thus, understanding itself depends on the context of speech, the Wittgenstein language game. So it is only in certain situations that the assertion "Fedor appreciates black tea" will be taken as a truth. Questioning the necessary conditions for the performance of the illocutionary act behind the statement "You are not feeling mouldy", Austin (1979: 249) points to the importance of the epistemic authority of the speaker. Indeed, apart from me, only a doctor can decide my physical condition. As Fedor's best friend, who better than I to say whether he likes black tea or not? Anyway, one can fail to reassure the listener who bought a box of lapsang souchong for Fedor by stating that "Fedor enjoys black tea." The perlocutionary act refers to the unnecessary consequences of the happy illocutionary act: I say, I affirm, but I do not reassure my interlocutor.

6 The drive to explain social situations by returning to local circumstances owes much to the ethnomethodological work of Harold Garfinkel (1967). See Knorr-Cetina (1981).

7 The idea of constructed scientific facts is a classic in the history of science, often associated with Gaston Bachelard in France: "We only have to speak of an object in order to believe ourselves objective. But in our first choice the object designates us more than we designate and what we believe our fundamental thoughts about the world are often secrets about the youth of our mind. Sometimes we marvel at the chosen object; we accumulate hypotheses and dreams; we form convictions which have the

appearance of knowledge. But the original source is impure: the first evidence is not a fundamental truth. In fact, scientific objectivity is possible only if one has first broken with the immediate object [...], if one has stopped and contradicted the thoughts arising from the first observation" (Bachelard, 1949: 9; our translation). It is above all on the methodological framework that Latour distinguishes himself from his French predecessors, who are too rationalistic and attached to a too cumulative perspective of science for his taste (Latour, 1989: 12). It is not surprising when we read from Bachelard's pen: "The history of science, meditated in the values of progress and in the resistances of epistemological obstacles, truly gives us the integral man. If this history has a manifest reality, it is precisely because one feels that it is one of the profound traits of man's destiny" (Bachelard, 1971: 173–174; our translation).

8 Without going into details, Brownian motion consists of a random movement (here, that of prices), and one of its characteristics is that the logarithm of variations follows a normal distribution (see Chapter 7).

9 It is of paramount importance to specify that translation is never neutral, it is synonymous with the mobilisation of resources – diversion of agents, as well as reappropriation by the latter. As such, more than just intermediaries, the devices are considered mediators.

10 The notion of device is borrowed from Deleuze (1989), who found it in Foucault. More precisely, the notion of layout serves essentially to qualify the influence of the "macro-power" (State) in the creation and diffusion of social norms, to the benefit of sets of "micro-powers" contained in more localised socio-technical devices.

11 "To determine the objectivity or subjectivity of a claim, the efficiency or perfection of a mechanism, we do not look for their *intrinsic* qualities but at all the transformations they undergo *later* in the hands of others" (Latour, 1987: 258). More recently, Latour (2012: 17–18; our translation) stated: "We wanted to understand by what instruments, machinery, tangible conditions, historical and anthropological conditions it was possible to produce objectivity. Without appealing to some transcendent certainty that would have suddenly and without discussion, aimed Science with a big S against the idea. In our view scientific objectivity is too important to be left to the sole defence of what I'd called mix-all 'rationalism' which too often interrupts irrationally insistent opponents."

12 It should be noted, however, that making Dupuit a figure of extra-academic thought is an anachronism. If one can rightly characterise his approach as based on practical cases, he nevertheless remains a prominent figure in the history of theoretical thought (Etner, 1987; Ekelund and Hebert, 1999).

2 The theory of performativity

A double remoteness

> Nature does not care – so we assume – whether we penetrate her secrets and establish successful theories about her workings and apply these theories successfully in predictions. In the social sciences, the matter is more complicated and in the following fact lies one of the fundamental differences between these two types of theories: the kind of economic theory that is known to the participants in the economy has effect on the economy itself, provided the participants can observe the economy, i.e., determine its present state.
>
> However, the distribution of the kind of theory available, and the degree of its acceptance, will differ from one case to the other. This in turn will affect the working of the economy. There is thus a "back-coupling" or "feedback" between the theory and the object of the theory, an interrelation which is definitely lacking in the natural sciences.
>
> (Morgenstern, 1972: 707)

> We are suffering the most unbearable thing. They try to cover us with lice, larvae, caterpillars. The air of microbes has been populated (Pasteur). We can now drink and eat in pure water.
>
> The print multiplies. And there are people who find that all this does not swarm enough, who make verses, poetry, surreality, which add up.
>
> Dreams (it seems that dreams deserve to enter the dance, that it is better not to forget them). Reincarnations, paradises, hells, finally what: after life, death still to live!
>
> Francis Ponge, *La mort à vivre.*

Francis Ponge's poem *La mort à vivre* illustrates the epistemology of the performativist approach: it is a question of understanding these devices, concepts, tools created by economists, which become autonomous and are part of the mediation between actors and the world around them. The economist populates the world with new entities in the same way Pasteur populates the world of microbes (Latour, 1993b). Morgenstern reveals a more classic view. The link between theory and world is approached in the light of an epistemological question: what to do with the influence of our theories on our objects of research? On the one hand, there is the construction of the social world through the implementation of technical devices; on the other hand, there is the effect of scientific knowledge on the social benchmarks of agents. These are two ways of considering the "performative phenomenon" symptomatic of what performativist sociology is moving away from.

The aim of this second chapter will be to clarify this remoteness by giving substance to what Callonian sociology opposes. To do this, I will position the theory of performativity with respect to two poles. The first pole is the critique of economic sociology toward mainstream economics. It will be argued that this criticism has as background the opposition introduced by Karl Polanyi between formal economics and substantive economics, and more particularly, the notion of social embeddedness of the economic sphere. It will be apparent from this positioning that the major characteristic of the theory of performativity, in addition to its focus on technical devices, is the rejection of the idea of social embeddedness – a concept that can be (as I will try to bring to light) seen as the analytical heart of economic sociology. This setback is intimately linked, first, to a desire to support an ontology devoid of social or cultural categories of a macro-social order, and second, to the assumed absence of a critical perspective with regard to economic theory.

The second pole is that of the standard conceptions of the social influence of economic theories, bringing together both sociologists and economists. An attempt will be made to combine these approaches around the use of the notion of convention. Economic theory has indeed engendered an important debate about the effects of the social influence of the theorist's discourse on his ability to tell the truth. In an epistemological framework, reducing the value of truth to predictive ability, to say that the economist can generate or destroy the reality he claims to describe, is not without its issues. From this perspective, an economic theory influences the social world in that it becomes a convention around which the agents coordinate. Sociology has also turned its attention to what is customary to name, after Bourdieu, the "theory effect": a social theory leads to reality by creating new norms of representation of the social world. The sociological approach here takes the position of considering such an effect as a new object of analysis, unlike economics, which considers it as an epistemological problem. Nevertheless, as I will demonstrate, the social influence of theories is always considered from a conventional angle: a theory becomes a conventional reference point guiding the agents in their decision-making. This mapping work, which will be carried out in the first two sections of the chapter, will be followed by an illustration using the examples of Karl Polanyi and Marie-France Garcia-Parpet, whose work, although not from the milieu of performativist sociology, is often considered as a founding act.

First remoteness: economic sociology and social embeddedness

The notion of social embeddedness has played a major role in the history of economic sociology. The course of this discipline can be seen as a long work on the idea that the economy, as a sphere of activity, is necessarily embedded, according to Polanyi's term, into the wider social sphere. The distinction between formal economics and substantive economics, deeply linked to the notion of the social construction of the economy, will allow us to think of a certain unity of economic sociology, the unity that the performativist sociology breaks. The rejection of the notion of embeddedness is also what distinguishes the performativist approach from standard approaches to the social influence of economic statements. This will be studied in the next section. The primary purpose of this section is to emphasise the central role of the idea of the social embeddedness of the economic sphere. If this notion finds its moment of glory only when it is recovered by the new economic sociology, it will be shown that those who are often considered the founding fathers of economic sociology (Durkheim, Weber, Pareto, Tönnies) adopt a similar perspective which Polanyi inherits. There is no claim in the matter of the history of ideas. As in the context of the philosophy of language, the objective is above all to situate clearly the sociology of performativity by emphasising the major break it constitutes with regard to almost all of the sociological tradition. Following a relatively classic reconstruction, it will be shown that the different constitutive approaches of contemporary economic sociology can be considered as so many variations of the general notion of embeddedness. It is a homogenisation whose only objective is to outline the strength of the divorce between economic sociology and performativist sociology.

Economic sociology: the market as a social structure and the enrichment of Homo economicus

The idea that the economic sphere fits into broader social spheres is intimately linked to the desire to enrich and even compete with economic reasoning centred on rational action. In this case, what is regularly referred to is an approach that is both individualistic and rationalistic as it crystallises in the early neo-classical authors: Jevons, Marshall, Menger and Walras.[1] John Davis (2003: 25–26) thus summarises their conception of the individual:

- Individuals are the basic unit of any economic analysis because only their behaviours can be understood in terms of choice.
- Individual choices can only be understood in terms of internal states, tastes and desires. Agents seek to maximise their utility.
- Individuals are able to discriminate among the options available to them by applying marginalist principles.

We shall have the opportunity to return in greater detail to this theory of the individual in Part III. The point is that such a perspective implies on the one hand that economics is defined as the science of choice, and on the other hand that this choice is only the result of a process of internal deliberation. Thus, the theoretical market is above all the abstract place of encounters of individuals seeking to maximise their respective utilities through the exchange of goods which constitute their initial endowments. It then remains to determine the rules of interactions. In the standard theory of general equilibrium, it is the price (or rather the price set for each good and each period) that mediates between a multitude of rational agents.[2] There is therefore a consubstantial relationship between the theoretical market and the equally theoretical economic agent: the theoretical market establishes an arena within which rational behaviour can unfold "freely". The representation of the agent and of the action developed by the neo-classical economics from the beginning of the twentieth century has given rise to many criticisms. A large proportion of these are built into the sociological field, leading to the emergence of a competing literature in the analysis of economic phenomena: economic sociology. The reprimand which is of interest to us here, against economic analysis, touches on a conception considered too narrow (absence of context of socialisation) and too broad (the whole of the market mechanism rests on its shoulders) with regard to individual behaviour. This would imply that:

- economic agents are endowed with uncommon cognitive abilities so that they can arbitrate between all the goods in an economy;
- they hold relevant information on all of these goods;
- the market describes the only relevant institution of economic coordination.

From the outset, economic sociology has given itself the aim of showing that the agent can only really act in society if his behaviour is regulated by norms of representation and behaviour. It also argues that the market is only one type of institution among others. It enriches the economic agent through the social, and the economy is only a segment of the social world in which it is inserted.

Vilfredo Pareto considers, for example, a methodological complementarity between economics and sociology, while stipulating that, nevertheless, sociology attains a more advanced stage of scientific research:

> Human society is the subject of numerous studies. Some have special names; law, history, political economy, the history of religions, and so on. Others embrace still confused matters, the synthesis of which are already distinct, aims at studying human society in general. We can give this group of studies the name Sociology.
>
> (Pareto, 1917 [1968]: § 1; our translation)

It thus leaves room for economic analysis, considering that the latter, regarded as pure economics, is nothing but a first approximation of reality, the three approximations being pure economics, applied economics and, finally, sociology: "We proceed by successive approximations; that is to say, by firstly considering the phenomenon as a whole, deliberately neglecting details of which we shall take account in the following approximations" (Pareto, 1917 [1968]: § 69, 9; our translation). If theoretical economics is considered as a first stage of the perception of reality, it retains all its legitimacy insofar as it is supplemented by another type of approach, dwelling on phenomena outside the sphere of logical actions (specific to the economy). If Pareto retains an individualistic approach, he has the merit of thinking about the interaction of behaviours from different spheres of activity.

Since the disciplinary field was already largely marked by the works of Weber and Durkheim, Paretian sociology has never really been able to impose itself as a reference. The works of these illustrious contemporaries are now more widely used. In my view, they combine two main characteristics that can be found in the new economic sociology: (i) to define the economy not as the sphere of rational choice (formal economics), but as a type of activity defined by its place within the social space (substantive economics); (ii) to consider this economic sphere as embedded within social institutions beyond these activities alone. These two points justify both the consideration of the market sphere as a social structure and the strong rationality of agents as an unnecessary hypothesis.

Durkheim and his school (mainly Marcel Mauss and Francois Simiand) are at the outset an alternative to economic theory, and in fact to the whole of the social sciences taken as special sciences in the face of a general sociology (Steiner, 2005a) that goes so far as to use the term "Durkheimian imperialism". When he founded *l'Année sociologique*, Durkheim defined the object of the social sciences according to a division of labour, of which sociology is the central hub. In this perspective, sociology aims to replace economics by imposing an alternative explanatory mode whose central concept is social facts. The latter are defined as "manners of acting, thinking and feeling, external to the individual and endowed with a power of coercion by virtue of which they exercise control over him" (Durkheim, 1895: 97; our translation). A notion which is the starting point of the Durkheimian critique of political economy, which can be reconstructed in two points: a critique of the notion of economic facts, and a critique of explanation based on the desire for wealth. Durkheim, in his first major work on sociology, *De la division du travail social* (1893 [1930]), attacks a vision which Karl Polanyi would have described as an economistic view, namely that the division of labour must, above all, be considered in purely economic terms: it is a way to improve productivity and increase the wealth of human society. Durkheim grasps the division of labour as a "total social fact", to use the terminology of Marcel Mauss – that is, those facts which "in some cases set in motion the whole of society and its institutions [. . .] and in other cases only a very large number of institutions, especially when these exchanges and contracts relate more to individuals" (Mauss, 1902–1938 [2006]: 274; our translation). For Durkheim, more than a mere economic configuration, division of labour is not only a social organisation producing solidarity, but also a system of images – that is, a constitutive representation of a common consciousness. This configuration, as a system of representations, imposes itself on social actors as an external object. They abandon themselves spontaneously, alienating part of their personality (Durkheim, 1893 [1930]: 69). The economic sphere is therefore embedded in a moral and cognitive sphere (a representation of the world).

The division of labour is consubstantial with a type of solidarity that Durkheim calls organic, which is opposed to the mechanical solidarity of traditional societies, and which is the basis of a legal system needed for commercial economic life. Economic activity is part of a system of representations resulting in a set of rules that guarantee the proper functioning of society and the economy. This is particularly the case when Durkheim discusses the possibility of contractual exchange: "Every contract presumes [. . .] that, behind the committing parties, there is a society ready to intervene to enforce commitments that have been taken" (Durkheim, 1893 [1930]: 82; our translation). Thus, the sociologist places himself as a precursor to contemporary institutionalist approaches: the difficulty of an economic exchange based on necessarily incomplete contracts makes an economic sphere detached from other social spheres unthinkable. In this way, the division of labour, like the gift-giving practices of Mauss, is above all a foundation of society rather than a particular social sphere.

Durkheim thinks on the one hand that economists wrongly consider some social facts from the exclusive angle of the economy (the division of labour), yet on the other hand that they tend to put economic life first. To view, as Spencer and J. S. Mill do, society as a set of freely passed contracts is to confuse causes and effects (Durkheim, 1895 [1930]: 188). Contracts are not at the basis of society – it is the latter (and its cognitive, moral and legal apparatus) that is the condition of the former. This reasoning leads Durkheim to question the image of the individual associated with the economic perception of society:

> Man is double. In him there are two beings: an individual being who has his base in the organism and whose circle of action is, by this very fact, narrowly limited, and a social being who represents in us the highest reality, in the intellectual and moral order, which we may know by observation, I mean society. This duality of our nature results, in practical order, from the irreducibility of the moral ideal to the utilitarian motive, and, in the order of thought, the irreducibility of reason to individual experience. As long as he participates in society, the individual naturally transcends himself, both when he thinks and when he acts.
>
> (Durkheim, 1912 [1960]: 23; our translation)

The agent, by its social essence, does not have to carry the whole weight of the market system as it does (according to Durkheim) in the individualistic approach of political economy. In accordance with the saying, one must explain social facts using social facts.

Beyond economic necessities, Durkheim therefore envisages the emergence of modern capitalism in terms of the emergence of new social and societal configurations. The process is well known: societies with strong mechanical dominance give way to societies structured by organic solidarity, characterised by a strong social division of labour. Unable to directly observe these "types" of solidarity, Durkheim uses as an indicator the nature of the legal system, and this refers to the way individuals relate to the society to which they belong. Durkheim identifies two types of law: repressive law, which punishes criminals, and restitutive law, which consists of simply restoring the social order. The first type is the equivalent to the expiation of a crime by a society united around a common consciousness: "The punishment therefore consists essentially of a passionate reaction, of gradual intensity, that society exercises through a body constituted by those of its members who have violated certain rules of conduct" (Durkheim, 1893 [1930]: 64; our translation). This is a society that punishes: a society made up of identical individuals united by a common consciousness to which they alienate their personality (Durkheim, 1893 [1930]: 69). Solidarity rests on the resemblance of individuals who share everything and who ultimately have no margin of freedom, no subjectivity.

The second type of law, called "restitutive" (for example, expectation of damages), no longer concerns the whole of society as a uniform body, but rather a part of it, an autonomous subgroup (for example, commercial law and the sphere of commerce). Restitutive law is part of a type of solidarity which presupposes a differentiation of tasks, which itself presupposes that individuals are given a sphere of freedom conducive to the constitution of their own personality. Organic solidarity is therefore the counterpart of the division of social labour. Thus, the division of labour is not an obstacle to solidarity; on the contrary, it is the foundation. The most important thing here, as far as we are concerned, is that the division of labour, as an economic fact, is necessarily embedded in the division of labour as a social institution. This is a force of the social fact that is rejected by performativist analysis, recalling that Latour makes Gabriel Tarde, Durkheim's theoretical historical enemy, a tutelary figure.

It is customary to contrast the works of Emile Durkheim with those of Max Weber according to an epistemological dividing line between holism and methodological individualism. Indeed, while the starting point of Durkheim is the study of social facts using social facts, Weber (1921 [1978]: 4) defines sociology as:

> a science concerning itself with the interpretive understanding of social action and thereby with a causal explanation of its course and consequences. We shall speak of "action" insofar as the acting individual attaches a subjective meaning to his behaviour–be it overt or covert, omission or acquiescence. Action is "social" insofar as its subjective meaning takes account of the behaviour of others and is thereby oriented in its course.

Since a social study starting from the whole society – he speaks of a functional analysis (Weber, 1921 [1978]: 18) – can only be a preliminary, Weber seems to base his sociology on individual action alone. Thus, the social fact of Durkheim disappears in favour of a reduction to individual action. Nevertheless, if the Durkheimian thing (the social fact) disappears, it is only to be redistributed within individual consciousness. Indeed, if Weber starts from the individual, the latter is necessarily viewed from a social point of view. For example, when he speaks of the way sociology treats the state, Weber (1921 [1978]: 14) writes:

> [F]or sociological purposes, there is no such thing as a collective personality which "acts". When reference is made in a sociological context to a state, a nation, a corporation, a family, or an army corps, or to similar collectivities, what is meant is, on the contrary, only a certain kind of development of actual or possible social actions of individual persons. [. . .] These concepts of collective entities which are found both in common sense and in juristic

> and other technical forms of thought, have a meaning in the minds of individual persons, partly as of something actually existing, partly as something with normative authority. This is true not only of judges and officials, but of ordinary private individuals as well. Actors thus in part orient their action to them, and in this role such ideas have a powerful, often a decisive, causal influence on the course of action of real, individuals.

Here we are very close to Durkheim's position, which, let us recall, speaks of an alienation from the collective categories. This perspective refers to support for ontological individualism: social fact is above all a category of thought, not a reality independent of individuals. Without actors, there are no social facts. For Weber, if individuals are the essence of social life, their behaviour is oriented in relation to sets of representations – that is, of maxims which they expect to see observed by *others*. These maxims are respected in that they represent a legitimate order inherited from custom or constituted by interest (not to be *boycotted* by *others*). The basis of this legitimacy can be, according to a well-known typology (Weber, 1921 [1978]: 36), tradition, affective beliefs and rational beliefs in value or legality – that is, submission to a formal status. What do these maxims condition? Mainly two things: the existence and the scope of the sphere of the economy. The existence of an economic sphere requires, as in Durkheim, a legal sphere guaranteeing ownership and respect for contracts. Social conditions also influence the configuration of material needs and the means to satisfy them. In other words, the different orders legitimise and define the economic sphere from the moment when it constitutes a stack of specific meanings and activities. Weber (1921 [1978]: 68) takes the example of goods:

> It is necessary for the purposes of a sociological theory of economic action to introduce the concept of "goods" at an early stage [. . .]. For this theory is concerned with a type of action which is given its specific meaning by the results of the actors' deliberations, which themselves can be isolated only in theory [but cannot be observed empirically, admitting that] [e]conomic theory, the theoretical insights of which provide the basis for the sociology of economic action, might (perhaps) be able to proceed differently; the latter may find it necessary to create its own theoretical constructs.

In this way, Weber calls for an avoidance of confusion between the economic orientation of an activity, defined by the aims of the activity in question, and its technical orientation, exclusively focused on means. If means–end rational action seems to be the cornerstone of its analysis of modernity, it is through values that he studies the structuring of the modern economy. In his study *The Protestant Ethic and the Spirit of Capitalism* (1904–1905 [2001]), the notion of *Beruf*, the task imposed by God, serves as a stepping stone to economic rationalisation: "The only way of living acceptably to God was not to surpass worldly morality in monastic asceticism, but solely through the fulfilment of the obligations imposed upon the individual by his position in the world" (Weber, 1904–1905 [2001]: 40). Another entry point in Weber's economic sociology is that of the market.

To understand the way in which Weber envisages it, it is first and foremost essential to return to a major distinction in his work between communal relationship and associative relationship (Weber, 1921 [1978]: 40). Communal relationship refers to a social bond based on the traditional and affective feeling of belonging to the same community. Associative relationship refers to a relationship based on the compromise or coordination of rationally motivated interests. This distinction inevitably suggests Ferdinand Tönnies' distinction between community and civil society. The community defines a group in which each person moves by a "will of the community", like the family, and is also based on a sense of belonging in communities. In a society, "[n]obody wants to do anything for anyone else, nobody wants to yield or give anything unless he gets something in return that he regards as at least an equal trade-off" (Tönnies, 1912 [2001]: 52). However, unlike Tönnies, Weber does not argue for historical sequencing between the two types of organisation. It is a strong point of his approach to the markets, which, if they seem to be only in an associative relationship (coordination of interest), also belong to communalisation (the feeling of belonging to the community). For Weber (1921 [1978]: 635), it is possible to speak of a market "wherever there is competition, even if only unilateral, for opportunities of exchange of a plurality of potential parties". Yet each of its components, namely exchange and competition, can only take place over time if there is a market community (Swedberg, 1998). As in Durkheim, the market exchange will find its place only if it is based on a community (in the sense of communalisation) around its different components. Monetary exchange, for example, requires that a common space of legitimacy opens up, a community order:

> [A]ny act of exchange involving the use of money (sale) is a social action simply because the money used derives its value from its relation to the potential action of others. Its acceptability rests exclusively on the expectation that it will continue to be desirable and can be further used as a means of payment. [. . .] Money creates a group by virtue of material interest relations between actual and potential participants in the market and its payments. At the fully developed stage, the so-called money economy, the resulting situation looks as if it had been created by a set of norms established for the very purpose of bringing it into being.
>
> (Weber, 1921 [1978]: 636)

Sociation and communalisation are therefore intimately linked, as the market is embedded in a community sphere which is a condition of its existence and a way of "making society" (François, 2008).

A fundamental contribution of the founders' economic sociology is therefore to insist on the necessary "embeddedness" of market relations within a particular social (and symbolic) environment. The notion of embeddedness is intimately linked to the name of the Hungarian economist Karl Polanyi. He will make the link between old and new economic sociologies, which will make it possible to emphasise that when rejecting the concept of embeddedness, it is this whole tradition that performativist sociology rejects.

Formal economics versus substantive economics: Karl Polanyi

The case of Karl Polanyi is particularly interesting, in that his work profoundly influenced the revival of economic sociology in the early 1980s. The famous article by Mark Granovetter, "Economic action and social structure: the problem of embeddedness" (1985), considered a foundation of what we have come to call the new economic sociology, is a direct reference to the concept of embeddedness. Steiner (2007) also points out that Polanyi remains one of the most cited authors in economic sociology. Moreover, Michel Callon regularly refers to the notion of embeddedness in order to explicitly detach himself from it, hence our interest. As with Durkheim and Weber, Polanyi adopts an institutionalised, embedded vision of the economy.[3]

Two definitions of economics

In *The Great Transformation* (1944 [2001]), and in a chapter entitled "The economy as instituted process" (1957), Polanyi first tackles economic theory as it is then practised, concentrated solely and obsessively on price as the economic fact *par excellence*, thus describing the whole economy as determined by the choices prompted by the scarcity of means (Polanyi, 1957). He describes this type of economic theory as "formal". In general, this definition of economics refers to that provided by Lionel Robbins in *Essay on the Nature and Significance of Economic Science*:[4] "Economics is the science which studies human behaviour as a relationship between ends and scarce means which have alternative uses" (Robbins, 1932: 15). The object of economics is thus reduced to a constraint choice. Polanyi wants to embark on a different path: that of substantive economics. This new meaning refers to economy as an institutionalised process, as a set of constant interactions between the human being, acting in the quest for his subsistence, and his physical and social environment. Two notions are invoked: that of process and that of institution. The first refers to an analysis in terms of material movements encompassing the production, distribution and appropriation of goods. The second is the fact that these movements take shape within a structure of interactions that come under custom and law – in other words, institutionalisation. Hence the institutionalised nature of the process:

> The instituting of the economic process vests that process with unity and stability; it produces a structure with a definite function in society; it shifts the place of the process in society, thus adding significance to its history; it centres interest on values, motives and policy. Unity and stability, structure and function, history and policy spell out operationally the content of our assertion that the human economy is an instituted process.
>
> (Polanyi, 1957: 249–250)

Polanyi's main criticism of formal economics is that when the latter undertakes to study particular economies through the "universal" principle of choice, it neglects the equally universal need for human communities to organise (that is, to institutionalise) their subsistence on the basis of a historically located definition of needs. This oversight leads to two biases that constitute the economistic fallacy (Polanyi, 1977a). This error is in fact the confusion of the two possible meanings of economy:

- By ignoring the necessary institutional structures particular to each social group, formal economic theory comes to consider implicitly the present arrangement as universal, and in fact the touchstone of all analysis. Among these universalised particular rules, one finds on the one hand that of scarcity, on the other hand that of generalised commodification, illustrated in *The Great Transformation* by the commodification of land, labour and money.
- Just as they look at others on their own, economists see their own societies as steered by unchangeable rules to which human beings would be subjected. As such, Polanyi argues that "the market system violently distorts our views on man and society", the latter two appear to be subject to "economic determinism" (1947a: 96).

In order to avoid these biases, Polanyi launches the substantivist project to study the institutionalisation of economic processes. It is a question of parting from economic analysis starting only with individual maximisation behaviour towards an institutional analysis. For Polanyi, pure individualism has the property of analytically fixing institutions because it amounts to considering as belonging to the human what is in reality relative to the historically located institutions that frame its action. It is therefore necessary to accompany the study of individual behaviours with a study of their institutional environment. In other words, where the formal economy sets scarcity and choice as ahistorical facts, the substantive economy:

> implies neither choice nor insufficiency. Man's livelihood may or may not involve the need for choice. Custom and tradition, as a rule, eliminate choice, and if choice there be, it need not be induced by limiting the effects of any "scarcity" of means.
>
> (Polanyi, 1977b: 27)

It is to these institutions that Polanyi proposes to return with the aid of a conceptual toolbox discussed in detail in the next section.

The role of institutions

An examination of the means by which the economy, in the sense of economic reality, acquires its stability, or the recurrent interdependence of its members through its institutionalisation, has to focus on a "combination of a very few patterns which may be called forms of integration" (Polanyi, 1957: 250). A first taxonomy of these forms is born in *The Great Transformation*. This will be repeated and modified in "The economy as instituted process" (Polanyi, 1957). In the latter text, three forms of empirically observable integration emerge: reciprocity, redistribution and exchange. This triptych relates very precisely to the movement of goods, namely movements in physical space and changes in ownership (Maucourant, 2005: 62). Each of these forms of integration refers to a type of arrangement (symmetry, centrality or market). These systems are much more than the mere aggregation of individual acts: "Reciprocity behaviour between individuals integrates the economy only if symmetrically organized structures, such as a symmetrical system of kinship groups, are given. But a kinship system never arises as the result of mere reciprocating behaviour on the personal level" (Polanyi, 1957: 251). These structures are heuristically necessary for the regularity of the movements observed using integration forms:

a Reciprocity is only possible if there is a principle of symmetry such as Polanyi explicitly finds in the work of the anthropologist Bronislaw Malinowski, *Argonauts of the Western Pacific* (1922). He describes a principle of Melanesian intertribal exchange known as *kula*, popularised in France by the works of Marcel Mauss (1923–1924 [2007]). The principle is, briefly, as follows: during large maritime expeditions, the sailors used exchanges of precious objects according to a temporal frequency and a precise direction of rotation. These exchanges were subject to the obligation of reciprocity of the gift-exchange type – that is, the obligations to receive and to reciprocate: the person who receives is obliged to return on a subsequent journey. Within the setting of the *kula*, the reciprocal movement of goods is possible only if each individual "possesses" a correspondent in another island. In other words, reciprocity cannot emancipate itself from a symmetrical social structure.

b Redistribution, which Polanyi describes as a movement of appropriation in the direction of a centre and then towards the outside, is subsumed by the establishment of a merging of wealth by virtue of custom. The society must be structured around a centre.

c The third form of integration is exchange. It requires, in order to be envisaged as such, the support of a market that creates prices. Polanyi distinguishes three types of exchanges: operational exchange (simple passing from hand to hand), decision-making exchange (fixed-rate appropriation movement) and integrative exchange (appropriation movement at a negotiated rate).

The social movements offered to the observer with the aid of the three mental tools of reciprocity, redistribution and exchange (these three forms of integration being heuristic tools, and not *per se* external realities) require special institutional arrangements. Individual action is possible only if there is an appropriate institutional structure:

> Broadly, the proposition holds that all economic systems known to us up to the end of feudalism in Western Europe were organised either on the principle of reciprocity or redistribution, or house holding, or some combination of the three. These principles were institutionalised with the help of a social organisation which, inter alia, made use of the patterns of symmetry, centricity, and autarchy. In this framework, the orderly production and distribution of goods was secured through a great variety of

> individual motives disciplined by general principles of behaviour. Among these motives gain was not prominent. Custom and law, magic and religion cooperated in inducing the individual to comply with rules of behaviour which, eventually, ensured his functioning in the economic system.
>
> (Polanyi, 1944 [2001]: 57)

It follows from this analysis that the economic sphere, if one reduces it to the market-oriented sphere, only exists when it is integrated in a system of representation (the supporting structures) conditioning its existence. Such are the origins of the notion of social embedding of commercial activity. The next section will be devoted to its reception by the new economic sociology. It sets the ground for the rest of our work: to show how the role of economists in the construction of the social world has been theorised from a particular modality of embeddedness within the approaches of the economic theories' social influence that reject the performativist sociology.

Contemporary economic sociology: different modalities of embeddedness

The renewal of economic sociology since the 1970s does not seem to call into question the primary principle of the founding fathers: economic organisation, essentially the market, maintains intimate relations with other spheres of society. The lexicon of embeddedness is now common, and Polanyi a reference author. If one focuses specifically on the market, it should be understood as a social structure (Steiner, 2005b), like a set of regularities of interactions maintained by various mechanisms. Swedberg (1994) focuses on this element:

> My main emphasis, however, will be to look at markets from a particular perspective, namely as a specific type of social structure. Social structure can be defined in a number of ways, but what is usually meant by this term is some kind of recurrent and patterned interactions between agents that are maintained through sanctions.

We shall follow here Ronan Le Velly (2012), who makes the decision to map the field of the new economic sociology by referring to the different conditions for embeddedness of markets mobilised by sociologists.[5] This approach introduces the continuity I seek here to emphasise between old and new economic sociology. I will concentrate on three different conditions of embedding: social networks, formal rules and cultural meanings. In the end, the focal point of economic sociology is that the encounter of supply and demand, as well as the underlying anthropology necessary for the market mechanism, implies specific investments relative to these conditions. In order to clearly specify the context in which performativity sociology emerges, briefly detailed here are examples for each of the conditions of embeddedness.

Embeddedness and networks

The name of the American sociologist Mark Granovetter is systematically associated with the emergence of the notion of network in sociology. This refers to the links between social actors: economic action is socially situated, and can only be understood insofar as it takes place within a network characterised by its density, form and the nature of its ties. The last characteristic refers directly to the fact that a network is ultimately only a set of bilateral links. In his well-known article "The strength of weak ties", Granovetter (1973) shows that the strength of a tie (assessed according to the duration of the relationship and its emotional task) is an essential element of understanding market relations: "As in other parts of economic life, the overlay of social relations on what may begin in purely economic transactions plays a crucial role" (Granovetter, 1985: 498). Granovetter shows, by way of illustration, that the chances of finding a job are all the stronger because we maintain a large network of weak ties. This intuition was later developed by Ronald Burt (1992). The strength of weak links is essentially the fact of a privileged place within a network: it is the opportunity to make the link between two disconnected subgroups. The actor who comes to fill what Burt calls a "structural hole" via a weak tie enjoys an advantageous situation (under the assumption that an actor cannot maintain strong links with two other actors without sharing with them at least a weak link). Granovetter (1974) notes, in his executives' labour market survey, that in the Boston area 56% of respondents found employment through personal relationships, compared with just under 20%, respectively, through formal procedures standards or spontaneous applications. A closer look reveals that almost 30% of the sample had their latest job even though no research was under way. Thus, the matching of offers and jobseekers does not seem to be explained by the price variable (wage) alone. The place an individual occupies within various networks (family, friendship), as well as the informational advantages it confers on him, are elements of the first order. The embeddedness is therefore both reticular and structural: it depends on the links and the overall structure of the network. The work of Brian Uzzi (1996) on the New York-based ready-to-wear industry is a perfect example of reticular embeddedness. The author unveils a systematic link between the degree of embedding and the probability of bankruptcy. This connection takes the form of a U-shaped curve: if the strength of the ties that unite the producers with their suppliers and their customers is first and foremost an asset, it becomes a handicap as it imposes too much demand on relationships. On the one hand, customised and recurring links establish a relationship of mutual trust, facilitating contractual negotiations and allowing more precise information about customers and suppliers to be stored. On the other hand, shutting oneself up in too dense a network, cut off from the rest of the market, risks bypassing interesting opportunities. According to classic economic sociology, markets are embedded in social relationships; here, they are characterised by structured networks.

Embeddedness and regulation

As we have seen earlier, both Durkheim and Weber grant law a central role in the structuring of the economy. It regulates exchanges and establishes the space of the rules of commercial relations. The study of legal systems has of course also been a central element of economic thought since its emergence. Thinkers like John Roger Commons (1924) place emphasis on the law as a system of rules necessary for the establishment of the market.[6] Commons studied the various stages that led from feudal systems to American capitalism at the beginning of the twentieth century. The institutional dynamic is essentially based on the mutation of definitions of concepts and terms used within the legal apparatus that regulates economic activity while resolving legal conflicts.

For Commons, the evolution of the rules, by a constant redefinition of the terms following conflicts between parties, is the basis of an institutionalism founded on legal evolutionism: common law is the vital element of evolution of economic systems, in that it combines the use of precedents and takes into account historical circumstances. This therefore ensures, for Commons, both the continuity and evolution of the law and economic regulation:

> In general it is precedents that are described as the "unwritten law", while statutes, by-laws, corporation charters are the "written" law. But the written law is only words. The "unwritten" law is written in the decisions of disputes which construe the written law in particular cases. It is practices, customs, and precedents – in short, this unwritten law – that is the living law. This is the common law method of making law.
>
> (Commons, 1934 [2005]: 707)

Subsequently, Commons develops a theory of economic stages based on the evolution of the concepts of freedom's definitions, ownership and the secure process of law (due process of law). Let us focus on the case of property. For Commons, the transformation of feudal societies towards Anglo-Saxon capitalism in the early nineteenth century was essentially based on the shift from a definition of property based on use value to a definition based on exchange value. This process took place through a succession of disputes calling for decisions by the judicial authority. In the case of *Slaughter House* (Commons, 1924: 11), in 1872, the State of Louisiana granted a butchers' corporation a monopoly on slaughter in New Orleans, and thereby regulated the price paid to other butchers for slaughter. The latter then lodged a complaint with the Federal Court, arguing that the Fourteenth Amendment of the American Constitution, prohibiting any state interference leading to depriving individuals of their "life, freedom, or property", had been violated. Faced with the vagueness of this rule, the Supreme Court had to decide between two definitions of the term "property": if property means the ownership of an exchange value (freedom of sale of the thing[7]), then the Federal Court would have been obliged to intervene. In defining property in relation to commerce, monopoly is thus presented as a deprivation of individual property by the state. If, on the other hand, property means property of a use value (freedom of physical use of the matter), then there was no reason to oppose this monopoly, with the decision of the court setting a precedent under common law. The conflict of interpretation among the judges of the Federal Court first turned in favour of the second definition, supported by Judge Miller, at the expense of the first. The latter did not, under a system of jurisprudence, find any origin. The change would occur in 1884, when the Slaughter House

Company in turn complained against the state of Louisiana for opening the market to another company. In the absence of being able to justify itself by the force of precedent, the minority interpretation in terms of ownership of an exchange value, supported by Judge Field, found in Adam Smith the origin of such a definition: "Justice Field now stated that this meaning of property was derived from Adam Smith" (Commons, 1924: 14).[8] If, in this second case, the two interpretations led to the same opinion as to the legitimacy of breaking the monopoly, it was a chance to introduce the idea of the legitimacy of a new interpretation of the notion of property which would take a number of years to establish. It is here that the very notion of competition is being challenged:

> Competition is not Nature's "struggle for existence" but is an artificial arrangement supported by the moral, economic, and physical sanctions of collective action. The theory of free competition developed by economists is not a natural tendency towards equilibrium of forces but is an ideal of public purpose adopted by the courts, to be attained by restraints upon the natural struggle for existence.
>
> (Commons, 1935: 713)

In line with Commons' work, the economic analysis of law has rediscovered in recent years the role of law as a structuring factor in the economy. The recent work of economic sociology nevertheless makes a further step in the study of this modality of embeddedness. On the one hand, it goes beyond the role of law to take an interest in regulation as such, and on the other hand, far from considering the latter solely as what permits the exchange, we make it a constituent in its own offers and wants. Le Velly and Bréchet (2011), in a study of the organisation of collective catering supply, go so far as to envisage this meeting between supply and demand as an encounter between different regulatory activities (that of producers and that of municipal kitchens): "the meeting of their regulatory activities structures the uncertainties supported by some, the margins of manoeuvre at their disposal and the relations of strength which bind them" (Le Velly and Bréchet, 2011: 485; our translation). Public catering, for example, is subject to both the public procurement code and the nutrition recommendations of the Task Force on Food and Nutrition Markets (Groupe d'étude des marchés de restauration collective et de nutrition). For example, in the case of a call for tenders, applications containing these standards govern the various offers. The work of Le Velly and Bréchet tends to show that the adjustment between supply and demand can therefore be considered as an adjustment between both sets of regulations. They studied the case of the central kitchen of the city of Nantes, which in 2006 wanted to develop the purchase of both organic and locally produced products. However, it was constrained by the Public Procurement Code (Code des marchés publics), which considers the inclusion of locality criteria as discriminatory. It was therefore necessary to convene an experimental contractual framework in order to circumvent national rules. This example, for the authors, "testifies to the ability of the actors to cope with the regulations of control, including when they come under the law" (Le Velly and Bréchet, 2011: 485; our translation). Economic sociology is moving more and more towards these notions concerning the modification of regulatory systems.[9]

Cultural embeddedness

Beyond regulations, the economy, and *a fortiori* the markets, are delimited and produced by culture, namely a set of normative representations. This is the meaning of the notion of "fictitious commodities" defined by Karl Polanyi as not having been produced for sale. A line is drawn between what can (or "must") legitimately be exchanged on a market, and what cannot. DiMaggio, in "Cultural aspects of economic action and organisation" (1990: 113), provides a general view on this with an explicit focus on the network approach:

> I suggest that economic behaviour is embedded not only in social structure, as Mark Granovetter has argued [. . .], but also in culture. [. . .] I use "culture" to refer to social cognition, the content and categories of conscious thought and the taken-for-granted. Culture consists of shared cognitions that vary within some theoretically relevant population.

Through shared classification systems, culture acts on several levels as "normative scripts". DiMaggio identifies three different ones: the classifications delimiting the field of economic action, the rituals and symbolic systems that constitute the roles of each and every one in an economic system, and the tastes of the actors.

The place of an individual within a cultural system is, unlike the one within a network, linked to a set of normative conceptions. These conceptions affect the place of individuals *vis-à-vis* others, objects and places. DiMaggio considers the example of a grandmother and her grandson trading sexual favours in a temple. This vision shocks the standard representations of the economic sphere in four ways: (1) one does not trade with a member of one's immediate family; (2) paid sex is in many countries considered immoral: physical intimacy is not considered a commodity; (3) mercantile exchanges within a place of worship are inappropriate (think of the biblical Cleansing of the Temple); (4) one does not have a sexual relationship with one's grandmother. In each of these, a culturally established categorisation is violated: that of the inside and the outside of the circle of intimacy, that of the market and the non-market, and that of the profane and the sacred, to use Mary Douglas' (1966) expression. These boundaries only make sense if the different actors of economic life find themselves in relation to them. If it is unthinkable to sell services to one's grandmother, it is because one assumes the role of granddaughter or grandson. Economic rationality is circumscribed to institutional spheres considered as economic. Linked to a role that one endorses within these spheres, it is experienced as a ritual, it functions as a myth linking behaviour to this sphere (Meyer and Rowan, 1977). Berger and Luckmann (1966: 91) define the role as a "typification" which defines the right attitude in the right situation:

> We can properly begin to speak of roles when this kind of typification occurs in the context of an objectified stock of knowledge common to a collectivity of actors. Roles are types of actors in such a context It can readily be seen that the construction of role typologies is a necessary correlate of the institutionalization of conduct. Institutions are embodied in individual experience by means of roles. The roles, objectified linguistically, are an essential ingredient of the objectively available world of any society. By playing roles, the individual participates in a social world.

Finally, these social roles are intimately linked to the agents' preferences. Many are sociological works highlighting the intimate link between the cultural structuring of a society (set of classifications and roles) and types of consumption. Thorstein Veblen's famous publication *The Theory of the Leisure Class* (1899) is regularly considered as the first study of the socio-cultural role of consumption. For his part, Bourdieu seems to go further by linking consumption and legitimacy within the cultural space: consumption is a means of distinguishing oneself in a specific field and of perpetuating one's domination by the accumulation of symbolic capital.[10] This accumulation is the strategic element of dominant tastes. On the supply side, the mechanism responds to the same processes: production is the production of culture, a field of cultural domination.

If one can consider the embedded market in a set of cultural classifications, it can also be considered from the angle of overall cultural representation (Le Velly, 2012: 44). This principle has become an interest to Virtualism, a sociological trend developed by James Carrier and Daniel Miller (1998): if the market as a thing does not exist, it is quite different from the market representation of the world. The idea of fictitious commodities seems closer: merchandise in the commercial sense of the term does not exist, there are only commercial representations of the goods. From this viewpoint, it seems that the notion of embeddedness (whether explicit or not) structures the field of economic sociology. It goes without saying that this judgement is based on a very general definition of this concept – a generality, stemming mainly from the fact that it is built above all as a critical weapon towards formal economics, that is understood as an individualistic science of choice.

This rapid reconstruction allows one to grasp the importance of the rupture made by performativist sociology when it distances the concept of embeddedness.

A distancing of the embeddedness principle

Callonian performativist sociology refuses both to conceive performativity as an ideal movement (a "psychogenic" movement) and to think of society in terms of the notion of embeddedness. This is a strategic position based on a social ontology devoid of collective categories and resulting from an epistemological perspective that I have already had the opportunity to explain in the previous chapter: markets should not be considered as social structures welcoming actors willing to exchange; they are, on the contrary, many places technically equipped, created by exchange, considered as processes of individuation, and the qualification/disqualification of singular goods. This rejection of the market as a social structure naturally leads Callon to reject the very idea of society:

> Society is imagined as a context or as a frame. Society is out there and you imagine how to put this strange beast, the market, in this frame. It's another version of the infrastructure and superstructure metaphor. You have realities that are called markets or economic activities or society and what you try to imagine is the respective positions of these realities. Developing an argument made in the anthropology of science and technology, you must not imagine society as a context for different types of activities including economic activities; you have to imagine the process through which collective relations are constructed, including relations that can be called economic relations.
>
> (Callon et al., 2002: 291)

He explicitly positions himself against the concept of embeddedness:

> The organisation of markets depends on the nature of technologies, the nature of professional activities that are involved in the markets and so on. I think that the other way of making the point is to link this debate to the question of the commodification of life. It's not a new question but it's a very central issue and the way of answering this question is I think profoundly different now from the way we used to phrase this question and to imagine answers to this question. The metaphors of infrastructure and superstructure and the metaphor of embeddedness are not helpful if we want to find answers to these questions. What I tried to do in *The Laws of the Markets* was to replace these old metaphors by a new way of describing transactions or relations that involves a double process of entanglement and disentanglement.
>
> (Callon et al., 2002: 292)

He evokes the constitution of the social world from below by the stabilisation of networks that integrate human and non-human actant. This principle leads, for example, to a particular vision of rationality that could be described as both extrinsic and material: extrinsic because individual decision-making relies on external entities; material because, in line with ANT, the point of view focuses on technical devices as rationalisation factors. Once again, performative sociology moves away from, first, the idea of mainstream economics, focusing its analysis on an intrinsic rationality, and second, from mainstream economic sociology, which attempts to enrich rationality through the integration of social factors. Far from wanting to enrich the economic model of human acting, Michel Callon's approach is rather oriented towards the question of what makes rational calculation possible? Hence his assertion that *Homo economicus* really exists, even if he is the result of a techno-social construction historically located as part of the economics discipline (Callon and Latour, 2013). This is where an affirmation refers back-to-back to economic sociology and economics. Disagreement concerns, primarily, identifying the relevant factor in the understanding of the economic sphere: technical devices on the one hand, social embeddedness on the other; learning from actors on the one side, critical unmasking (*dévoilement*) of the social structures on the other: "The sociology of unmasking (the sociologist makes visible links that actors do not see) is succeeded by a sociology that can be described as constructivist which it would be more accurate to call performative" (Callon, 1999: 71; our translation).

The debate around the notion of "quality" exemplifies the divergences between Callonian sociology and standard economic sociology. Today, much debated (Musselin and Paradeise, 2002), the question of how agents manage uncertainty about the quality of products, from the outset, is a relatively strong criticism of standard economic theory and its approach to goods. Goods, as a starting point for economic models, are regularly considered as given: their quality is not contested. Introducing doubt about goods through information asymmetries undermines the foundations of such representation. It is a perspective that could theoretically lead to the disappearance of markets (Akerlof, 1970). Faced with this, many studies have sought to theorise the relationship of individuals to this uncertainty, the procedures used for the qualification of goods. Lucien Karpik's (1989, 2010) analyses of the lawyers' market are often the starting point for this model. In this market, as competition can hardly be based on prices (these are very difficult to obtain), the focus is on quality. However, the technical nature of the legal service means that the client is often poorly equipped to judge the competence of the lawyers consulted. Nevertheless, contrary to Akerlof's information asymmetry model, the average quality of the lawyers' market remains good. For Karpik, because of its embeddedness at the heart of a social structure that restores trust between the principal and the agent, the coordination between offerers and demanders exists beyond the uncertainty of quality. These are, primarily, authorities from the public domain as professional, true "guarantors of trust" (Karpik, 1989: 199). Although different, the approach proposed by François Eymard-Duvernay (1989) follows a similar logic: the recognition by individuals of equivalence relationships, between heterogeneous goods, is via a conventional process of common valuation based on a shared idea of what is a fair exchange.

The stance of Michel Callon (2002; Callon et al., 2000) is symptomatic of what separates him from more conventional economic sociology: understanding exchange requires that one abandons the idea of a social embedding overcoming circumstances of uncertainty about the intrinsic qualities of the goods. This is in favour of an approach that determines that each bilateral exchange is a process of singularisation and of particular qualification: the market, a socio-technical device, in constant reconstruction, is a result and not a framework. Each exchange is an innovation:

> To sum up the differences between both traditions, one could say that both are interested in the felicity conditions of the market transaction, but, for the first one, the threat is due to the existence of uncertainties on the qualification of goods, whereas, for the second, the threat is the lack of individualisation of the goods. In one case, what is first is the competition; in the other case, it is the realisation of the preference of a particular good by a particular agent.
>
> (Callon, 2002: 263; our translation)

This passion for the singularisation of goods as the agent reflects the deep rejection of the Bourdieu tradition, that of the objectification of the subject (Bourdieu, 1997 [2000]). For Callon, moreover, it is about subjects teaching the sociologist. The questioning of the subject cognitive privilege is, in economic sociology as in mainstream economics, the result of immersion in a higher-order setting: social embedding on one side, and the process of competition on the other. To reiterate, the "social" in the socio-technical devices of the Callonian approach has nothing to do with the social of the "sociologists of the social", to use Latour's expression. While in the latter case the social is a structure holding a certain inertia preceding action, it is, within the framework of performative studies, a singular arrangement between human and non-human actants. In response to Callon, Eymard-Duvernay (2002: 271; our translation) comments: "These analyses of action, in my opinion, present the defect of projecting on the excessively flexible notion of network the tension between action and justification. The emerging local judgment of interpersonal relationships cannot be understood without considering general qualifications." We will see later that this criticism touches the heart of the theory of performativity's difficulties. To refuse to consider the social as an entity formatting behaviours is to deprive oneself of an essential informative element.

*

This first section has made it possible to relocate performativist sociology within economic sociology. Its singularity rests on the pure and simple rejection of the notion of embeddedness: the market is a process of individuation, not a space determined by external social forces. We will now address a more precise positioning by considering economic and sociological approaches in relation to the social influence of economic theories. We will see that the point of arrival will be the same: a refusal to consider the social world through the prism of macro-social entities. On this occasion, we will move from the broad notion of embeddedness to the more precise one of convention: both economists and sociologists who considered a phenomenon close to performativity before Callon's works think that economic theory forms the social world by becoming a convention.

Second remoteness: from the standard approaches to the social influence of economic theories

The influence of their discourses on the phenomena they study is a problem shared by sociologists and economists. As Anthony Giddens (1990: 15–16) points out:[11]

> The development of sociological knowledge is parasitical upon lay agency concepts; on the other hand, notions coined in the meta- languages of the social sciences routinely reenter the universe of actions they were initially formulated to describe or account for. But it does not lead in a direct way to a transparent social world. Sociological knowledge spirals in and out of the universe of social life, reconstructing both itself and that universe as an integral part of that process.

Ian Hacking (2001, 2004) makes this influence the first characteristic of the social sciences. Contrary to the facts studied by the "hard" sciences, social actors react to the way they are inserted in scientific classifications. If the interaction between subject and object is the fruit of any empirical science, in that the tool of observation is always part of the world of the object of the same observation, there is nevertheless a considerable difference between the problem of measurement in quantum physics and what we see in the social sciences: the object of the latter not only reacts mechanically, it acts strategically by relying on an informative base including human sciences themselves. Alain Boyer (1994: 237) provides a supporting example of this distinction between nature's reaction and the action of the human: if someone at the foot of a snowdrift screams loudly enough to a partner "An avalanche is about to happen!", there is a probability that this statement will be self-fulfilling. However, this chain reaction is not the result of an interpretation by the upper layer of snow. This event is not due to the meaning of the statement, but to the sound volume of the speech.

Developed by Robert K. Merton, the notion of self-fulfilling prophecy provides an eloquent illustration of this phenomenon. Such a prophecy "consists of a false definition of the situation, giving rise to a new behaviour that invalidates the original conception"; it is, at root, "a *false* definition of the situation evoking a new behavior which makes the originally false conception come true" (Merton, 1948: 195). As an example, he examines the exclusion from trade unions in the 1920s of black workers, who were considered untrustworthy, "traitors to the working class, thus as potential strike-breakers" (Merton 1996: 187). This is an exclusion compelling them to agree to work for lower wages and, moreover, during a strike. The original opinion of the trade unionists is then confirmed. In other words, a belief, by the habits it engenders, confirms (or at least does not refute) itself. Merton is inspired here by William I. Thomas' situational theory. Merton cites Thomas and his theorem: "If men define situations as real, they are real in their consequences" (Merton, 1948: 193).

In other words, social actors do not react to the objective conditions of a situation, but to the meaning they give it. Thus, trade unionists do not exclude African American people because they are really strike-breakers, but because they *think* they are. This belief ultimately has effects on the real world, in this case forcing African American people to effectively break strikes: a theory leads to its own realisation. Merton also considers the case of bank panics: the collective definition of a situation, here a rumour of insolvency, becomes an integral element of this same situation and influences its course by provoking agents to withdraw their funds, which will actually lead to a bank panic. This concept is well known in economics, at least since Keynes and Chapter 12 of *The General Theory of Employment, Interest and Money* (1936 [2013]), where he emphasises the necessarily conventional aspect of long-term investment practices due to a state of fundamental uncertainty.

The notion of self-fulfilling prophecy owes much of its fascination to the famous example of the Pygmalion effect. Rosenthal and Jacobson (1968) describe an experiment conducted in a class, consisting of a series of tests supposed to identify students with a higher potential for progression. The results were communicated to the teacher. One year later, the researchers found that these students had improved their results to a higher degree than the other students. However, the tests had randomly selected the students. These results were explained by the effect of the prophecy on teachers' behaviours: they tended to pay more attention to "high-potential" students.

If we apply the Merton concept to the scientific domain, we conclude that the social sciences have the capacity to influence the world because of the reactivity of the actors in relation to the speech they produce.[12] The notion of theoretical discourse here refers to all the constitutive discourses of social theories likely to be taken into consideration by social actors: classifications, hypotheses (for example, that of rationality), concepts rallied as the end of analysis (like the notion of equilibrium in economics) and theories as a whole. Before the emergence of performativist sociology, two theoretical corpuses had considered and studied this particularity. On the one hand, economic science examined what such a phenomenon implied about the nature of its own theoretical propositions. On the other hand, some sociologists have studied the way in which theoretical discourses influence the construction of the social world. The economic corpus addresses the problem of the influence of economic discourse on the economic world from the epistemological angle of self-destruction and the possibility of prediction: what are the effects of the social influence of economic theories on their predictive power? This reflection is based on widely used concepts: those of equilibrium, fixed point or self-realisation. Economic sociology endeavours to understand the influence of economic statements by referring to the actual practices of agents and to the social construction of markets. The aim of this section will be to unify these two approaches in the face of performative sociology, in order to show that, again, it is in the relation to the social that the nuance is played out:

> One might ask, to begin with, in a very general way, if there is a social or human science that is not normative. [. . .] But the philosopher could declare in principle that Human science is normative by definition, and in support of this proposition he can deny either that our social science is really a science, or that it be truly free from value judgements.
>
> (Dumont, 1985: 46–47; our translation)

Louis Dumont gathers here both debates which took place regarding the particularity expressed above: that of scientificity and that of normativity. From these two issues emerges the difference in process of the social influence of economic statements respectively by economics and by economic sociology. After presenting it in a precise way, I will refine the taxonomy beyond a disciplinary dichotomy by identifying on the one hand a strategic approach to the social influence of theoretical statements, focusing on the integration of the economist's discourse within coordination models, and then an interpretative approach. The issue will be brought closer to the influence of the economic discourse of the notion of convention: from one perspective, the economic approach considers economic theories as coordination conventions, Schelling focal points, and from another, economic sociology considers them as interpretative conventions – for example, factors of formation of individual and collective beliefs. In both cases, we have to deal with a conventionalist approach to the social influence of economic theory on the social world: a theory influences as it becomes a social entity transcending individuals. It is precisely this type of representation that performativist sociology rejects, in that the idea of convention is ultimately only a modality of social embeddedness, assuming that behaviours take place in a structured social environment:

> The thesis of performativity, which I understand gives rise to many misinterpretations, becomes clearer and more interesting when placed in relation to other notions which have been or are being used to describe the relationship between economics and economy, like those of self-fulfilling prophecy, the prescriptive or normative dimension of economics as well as performance (in the sense of the English term). The notion of self-fulfilling prophecy, if one adheres to it, argues that economic theory is at the same time wrong (it does not describe the reality of the markets) and effective (it has an impact on the behaviour of the agents and makes possible the functioning of markets): theory is a coordinating tool in situations where agents lack common landmarks. The theory plays the role of a convention: if people believe that the others believe that they believe the theory is true [. . .], then there is a convention that allows coordination. The fundamental difference perceived with the thesis of performativity is the relationship to/with the truth. Performativity presupposes socio-technical agencements that lead to an effect on behaviours.
>
> (Callon, 2006a: 26; our translation)

We will show that, although based on different ways of questioning, the economic and sociological perspectives refer to the same representation of the social influence of economic theories in conventional terms.

From scientificity of social sciences to economics as focal point: the economists' approach

It is essentially from the 1930s that economic theory gradually incorporated the idea that the information supposed to describe reality generates or modifies it. Thus this "reality" will in fact be determined in part by the representations social actors make of it. In a context where the predictive capacity of theories is at the heart of the expression of the criterion of truth, the question of the social influence of statements of economic theory is approached from the angle of the scientificity of social disciplines: do they still have things to say? Karl Popper sets out a means to measure the particular epistemological context that will lead to this specific process. The starting point of the process can be identified in Morgenstern (1928, 1935b, 1972), the first to raise the possibility of predictions being given the social influence of theoretical statements. Morgenstern would inspire a series of works (Simon, 1954; Grunberg and Modigliani, 1954) qualifying the proposition of the logical impossibility of any forecast. We will see that the answer given by these authors is one of the starting points for the hypothesis of rational expectations, a concept that is central to contemporary economics.

Popper, Morgenstern and the problem of scientificity

In *The Poverty of Historicism*, Popper (1944: 13) defines the Oedipus effect:

> the influence of the prediction upon the predicted event (or, more generally, for the influence of an item of information upon the situation to which the information refers), whether this influence tends to bring about the predicted event, or whether it tends to prevent it.

For him, this effect is the reason for renouncing scientificity on the part of the theories which he labels "historicist". Indeed, in the context of the Popperian epistemology of empirical sciences, any discourse leading to empirically refutable predictions is considered scientific. It is understood that the Oedipus effect, if generalised in a self-destructive sense, carries with it the potential to undermine any scientific claim of social disciplines by depriving them of their predictive ability: social theories would still be falsified, and consequently, could never be corroborated.[13] More generally, the Oedipus effect[14] deprives the scientist of his capacity for external observation.[15]

In a similar position to Popper's, it is through the prism of predictions' self-destruction that the social influence of theoretical statements is firstly perceived in the field of economic theory. Morgenstern is often considered the first to introduce this old debate into economics.[16] In three fundamental texts, Morgenstern (1928, 1935a, 1972) develops the idea of the logical impossibility of any public forecast from the social sciences. The reasoning, leading to what is commonly called the "Morgenstern paradox", can be summarised as follows: the economist, following the analysis of an economic system, wishes to issue a forecast. To do this, he must take into account the reaction of this system (reaction of the agents) to his own forecast, which leads him to produce a new forecast that will itself be considered by the agents. Morgenstern thus arrives at the conclusion that infinite specularity prevents any decision-making, and therefore any prediction. This reasoning inevitably brings us back to the problem of scientificity when we read Morgenstern's work (1972: 704): "The aim of a good theory is prediction and in prediction lies the ultimate test of validity." This argument is at first sight an extrapolation of the problem, highlighted by the author himself, arising from decision-making in the context of a strategic game like the one found in the now famous parable of the pursuit of Sherlock Holmes by Moriarty (Morgenstern, 1928, 1935b; Von Neumann and Morgenstern, 1944). Conan Doyle's Sherlock Holmes, while waiting for the train from Victoria Station to Dover, recognises Moriarty, who is pursuing him. Holmes then faces an infinite speculation: he can decide to deceive Moriarty, to get off at Canterbury station instead of Dover. Nevertheless the pursuer can anticipate this behaviour and leave the train at Canterbury too. In the latter case, Holmes may then decide to finally get off, as expected, in Dover, unless, again, Moriarty anticipates Holmes' anticipation. One then falls into a phenomenon of infinite specularity of the type "I know that you know that I know, etc.", in accordance with game theory. In this case, the introduction of mixed strategies is often considered as one of the potential solutions.

It seems at first that Morgenstern's paradox agrees with the general principle of infinite specularity set out above. In both cases, it is the reflexive nature of the economic reality (I am in the other's head, and vice versa) which causes the regression. Nevertheless, let us note that with Lehmann-Waffenschmidt (1990), unlike the Morgenstern paradox, the Holmes/Moriarty dilemma is based on a strategic adjustment between two agents with diverging interests. As such, the problem is different enough to join a panel of different solutions.[17] This is the task of the Morgenstern continuators.

Fixed point and the logical possibility of economic forecasts

The answer to Morgenstern's scepticism will come in two steps. Grunberg and Modigliani (1954, 1965), as well as Simon (1954), were the pioneering authors of a series of works mobilising the concept of a fixed point in order to prove the existence of at least one public forecast that leads not to its own destruction, but to its making. For this purpose, the authors endeavour to show that the forecasting function of the agents, supposedly known to the economist and containing a public forecast, accepts at least one fixed point – for example, a point where the economist's prediction leaves the reaction of the agent unchanged. A "good" theory is possible if it affects the world in its way. In the Grunberg and Modigliani model, in a given market, producers adjust their production in period $t + 1$ according to forecasts made at period t of the price of the good produced. The reaction function of the agents, or the representation of how they anticipate future prices, can be written as follows:

$$p_e = E(p_t, P)$$

where p_e, the anticipated price, depends both on the price of period t and on P, a public price forecast in $t + 1$ carried out in t.

Positing that the actual price in $t + 1$ (p_{t+1}), is a function of p_e – that is, that the price, as a social fact, depends on the agents' expectations of it – we can use the function of reaction as the function which associates with p_t as well as with each public forecast, a value with the anticipated variable:

$$p_{t+1}(p_e) = F(p_t, P)$$

Grunberg and Modigliani then endeavour to show that under the assumption of the existence of at least one correct forecast, that is to say agents always have the ability to forecast prices if there is no public forecasting (that is, if $p_e = p_t + 1$), there is at least one correct public prediction, for example a prediction which, even if it is integrated within the beliefs of the agents, remains correct under two conditions: first, that the anticipated variable has a minimum k and a maximum K; second, that the reaction function is continuous and defined over the interval $[k; K]$. If we consider the private prediction possible, any variation of $p_t + 1$ is the result of a variation of P (the public forecast). So we have a new reaction function:

$$p_{t+1} = G(P)$$

This is shown by the curve in Figure 2.1. If the above hypotheses are accepted, then there is at least one point (here, three) at which the curve p_{t+1} intersects the diagonal, this one representing the equality between price anticipated by the agent and the actual price. At this point, $p_{t+1} = G(P) = P$. In other words, this point represents a fixed point in the reaction function of the agents.[18]

The possibility of a valid private forecast is central here. As such, there is no mistaking the purpose of Grunberg and Modigliani's contribution. It is twofold: it is certainly a question of answering the impossibility of Morgenstern, but also of showing that the real problem, in a complex system, is not so much the public forecast as the private forecast (Grunberg, 1986: 479).[19]

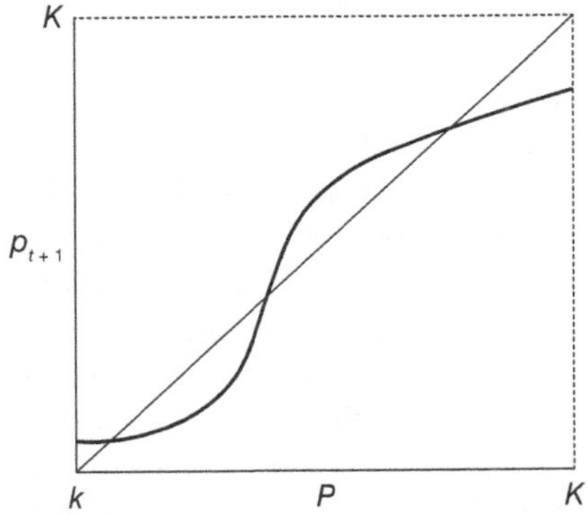

Figure 2.1 Graphical representation of the fixed points of a reaction function

Rational expectations and sunspot models

The second stage of reaction to Morgenstern's scepticism is the elaboration of the canonical hypothesis of rational expectations. The hypothesis of rational expectations can indeed be considered as an attempt to solve the problem related to the availability of new information and the unremitting variation of theoretical representations of agents. This concept, which has been current in economic theory since the 1970s, initially considers that agents use the theoretical representations of the economist himself. In his seminal article "Rational expectation and the theory of price movements", Muth (1961) underlines the lack of relevance of the models of fluctuations neglecting the formation of expectations. It is to remedy this gap that he introduces the hypothesis of rational expectations, which he then defines as follows:

> The hypothesis asserts three things: (1) Information is scarce, and the economic system generally does not waste it. (2) The way expectations are formed depends specifically on the structure of the relevant system describing the economy. (3) A "public prediction", in the sense of Grunberg and Modigliani (1954), will have no substantial effect on the operation of the economic system (unless it is based on inside information).
>
> (Muth, 1961: 316)

Muth explicitly places the effort of Grunberg and Modigliani (Muth's thesis director) at the heart of his argument. He considers the hypothesis of rational expectations as avoiding the problem of public forecasts.[20] It seems here that the representations of the agents and the economist are attached to a "relevant" representation of the economy. One can legitimately wonder what this notion of "relevant system" means. It makes it possible to consolidate the hypothesis of rational expectations and the problem of predictability: if the agent, like the economist, knows the true nature of the model – if there is symmetry between them at this point – then there is no longer a problem concerning self-destruction theories (Sent, 2002: 299). To understand more explicitly the significance of the relevant character of the economy's representation, one must turn to another great contributor to rational expectations. Thomas Sargent (1993) suggests two components to the hypothesis of rational expectations: (1) maximising rationality, and (2) the coherence between the different agents' forecasts. It is at the level of the second part that the notion of "relevant model" becomes clearer. Representations of agents are consistent when each, seeking to estimate the value of a variable – for example, the average production of other agents to determine its own level of production – produces a quantity x, expecting that others will do the same, being themselves convinced that the agent in question will also produce x. Then we enter again into an infinite specularity game like "I know you know that I know you know . . .". Formally, this gives:

$$x = h\ (X) = X$$

Here, x is the individual production level, X is the average production level, and $h\ (X)$ is the production function that maximises the agent's revenue.[21] The rational expectation of the variable X is therefore, as with Grunberg and Modigliani, a fixed point of representation: the agent chooses to produce $x = X$ – this is his best answer according to the first principle of rational expectations – thinking that others will do the same. Thus: X is *common knowledge*. He then takes X as given (he knows X). There is, at first glance, a concordance between expected average production and actual average production, in that both the aggregate of agents and the economist modelling the system take as given the value of X in question. This estimate is what Muth calls "relevant" representation, the anticipation common to all agents as well as to the economist of a particular variable. Anticipation is finally being confirmed. Note that the agents take as exogenous a variable depending on their own decisions and that their projects are realised (the other agents actually produce X). This representation is by definition self-fulfilling: it is true (not refuted) only to the extent that everyone thinks it. In this view, the coordination point is the economic theory itself (the representation of the modeller of the variable X).

The argument of Muth and Sargent is also the backdrop for Lucas' (1976) renowned criticism of Keynesian macroeconomics. This criticism focuses in part on the lack of consideration of the agents' reactions to economic policies (an absence that makes the calibration of models based on the observation of past values sufficient). Lucas criticises mainly the model of adaptive expectations, *à la* Friedman, that generates systematic errors from the agents. It assumes that in a reactive market, agents always end up knowing the economic theory if it is used by the public authorities. As such, a model with adaptive anticipations can only ultimately be contradicted by the facts, whereas the hypothesis of rational expectations would offer the advantage of founding "true" theories, which remain true even when agents integrate them into their knowledge base.

Muth, Lucas and Sargent only give substance to the intuition of Grunberg, Modigliani and Simon: the right economic theory is the one that does not self-destruct. It must remain valid if agents are aware of it and use it to build their forecasts. To put it simply, there is symmetry between agents and economists here (Sent, 1998, 2001, 2002).[22] The hypothesis of rational expectations seems to answer the problem of scientificity evoked by Morgenstern: a true economic theory (predictive or descriptive), or at least one not contradicted by the facts, can be possible. However, there seems to be a significant shift: the starting point of Morgenstern is that of forecast impossibility. If Grunberg, Modigliani and Simon are still in agreement, rational expectations intend to establish a determining model for a unique coordination equilibrium. Thus two questions emerge: an epistemological question, evoked by Morgenstern and resolved (so far in this presentation) by Grunberg, Modigliani and Simon, as well as a question relating to the explanatory capacity of economic models (how to think of market clearing as a single equilibrium) in which agents have an ability to theorise what they observe. It is because of this second question that the hypothesis of symmetry between the representations of the agents and those of the modeller is introduced.

The answer given by the hypothesis of rational expectations to the Morgenstern paradox is in fact relatively weak. Assuming that the agents have the capacity to predict, with the information they have and on average, the results of the model in which they operate, and that the agents' expectations are in accordance with the predictions of the theoretical model, and thus that the hypothesis of rational expectations entails a self-fulfilling theory, it is still possible that several theories exist (thus several variations of the model in which the agents evolve) that are not compatible with each other, as there may be several possible values of X. If a theory is true because it helps to bring about the situation it predicts, one inevitably falls back on the question of indeterminacy, as that there is no single self-fulfilling theory. A series of works illustrate this idea using so-called sunspot models. The objective is to study the possibility of the existence of a multitude of equilibria of rational expectations in the framework of infinite horizon models; each equilibrium will correspond to the influence of an exogenous variable (having *a priori* no impact on the fundamentals of the economy) on agents' expectations: for example, the appearance of sunspots. One could expect the reference theory, the "true" theory, to be one that does not allow any room for extrinsic factors. However, Azariadis and Guesnerie (1982), adopting the reference model developed by Azariadis (1981), show that there can exist, in a deterministic model with rational expectations, sunspot equilibria. If there are a multiplicity of equilibria, self-realisation as a criterion of truth is not sufficient to remove the indeterminacy coordination. Yet it is necessary to select a single equilibrium corresponding to a particular theory. From there, the theory's truth remains conditional on its hegemony; it is only true to the extent that it is considered as such (Chiappori, 2004). This conclusion poses a conventional problem: if the theories used by the agents are benchmarks allowing them to coordinate, how can we explain the choice of one of them at the expense of others? In itself, the hypothesis of rational expectations solves the problem by considering the economic theory of the modeller as a coordination marker, but what if there are several rival theories? The literature corresponding to sunspot equilibria was later consolidated by integrating learning algorithms into the models (Desgranges and Negroni, 2001). Nevertheless, the difficulty remains the same: how to choose one model of learning rather than another?

Economic sociology seems to move away considerably from the issue of scientificity by going beyond the framework of forecasts or models of coordination. Economics is no longer a coordinating landmark, but creates a more general interpretative framework. It will become clearer later that this approach tends to take another step in the context of the problem raised by economists.

From social sciences normativity to economics as an interpretative framework: the sociological approach

Beyond the problems of scientificity mentioned above, the social influence of theoretical discourse implies a blurring of the boundary between positive and normative statements. For a long time, following an interpretation of Hume's guillotine, normative statements have been rejected from the register of science by affirming, like logical positivism, the axiological neutrality of theoretical systems. New epistemological approaches prefer to see science as "taken from diversified activities and social relations, meeting multiple objectives" (Pestre, 2006: 5; our translation). These new approaches are called *science studies*, driven by the desire to operate on a social deconstruction of science. One of these, the Edinburgh School's Strong Programme, points to social struggles as external determinants of scientific controversies. Science takes place in a pre-existing social space that has to be studied in order to understand the emergence of theories. If science studies focus their attention as much on the natural sciences as on the social sciences, the problem of the social influence of the theoretical statements makes it possible to take another step concerning the manipulation of the social world by the scientific world: the observing scientist becomes a manipulator of the social order (consciously or unconsciously).

As we have seen above, Pierre Bourdieu particularly focused on this phenomenon in his studies on the power of language (1981, 1991). He discusses what he calls "theory effect": "The most strictly scientific description is always exposed to function as a prescription capable of contributing to its own verification by exerting a theoretical effect in favour of the advent's announcement" (Bourdieu, 1981: 72; our translation). Bourdieu's analysis of the power of scientific language is embodied in his general conceptualisation of social space: a set of fields in which actors are positioned according to a hierarchical situation determined by their capital endowment (economic, cultural, social). Such social fields are places of confrontation for domination, the weight of each actor depending on its competitive advantages (volume and capital structure of different kinds). This domination equates to a greater power over the structure of social reality, like a greater influence on the setting of the rules of the social game. To be dominant is therefore to acquire symbolic legitimacy in the determination of social differentiations according to the capital endowments of each (legitimate/illegitimate, dominant/dominated, strong/weak, etc.). This position is a sign of a strong symbolic capital endowment, defined as "the shape that any kind of capital takes when it is perceived through categories of perception which are the product of the incorporation of divisions or oppositions within the distribution structure of this type of capital" (Bourdieu, 1994: 117; our translation). The struggle for symbolic capital is therefore the struggle for the application of a social field vision. This vision can ultimately find its objectification in various institutional rites marking social differentiation, graduation, marriage and investiture, which Bourdieu (1991: 119) takes as an example:

> The process of investiture, for example, exercises a symbolic efficacy that is quite real in that it really transforms the person consecrated: first, because it transforms the representations others have of him and above all the behaviour they adopt towards him (the most visible changes being the fact that he is given titles of respect and the respect actually associated with these enunciations); and second, because it simultaneously transforms the representation that the invested person has of himself, and the behaviour he feels obliged to adopt in order to conform to that representation.

Beyond the formal recognitions, the balance of forces for the appropriation of symbolic capital are cognitive acts setting up representation norms (Bourdieu, 1994: 124). The scientist produces categorisations of the world, classifications, and is one of the "professionals of the symbolism [who] clashes, in combats for the imposition of the legitimate principles of the division of the natural and social world's vision" (Bourdieu, 1994: 91; our translation). He bears the representations of the world within a particular social order. He either tends to legitimise it in time, producing an acknowledgment ("dominant discourse"), or break the adhesion ("heretical discourse"). As such, science and politics overlap. Political action is only possible to the extent that the actors make representations of the world around them, and that we can influence the social world by introducing new ones (Bourdieu, 1981: 69). What is meant here by normative, beyond the affirmation of what ought to be, is the imposition of a vision of the world, of a legitimate representation norm and of the social field's rules. In his study of the field of social sciences, Bourdieu (2001: 173; our translation) concludes that "the analyst is part of the world he seeks to objectify, and the science he produces is only one of the forces that compete in this world". As noted earlier in this chapter, Anthony Giddens also makes the social influences of sociological statements an essential point of institutional dynamics. In *The Consequences of Modernity* (Giddens, 1990), this influence is considered as a peculiarity of modern societies whose mechanics are deeply linked to agents' trust in expert systems.[23] If Giddens and Bourdieu seem to agree on this basis, the first puts an additional emphasis on the meeting point between scientific ideas and systems of representation. He calls these places "access points", and adds that it is as much a matter of shifting ideas as building confidence in expert systems:

> Sociological descriptions have the task of mediating the frames of meaning within which actors orient their conduct. But such descriptions are interpretative categories which also demand an effort of translation in and out of the frames of meaning involved in sociological theories.
>
> (Giddens, 1984: 284)

Giddens opens the door to the translation link between theory and secular knowledge where Bourdieu's sociology has been criticised for its lack of consideration of the work of reappropriation and reinterpretation by social actors of the propositions; even the notion of the social influence of theoretical statements is consubstantial with the reflective agents' capacity (Boltanski, 2011). It is vital to detail how a scientific convention becomes a convention for individuals outside the strict scientific field. We can consider that performativist sociology advances this project to completion.

Two conventionalist approaches

Placing in perspective the ways economics and sociology deal with the phenomenon of the influence of economic discourse on the world it describes has made it possible to situate these two paths within different problems. Economic theory has focused on the predictive difficulty generated by the potential self-destruction of its statements. In a Popperian epistemological context, such self-destruction would be synonymous with a suspension of the discipline's scientificity. The sociological point of view is oriented towards an in-depth study of the social influence of scientific discourse. This division finally leads us to a correspondence between the idea of the social influence of the theoretical (here economic) speech and the idea of convention: in both cases, the theory influences the social world by implanting a new conventional reference. Conventionalist authors, particularly those who participated in the collective work *Théorie des conventions* (Batifoulier, 2001), insist on the distinction between two types of convention: strategic and interpretative.[24] Although this dichotomy may be questionable in a number of ways (Orléan, 2004a), two different states of mind are defined regarding the issue of the social influence of theoretical statements, and we will see later that performativist sociology has opposed this representation by rejecting the use of conventions.

Social influence of theoretical statements' strategic approach: economic science as a coordinating landmark

The problem of the influence of theoretical statements on social phenomena is treated in economic science by a failure to explain the coordination of agents in a world integrating the knowledge of the economist himself. The hypothesis of rational expectations introduces as such a strong idea: a good theory is essentially self-fulfilling; it remains valid even by integrating this knowledge with the beliefs of agents. However, nothing is said about the learning of rational expectations. This last point becomes important with sunspot models, where several potential equilibria coexist. The economic theory in place in a particular historical context becomes a coordinating landmark discriminating a single coordination equilibrium. This theory is a convention in the sense of Sugden (1986: 12): it is a representation of the world entailing a shared behaviour within a group because everyone shares it. We answer the question "Why is everyone doing *R*?" with "Because everyone is doing *R*."

This definition takes place within the framework of evolutionary economic analysis, and considers the convention as the little thing (*le petit plus*) that makes the difference, solving the problems of indeterminacy in coordination. As such, the convention begins where the single maximisation of utility is no longer sufficient. This "strategic" approach develops mainly from the study of coordination games and starts from the observation that in order to coordinate, economic agents need rules stemming from contracts, constraints and conventions. These are considered salient solutions to coordination acts – in other words, theory is a focal point (Schelling, 1960). If there are several potential relevant theories, as the sunspot models show, then the choice of the theory is a conventional fit: "The truth of the theory remains conditional on its hegemony; it is only exact to the extent that it is considered as such" (Chiappori, 2004 112; our translation). Interpreted this way, the truth of a theory remains relatively volatile: it can indeed be a victim of a reversal of convention (Orléan, 1989).

Interpretative approach to theoretical statements' social influence: economics as a conventional valuation model

Bourdieu and Giddens' sociologies adopt a different position. The departure point is no longer the coordination itself, but the constitution of a context of interpretation rooted in the classifications of economics. This approach certainly refers to the notion of convention, but this time taken in a different direction: the convention as an interpretative framework, as a model of conventional interpretation. If the conventions' strategic approach allows the convergence of the agents' expectations at a local scale, convergence materialised by the discrimination of equilibria, then the interpretative conventions are at a higher level of abstraction: because the agents' limited cognitive abilities imply an impossibility for them to know all the ins and outs of their actions in the social world, the conventional rules (the conventions in the strategic sense of the term) are necessarily incomplete. The economics of the conventions raise the primary role of interpretation: faced with a complex situation, the agent refers not to the entirety of the information available, but to an interpretive model that he shares with his peers, a normatively charged conventional evaluation model. This common context of interpretation marks off the field of possibilities and facilitates the choice of the agents. Luc Boltanski (2011: 25) speaks of "cognitive and deontic equipment", which are skills we must assume if we want to understand how agents manage to coordinate. The theory is no longer a salience to which agents coordinate, but an epistemic factor: it models the perception of the world more than an explicit reference point. As we have already observed, to reduce the notion of performativity to that of convention is not self-evident. The sociological consideration of theoretical statements' social influence, in that it is included in the details of the influence of scientific categorisations on the formation of interpretative conventions, breaks the direct link of the approach by rational expectations. The latter focuses on the economic actor as a simple calculating machine unfit to entertain thoughts about the collective. Boltanski (2011: 25) emphasises that cognitive equipment, here the conventions of interpretation, helps the coordination between the actors, "notwithstanding the disputes that oppose them or even, to be more precise, through the very intermediary of these disputes".

*

Unifying economic and sociological approaches to the social aspects of economic theories' influence around conventions makes it possible to give substance to the various tensions discussed earlier concerning the types of performativity (see Chapter 1) and to emphasise the exact nature of the setting aside of the concept of embeddedness. Ultimately, the four tensions show a clear line between the conventionalist approach of the social influence of economic theories and the Callonian approach. On the side of conventionalist approaches, performativity is ideal, as it is apprehended in terms of representation, and collective, as long as it is part of a conventional embedding process. The first point is shared by economists and sociologists. The second calls for a nuance via the conventions' duality: among the economists studied, the notion of collective is reduced to a common landmark classed as a hypothesis in the case of rational expectations, whereas sociologists summon a collective acting through shared representations of the world. This last point delimits another frontier between the conventional approach and the performative approach: the status granted to collective entities. It is here with the whole of economic sociology that the theory of performativity seems to disintegrate.

Chapter 1 sought to define the theory of performativity, leaving a glimpse of what was not performativity, but what it had been constructed against. At the end of these two sections, we can say that performativity concerns economic sociology and the social influence of economic theories' classical approaches (economic and sociological) that the theory of performativity disintegrates. By rejecting the notion of markets' social embeddedness, by refusing to approach the social world as structured by macro-social facts necessarily framing the exchanges, performativist sociology is prohibited to approach the performative movement as a conventional movement. Economic participation theory focuses on the construction of social world embedded markets – all this for the benefit of a technical vision of the social world. The next section will illustrate this profound breakthrough by focusing on two emblematic works from each perspective: on one side, economic sociology and the conventional influence of theories, on the other, the performativistic perspective.

Two examples of double fractures

In order to illustrate the singular aspect of performativity theory in relation to a more classical approach to the social influence of economic theories, two examples will be analysed: (1) *The Great Transformation* of Karl Polanyi, from a classic case study of economic sociology, and (2) the study of Marie-France Garcia-Parpet of the establishment of an auction market, which supporters of the performativist approach regularly call the first study of its kind (even though Garcia-Parpet clearly claims his affiliation to the work of Bourdieu).

Polanyi and The Great Transformation

Karl Polanyi's notoriety owes much to *The Great Transformation*.[25] This text has sparked a number of debates, one of which has particularly marked the history of economic ideas: opposing two interpretations of the concept of disembeddedness. In *The Great Transformation*, Polanyi reconstructs the history in the nineteenth century of the attempt to set up a market society supporting a new system of trade coordination, a large self-regulating market. Such a system would have had as a characteristic a progressive disintegration of the economy compared to the traditional social structures. For instance, we gradually transform and commodify labour by disembedding it from traditional solidarity systems in order to create a large supply of labour to feed a labour market. By foregrounding the history of this main change in the course of social life, Polanyi in *The Great Transformation* considers the link between an institutional dynamic and representations disseminated by political economy: "In order to comprehend German fascism, we must revert to Ricardian England" (Polanyi, 1944 [2001]: 32). According to this reading, the idea of economic theories' social influence is for Polanyi intimately linked to embeddedness. *The Great Transformation*'s history is that of the growing but never total domination of the market over other forms of integration. Market exchange would have gradually broken away from the rest of social relations to move towards the constitution of a large self-regulating market requiring the institutional support of all the social structures: "[T]he control of the economic system by the market is of overwhelming consequence to the whole organisation of society: it means no less than the running of society as an adjunct to the market" (Polanyi, 1944 [2001]: 60). Thus, an institutional model supported by a single type of motivation would be applied to society as a whole: greed, fed by the spur of hunger. Polanyi explains this evolution by the emergence of a belief about the natural and inevitable character of this institutional change, a belief disseminated by formal economic science (which will crystallise later in the definition of Robbins). Adam Smith's discourse, which considers the origin of the division of labour as being an individual propensity to barter, has performative effects on collective mentalities. It is precisely from this "market mentality" (Polanyi, 1947b) that Polanyi makes history. This market mentality, necessary for the proper functioning of a large self-regulating market, consists of two types of beliefs:

- beliefs relating to the primary motivation of humankind: we gradually build the image of a human being governed solely by a type of rationality of the means–end type in a natural context of scarcity;
- beliefs relating to the general laws of the economy, mainly to the determination of wages.

These two types of beliefs have transformed the image of society, which is now considered a simple auxiliary to the market. This is how social objects are gradually considered as commodities. However, for Polanyi, these anthropological and institutional characteristics are above all historically situated, crystallised by economic science's naturalistic discourse fuelling the market mentality. The formal economics description does not become a reality, it simply justifies the preservation of a particular institutional system, the origin of which is to be sought outside the scientific discourse, namely the extension of the place of the machine in the productive process.[26]

The penetration and the diffusion of the machine have made mass production necessary in order to optimise the depreciation of these expensive installations. This new industrial structure then forces the substitution of the motive of subsistence for that of profit, so more production becomes the very condition of production: profit and subsistence become synonymous. At this stage, a first theoretical mistake of ethnocentric generalisation is made by formal economic theory: it is by observing this phenomenon that Adam Smith constructs a human fable naturally inclined towards barter with his "market psychology" (a term used by Polanyi). The anthropology is then naturalised, yet (according to the substantive economics) historically located: "However, principles of behaviour such as these cannot become effective unless existing institutional patterns lend themselves to their application" (Polanyi, 1944 [2001]: 50–51). This error will be the basis of a moral legitimisation of the sole search for individual interest:

> Scholars had proclaimed in unison that a science had been discovered which put the laws governing man's world beyond any doubt. It was a the behest of these laws that compassion was removed from the hearts, and a stoic determination to renounce human solidarity in the name of the great happiness of the great number gained the dignity of a secular religion.
>
> (Polanyi, 1944 [2001]: 106–107)

The consequence of the machine's high cost, and of the behavioural model to which it is favourable, is the obligation to guarantee the regular supply of production factors –labour, land and money.

As far as labour is concerned, this commodification happened in two legal stages.[27] The first entailed the separation of man and land through the Enclosure Acts of 1801. They drove needy farmers out of agricultural practice and allowed the creation of a mass rural proletariat. The cost of the enclosures led to a redistribution of the land, but especially the end of common land, an essential device for the survival of rural communities. This movement to commodify land was growing, especially with the end of the *majorat* and the introduction of a right to buy back the land (provisions that Bentham defends). It had the effect of swelling the ranks of a rural factory proletariat: the constitution of a consequent job offer. The second step was the Poor Law Amendment Bill of 1834 – according to Polanyi, the true starting point of modern capitalism. It ended the Speenhamland system, which guaranteed everyone a subsistence income. In this way, the reserve army of labour engendered by the Enclosure Acts led to the vital obligation to be present at the doors of factories, guaranteeing the producers a continuous supply of labour.[28]

So far, we have seen how the introduction of the industrial machine has influenced (1) the individual behaviours and the usual assumptions as well as the conditions of survival (one must produce more, one must offer one's work to the nascent industry), (2) the content of economic theory (the theoretical generalisation of a particular fact) and (3) formal institutions (the introduction of new laws). In accordance with the issues discussed here, it is important to focus on the feedback mechanism between economic discourse and institutional structures. Indeed, if reforms are put in place, it is partly thanks to the mediation of economic theory that looks towards society:

> [T]he mind of man turned toward his own community with a new anguish of concern: the revolution which the justices of Berkshire had vainly attempted to stem and which the Poor Law Reform eventually freed shifted the vision of men toward their own collective being as if they had overlooked its presence before. A world was uncovered the very existence of which had not been suspected, that of the laws governing a complex society.
>
> (Polanyi, 1944 [2001]: 88)

This view, which constitutes classical economic theory (Polanyi evokes mainly Smith, Bentham, Malthus, Ricardo and J. S. Mill), takes shape in England during the period before the Poor Law Amendment Bill, during the Speenhamland system. Between 1795 and 1834, a salary supplement scale was set up that was indexed on the price of bread. According to Karl Polanyi, this grading scale had the real effect of bringing wages down to subsistence level, because "under the new regime of the economic man, nobody would work for a wage if he could make a living by doing nothing (or not much more than nothing)" (Polanyi, 1944 [2001]: 82) as part of a system where wages rarely exceeded the minimum subsistence provided by Speenhamland. As such, "[w]ithin a few years the productivity of labour began to sink to that of pauper labour, thus providing an added reason for employers not to raise wages above the scale" (Polanyi, 1944 [2001]: 83). The second economic error, after the naturalisation of greed, was to consider wage stagnation at the level of subsistence as the result of natural economic laws. The law of diminishing returns and the law of population, then the naturalist foundation of classical economics, were a consequence of the conditions of the Speenhamland system. The discovery of social laws was the accelerating factor of change in enacting the Poor Law Amendment Bill. If Smith, says Polanyi, tells us that the economic sphere is not subject to its own laws, its functioning being in agreement with human nature, then for a new generation of social thinkers (Townsend, Ricardo, Malthus), the external and natural laws are imposed on human beings:

> By what law was the labourer ordained to obey a master, to whom he was bound by no legal bond? What force kept the classes of society apart as if they were different kinds of human beings? And what maintained balance and order in this human collective which neither invoked nor even tolerated the intervention of political government?
>
> (Polanyi, 1944 [2001]: 120)

To answer these questions, we invoke the aforementioned economic laws. It is on behalf of Ricardo and Malthus' law that the abolition of regulations on the poor is articulated. For these two authors, the disastrous social situation that accompanied this period of history (contradicting the Smithian proposition that abundance affects people) was the result of the conjunction between a bad legal system (Speenhamland) and a tendency of the economy to bring wages back to subsistence level. On the one hand, wages were maintained at a subsistence level, as it could not be otherwise. On the other hand, Speenhamland was nonsense, and it disincentivised work and hindered the natural growth of the market economy. But if for these authors it was advisable to reform, taking into account the economic natural laws as well as a socially defined goal (for example, the greatest happiness for the greatest number), it was quite different to Joseph Townsend, who moved economic cynicism further. He observes in his *Dissertation on the Poor Laws*:

> Hunger will tame the fiercest animals, it will teach decency and civility, obedience and subjection, to the most perverse. In general it is only hunger which can spur and goad them [the poor] on to labour; yet our laws have said they shall never hunger.
>
> (quoted in Polanyi, 1944 [2001]: 118)

From 1840 onward, activism ceased to be driven by the desire to improve a socio-economic situation in order to integrate it within a real faith. Any obstruction of the laws of the market was counterproductive and harmful:

> For the self-regulating market was now believed to follow from the inexorable laws of Nature, and the unshackling of the market to be an ineluctable necessity. The creation of a labour market was an act of vivisection performed on the body of society by such as were steeled to their task by an assurance which only science can provide. That the Poor Law must disappear was part of this certainty.
>
> (Polanyi, 1944 [2001]: 132)

Polanyi's primary idea is therefore that classical economists have shifted to society a biased view by being trapped by the institutional system of Speenhamland: although greed, the law of diminishing returns and the law of the population are explanatory concepts forged in and for a precise institutional system, they are naturalised and act in return on institutional evolution by feeding social reformism and the diffusion of a market mentality. For Polanyi (1944 [2001]: 171), Speenhamland gave the phenomenological appearance of a market economy to what was in reality only a kind of non-market capitalism. Parallel to this movement of transformation, structured and amplified by economic theory, Polanyi identifies a counter-movement based on a similar dynamic. New institutional structures designed to respond to the stimulus of the machine would create new living conditions, leading to a reaction from people. If labour is transformed into a commodity, it is only a fictitious commodity, in that it cannot be manipulated without affecting the person who is its bearer:

> To allow the market mechanism to be sole director of the fate of human beings and their natural environment indeed, even of the amount and use of purchasing power, would result in the demolition of society. For the alleged commodity "labor power" cannot be shoved about, used indiscriminately, or even left unused, without affecting also the human individual who happens to be the bearer of this peculiar commodity.
>
> (Polanyi, 1944 [2001]: 76)

The self-regulating market was the result of the meeting between a specific state of European history and a mentality replaced by social theories. As Jérôme Maucourant (2005: 130) recalls, the great thesis of the Polanyian account is "the structuring role of representations in the fabric of society". Collective representations were a powerful driving force of the mid-nineteenth-century movement, the performative vector of liberal ideologies, which led Hutchison to observe in 1851 that the world was now led by philosophers and economists (Maucourant, 2005: 130; our translation). For Polanyi, the term of a large market's construction is manifested by the culmination of the counter-movement. Four major events form its manifestation: the New Deal, the *Front populaire*, sovietism and fascism, which induce new social relations. Polanyian historiography therefore clearly integrates economic discourse as a factor of institutional evolution, playing on both mentalities and legal structures.

Socio-technical construction of a strawberry market

The Polanyian approach to the social construction of a large self-regulating market is emblematic of how economic sociology views market phenomena as well as the social influence of economic theories. As we have seen earlier, performativist sociology diverts from the traditional approaches of economic sociology, considering that the social influence of economic theories can be considered as an experimental, materially distributed and extended process. To illustrate this approach, we will focus on the canonical study of Marie-France Garcia-Parpet, who in 1986 published a work with the evocative title "The social construction of a perfect market" in which she followed step by step the creation of a Dutch auction in Sologne in the early 1980s. Exemplifying the theory of performativity through the work of Garcia-Parpet may seem strange. Not only does her work not belong properly to the performativist corpus (which formed later), but Garcia-Parpet clearly adopts a Bourdieusian vocabulary, far from the Callonian perspective. She largely analyses the construction of markets through the prism of their embeddedness within particular social structures, being clearly placed in traditional economic sociology. She also clearly claims her Bourdieusian heritage (Garcia-Parpet, 2014).

Nevertheless, this work represents a turning point in the analysis of the social influence of economic theories. In his founding text, Callon (1998: 20) cites Garcia-Parpet's work as a reference: "One of the best studies I know is that of Marie-France Garcia on the transformation of the table strawberry market in the Sologne region of France." The text would even be reproduced in a collective volume concerning the performativist perspective (MacKenzie, Muniesa and Siu, 2007b: 8):

> Garcia-Parpet's chapter is paradigmatic in its suggestion that economics, sociology and anthropology should focus on how markets are constructed and maintained (and on the role of economic theory, material devices, producers, physical architectures, linguistic codes, and so on, in the construction and functioning of market), rather than focusing simply on demonstrating ways in which the concrete marketplace differs from economists' "abstract" markets.

Garcia-Parpet's work has therefore attracted the attention of performativity sociologists, so much so that they have integrated it into the history of their own theoretical corpus. It therefore seems relevant to understand why it has become retrospectively a representative text of the performativist approach. The idea of this section is therefore not so much to retrace Garcia-Parpet's argument as such, but to consider how it has been reproduced in performativist studies.

In 1981, the strawberry market in the department of Loir-et-Cher in France suffered a fundamental change following the establishment of a Dutch auction system in the town of Fontaines-en-Sologne:

> The marketplace is characterized by the way in which it makes use of up-to-date technology – transactions are performed through an electronic scoreboard, and take the form of a descending-price or "Dutch" auction [*marché au cadran*], in which the auctioneer starts with a high price and then gradually lowers it until the goods in question are sold.
>
> (Garcia-Parpet, 2007: 20)

Garcia-Parpet's objective is admittedly to show that this market perfectly mimics the theoretical model of the neo-classical market, based on perfect competition, but she also identifies the construction process, based on logics that do not emanate from the academic field as such. The Fontaines-en-Sologne market is primarily presented in the form of a physical architecture divided into four parts:

- a cabin equipped with a computer in which an auctioneer is situated; he centralises the information and displays the prices of the batches of fruit for sale on a screen located outside;
- a room where the producers are situated and the screen is visible;
- a room where the buyers sit, equipped for remote-control participation in the auction; the screen is also visible here;
- a display area for products (baskets of strawberries) that will be exchanged.

From the cabin, the auctioneer can see the sellers' and buyers' rooms, the latter seeing only him. The sales process is as follows: after viewing the lots, producers, buyers and the auctioneer go to their respective locations. The basic principle of the sale is that of the Dutch auction, a degressive auction where the first bid wins the lot. For each quantity, the auctioneer announces a price before lowering it until a buyer bids with his remote control. The producer can then accept the price displayed on the screen, or refuse it with a gesture to the auctioneer. For Garcia-Parpet, this market exemplifies the assumptions of perfect competition.[29] She identifies four of these: the agents as price-takers, homogeneity of the products, fluidity of the market (free entry and free exit), as well as transparency (common knowledge of the quality and the quantity of the goods). These conditions are, at first glance, respected:

- The limited number of suppliers (35) and sellers (10) is offset by the unit sale of lots, which has the effect of ensuring competition by bringing it into play for each lot.
- The market only deals with strawberries that meet strict quality criteria. The hypothesis of homogeneity therefore seems to be respected.
- Transparency is ensured by the viewing period of the products preceding the auction.
- Free entry and free exit are ensured by the possibility for producers to refuse sales.

The performative aspect of such a market establishment becomes evident when we know that its implementation was largely orchestrated by an economic adviser to the regional chamber of agriculture, having just finished his studies, during which he had been taught the neo-classical theory of perfect competition. From a performativist perspective, we understand the interest of such a case: the performance is not a simple story of economic beliefs. Once the market technical device (the architecture of places and the electronic devices) is set up, the actors are led to behave in a direction dictated by it: they accept the price, and they communicate only through it. The market mechanism is also backed up by other mechanisms ensuring the approximation of perfect competition assumptions. The homogeneity of goods is, for example, the result of a construction process based on multiple devices. This process took shape in the early 1970s with the establishment of a campaign to increase the quality of production by advocating a reduction in the strawberry plant varieties used, as well as the Chamber of Agriculture formulating a set of agricultural standards. These recommendations were conveyed to farmers through leaflets setting out the "13 Commandments" of the good strawberry producer. This campaign finally led to a major innovation: the creation of a quality label, "Strawberries of Sologne". These innovations made it possible to change the way Sologne's strawberries were viewed: they were now homogeneous goods supported by a specific device. One quickly understands why this analysis aroused the benevolent interest of Michel Callon. On one hand, it constitutes an important contribution to the study of markets as spaces of calculation independent of the calculating capacities of the participants. On the other hand, it focuses on: an experimental performative process where the young economic adviser plays the role of market designer; material, because of the central role given to technical devices; and distribution, since the performative process is the result of distinct actions (homogenisation on one side, setting up the market on the other). The role of market architecture would eventually become a focus of performativity theory (MacKenzie, 2006a: 15).

Two significant examples of a fracture

The two cases described above have the merit of providing an illustration of the double fracture that the performativist approach operates in relation to the social influence of economic theories. Karl Polanyi provides the perfect example of a process combining a classical critical perspective of economic discipline with a conventional approach to the social influence of economic theories. The concept of embeddedness, at the centre of its analysis, is often an opportunity to emphasise the social aspect of human behaviour needed. From a *Homo economicus* whose behaviour is governed only by the expectation of gain we move to an intrinsically social vision of the individual: institutions regulating the production, consumption and distribution of means of subsistence require, in order to function, that individuals have integrated conventional apparatus, "supporting structures". As such, the economy (in the substantive term) is necessarily regulated by behaviours that, in the final analysis, are the fruit of a process of socialisation:

> Aristotle was right: man is not an economic, but a social being. He does not aim at safeguarding his individual interest in the acquisition of material possessions, but rather at ensuring social good-will, social status, social assets. [. . .] *Man's economy is, as a rule, submerged in his social relations.*
>
> (Polanyi, 1947b: 112)

In this perspective, economic behaviour is subordinated to social structures (tradition, religion, etc.). If the interpretation of Polanyi's work is debated (Brisset, 2012b), he seems at first sight to report the under-socialised aspect of economic man as he is, according to him, presented by the formal economic theories. To use a more contemporary expression, economic rationality is systematically located in an environment whose specificities must be taken into account. We therefore link the idea of social enrichment of *Homo economicus*. From this point of view, the intervention of economics in the real economy leads to the constitution of social conventions on which the economy is built: classical economists model the economy through the dissemination of a market mentality, an interpretative convention.

As mentioned above, sociologists' interest in performativity in Marie-France Garcia-Parpet's work is because she abandons a critical position regarding the economic concept of the rational agent in order to focus on particular socio-technical devices allowing it to act in an uncertain world, according to market logic. The rational agent is a combination of the human and non-human. From this aspect, the market is no longer an organisation based on a social environment defined in terms of beliefs (the "market mentality" of Polanyi), but a calculating device to which the actors abandon decisions – a device emerging from the theorising practices of economists:

> The word calculus must not be taken metaphorically, as if there existed from all eternity, in the minds of the agents, a kind of "mental calculus" which would only find "to apply", to "materialise", "to concretise" in real calculations, on paper, on accounts book. [. . .] [I]t is necessary to take the calculation in the material sense of what is done on a table about figures with graphical instruments [. . .]. It is the metrology of economic calculation as the metrology of the meter or the kilo: before the establishment of benchmarks and the meticulous intercomparison of their replicas, we cannot take any measure at all.
>
> (Callon and Latour, 2013: 16)

There is therefore a side-lining of both social conventions, taken as collective beliefs, necessary for the establishment of the market organisation and for the intervention of the economist in terms of beliefs. The social world is not "already here". It is built through devices whose development can be informed by economic theories. Here are the two performativist precepts inherited from actor-network theory:

A Economics performs through socio-technical devices making individuals carry out actions (see Chapter 1).
B There is a refusal to consider macro-social sets in favour of socio-technical devices (see earlier in this chapter).

In a recent contribution, Michel Callon (2013) summarises his position by opposing a market approach as an interface between offers and requests formulated by given agents (on given objects) to a market approach as market organisations: places in perpetual technical reconfiguration of translation and singularisation. Place within economic theory plays a key role, mainly through technical devices.

Conclusion: macro-social entities versus devices

This chapter continued the work begun in Chapter 1, exploring the place of performative sociology within the scientific field. It rejected both standard approaches of the social influence of scientific statements and traditional economic sociology as it is rebuilt around the notion of embeddedness. The point of fracture is systematically the same: Callonian performativist sociology intends to examine the way in which economists populate the world with technical devices forming a narrow socio-technical network in which individual decision-making takes place. Conversely, the approach that has been described as conventionalist focuses primarily on the macro-social entities that embed choices. To conclude these first two chapters, it has been shown that the role of the technical devices to *faire faire* ("make to act"), as well as the rejection of social entities of its explanatory pattern, are both pillars of performativist sociology. Beyond the classic opposition between holism and individualism, these characteristics are constitutive of what could be described as "methodological relationalism":[30] it focuses on networks where technical devices reflecting economic theories are integrated.

Notes

1 Let us emphasise the beginning of the assertion, "it is regularly referred to", for the outcome of this will shock, not surprisingly, many historians of economic thought. Indeed, it poses a certain continuity between four very different authors (emerging from heteroclite traditions and proposing opposing conceptualisations on many points) and the current economic corpus. I will refer, among other things, to this debate on the hypothesis of a marginalist revolution (Blaug, 1972; Jaffé, 1976), but also to work which strongly nuances the positions of the authors in question, particularly in the case of Walras (Baranzini et al., 2005; Baranzini et al., 2011) and Menger (Polanyi, 1957).

2 At least in his intuitive version. In fact, not only is there nothing to prevent the construction of a general equilibrium model with a small number of agents (as long as the price-taking assumption is respected), but it is also possible not to introduce an agent at all.

3 Once again, one should not forget that the various authors we are studying have strong specificities. For instance, we should keep in mind that Polanyi was much more influenced by Karl Marx than Weber. To say that all these authors share a common feature (the idea of embeddedness) is not to say they have everything in common. Far from it.

4 For definitions of economic discipline, see Backhouse and Medema (2009).

5 Reference could also be made to Beckert (2011), who follows a similar approach.

6 This sub-section contains some elements developed in Brisset (2013).

7 This is, for example, the position of Judge Swayne: "Property is everything which has exchangeable value, and the right of property includes the power to dispose of it according to the will of the owner. Labor is property, and as such merits protection. The right to make it available is next in importance to the rights of life and liberty" (Judge Swayne, in Commons, 1924: 13).

8 Commons is explicitly in line with Legal Realism, of which one of the tutelary figures is Oliver Wendell Holmes (Commons, 1924: 124). This current is opposed to a classical, mechanical and deductive view of law as an act of knowledge, and emphasises the essential role of the interpretation of the rule by the judge: "it is not true that in practice [...] a given word or even a given collection of words has one meaning and no other" (Holmes, 1899b: 297). The judge does not discover law, he creates it through decisions based on particular interpretative hypotheses. It is one of the roles of the social sciences to feed the legal interpretation, which cannot be self-sufficient: "An ideal system of law should draw its postulates and its legislative justification from science" (Holmes, 1895: 184). The rule of law is thus led to evolve according to the historical-social context and scientific theories that fuel the act of will which is legal interpretation.

9 For example, Trompette's (2008) work on supply–demand adjustment in the funeral market.

10 See Trigg (2001) on the link between Veblen and Bourdieu.

11 This section was first published in the *Revue de philosophie économique* (Brisset, 2012a).

12 What Barry Barnes call the "feedback loop or bootstrap": the social sciences are particular instances of referring activities. Accordingly, full independence of knowledge and its referents cannot be hoped for in the social sciences (Barnes, 1983: 524).

13 The logical empiricism of the Vienna Circle sets the verification criterion as a true dogma allowing the demarcation between science and non-science. Popper speaks of falsification and corroboration: a theory is corroborated when it resists attempts at falsification (Popper, 1935 [2005]). It is therefore understandable that a theory can never be verified, but only momentarily supported (it constantly bears the risk of being falsified). It should be noted that the discussion of the social influence of theoretical statements is more about empiricism than about the modalities of empiricism (verification or falsification). Indeed, it remains the same whatever the approach. Nevertheless, Popper was the first to integrate this type of reflection.

14 However, for Popper, if the Oedipus effect prohibits the constitution of a precise and public "detailed calendar of social events", this problem is similar to the one encountered by physicists (Popper, 1944: 14). The prediction of a physical phenomenon is in fact dependent on an artificial experimental isolation. If in physics, a forecast calls for similar conditions, in which experimental conditions are included, such an approach would then be applicable in the framework of the human sciences

through a conditional forecasting logic, according to the deductive-nomological model that we find throughout the work of Popper. As such, if Popper emphasises the subject–object link to work in the social sciences, he refuses to make it a particularity of the latter, and argues that the conditional method is a remedy for the difficulties engendered – for example: "Given such a law, change will go hand in hand with such other change." Isabelle This (1996: 560) points out that such an argument is not admissible: the distinction between conditional and unconditional forecasts absolutely does not solve the problem, and fundamentally nothing changes. Indeed, Popper seems to dismiss (without justification) the problematic of the Oedipus effect on the more general one of induction – an issue which became a particular concern developed in *The Logic of Scientific Discovery* (1935 [2005]). Following David Hume, Popper concedes that nothing assures the universality of an inference based on the observation of a finite number of cases. Any attempt at inductive justification is logically confronted with an infinite regression, because to justify an inductive statement – for example, "The farmer feeds his hens every day at 2 p.m." – it is necessary to firstly justify by induction the relevance of the inductive process itself: "Following the observation of so many cases of induction considered valid, I deduce the validity of the inductive process." This statement must itself be justified by induction. As such, it is never possible to establish with certainty the truth of an assertion from a finite collection of observations. To solve this problem, Popper summons the principle of *refutation*, linked to the condition of predictions: if it is impossible to verify, it is necessary to refute on the basis of conditional statements. However, the Oedipus effect imposes additional difficulties that cannot be reduced to only *Hume's problem*. Indeed, if it is possible to temporarily slip away from Humean criticism of induction by stipulating, for example, nature stability (physical or human) as a condition, the problem of reflexivity relates precisely to the non-stability of a particular component of human nature: that of social conventions, an element peculiar to the social world alone. Popper therefore criticises two different problems with the same tool without ever demonstrating its relevance. Whatever the outcome of this debate, this issue inevitably emerges when one evokes the notion of social sciences' reflexivity: the reflexivity forces the economist to look into the status of his models, whether these are explanatory or predictive.

15 The rhetorical process used by Popper in this text is very particular. He develops historicist arguments without any precise reference, going so far as to formulate "arguments in its support which have never, to my knowledge, been brought forward by historicists themselves" (Popper, 1944: 3).

16 Without dwelling on the subject, let me emphasise that the British logician John Venn (1866) was to my knowledge the first to introduce the notion of self-destruction.

17 See Boulding (1966).

18 Simon (1954) uses similar reasoning in looking at a voting example. The conclusions are exactly the same.

19 This point is also related to Grunberg's later work (1978) on the complexity of economic systems.

20 See Sent (2002).

21 This equalises marginal cost and price at a level dependent on the average level of production –; *h(X)* is the best answer to the given price.

22 The problem of symmetry between the economic agent, the economist and the economic agent is particularly salient in Sargent (1993: 21).

23 The idea that the critical activities of scientists have repercussions on the beliefs to which agents adhere had already been developed in *The Constitution of Society* (Giddens, 1984).

24 This distinction is also present, in a different form, in Favereau (2008).
25 This sub-section contains elements developed in Brisset (2012a).
26 This is not at the origin of the change, but it systematises a movement in progress: "We do not intend to assert that the machine caused what happened, but we insist that elaborate machines and plants were used for production. In a commercial society, the idea of a self-regulating market system was bound to take shape" (Polanyi, 1944 [2001]: 43).
27 The reading will be naturally truncated. We will focus here on the case of labour.
28 On this event, as well as on Polanyi's place in Marxist history, see Meiksins Wood (2002) and, of course, Thompson (1993).
29 Remembering that, in itself, perfect competition is generally defined by two assumptions – price-taking and the completeness of the market system – and that the ancillary hypotheses (large number of sellers and buyers, homogeneity, fluidity, etc.) only intuitively justify the preceding ones. Ignoring this distinction, Garcia-Parpet completely obscures the internal logic of the economic theory that estimated these assumptions.
30 The notion of "methodological relationalism" was pointed out to me by Philippe Steiner, whom I would like to thank.

3 Criticisms of the sociological approach to performativity

Since its first formulation, the theory of performativity has undergone a great deal of criticism. This chapter will show that this criticism justifies rethinking economic theories' social influence within a different theoretical framework. In the first analysis, most of the attacks on performativist sociology focus on its critical poverty, which is assimilated with a genuine allegiance to mainstream economic theory. This argument will not address mainstream economic theory as it poses a certain number of substantial and formal problems (is there a clean and unified analytical heart for mainstream and heterodox economics?). It is above all a question of how critics of the performativist approach position themselves in the economic field (Philip Mirowski, Edward Nik-Khah, Ben Fine, Geoffrey Hodgson) or sociological field (David Miller, Patrik Aspers, theorists of the Edinburgh School) towards the economic theory they consider orthodox: neo-classical theory as formal economics' archetype.

What is criticised in the theory of performativity is the consideration of the categories of neo-classical economics as relevant from the point of view of the analysis, as long as they participate in the construction of the social world.[1] This judgement amounts to attacking an assumed position of Callonian sociology, which has been extensively discussed in the previous chapters: the refusal to consider social entities (institutions, conventions) as categories relevant from an ontological point of view. If, in line with ANT, this point is the strength of the theory of performativity, in that it allows us to focus the analysis on the techniques as performative vectors, it is also its Achilles' heel. Fundamentally, what is considered an allegiance to neo-classical economic theories comes primarily from the fact that markets or agents are no longer treated as social entities, but as simple calculating devices: the market is approached almost exclusively from the angle of its technical materiality, and the economic agent from the angle of its calculating equipment (therefore, its position in the market). This is a position that would also be shared by standard economic theory. Considered as such, markets and agents become malleable, an approach of the social world leading to a particular relativism from the point of view of those who intend to criticise the standard economic approach. First, this relativism will render impossible any criticism of performed economics (from a positive point of view), and secondly, it will undermine the very claims of performativist sociology by preventing thought about conditions of failure. Remember that performativity downfalls were the foundation of Austin's definition: a performative utterance is a statement that can fail to do something. By discarding the definition of performativity by its possibilities of failure, performativist sociology seems to empty the heuristic content of this concept. Why does performativity not always succeed? In this chapter, we will start by looking at the various criticisms to which the theory of performativity has been subject. We will study three of them, which we consider particularly representative: British anthropologist Daniel Miller, whose work gave rise to a direct confrontation between the sociology of performativity and virtualism (a framework of competing analysis); Marxian economist Ben Fine, who focused on the constructivism, considered unfounded, of Callonian sociology; Philip Mirowski and Edward Nik-Khah, who systematised the points of view of the two previous authors by defending the theoretical conservatism of performativist sociology because it stems very precisely from the special place it confers on the role of technique. These criticisms, far from being novelties, replay the debate that had enlivened actor-network sociology in the early 1990s. The accusation of relativism is a little premature, in that Callon and Latour evoke the "tests of truth" a technical device must pass to fit into agents' practices. Nevertheless, insisting in particular on the technical aspect of this insertion, Callon seems to miss part of the story: social truth tests.

The controversy between some among the Edinburgh School and ANT (principally in the works of Bruno Latour and Michel Callon) also focuses on the role conferred on technical objects in sociology of scientific knowledge, and more particularly on what is commonly called the "generalised principle of symmetry" between the human and the non-human (the technique) in the constitution of scientific networks. The second section of this chapter will show that all the criticisms referenced point towards a blind spot of performativist sociology as it empties its ontology of structuring social entities, sets of conventions imposing agents, therefore precluding thoughts of integrating a number of possibilities of performativity failures. This point has been raised by some of the most important thinkers of performativity, in its general sense, such as Judith Butler. These stress the interest of the concept of "counterperformativity". Nevertheless, the idea that such a concept cannot find its place in a strictly performativistic framework will be defended. In the end, what will be demonstrated is the link maintained by the following three elements:

A Economics performs through socio-technical devices making individuals carry out actions (see Chapter 1).

B There is a refusal to consider macro-social sets in favour of socio-technical devices (see Chapter 2).

C There is difficulty in thinking about performativity failures.

Recurring criticism of the notion of performativity

When Michel Callon commenced the project of studying the role of economists in the construction of the social world, he clearly placed himself regarding the fields of economic sociology and economics. This positioning, studied in detail in the previous chapter, leads to a strong affirmation: economic theory is considered as an element of the social world, and it is necessary to discard any critical attitude towards it:

> There are two positions we have to abandon. The first is the idea of critique of hard economists, which is intended to show them that they are wrong. And the second position is to describe markets just to say that they are more complicated than economists or political decision-makers believe. [. . .] Let us stop criticizing the economists. We recognize the right of economists to contribute to performing markets, but at the same time we claim our own right to do the same but from a different perspective. [. . .] What is very important is to abandon the critical position, and to stop denouncing economists and capitalists and so on. Instead, we need to engage with debates on specific markets.
>
> (Callon et al., 2002: 301)

In doing so, he breaks with the project of unmasking, associated with critical sociology – a project based largely on the ideal type of sociological standing as "free-floating intelligentsia" (Mannheim, 1936). In this last perspective, the sociologist brings the actor to awareness of the reality of a social world that escapes him. Callon observed that: "Nevertheless, the liberalism of these sociologists does not extend to allow the actors studied to discuss society and its constituents in an open manner" (Callon, 1986b: 197). This position echoes that of Bruno Latour, who distances himself from the Kantian criticism which is at the root of modern sociology (Latour, 1992). In his desire to awaken the social actor to the current confusions between noumenal order and phenomenal order (the economic error that Polanyi condemns), the sociologist places himself in a position of unjustifiable overarching transcendentalism: "Let's say that our sociology prefers a local history whose frame is defined by the actors and not by the investigators" (Latour, 1993a: 24; our translation). The refusal to censor actors in the name of a so-called superior discernment ability is an important contribution of ANT.[2] It is nevertheless what is more problematic: the main justification for rejecting the employment of (transcendent) social categories, marking the transition from the social context to the network: "A technical project is not in a context, sometimes it gives itself a context, or not. We must not "set the projects in their context", as we say foolishly, but follow how the project contextualises and decontextualises itself" (Latour, 1993a: 115; our translation). This position, when adopted by performativist studies, attracts the wrath of both the critical sociology of economics and the economists themselves (especially when they are positioned in heterodoxy). Based on several of these criticisms, it will be shown that the fundamental point of disagreement lies in the way of viewing the social: whereas, as we have seen, many of the critics of formal economics focus on forgetting the social, the performative approach seems to share with formal economics an under-socialised vision of the actor, putting at the centre of its analysis technological tools as a means of calculation.

Criticism of non-criticism: economic theory allegiance

The interest of the British anthropologist Daniel Miller's criticism (2005) lies in the fact that he shares the same starting point as Michel Callon. Both reject a constative view of economics; both question the role of economists and their theories in the construction of the social world; and both focus on the role of *Homo economicus* and the market as pure abstractions participating in the reconfiguration of individual behaviours and economic arenas. Their affinities, however, end here. It is Daniel Miller who first shows the border between performativist sociology and the theoretical corpus of which he is one of the founders: virtualism. It draws on the status granted to economic theory in the social world: considering economic models as the heart of economic activity, Callon would operate an illegitimate reduction of economy to theory, imitating in this mainstream economists:

> I entirely concur with his initial warning that economists tend not to study economies, but rather attempt to project their models onto economies, Callon ends up ignoring this initial premise, and treating the economic model of the market as though it were core to actual economies rather than a projection of economists.
>
> (Miller, 2002: 219–220)

The controversial assertion of Michel Callon is that *Homo economicus* has his own existence because of the contribution of economics to the constitution of the economy. It is on this specific point that Miller distances himself. He refuses to consider that economic theory can call to reality the representations of which it is a carrier. He thus notes a substantial difference between the assertion that a particular economic theory contributes to the social construction of the world (even that the social world comes to mimic this theory) and that the social world intrinsically conforms to the descriptions which are made from it. For Miller, the theoretical market is above all an ideological model, and not the empirical core of economic systems. He bases his criticism on his analysis of the Indian Jajmani system (Miller, 1986), which has become part of classical anthropology since the work of Louis Dumont (1971). This organisation is based on a system of mutual obligations linking different castes (landowners and workers). Miller looks more specifically at how the caste of potters organises the distribution of production in a village. When someone becomes a potter, he is destined to it by virtue of a symbolic order emanating from the nature of things (*dharma*). Miller shows the way in which a ritual distribution system co-exists, independently of individual needs, with a market system allowing the first system to work. The market is a social reality with a particular function in a distributive values system.

Starting with this example, Miller defends the idea that markets are necessarily embedded within ritualised configurations that take root in specific ideologies. In the potters' example, the market is only the support of another mode of symbolic distribution, and would not function without it (the market is only a protective circle). This type of analysis remains relevant for contemporary economic systems. In most contemporary capitalist systems, the market, as the main mode of distribution (like the pot distribution system in India), is necessarily supported by a system of values that standard economic theories do not take into consideration. In other words, Miller re-enacts the opposition between formal and substantive economics: a trading system, whatever it may be, is not comparable to a state empty of any social institution. It is not a simple technical allocation device, as it needs to be embedded in a symbolic order – precisely what Callon refuses to consider. The reference to Polanyian embeddedness is explicit and in line with economic sociology. To understand Miller's criticism, it is necessary to explain his interpretation of the concept of disembeddness. According to followers of new economic sociology, the concept of disembeddness carries a powerful ambiguity. Indeed, it would lead us to think of the economic world outside social institutions. This controversy was initiated by Mark Granovetter (1985), who criticised Polanyi, who would in fact come to accept a dichotomy between the economic and relational spheres by the very evocation of a process of disembedding. Barber clearly summarises this proposition: Polanyi describes the market as no longer embedded in the other socio-structural and socio-cultural elements of society. This proposal, unlike Polanyi's, is that all economies are inevitably embedded, and to continue: "Calling the market 'disembedded' leads analytic attention away from just what this interdependence is" (Barber, 1995: 400). Polanyi would therefore give the economic actor an under-socialised vision, whereas economic sociology would rather enrich the simplistic vision of the economic agent. The disembeddedness is here understood as the end of the social as a macro-social element (redistribution, reciprocity). Contrary to this position, there are a number of commentators who opt for an ideological view of disembeddedness (Block, 2003; Maucourant, 2005: 92–95; Brisset, 2012b; Maucourant and Plociniczack, 2013): the disembedded economy is not a state of affairs, but a utopia in progress – a utopia in believing that all subsistence problems are soluble within the mechanisms of the market. Indeed, Polanyi defends himself from *de facto* disembeddeness: "We are not dealing here, of course, with pictures of actuality, but with conceptual patterns used for the purposes of clarification. No market economy separated from the political sphere is possible" (Polanyi, 1944 [2001]: 205). The terms of the disagreement between Miller and Callon are ultimately only an extension of what revolves around Karl Polanyi's work. This point is particularly clear in the following statement:

> In short, to understand how markets operate requires the historical and ethnographic study of entanglements, since neither the players involved nor us as academics are faced by a market situation characterized by disentanglements, unless we choose to portray things that way in order to better fit the models of economics.
>
> (Miller, 2002: 223)

To simplify, whereas Miller considers formal economics as an ideology, Callon approaches it as a reality in power. This point crystallises for Miller the main difference of approach between the sociology of performativity and virtualism (Carrier and Miller, 1998), a current sociology that is also trying to understand the role of abstraction forms in the evolution of the social world. Ben Fine (2003, 2005), who contributed to Carrier and Miller's collective book *Virtualism* (Fine, 1998), adopts a similar position. According to him, because of Callon's refusal to consider the world as a set of macro-structures, Callonian sociology suffers from the same limits as standard economic theory. As in Miller, the "standard" theory is assimilated to a "formal" economic theory. Fine reacts particularly to the denial of existence of capitalism as a social system integrating markets:[3] "It's probably also a notion we have to get rid of [. . .] I think it's a very important point. Capitalism is an invention of anti-capitalists" (Callon et al., 2002: 297). It is understandable that such an affirmation may irritate an author who adheres to Marxism, in that it removes all critical possibility:

> Callon's stance is to brush this all aside with the dictum that 'capitalism does not exist', a phrase with striking resemblance to Baudrillard's denial of the Gulf War. This might be helpful in deconstructing the material world but it is a recipe of more or less arbitrary description at the expense of theory and explanation. What are the strategic implications for social science? For Callon, because capitalism does not exist, there is no need for an alternative economics in the form of political economy.
>
> (Fine, 2003: 481)

In a similar category, Mirowski and Nik-Khah (2007)[4] go so far as to evoke a real pact between performativist sociology and neo-classical economics. They reconstruct the general theory of performativity around the following points:

i Markets are of various forms and centred on calculation entities.
ii From (i) it is argued that markets are neither more nor less than techno-scientific phenomena, like microbes, scallops or hotel keyrings.
iii From (i) and (ii) we draw the thesis of performativity: if markets are only technological devices, they are easy to handle.
iv From (i), (ii) and (iii), the illegitimacy of any criticism of the truth of economic theorisations emerges.

The authors illustrate this distance from any critical claim by raising the heuristic poverty of the performativist approach. To this end, they revisit the study by Francesco Guala (2001) on the auctioning of electromagnetic spectrum licences in the United States in 1993 by the Federal Communications Commission. The agency turned to economists to set up a bidding system that was both efficient and fair (guaranteeing technological availability for all Americans). Two bodies competed with one another: game theorists (Binmore and Klemperer, 2002) and experimental economists (Charles Plott). While the former focused on the way in which an auction mechanism leads to equilibrium insofar as agents have all the relevant information, for the latter it was the bidding mechanism itself which was the centre of optimum calculation.

The main difficulty with wireless spectrum auctioning is the interdependence of licence values in different geographical areas. Without going into details, while the experimentalists proposed the auctioning of lots so that their values were revealed, the game theorists opted for a multiple and simultaneous auction of the operating licences on each frequency range in each zone: to reveal relevant information in one case, and to design good coordination rules in the other. Several representations are here in competition for performance of the social world; how can we explain that one vision is necessary and not the other? In this case, how can we explain that it was finally the recommendations of the games theorists that got the upper hand? Nothing in the theory of performativity would make it possible to understand this, according to Mirowski and Nik-Khah, since it concentrates its attention on theoretical black boxes without considering the social conditions in which the theorists act. Callon is therefore led to consider performativity as a simple game of a confrontation between several theoretical corpuses. Mirowski and Nik-Khah particularly insist that the solution of game theorists was more conducive to generating short-term benefits for major operators, as well as for the government, to the detriment of users' interests in terms of distribution and pricing.

Miller, Fine, Mirowski and Nik-Khah's critics are representative of a predominant criticism of the performativist corpus (Aspers, 2007; Dequech, 2008; Santos and Rodrigues 2009; Hodgson, 2009; Roberts, 2012; Mirowski, 2015): a lack of critical behaviour rooted in a poor and malleable vision of the social world. Indeed, the sociology of performativity shares with standard economics a view of the economy through the prism of calculation and calculability. Muniesa and Callon (2003: 193) define economic markets as "organized collective devices that calculate compromises on the values of goods".[5] Given the refusal to approach the social apparatus, one is first led to insist on the technical aspect. By substituting technical embedding for social embedding, the theory of performativity abandons any heuristic criticism of economic theory and overestimates the plasticity of the social world:

> The question is no longer "Is this anthropology true or false?", but "Is this anthropology able (Where? How? For how long and in which spaces?) to perform, to enact, a reality corresponding to what it says?" This type of

> question, that may seem strange to a positivist mind, becomes meaningful when we accept the conception of agency presented above. The forms of agency are variable and, to some extent (but only to some extent), plastic and adjustable.
>
> (Callon, 2005: 10)

The criticisms of performativist theory focus mainly on its refusal to adopt an offensive posture in the face of neo-classical economics. As such, this trial has limited value for anyone interested in how economic theories contribute to the construction of the social world. The relevance of the performativist approach to its own objectives should be considered (Muniesa, 2016). The criticisms that have been mentioned nevertheless reveal a deeper problem which can reduce the heuristic capacity of this approach according to the criterion it has set for itself: to determine the mechanisms leading to the congruence between descriptions conveyed by theories and social reality. Indeed, leaving the collective categories out of the analysis offers the world greater plasticity than it would have had by integrating them, so that the ability of economic theory to influence the social world has been greatly neglected by economists; it is, on the contrary, overestimated by performativist theorists. In a recent very interesting contribution, Muniesa analyses the critics of Miller, Mirowski and Nik-Khah. According to him, defending a critical analysis of neo-classical economic theory against the notion of performativity "ends up enforcing a strange alliance between economic science and economic criticism" (Muniesa, 2016: 121): they indeed share a naturalistic view of the economy. Muniesa then emphasises the paradox of criticism of an economic theory that has no performative capacity: "In short, economics is wrong but does not matter. So why then should we waste time criticizing something that does not matter ?" (Muniesa, 2016: 121). It seems clear that no critical economist would claim that economic theory has no effect. What is really at stake is the ability to influence the social world in the sense of greater conformity.

Focus on the object or oversight of the social

If its establishment in ANT is considered the main originality of the theory of performativity, it is important to update the criticisms, especially since, as Mirowski points out, it is precisely the focus on techniques that serves as a justification for abandoning social structures as a framework for analysing markets and agents. In accordance with what was written in Chapter 1, the concentration on technical objects as performative means is based on two fundamental ideas: on the one hand, the technical object has the particularity of forcing agents to act without their having awareness of the technical mechanisms put in motion; on the other hand, it is possible to consider a symmetry between the human and the non-human without a relationship of subordination between them. These two ideas will be addressed separately. I will begin by showing that the first thesis does not allow us fundamentally to differentiate macro-social entities from technical objects, in that they both display this same characteristic. This will then lead me to question the relevance of the principle of symmetry: is it possible to understand the inclusion of techniques in practices regardless of the social relations in which they take place? Not at all. The conclusion at the end of this section will be that the refusal by the performativists to consider social structures is the recurring point of all the critics of this theory of performativity, and that these criticisms are valid.

The object as a cognitive crutch

A key idea, common to actor-network theory and performativist sociology, is that the technical object acts as a crutch for anyone who uses it from the moment it becomes a black box – that is, a cognitive support whose relevance is not questioned: "Cognitive abilities do not reside in 'you' but are distributed throughout the formatted setting, which is not only made of localizers but also of many competence-building propositions, of many small intellectual technologies" (Latour, 2005: 2011). From the perspective of ANT, this point explains why we are interested in objects as providing stability for networks (a blind spot of classical sociology); from the perspective of performativity, we reject the standard approaches of the influence of the economics on the social world (self-realisation, conventions, institutions, norms of representation) in favour of a socio-technical approach. As we have seen above, this point is the originality of the notion of performativity. As in the example of the car engine, where the user ignores its operation and the physical theories it embodies, when an incompatible recipient-organ donor pair approach institutions such as the Kidney Exchange Clearinghouse in the United States in order to be linked to other pairs so that they can exchange kidneys between the respective donors, they rely entirely on matching software developed by economists (Steiner, 2010a, 2010b). They use them as black boxes, in the sense that the two people do not need to know the functioning of these systems, bringing together complex theoretical knowledge, such as the Gale and Shapley algorithm (1962) or the model of matching developed by Roth et al. (2004, 2005). It is precisely because they do not need to master these theoretical elements that this technical design can serve as a cognitive crutch for the actors or users. Once set up, such a system need only collect the necessary information (*input*) in order to put together the individuals in relation (we speak of a *matching market*) to each other (*output*). Beyond a simple performativity by the production of a set of economic beliefs, the economist, as an engineer, impacts the agents' practices without there being any need to educate them:

> Many dispositifs exist in which economic knowledge, formally-rational economics included, is embodied in such a way that economic action implements what economic theory predicts will occur, even where there is complete ignorance on the part of the agent of such economic theory.
>
> (Steiner, 2010a: 248)

Two arguments come together to characterise the role of the non-human as a specificity of the theory of performativity. Technical devices are facts of which no one needs to understand their components in order to use them, and cognitive crutches which help in decision-making. Are such features the techniques' own?

These two characteristics might not be sufficient to oppose performativity by collective belief and performativity by object. It is indeed possible to show that these two characteristics can very well be applied to collective beliefs, to conventions – that is, to the explicit or implicit rules, formulated or tacit, which allow people to coordinate. This definition fits, as seen earlier, in the context of the problem of indeterminacy of the result of a process of coordination between agents (Lewis, 1969; Hardin, 2003). To decide to drive on the left or right, I have to believe that another motorist will do the same, which means that I think he thinks I think . . . I will drive on the left or right. It is to respond to this indeterminacy, linked to the existence of multiple equilibria and to the common knowledge of rationality, that the idea of convention (especially in game theory) is often invoked. For Mary Douglas (1986: 46), this definition has the disadvantage of neglecting the conditions of self-application of the conventional rule: "We want conventions about pedestrian crossings to exist, but we will violate them ourselves if we can do so with impunity." This raises the question of convention legitimacy: in order for a convention to be respected (at least by those who enforce it), it is first necessary that it is based on a deeper convention.[6] In other words, for a conventional rule to persist, a common legitimate representation of the world to support it is necessary. The convention therefore takes on a phenomenological aspect (Berger and Luckmann, 1966) that relies imperatively on a community of beliefs *vis-à-vis* the physical and social world. As such, a convention is both a rule and a cognitive element weighing on the legitimacy of its application.[7] We return to the sum of the two types of convention: strategic and interpretative.

Starting from this definition, two observations are available to us:

i A convention is an object solving coordination dilemmas that an isolated mind cannot solve. Indeed, without the external mediation of a social object discriminating one strategy among others, no individual decision could be taken.
ii Defined as a cognitive framework, the convention acts as an *automatic pilot* (Douglas, 1986). As such, it is a fact, a black box to which individuals leave their decisions.

It is therefore clear that, in this context, characteristics that performativist sociology lends to non-humans can just as easily be lent to the social world, to conventions. If a social convention is inspired (via, for example, learning) from a particular economic theory, nothing allows us in principle to differentiate it from a non-human actant according to the criteria given above.

Thus, the rejection of approaches by the conventions of social influence of economic theories cannot be justified by a specific originality of technical objects. A convention is (but not uniquely) a special device for decision-making, a black box that is reopened in times of crisis. When Karl Polanyi considers the history of the market society, he shows how economic knowledge, carried by classical economists, favours the establishment of a mentality that supports the institutional system of the market. If the major characteristic of the market society is the commodification of social elements formerly governed by other organisational models (labour, money and land), the market becomes an institution only when it is supported by the social convention of the market mentality when it is considered an ahistorical reality. It then becomes a device: agents ignore the exact content and abandon their daily decisions, precisely by virtue of a conventional process. However, like all the devices analysed by ANT, a crisis can justify the reopening of the device, as well as the questioning of its objectivity. This process is the backdrop for *The Great Transformation*: as humans were being shaken up by the blind forces of the market, a counter-movement of reintegration of economic activities within more human social devices was taking shape, particularly under the authority of the socialist reformer Robert Owen. The relevance of an approach centred on technical devices was not questioned, but only the argument of a fundamental originality of these devices, justifying the rejection of other approaches.

Back to the principle of symmetry

It has been shown that, in itself, the argument of the cognitive crutch does not justify the granting of a special status to non-humans, with respect to the classical collective categories, in building the social world. We will now examine the relevance of a symmetrical relationship between the human and non-human, between the social and the technical. According to Bruno Latour, it is unproductive to consider a society "already there" onto which the technical arrangements would be grafted. In such a belief, a technology would only reflect a higher order of social order. On the contrary, it would be necessary for Latour to understand the society under construction like the agglomeration of technical and human elements that stabilise the social. This idea has been subject to strong criticism, especially from supporters of the sociology of scientific knowledge, and we will review three of them.

For Winner (1993), to focus excessively on the construction and stabilisation of technical devices, not only would ANT not capture the multitude of potential uses of technical objects, but it would also be a heuristically weak tool in understanding technologies' impact on social relations. On the one hand, the social context is essential to understand the devices' social use, for to remove society is to miss part of history. On the other hand, in neglecting the social relations underlying the context of scientific discovery, ANT would fall back into Whiggism's outlook – to make the history one of winners and dominant social groups, considering the scientific devices only in terms of their orthodox social uses. ANT is reproached here in considering non-humans only for themselves. This point is the centre of Collins and Yearley's criticism (1992a, 1992b). Beyond the question of the conservative nature of the history of science produced by ANT, Collins and Yearley approach the problem of technical devices' relative autonomy while defending the idea that these are necessarily intimately bound to their contexts. The use of an object requires know-how conferred by the community in which it takes place. When a technical tool supports a scientific procedure, such as a mass spectrometer (Collins and Yearley, 1992a: 311), it is necessary to interpret the results according to rules specific to the scientific field. In the example of the pricing equations cited above, the price-sheets provided to the arbitragers require know-how as well as an ability to interpret the results of the calculations they make possible. Similarly, a device aimed at coordinating individual acts needs to be understood by the actors in question: we do not learn from a "no smoking" sign the reasons that push actors to respect or ignore the rule (Collins and Yearley, 1992a: 318). These examples testify to the necessary mediation by social conventions between individuals and devices. This point of view is also shared by David Bloor (1999: 88): "Systems of belief, that is, shared institutionalised forms of knowledge, are the medium through which people co-ordinate their shared interactions with non-social nature."

Bloor bases his criticism of ANT on his studies of Wittgenstein's work (Bloor, 1997). As seen previously, the use of a device requires rules, whether they are procedures of use or methods of interpreting the results. As Wittgenstein has illustrated, a rule, if reduced to its linguistic form, is necessarily incomplete in that neither the verbal definition of language (which makes us go infinitely from word to word) nor its ostensive definition (in that some words simply cannot be shown: "one", "number") are operative (Wittgenstein, 1958). In this way, rules cannot be apprehended as rails (Wittgenstein, 1953: § 218) determining ways of acting, since all possible ways of acting could flow from the same rule. Wittgenstein's solution to the definition of language problem (especially rules) is to re-anchor it in practice via the notion of a language game: "the whole, consisting of language and the actions into which it is woven" (Wittgenstein, 1953: § 7). Similarly, "'obeying a rule' is a practice. And to *think* one is obeying a rule is not to obey a rule" (Wittgenstein, 1953: § 202). Notions of language game and convention thus ultimately have the same purpose: to dissolve the arbitrariness of the rule (rule of language on one side, and of coordination on the other). It is also to solve the dilemma of language's origin, raised by Willard Van Orman Quine, that David Lewis mobilises the notion of convention. In his preface to Lewis (1969: xi), Quine reformulates his paradox in a playful way:

> When I was a child I pictured our language as settled and passed down by a board of syndics, seated in grave convention along a table in the style of Rembrandt. The picture remained for a while undisturbed by the question what language the syndics might have used in their deliberations, or by dread of vicious regress.

It is in a practical relation to the world that the conventions manifest themselves. The notion of *habitus* has been used elsewhere to give substance to this ANT criticism (Brisset, 2012c). Defined as a "given system of preferences, principles of vision and division [. . .], long lasting cognitive structures [. . .] and patterns of action that guide the perception of the situation and the response adopted" (Bourdieu, 1994: 45; our translation), the *habitus* is a social complement necessary for the use of a device.[8] In this respect, it is simply impossible to reject, as Latour does, the old sociological collective categories since they are necessary to understand the use of devices. If a social representation is expressed by a relation to a thing, it cannot be reduced to it.[9] The technical object used in the social world is in the end only the expression of an underlying conventional world. The result is an inversion of the performativist project. It seems, therefore, that ANT can be subject to two types of criticism: first, relative to the specificity of non-humans with regard to social conventions; and second, concerning the symmetry between humans and non-humans. Since it is ultimately an extension of ANT, performativist sociology is subject to the same considerations, especially since, as we saw in the previous chapter, the Callonian theory of performativity focuses primarily on non-humans, on techniques, thus unbalancing symmetry in favour of non-humans.

The criticisms produced by SSK supporters towards ANT may nevertheless appear to be partly unfair. Firstly, if ANT grants great importance to technical devices, it is only because it exists within a field that aims to study them. Second, from a methodological point of view, as we saw in Chapter 1, ANT does not exclusively focus on technical devices, but on the socio-technical too, like assemblies of techniques and knowledge. The important point of criticism must therefore not be the negligence of social mediation between humans and devices, but the nature of this mediation. Michel Callon is extremely clear on this point when he evokes the principle of symmetry: it is a question of considering the technical and the social with the same theoretical tools, without a relationship of subordination between them. For example, the idea of "making to act" can very well be applied in the human/non-human sense – that human actors make techniques act. Nevertheless, such an approach has precisely the characteristic of removing from the social all that makes its definition among sociologists as well as economists, expressly a set of categories of thoughts imposing themselves on agents and necessary for social life. The notion of socio-technical devices thus reduces the social to its congenial part, namely the human taken out of society (whose construction is to be understood). As a result, performativist analyses do not envisage much more than the technical inclination of performativity, the human being reduced to the actor using technique.

Callon et al. (2001: 180; our translation) address the question of the common world. The project is then explicitly to understand the construction of socio-technical networks instead of presupposing them: "One group never victoriously pop ups out of the blue. He experiences himself, gropes around, looks for himself, navigating amid uncertainties." This perspective is entirely consistent with what was already defended by Callon (1986a) in his famous article on the domestication of scallops, where he addressed the study of scientific controversies.[10] In both cases, the ambition is to give voice to the actors themselves, letting them express how they understand and manage the uncertainty inherent in the social. The desire to give back their voice to the actors was invaluable while sociology tended to systematically adopt an overarching position.[11] Nevertheless, the position defended here is that it is impossible to understand the constitution of a common world without starting from a common world: if the actors have the capacity to doubt the stability of the world around them, they must still imagine a certain stability. As Peirce (1868: 265) observed about philosophy:

> We cannot begin with complete doubt. We must begin with all the prejudices which we actually have when we enter upon the study of philosophy [. . .]. A person may, it is true, in the course of his studies, find reason to doubt what he began by believing; but in that case he doubts because he has a positive reason for it, and not on account of the Cartesian maxim. Let us not pretend to doubt in philosophy what we do not doubt in our hearts.

We have seen that to function, the mediation between the human and the technical necessarily outflanks the human faced with the non-human: a rule of use or interpretation is only operational insofar as it takes place within a language game common to all. As such, unlike Latour and Callon's approaches, the social world is necessarily an "already there". It is also remarkable to note that the principal position against any form of dualism (agents/social, nature/society) is difficult to maintain. This is what Fine claims in his excellent article "From actor-network theory to political economy":

> ANT has been enabled to exercise its own version of what I term "-/ismitis". As it claims to have abolished (all) illegitimate dualisms, so it can read off all other contributions through the prism of having failed to do so. Anyone who explores the distinction between nature and society, even to discover how they are integrated, is liable to be found guilty of dualism. The parallel is with accusations of functionalism, structuralism, instrumentalism, economism, etc. against those who dare to suggest that function, structure, instrument, causation and economic factors prevail in society.
>
> (Fine, 2005: 97)

Separating, as Callon does, an explanation in terms of beliefs and conventions of an explanation by the device has little meaning: it is simply not possible to start from a social world emptied of all categories if we want to understand the use of non-human agents by human agents. Whereas the common world of Callon boils down to an organisation (network) of non-human and human actors leading to a redefinition of the actors themselves (which, for a human actor, goes through a production of his own subjectivity), the common world that is a convention constitutes an epistemic base necessary for any organisation, any network. By erasing the priority of the human over the non-human in explaining social phenomena and by considering technical objects outside the social practices of which they are the centre and which precede them, performativist sociology can upset the balance of the relationship between humans and non-humans in favour of the latter. As we have seen, among performativists, it is the techniques that explain that behaviours of human actors conform to economic theories.

*

At the end of this study of criticisms of performative sociology and the ANT, it is noteworthy that the recurring point is the lack of consideration with regard to the social world in which social actors evolve. Beyond the fact that in both cases this position leads to a certain allegiance to the prevailing science, it seems that such a position is hardly plausible from an analytical point of view if one wishes to understand the way theories shape the social world, especially when it comes to thinking about the failure of performativity (Butler 2010, Brisset 2011). This last point, which will be the subject of the next section, seems to be the true heart of the debate revolving around Callonian theory.

The heart of the problem: relativism

The various criticisms detailed above call into question (more or less explicitly) the social ontology carried by the theory of performativity. The absence of a common world considerably reduces the role of humans in socio-technical devices, giving way to techniques. However, considering markets from a mainly technical angle, the theory of performativity presupposes the validity of economic theories in shaping the social world more than it theorises them. The relationship between science and society becomes similar to that of a mechanic with a car. Nonetheless, this position is considered by some performativity theoreticians to be far removed from the Callonian approach as an intrinsic limit of this approach. It is, for example, the position of Judith Butler, who, in a particularly acrimonious article (Butler, 2010), points to the failure of Callon's theory of performativity when it exclusively considers the phenomenon of performativity by investigating its performance:

> Although this notion of the variability of economic practice and relation disturbs the idea of the economy as a singular notion, it does not precisely tell us how performativity works to effect that disturbance or, indeed, to what alternative conception that disturbance leads. Neither does it tell

> us when and why performativity fails to work, when it invariably does. Indeed, if we accept that there are variable modes by which economic life is organized, and even that theories contribute to those organizations and hence are part of the organizing mode itself, then that only tells us that theories are performative in the sense that they help to organize the objects they theorize. Theorists may then endeavor to think more carefully about how their own work contributes to the organization of the market, but two questions remain: what happens when disjunctions emerge between theory and economic activity? And on what grounds would theorists conclude that it is better to contribute to the making of the economic sphere in one way rather than another? In a sense, both the breakdown of performativity and the normative horizon of its aspirations still remain to be explained and understood.
>
> (Butler, 2010: 149–150)

Butler blames Callon for treating the performative act as a whole, without distinguishing the performative action from its effect on the real world. However, analytical tools belonging to performative theory do not allow these effects (in the vocabulary of the philosophy of language, to discriminate failures of illocutionary and perlocutionary acts). Donald MacKenzie (2009: 57), who has a different perspective on performativity, stresses this limitation:

> The task of tracing an agencement in an interconnected world is formally endless, and the notion could become simply a jargon into which to translate banal description and narrative, as happened to some degree when actor-network concepts first became fashionable in English-language science and technology studies some twenty years ago.

To overcome this problem, MacKenzie (2007: 55) chooses to define groups and subgroups of performativity. He starts with the widest possible definition of what he calls "generic performativity": economic theory used by actors in economic and social processes. Within this broad set, he distinguishes a first subset, which he calls "effective performativity". The use of this theory has effects on the economic and social process, and this subset is divided into two subsets:

- *Barnesian performativity:*[12] the use of a theory makes the social world similar to the description made by the latter;
- *counterperformativity:* the use of a theory distances the social world from its description.

For MacKenzie, these two sets must constitute the heart of the theory of performativity, the generic performativity ultimately informing little about the construction of the social world. However, he does not theorise any potential counterperformativity mechanism. Butler considers this approach superficial in the sense that the failure of performativity has always been set aside from the theory of performativity. She reproaches MacKenzie (Butler, 2010: 152):

> There is a difference between claiming (a) that breakdown and disruption of performative operations can happen, and (b) that the risk of breakdown and disruption are constitutive to any and all performative operations. The first is empirical, but the second is structural.

Although it is the question of the failure of performativity that is reflected in the criticisms cited above, Daniel Miller supports this point when he is more interested in failures than in achievements in performativity (Miller, 2005: 8). It is particularly interesting to note that performativist sociology breaks away from Austin's original definition. Remember that the starting point for the philosopher was the fact that certain statements fail when they have no impact on the world. This leads him to place the performative felicity conditions at the heart of the definition, and therefore, the possibility of failure. This is because the Callonian approach, with its technicist vision, expels the ideas of social felicity conditions that exclude performative failure. So here we are, beyond a simple constructivism that could both admit that economists could participate in the construction of social reality and fail to do so, in a hyper-constructivist perspective: nothing seems to prevent performativity. This problem is discussed today in the literature related to performativity in economics (Svetlova, 2012).

In line with the theory of self-fulfilling prophecies developed by Merton, the notion of performativity seems to lead to the conclusion that any theory can become true (or at least not invalidated) on the condition of performing the world through individual decisions. By its silence, performative theory tacitly accepts this principle. It is this conclusion that has given rise to strong criticisms of the "conservative" character of the theory of performativity, which, unlike many sociological theories, does not seek to enrich the concepts of economic analysis, but rather to adjust them by considering that this theory forms the world in its image, and consequently becomes true. One debate typifies this tension. Ferraro et al. (2005) studied the effect of managerial theories on managerial and identified three ways the theory can come to self-realisation: institutional design, social norms and language. The idea is that under the condition of the combination of these three notions, any theory can become true in the sense that it provides economic agents with a good heuristic tool for making their daily decisions. Felin and Foss (2009a, 2009b) provide a somewhat provocative answer by arguing, on the contrary, that only true theories can prevail, and thus influence the world, in the struggle between conflicting theories. This is for them the main limit of the performativity effect. The argument of Felin and Foss lacks a definition of what is a "true" theory.[13] As seen in Chapter 2, an abundant literature has indeed been devoted to showing the way in which a theory which is absurd at first glance – for example, how the appearance of sunspots influences the variations of prices of certain types of financial securities – may self-realise even if it seems that there is no link between the two phenomena.[14] Nevertheless, Felin and Foss raise a most pertinent question, one well known to economists: that of the selection of a single equilibrium in the case of a multiplicity of potential equilibria.[15] One of the consequences of the existence of self-fulfilling equilibria is that there are as many potential equilibria as theories circulating in a population of agents. More generally, it can be said, following Kjellberg and Helgesson (2006), that "the multitude of practices that constitute markets suggests the presence of many efforts to shape markets". Chapter 2 covered these discussions, which will be subsequently developed around the idea of the limit of performativity. Can we affirm, according to Felin and Foss, but also Hodgson (2009), that a theory is true when it is considered as such, and especially when it is used as a heuristic tool in decision-making (it generates beliefs that will allow action, and there are limits, even shifting ones) to the diffusion of an economic theory within a population? In the framework of a bilateral coordination, if the forecast of each one about the strategy of others is that it acts according to a precise economic theory, then the theory becomes a norm like a coordinate mark, a focal point in Schelling's sense (1960). Thus perceived, a theory seems to be able to become true as long as it is used by individuals. The comparison between the thesis of performativity and a number of economic issues relating to the general notion of convention (self-realisation of beliefs, focal point, coordination convention, etc.) allows here a considered response to significant criticisms. It is precisely because Callonian sociology refuses such a merger that it cannot satisfy its critics. The refusal to tackle the problem of the relationship to the truth and the absence of a pre-existing common social world undermines the understanding of the performative phenomenon as a barrier to the conceptual development of counterperformativity: for a theory to serve as a decision-making tool, it must be accepted as true by actors evolving within a pre-existing conventional world. This necessary condition, a blind spot of Callonian performative theory, would nevertheless support the notion of "truth test" at the heart of Callon and Latour's approaches. The proposals of Muniesa and Callon have already been mentioned in the introduction to this work: "It is because they [the economic sciences] produce models and representations, which involve proofs of truth, that they can efficiently intervene in these designs and learn from the experiences that they organise" (Muniesa and Callon, 2009: 319).

If the notion of failure is thus constitutive of the theoretical DNA of performativist sociology, it is considerably weakened by a social exclusion that implies a de-symmetrisation of the analysis in favour of the techniques. From here, it is a question of explaining why one theory propagates and shapes the social world more than another and, consequently, why coordination takes place at one point rather than another. Giving flesh to the notion of counterperformativity consists very precisely in exploiting this idea by answering the following question: if the social world depends on the representations one has, how can one think of the existence of truth tests for economic theories that introduce new representations? For this purpose, we must equip performative theory with social world theory, in order to find what seemed to be a major element of the ANT's sociology, little by little obscured:

> I wanted to show the technicians that they could not even conceive a technical object without taking into account the crowd of humans, their passions, their policies, their poor calculations, and that by becoming good sociologists and good humanists, they would become better engineers and wise decision-makers.
>
> (Latour, 1993a: 8; our translation)

The work of the philosopher John Searle will provide a first approximation of a new approach to performativity. We will see that it allows at least two limits to performativity, two ways in which the social world puts pressure on the performative mechanism, even in a constructivist framework: that of physical facts and that of social phenomena. Even if the thesis of performativity is often an opportunity to emphasise the eminently rhetorical aspect of economic theories (for a theory to avoid refutation, it is enough to convince agents to use it), the analytical content counts. Indeed, the link between agents' representations and scientific knowledge is never direct: these agents must choose an explanatory theory of the world while they are confronted with elements they have not mastered. Supporting this argument will require understanding how economic theories, through the phenomenon of performativity, participate in the construction of social reality (Searle, 1995). Only once this explanation has been set up will it be possible to qualify the effects of the performative phenomenon.

Conclusion: the problem of counterperformativity

The main result of this chapter is to have made the link between the fundamental characteristics of performativist sociology highlighted in the first two chapters (the concentration on the role of objects and the discharge of the social) and the criticisms levelled at it; the main criticism is the lack of perspective on so-called standard economic theory. Beyond this point, which does not in itself constitute a convincing attack inasmuch as this position is clearly claimed by Callon, the systematic examination of the attacks on performativity revealed a deeper difficulty, intimately linked to characteristics A (economic science is performative through socio-technical devices) and B (the refusal to consider macro-social ensembles in favour of technical devices):

C the difficulty of considering failures of performativity.

This ends the critical reconstruction of the theory of performativity and indicates a problem requiring an alternative approach to ANT methodology. In studying the limits of performativity, these potential failures, and thus giving more substance to notions such as truth tests or counterperformativity, the performativist tools become insufficient in that they have gradually led to what Razmig Keucheyan has called a "non-social constructivism" (Keucheyan, 2007) – that is, an approach centred on both techniques, considering the social first and foremost as a process, and not as a still frame. If there is a lesson to be learned from the original definition of the notion of performativity posited by John Austin, it is good that the performative act, the fact of "making to do" (whether by words or by techniques), requires that some social conditions should be met: to perform a marriage, one must be licensed – one must have a specific place in the social field in which I am projected, both me and my speech. In that capacity, denying the social the status of explanans (not considering that a theory operates in a social context that precedes and imposes itself onto it) amounts to ignoring some conditions necessary for performativity, consequently preventing a grasp of the question that runs through this book, which questions the reasons for the performative failures of singular economic theories.

Notes

1 As we shall see, this criticism is not entirely relevant, in that the refusal to adopt a critical position towards economic theories is a position of principle, and not a result of the theory of performativity.
2 We can also find this position in Boltanski (2011, 2012).
3 See also Callon and Latour (2013)
4 See also Nik-Khah (2006) and Mirowski (2013, 2015).
5 Computability can be at two levels of analysis deriving from the origins of mathematical economics through the debate between Walras and Edgeworth (Bridel, 2008). Whereas the first considers the market as an algorithmic structure (trial-and-error) determining the economic equilibrium (*market machine*), the second offers instead the rational agent (*pleasure machine*) as the starting point of reasoning in the absence of structure (Debreu and Scarf, 1963). In the first perspective, it is the market that acts as a computer centre; in the second, it is the agent. This type of analysis duality is still widely present today (Mirowski, 2007), and aptly illustrates the fields of the different performativist works: one studies the ways in which the agents are paired individually, or the way in which they are placed in a calculation structure.
6 See the idea of *deep convention*, Marmor (2009).
7 This definition of convention, integrating both the idea of rule and legitimacy of the rule, goes beyond the simple framework of coordination. Douglas also emphasises the essential role of institutions in cases of moral crises. This is, for example, the case when the survival of a group requires the death of one of its members: an institution is often summoned to make the decision, instead of an individual. No one has to take responsibility for a socially overbearing decision.
8 One can also consider a great proximity between the thought of Bourdieu and that of Wittgenstein. Both start from the same observation: the idea of rule is not sufficient to explain human actions. Practice (the habitus or the play of language) is not reducible to the statement of an action rule.
9 As Batifoulier and Thèvenon (2001: 249; our translation) point out: "Objects would impose sufficient constraints to coordinate not only by the mediation format they

induce, but also because they would be nothing more than the tip of an evaluation model, crystallising a particular form of judgement capable of guaranteeing the desired objectivity."

10 "We want to show in this paper that the analysis can be continued with a society that is considered uncertain and questionable [...]. Our goal is to show that it is possible to doubt the society itself as well as the actors, and that this does not lead to chaos or absurdity" (Callon, 1986a: 175–177; our translation).

11 A will that can also be found in Boltanski (2011, 2012).

12 Reference from British sociologist Barry Barnes (1983).

13 As for Merton's case

14 On the theory of sunspots, see Azariadis and Guesnerie (1982) and Chiappori (2004).

15 As Dupuy (1992: 231–232; our translation) underlines: "An 'equilibrium', a fixed point of the self-referential process, is obtained when the actors' reactions to the representations they make of the reality in which they are immersed generates, by composition, a reality in conformity with these representations. It is, again and again, the logic of the self-fulfilling prophecy."

Conclusion to Part I

At the end of what constituted our entry into the theory of performativity, three important stages marked out our course. Proposing a reconstruction of the history of the notion of performativity between the philosophy of language and actor-network theory has made it possible to explain the central idea of performativist sociology, specifically the importance of devices in the construction of the social world. In this perspective, the different economic theories execute the world they claim to describe, embodied in multiple technical devices forming a vast network to assist individual decision-making. Thus, these decisions lead social actors to perform as if they conformed to the theories integrated into the techniques. The refusal to adopt the perspective of "sociologists of the social" – in other words, of those who confer on macro-social sets (conventions) the status of interpretive elements of the first order in the heuristics of the social world – is the technicist approach equivalent of performativist sociology. However, this methodological characteristic underlies an important weakness of the performativist corpus: its difficulties in considering performativity failures. As a matter of fact, the principles of use of a technical device and the reasons why the actors coordinate on a device do not emanate from the device itself. The device does not explain its influence on the social world, let alone its failure to influence it.

We have finally seen that this theoretical difficulty threatens the heuristic efficiency of the theory of performativity. The economists who have studied this theory have not been mistaken. After this reconstruction work, we can, in the next part, begin the phase of theoretical elaboration.

Part II

A conventionalist approach to performativity

Introduction to Part II

Part I of this book provided an opportunity to review the theoretical characteristics of performativist sociology, its roots and its complications, by focusing on its three principal characteristics:

A Economics performs through socio-technical devices making individuals carry out actions (Chapter 1).
B There is a refusal to consider macro-social sets in favour of socio-technical devices (Chapter 2).
C There is difficulty in considering failures of performativity (Chapter 3).

These characteristics are closely linked: technical devices are valued more than social entities, which leads one to believe markets and agents to be mere technical devices, thus preventing consideration that the performativity of economic theory necessarily takes place in a pre-existing social environment. This observation calls for the reintroduction of social factors into the theory of performativity. Developing the ontology of social entities above individual representations will make it possible to theorise the limits of theories to be performed in the social world. This is a central focus of John Searle's social philosophy. Exploring social ontology will also enable a consideration of the performative structural movement of the social world and its resistance to this same world during this movement. By addressing social facts as entities that both surpass and constrain us, Searle's interest lies in producing a social ontology combining subjectivism and objectivism: social facts are ontologically subjective insofar as they depend entirely on representations we have of them (without humans, there are no state, businesses, church nor collective beliefs). Nevertheless, social facts are objective from an epistemic point of view: the knowledge of the institutional fact is under-determined by the representation one has as an individual. With this in mind, performativity can be redefined as the implementation of social facts inspired by economic theory within a social world that can nevertheless resist this process.

This development, however, is only an initial approximation of our analytical framework. It is thus necessary to implement Searle's approach in order to explain the mechanisms of performativity: how can one best understand how an economic theory can serve as a founding principle for a social fact? This question requires going beyond Searle by redefining social facts as conventions, viewed by philosopher David Lewis as social entities upon which individuals focus their beliefs. We will thus be able to derive a definition of performativity and identify the mechanisms of its failure. This definition, to a certain extent, will be a return to Austin: a definition of performativity based on the possibility of performative failures.

This approach will highlight three conditions which are essential to the performative process. In order to make the social world performative by becoming a convention, a theory must be: empirical, self-fulfilling and compatible with the conventional set already in place. The first characteristic refers to the ability of a theory to help agents make a choice among clearly identified alternatives. For example, if the theory of economic rationality becomes a conventional point of reference, it implies that a set of irrational behaviours can be identified. It also implies that acting rationally leads to results that conform to the expectations of agents conditioned by economic theory. In other words, the theory needs to be self-fulfilling. The second condition is essential, as is rationalises the claim that economics performs the world in the way of greater conformity. Finally, a particular theory will only become a convention if it does not contradict other conventions set in place. If, for example, agents deemed the Pareto criterion profoundly incompatible with the moral values of their community, it would be difficult to gain social acceptance of the implementation of a large market mimicking the function of general equilibrium.

These conditions will be deduced from a conventionalist approach allowing the elements that explain the failure of performativity to be identified, which Callon failed to recognise in his theory of performativity. Within this framework, these conditions are necessary but not sufficient for performativity to take place. A theory can fail to render the social world performative by not providing clear points of reference for the agents, by not allowing agents to achieve their goals, and by being faced with pressure from conventions that already exist (including normative conventions).

The third condition of performativity is the reintroduction of social factors into the theory of performativity, which is thus symptomatic of our approach. Performativity induces the emergence of a new convention on which agents coordinate in a world structured by other conventions. The exploration of this final condition will highlight the need for a structured ontology made up of conventions that are considered emergent effects. These are a result of individual representations which appear to individuals as external facts. Chapter 5 will attempt to unravel the debate of emerging social entities in order to epistemologically and ontologically justify the idea of conventions irreducible to individuals. Contrary to what Callon asserts, there is indeed a common world necessary for social life. This common world exerts pressure on emerging ways of thinking inspired by economic theory. In order to show this, this chapter will return to the way in which economists regularly treat institutional facts.

These institutional facts, while emerging from individual behaviours, are not reducible to them (see the section "The origins of the concept of the emergent effect"). The following sections ("Criticism of the notion of emergence" and "Institutions and epistemological irreducibility: how to endogenise the rules") will explore whether this concept is, indeed, problematic. It is possible to defend this conception as long as we consider a particularity of the social world, namely that it is made up of individuals seeking to coordinate, and that this ontologically creates the idea of institutional facts relying on agents as external entities (see the section "From epistemological emergence to ontological emergence"), thus slowing down the performative process.

The objective of this part will ultimately be to build an analytical framework that will provide a heuristically relevant perspective on performativity given the question: why do some theories shapes social reality and others not?

4 Changing perspective

Performativity, institutional fact and convention

> Men make their own history, but they do not make it as they please; they do not make it under self-selected circumstances, but under circumstances existing already, given and transmitted from the past. The tradition of all dead generations weighs like a nightmare on the brains of the living.
>
> (Karl Marx, *The Eighteenth Brumaire of Louis Bonaparte*)

The objective of this chapter is to redefine performativity in such a way that the difficulties inherent to the standard performativist sociology can be overcome. More precisely, this chapter will develop an approach to performativity that will better consider its failures. Searle's work, which develops social thought by reconciling subjectivism and objectivism, will serve as the philosophical foundation for my approach. Reviewing Searle's work is a necessary step towards developing an understanding of performativity as a construction of the social world that is also limited by the social world. This approach is built upon the concept of "institutional fact" and upon the evidence of a "metaphysical burden". The institutional facts come from individual representations that both make up society and impose a burden on it. This concept will be the basis of a new point on performativity: for performativity to take place, a new institutional fact must be implemented in a world that resists it. The definition of institutional fact deployed by Searle states that it is the support of the assignment of functions taking the form of "X counts as Y in a context C." An institutional fact is therefore a common representation of the world which allows certain decisions to be made. Following from the above, economics "performs" the social world as soon as it allows the emergence of new assignments of function – for example, "X counts as a commodity", which means that X will be treated and traded according to a set of rules rooted in a theory of markets. The question of the failure of performativity thus arises: how can a theory fail to become an institutional fact defined as an assignment of function? Searle's approach will prove to be inadequate in answering this question, particularly as his treatment of the way a function assignment becomes a benchmark for an entire community is too vague. As a result, it will be necessary to redefine institutional fact using the concept of convention borrowed from David Lewis, with the intention of understanding why individuals follow assignments of function. This work will be done in two stages. Firstly, it will clearly express Lewis' definition of a convention as an essential complement to the assignment of functions; secondly, it will highlight that this notion reveals three conditions necessary for the performativity of a theory: empiricism, self-fulfilment and complementarity with conventions already set in place within the social space. This work will require that we define what is meant by a theory in a conventionalist framework.

This chapter will thus provide: a new definition of performativity as a conventional assignment of function, a definition of theory as an element that can become an assignment, a set of conditions necessary for performativity. Exploring Searlian institutional theory is a necessary deviation given Austin's lack of reflection on the institutional integration of speech acts, and it has already been done throughout other works (Brisset, 2011; Herrmann-Pillath, 2010, 2012, 2013, 2016; Guala, 2016), but we will see that it will be necessary to go beyond Searle. Without exploiting his theory, this chapter will return to Austin by defining performativity by its conditions of failure (of felicity).

Social reality according to John Searle

The conceptual set constructed by Searle extends to fields as diverse as linguistics, philosophy and social sciences. In *The Construction of Social Reality*, Searle (1995) develops his theory of social reality. The theory is based on a fundamental distinction between brute facts such as "the moon causes tides" and social facts such as "this is money". The distinction between the two is made on the basis of a simple question: would this fact, or this characteristic, exist independently of our representations of it? This original distinction, constituent to Searlian realism, is an opportunity to remedy what Searle considers to be an epistemological error, associated with naive relativism: to deduce from the idea that individuals can never free themselves from their categories of thought when they observe the world (epistemological relativism) that the external world has no proper existence (ontological relativism).[1] For Searle, the existence of an irreducible gap between reality and concepts does not support any conclusion about the ontological nature of this same reality. This argument is at the heart of what he calls "external realism": despite being inaccessible for our knowledge by virtue of an insurmountable hiatus between the external world and our representations, there exists a reality independent of our representations – a reality on which the social world is built. Searle seeks to show that external realism is a condition of speech formulation: "[W]hen we attempt to communicate to achieve normal understanding with these sorts of utterances we must presuppose external realism" (Searle, 1995: 184). External realism is thus for Searle a condition of speech intelligibility. Even if there are no Diableret mountains or Lake Geneva, statements about them can be understood as dependent on an external reality. Institutional facts are a sub-category of social facts, and the three concepts making it possible to characterise them are: "assignment of function", "collective intentionality" and "constitutive rules". An institutional fact is, first of all, an object, a sign and an event to which a particular function is assigned. If the assignment of the function takes the generic form "X counts as Y in a context C", then the primary characteristic of institutional facts (unlike other social facts) is that they cannot be reduced to the physical characteristics of the entity to which they are attached. An institutional fact is rooted in a particular assignment of function based on a specific status conferred to the object. This can be defined as the "status function". For example:

(a) "A four-legged object on which it is possible to sit is regarded a chair."
(b) "Paper with certain characteristics is regarded as money."

Here, only affirmation (b) can be considered as a status function assignment, because contrary to assertion (a), the physical characteristics of the object (such as X: "paper") do not allow it to have the same function as money.[2] To enable this function, it is necessary to bestow upon a simple piece of paper a social power[3] issued from collective intentionality, which alone gives the paper its monetary function. This is what is missing from statement (a). On this basis, a social fact is essentially *self-referential*. For a type of object to satisfy the definition of a social concept, it must be believed that it satisfies this definition. Applied to the example of money, it can be said that money is considered as such when it is considered collectively. Collective intentionality, an essential characteristic of institutional facts, is taken from Searlian theory as a primitive fact necessary for collective action. Indeed, any action involving action from others requires a collective intentionality at a higher level:

> In order that two men should engage in a prizefight, for example, there has to be collective intentionality at a higher level. They have to be cooperating in having a fight in order for each of them to try to beat the other up.
> (Searle, 1995: 23–24)[4]

One part of this collective can be found by the acceptance of a system of rules in which a particular fact fits. It is precisely at this stage that Searle's famous distinction between constitutive and regulative rules comes into play. While the latter codifies an existing field (for example, the Highway Code is to regulate traffic), the former rules are consubstantial of this field. A game of chess, for example, whose existence is based solely on the rules that constitute it, is an emblematic example. On closer inspection, a constitutive rule is only the formalisation of a status function assignment: "X counts as a Y in a context C." In the final analysis, an institutional fact exists only in a set of consubstantial constitutive rules of the institutional architecture. As long as the institution allows the assignment of the function, it must be the result of an assignment of function conferring upon it the power to create institutional facts. In other words, a new constitutive rule can only emerge from a system of pre-existing constitutive rules. Here we find the essence of Bourdieu's criticism of linguistic performativity: for a statement to be enabled to act on the world, such as creating an institutional fact using a status assignment, it must take place in a previously structured social field.

Assignment of function and performativity

Searle's conceptualisation proves to be an invaluable tool for placing the theory of the performativity of theoretical statements within a theory of society containing social entities. Searle draws a comparison between his social theory and the theory of performativity taken from his linguistic meaning. First, he highlights that the institutional movement from X to Y by proposing that "X counts as a Y in a context C" is *ipso facto* a linguistic movement. The first characteristic of language is that it allows the representation of certain things that do not exist independently from language itself. The transition from X to Y is closely linked to language, and moves from brute fact to institutional fact (or from one institutional fact to another): "Without a language, we can see the man cross a white line holding a ball, [. . .]. But we cannot see the man score six points [. . .]" (Searle, 1995: 68). Indeed, the status function cannot be determined by the unique physical characteristics of X, it is in fact language that grants its existence.[5] Language creates the ontological categories of institutional facts and is crucial to the first stage of its creation. Beyond language, Searle focuses on the role of the "declaration" as an act of institutional creation. If language is a condition which is necessary for the assignment of function, a declaration is the act by which this assignment forms. As stated by Searle (2010: 11): "All institutional facts, and therefore all status functions, are created by speech acts of a type in 1975 [which] I baptised as 'Declarations'." A declaration is nevertheless a necessary condition for institutional creation insofar as in order to produce a performative statement – that is, to create the entity it announces – it must be delivered in a context and by a person to whom a particular status function has been assigned. For example: "the phrase 'I promise' is regarded as an obligation in an official context". It is at this stage that we will review the felicity conditions of John Austin.

It is thus possible to clarify the issue of the performativity of theoretical statements considering that economics plays the role of assigning status functions and that it has the socially recognised power to modify the assignment of functions already in place. This perspective considers the sciences in general, and in this case, economic science, as a means of fixing beliefs among other beliefs in keeping with pragmatist philosophy (Peirce, 1878b). As such, the main objective of science is to fuel individual and social habits of thought which influence the habits of actions taken by individuals. These thought habits can be considered as assignments of functions which take place on three levels:

- Individual representations: the actions of economic agents, through their practices with the economic and social world, are based on beliefs which can be assimilated with assignments of function. For example, in regard to financial expectations: "a massive restructuring of a listed company counts as 'a future rise in dividends'". These individual beliefs are influenced by economic theories, especially when they are incorporated with devices directly intended for decision-making (models of risk assessment on the financial markets, managerial theories, etc.).
- Formal rules: on this level, the formal rules of the human collective are explored. A number of studies have highlighted the importance of economics in the evolution of legal concepts. The American economist John Roger Commons provides a good example of such an approach. In his book *Legal Foundations of Capitalism* (1924), he describes the evolution of capitalism based on the gradual transformation of legal categories, namely property.[6] This evolution, among other things, takes place on the basis of the various theories of value developed by economists. In this instance, it is clear that the naming of the assignment of a new definition "carries with it the assignment of some new functions, for example, in the form of rights and responsibilities" (Searle, 1995: 88).
- For the formal rules to continue over time, it is imperative that they are relayed by a number of informal institutional facts (we can call conventions) – a system of representations and collective acceptance – and conventions will be explored by linking individual representations and formal institutions. For example, in order to render the legal code as more than mere written words, it must permeate collective representations. Karl Polanyi paves the way for changes to the European economic system in the nineteenth century in his work *The Great Transformation* (1944 [2001]). In this work, he established a certain market mentality supported by economists themselves.

This approach, however, still lacks the tools to consider the integrity of performativity, as it should include formal rules and individual and collective beliefs. The assignment of function shows its limits when the assignment is conceived as a collective fact. Performativity is indeed a relevant theoretical contribution as it reveals a connection between theories and a collective of individuals. We will come back to this issue in the next chapter.

Assignment of function and limits of performativity

In order to understand the limits of performativity, redefined as an assignment of function, it is necessary to understand the primary characteristic of an institutional fact. An institutional fact is a collective agreement, formal or tacit, embodied in social acts. Unlike physical objects, institutional facts do not become diminished the more they are used. In fact, their existence results from their use, which causes them to strengthen over time. Searle also finds that most of the time, institutions are not directly recognised by the people, and that it is only within practices that these appear. Individuals do not know social rules in their entirety, yet they are continuously practised by them. These social rules are part of what Searle calls the background: "In fact in many situations, we just know what to do, we just know how to deal with the situation. We do not apply the rules consciously or unconsciously" (Searle, 1995: 143). If the assignment of function only exists when it is supported by a set of individual and collective practices, the same can consequently be applied to economic concepts. Hence, an economic theory will only be performative if it is capable of establishing itself as a belief, and thus takes shape within a body of practices in which it would *in fine* only be a summary. If an economic statement can become true (or remain unrefuted), insofar as it integrates the practices of the agents, it is these same agents who thus perform the movement of integration. In order for a theory to establish itself, it must first provide an answer to practical questions which are deemed to be relevant. Theory then retains a scientific value, provided this value is judged on the basis of a criterion that is more flexible than usual: a valid theory, for example, is a theory that is retained by the agents because of the appeasement it provides to doubts relating to the outside world. In the eyes of the agents, some theories are more adapted than others. In order to understand performativity, it is necessary to understand this process of acceptance. As such, the crucial question here is: why use one economic theory over another? Searle provides us with two limits of the phenomenon of performativity: brute facts and institutional facts. This is a far cry from extreme relativism (any theory, at any time or place is able to perform its own reality as it is taken for granted by agents). These limits take shape within the framework of "external realism" and from the idea that if social reality is composed of facts dependent on our representations (which only exist due to the collective belief that they exist), then these facts are objective in the sense that they do not depend directly on individual representations. This point is an opportunity to draw a distinction between two meanings of subjectivity. From an ontological point of view, for something to be subjective, it depends ontologically on the experiences of the subject. The example of pain or money is as follows: to suffer depends entirely on the subject who is enduring the suffering, and "money" exists when the subject considers it to be money (buyers, sellers, tax collectors, etc.). Without a subject, there is no possibility of pain or money. From an epistemic point of view, subjectivity is above all a question of criteria of truth: truth does not exist inside facts, but as a result of an attitude towards them. In this regard, facts can be both ontologically subjective (their existence depends on the conscious subject) and epistemically objective (the knowledge of their characteristics does not solely depend on the representations of the subject that seizes them). The ontological meaning of the subjective–objective duality rests on the nature of the apprehended object: an object is said to be subjective if it depends on the representations one has of it. A market exists, for example, only because a human collective recognises it as such. On the contrary, for something to be objective (stones, mountains or stars), it is not reliant on individual representations or experiences one may have of it. The epistemic meaning does not refer to the nature of the object, but to the knowledge that the conscious being has of it. The question is thus as follows: if an object ontologically depends on its representation which allows a closer insight of performativity, is science still relevant? By following Searle's conceptualisation, it will be possible to answer. An ontologically subjective object can also be epistemically objective. Its understanding does not specifically rely on the person who is thinking about the object, but instead relies on a community of thinkers of a superior order. For example, to say that Van Gogh died in France is epistemically objective, even if the object "France" is ontologically subjective. On the other hand, to say that "Van Gogh is a better painter than Manet" is epistemically subjective (Searle, 2010: 21–22). From this distinction, it is possible to assume that there exists a pressure of epistemically objective social facts on individual beliefs, even though these two objects are ontologically subjective. Equipped with their representations, the agents are confronted with an epistemically objective world – that is, a social world imposing itself on their particular representations. The social world is thus not freely malleable. Take, for example, Searle's example of currency: "Facts about money can be epistemically objective even if the existence of money is socially constructed, and, therefore, to that extent, ontologically subjective" (Searle, 1995: 190). The justification of this statement takes place on two levels: first, a hierarchical relationship between brute facts and social facts; and secondly, an epistemically objective character of certain ontologically subjective social facts. The aim here will be to link this idea of selective pressure with the performativity of theoretical statements by introducing this concept into Searle's theoretical architecture. This will allow the modification of relativism, inherent to the problematic of the performativity of statements, in order to express the implications. These implications are social practices that select economic theory, allowing the social actors to complete their actions in an environment that resists them.

Brute facts and the assignment of function

Searle's conceptual system logically implies, in a manner consistent with external realism, the priority of brute facts over institutional facts. The social world is a narrow network of function assignments of type "X counts as Y in a context C", with the X of an assignment being the Y or C of another. Consequently, a hierarchy of institutional facts exists insofar as these facts are always intertwined within each other and there is ultimately always a status function assigned to something that is not a status function – that is, a fact whose existence does not depend on the beliefs one bears about it: a brute fact. It can thus be said without hesitation that Searle considers that "[t]he world of Supreme Court decisions and the collapse of communism is the same world as the world of the formation of planets and of the collapse of the wave function in quantum mechanics" (Searle, 1995: 120). For example, the physical characteristics of brute facts to which we assign functions influence the possibility of actions triggered by the assignment. Nevertheless, if the choice of an object to which we wish to assign a status remains important, the influence of the brute fact on the assignment remains variable: "There is a scale that goes from freedom to necessity, from arbitrariness to reason, in the items selected for the status-functions" (Searle, 1995: 86). If several brute facts can be adapted to a function assignment, then the choice remains social. Currency, for example, is an emblematic example of the importance of brute facts. According to Adam Smith, metal was established as currency in a large number of communities due to the ease with which metal was quantified and adjusted. As a store of value, currency must neither be alterable nor be damaged by contact with air, thus durable and possessing an advantage over conventional goods. A currency that does not adhere to these characteristics would not resist the social practices that designate its function. It would seem that there is the pressure of brute facts when it comes to the use of social objects in the daily lives of individuals, and thus on the self-reinforcing process of these institutional facts. Therefore, for a theory to perform reality, it is necessary that it takes place in a world containing brute facts that cannot be changed freely. In economics, the concept of the technical coefficient is a tool for representing the economic reality of physical characteristics and brute facts that do not exist solely because of human beliefs, but because they are imposed on them. A technical coefficient, which is included in production functions, is not self-referential. It does not depend on the representation others have of it, but on the physical constraints of the subjects treated. It is the same for the nature of the returns to scale characterising production functions; deciphering whether the quantity of output increases more than proportionally to the quantity of input is a technical question reliant on brute characteristics.[7] Similarly, the problem with integrating resource depletion into these same production functions is above all a physical constraint on economic theory itself. As such, a representation of the economic world integrating technical coefficients and a return that does not conform to a brute reality would quickly be abandoned by the agents. Here, it is important to note that the notion of device contains elements of brute fact, but is not reduced to it. A socio-technical device is the combination of purely physical characteristics and the social choice of its use. This notion is thus ineffective when it comes to reasoning a hierarchy between brute facts and institutional facts, especially as the pressure of the brute facts varies depending on the type of social object at play.

Social facts and the metaphysical burden

As a result, individuals are confronted with a number of brute facts (even if they are never and can never be perceived as such). This means a kind of selective pressure exists on assignments of function due to the ontological objectivity of the physical characteristics. However, these are not the only ones to escape individual representations. One can also consider that most individuals are unaware of the social structures and take their existence for granted. It would indeed be an insurmountable challenge for human beings to be wholly aware of the structures of the social world, and nor would it be possible to inform and consciously update oneself on the rules it is composed of. If social reality is ontologically subjective, bearing in mind that it is dependent on a set of individual representations, it can be considered as epistemically objective. Thus, when we discuss money, this object exists well outside our individual representation. Institutional facts are therefore to be considered as an ensemble of which the grasp of individuals is limited. Once recognised by a collective of individuals, the institutional fact imposes itself as an objective fact on all individuals even if they are only beginning to emerge:

> Consider a simple scene like the following. I go into a café in Paris and sit in a chair at a table. The waiter comes and I utter a fragment of a French Sentence. I say, "Un demi, Munich, à pression, s'il vous plaît." The waiter brings the beer and I drink it. I leave some money on the table and leave. An innocent scene, but its metaphysical complexity is truly staggering, and its complexity would have taken Kant's breath away if he had ever bothered to think about such a things. [. . .] Notice [. . .] that the scene as described has huge, invisible ontology : the waiter did not actually own the beer he gave me, but he is employed by the restaurant, which owned it. The restaurant is required to post a list of the prices of all the *boissons*, and even if I never see such a list, I am required to pay only the listed price. The owner of the restaurant is licensed by the government to operate it. As such, he is subject to a thousand rules and regulations I know nothing about. [. . .] If, after leaving the restaurant, I then go to listen to a lecture or attend a party, the size of the metaphysical burden I am carrying only increases ; and one sometimes wonders how anyone can bear it. [. . .] One reason we can bear the burden is that the complex structure of social reality is, so to speak, weightless and invisible. [. . .] They seem as natural to us as stones and water and trees.
>
> (Searle, 1995: 3–4)

It is as a result of this impossibility of considering all the assignments of function within their strategies that the social actor takes them for granted. Therefore, for a function assignment to incorporate individual beliefs, it must help the agents to evolve in a world on which they have a limited influence. As such, there is a selective pressure of institutional facts on the economic theories individuals adopt. Any theory can have no impact on the social world. We thus find the mechanisms at work in the case of the brute facts: it is indeed the practical reason which determines the diffusion and the collective acceptance of the assignments of function. The metaphysical impossibility evoked by Searle is nevertheless relatively vague. The question asked is as follows: is it cognitive (the social world is difficult to decipher) or logical (the impossibility for the actors of a social system to know the set of rules that structures this system)? This question remains unresolved: a justification for the "metaphysical" status of the burden is still missing. We will see in the next section that the concept of convention gives substance to the dual characteristic (the ontologically subjective and the epistemically objective) of social institutions. We will consider that the burden of the past is an important factor in rendering the notion intelligible, as explored by Boghossian (2006: 19):

> [C]onsider a case – like that of money – in which it *is* true that had we chosen not construct it, it would not have existed. This does suggest that, if we wished, we could make it the case that there ceases to be money in the future (although it would obviously be far from easy). But we cannot undo the past. Given that it is now true that there is money, no amount of our choosing to do things differently in the future can make it the case that there never was any money.

*

John Searle's theory of the social world allows one to consider the limits of performativity in the form of material and social pressures. The social limit will be of particular interest throughout the rest of this book, as Callon's poor development of ontology has impeded it being cogently defined to date. Latour, similar to Callon, states that the social only exists as a group of equipped individual agents and that nothing pre-exists this group ("there is no common world"; Latour, 2011). The social world is rendered extremely malleable as there is nothing in place to systematically explain performative failures. On the contrary, for a fact to acquire an institutional status, it must adapt to a pre-existing social system. Whilst keeping in line with the institutional economics, and to give substance to the principle of metaphysical burden mentioned above, it is appropriate here to use the notion of institutional complementarity – the idea that no institution is ever independent of other institutions that make up a social body in its entirety. Masahiko Aoki highlights that "a viable overall institutional arrangement, across different domains, is coherent and contains individual institutions that cannot be altered or designed in isolation" (Aoki, 2001: 225). In the context of game theory, Aoki refers to the notion of embeddedness: the agents participate in several games at the same time, concluding that the behaviours adopted in one type of game influence those in another type of game. For the purpose of what is to follow, it is important to remember that the notions of domain or type do not refer exclusively to different social spheres. Differentiating from the norm leads to a social cost which is fundamental to a selection effect arising from individual behaviours. Hodgson (2000a, 2000b, 2006) explores a double causality: downward causality in the case of a selection effect on the lower levels (customs or formal rules on individual actions), or upward causality when this selection effect occurs in the opposite direction (rules and customs must adhere to individual habits and behaviours). Because of the self-sustaining nature of the institutional continuum (by behaving in accordance with the rule or custom, the agent is able to reinforce them), a complementary relationship inevitably exists between its different strata. As such, any modification of one of the institutional levels is constrained by pressure from other levels, a pressure that originates from the traditional character of previous inherited institutions: to break the circularity of the causalities (ascending and descending) one is exposed at a significant social cost.[8] This cost can take the form of either a formal sanction designated by the law or an informal social sanction (for example, incurring repercussions in terms of reputation). Economic science, as an institution creating institutional facts through the phenomenon of performativity, is constrained by a pre-existing institutional set of rules.

Nevertheless, the idea of the pressure of a social world on the phenomenon of performativity is problematic. If the concept of the assignment of function provides the first attempt at a new definition of performativity, it does not allow a full grasp of the collective dimension of performativity, or the tools to consider the precise mechanisms of counterperformativity. However, the central point of this argument is to overcome the first problem while simultaneously overcoming the second, first, by clarifying that performative movement is a collective movement – that is, it is the implementation of a new assignment of function that simultaneously understands the conditions necessary for a theory to be able to perform the social world.

Beyond Searle: performativity as a conventional process

In order to explore the final mechanism of performativity as a function assignment requires that the latter concept is specified in order to truly grasp the distinctive characteristics of performativity. This will identify the failure of performativity, the moment when a theory fails to become an institutional fact. The notion of the assignment of function makes possible an understanding of performativity as the way an economic theory affects the representations of agents in their practices, yet this understanding remains too vague. What does it mean to "occupy a social function"? It simply means to be a social referent for the action: X counts as Y, so I act with X as with Y. At the end of the course of the function assignment, it engenders behaviour regarding X – it indicates a behaviour. The latter is the foundation to the proposed point, which is as follows: in keeping with the sociological and economic approaches to the social influence of theories, a theory is performative if it becomes a convention in the way Lewis defines it – that is, it is a convention if it fits into the social world as a point of reference so that it generates patterns of behaviour allowing actors to coordinate. We will then look at a definition of economic theories as a means of considering them as potential conventions. It will be shown by its formation that a theory can assume a conventional status within a population.

A conventionalist definition of performativity

A theory is at the origin of a new assignment of function, and this assignment of function becomes a convention which generates a regular and shared behaviour throughout a population. From here, we move away from the assignment of function to the monitoring of the assignment, what it indicates about the reasons individuals have for following it. To better gain an understanding of this, the concept of a convention as developed by David Lewis (see the next sub-section) will be explored before investigating how it can be adapted to a new theory of performativity (see the sub-section "From convention to performativity: a few adjustments").

From the assignment of function to convention

Lewis' work *Convention*, from a doctoral dissertation conducted by Willard Van Orman Quine, was written in order to respond to the claim that a definition of convention justifying the common ground in which language is a convention does not exist. Lewis' response is based on two arguments. The first consists of defending the possibility of agreements requiring no language that is tacit and therefore infra-verbal. The second argument is based on the dissociation between convention and agreement insofar as the convention precedes the agreement, and not the other way round. The final point of this book thus links the definition of convention and language:

> The language [someone] is using depends on the conventions he is party to. And these conventions are regularities in behaviour, sustained by an interest in coordination and an expectation that others will do their part.
> (Lewis, 1969: 208)

Lewis' definition of convention is constructed using game theory as support for his development – games of pure coordination, studied by Thomas Schelling (1960), a domain largely neglected by the standard approach developed by Von Neumann and Morgenstern (1944). This definition hopes to attain a generality beyond language as well as tools used for its definition. Here, we see a reason for Lewis' place in posterity in multiple fields such as decision theory, political philosophy, sociology or economic theory. Beyond Schelling, Lewis refers to the philosopher David Hume, who provided an early definition of "convention" as:

> A general sense of common interest; which sense all the members of the society express to one another, and which induces them to regulate their conduct by certain rules. I observe, that it will be for my interest to leave another in the possession of his goods, provided he will act in the same manner with regard to me. He is sensible of a like interest in the regulation of his conduct. When this common sense of interest is mutually expressed,

> and is known to both, it produces a suitable resolution and behaviour. And this may properly enough be called a convention or agreement betwixt us, though without the interposition of a promise ; since the actions of each of us have a reference to those of the other, and are performed upon the supposition, that something is to be perform d on the other part.
>
> (Hume, 1740 [1888]: 490)

Lewis thus starts from an intuitive definition of convention as a regularity of behaviour originating in the expectation that others will comply with it because of a common interest in this monitoring. Lewis uses this notion in coordination games (Figure 4.1).

In such a situation, characterised by a multiplicity of equilibria, an element must appoint itself to an environment that displays an obvious interest in coordination: a system of mutual expectations. This is what Lewis calls a convention. For Lewis, a regularity of *R* in the behaviour of population *P* acting in a recurrent situation *S* is a convention if, and only if, it is true and that it is common knowledge to *P*, known by almost all of *S*, among the members of *P*:

> 1) almost everyone conforms to *R*;
> 2) almost everyone expects almost everyone else to conform to *R*;
> 3) almost everyone has approximately the same preferences regarding all possible combinations of actions;
> 4) almost everyone prefers that any one more conform to *R* on condition that almost everyone conform to *R*;
> 5) almost everyone would prefer that any one more conform to *R′*, on condition that everyone conform to *R′*,
> where *R′* is some possible regularity in the behaviour of members of *P* in *S*, such that almost no one in almost any instance of *S* among members of *P* could conform both to *R′* and to *R*.
>
> (Lewis, 1969: 78)

The element that is essential to this definition is the notion of common knowledge among the agents. For an individual belief to become common knowledge, it is necessary that the reasoning done by agents – the way in which they choose one rule of action rather than another according to a set of preferences – is itself

		Player 2	
		A	*B*
Player 1	A	1 ; 1	0 ; 0
	B	0 ; 0	1 ; 1

Figure 4.1 Coordination game payoff matrix

common knowledge. In other words, one must be aware of the reasoning that leads others to respect the rule – that is, a common knowledge of the reasoning containing the rationality of the agents, but not being reduced to it: "[m]utualisation of some common inductive standards and background information, rationality, mutual ascription of rationality, and so on" (Lewis, 1969: 56–57). Lewis (1969: 56) defines common knowledge as follows: in a population of *P*, *x* is common knowledge in an *A* situation if, and only if:

a Everyone in *P* has reason to believe that *A* holds.
b *A* indicates to everyone in *P* that everyone in *P* has reason to believe that *A* holds.
c *A* indicates to everyone in *P* that *x*.

Condition (c) contains the common knowledge of the mode of reasoning. All agents know that *A* indicates *x* in population *P*. This basic definition presupposes two essential elements: on the one hand, that the agents share the same inductive norms representing it so that *A* indicates *x* to each one of them, but on the other hand, that agents share at least a minimum reserve of information. This last point, put forward by Lewis, was further developed by Aumann (1976; Hédoin, 2012a). If the convention, as well as the modes of reasoning, are common knowledge, then the logical conclusion is that the agents have constructed this common knowledge regarding the convention utilising the same reserve of common beliefs and information. Consider Aumann's reasoning: for example, if a disagreement exists regarding coordination, even though there is common knowledge of the mode of reasoning, it can only come from a different reserve of information. In order for coordination to be thought about, it thus requires common priors related to the state of the world, which presupposes an alignment of beliefs (Heap and Varoufakis, 2004). Thus, a convention is a shared social device incorporating the recognition of a state of the world. Moreover, if the common knowledge relates to the mode reasoning associated with each player (for example, by effectively inferring the respect of *R* from a social arrangement containing the conventional respect of promise), it also concerns the rules of the social game in which the action takes place: indeed, the agents must all possess the same representation of possible strategies. It should be noted, however, that Lewis excludes this latter point, at least as far as the definition in his 1969 work is concerned. In response to Quine's criticism, for whom a convention requires the use of other conventions, Lewis (1969: 87) states: "[A]n agreement sufficient to create a convention need not be a transaction involving language or any other conventional activity." Nevertheless, Lewis completed his definition of convention a few years later (1972 [1983]: 165) by substituting clause 3:

> 3) This belief that the others conform to *R* gives everyone a good and decisive reason to conform to *R* himself.

According to Olivier Favereau (2008), this substitution marks the passage from an individualistic and behavioural definition of "convention" (close to that of Hume's) to a definition that integrates an inevitably epistemic common world: I respect *R*, not because I know that others think that I think he thinks . . . that I prefer *R*, but because he has good reason to believe that I have good reason to believe that . . . *I* will choose *R*. These reasons, which are common to us all yet are not limited to individual preferences, belong to an epistemic community that contains a representation of the world, a sense of common interest and a common representation of the modes of reasoning of all individuals. These are conventional reasons. This change, suggested to Lewis by Jonathan Bennett in 1971, considers a scenario where not only do the agents have reasons to act, they also believe in the general conformity to *R* insofar as the agents believe in the general inference of *R* from the state of world *A* (Le Jallé, 2012). To argue here that this change is as profound as Favereau claims it to be is not appropriate; indeed, it would seem that the clause of common knowledge of the modes of reasoning already militated against a behavioural reading of Lewis. While common knowledge is based on the similarity of individuals regarding a procedural rationality, a common knowledge of Lewis' modes of reasoning relies on the ability to deduce common behaviour from a particular world. It thus supposes a set of already formed conventions (theoretical common beliefs). This, consequently, strengthens the notion of metaphysical burden as evoked by Searle. Lewis (1969: 83) writes:

> In agreeing face to face to conform to R, each of us is manifesting his (pre-existing or newly formed) propensity to confirm to R; and he is doing so under circumstances in which it is common knowledge among us that all of us are watching him.

Here we can see that it is the respect of a promise that ratifies respect for the convention. This respect can only function in a shared context where it is considered as a convention on the basis on which a system of deterrence has been established. Here it is not possible for anyone to inconsistently terminate an agreement because of a social convention putting pressure on contracting parties. This aspect will be developed in the next chapter. Beyond Searle, Lewis completes the notion of the assignment of function: it is the common (conventional) recognition of a state of the world that indicates an appropriate behaviour to adopt in a given situation. Lewis encourages the consideration of the epistemic conditions of assignment included in the clause of common knowledge. This will be of great interest in our approach to performativity.

From convention to performativity: a few adjustments

At this stage, the way in which a performative movement can be conceived as a conventional movement must be explained. Enabling performative movement renders possible the separation from the double removal referenced in the

Chapter 2 when setting up a convention in a population – that is, performativity becomes the introduction of a representation of the world as well as a shared belief about the behaviours to adopt. This perspective calls for a definition of performativity that will allow the integration of both the salient features of the Callonian approach and heuristically theoretical elements in order to identify the conditions of felicity from the performativity of economic theories. The performativist perspective devises the social influence of economic theories through the notion of a technical device. Theories are thus incorporated as a means of encouraging the agents to behave in a specific way. This encouragement causes social reality to behave according to economists' theories. Whilst the idea of "making actants act" must remain at the heart of performativity, we must still explore exactly what is meant by a theory which influences the social world by causing members of the population to act. In a study by MacKenzie and Millo (2003), which will be discussed in detail in Part III, Black and Scholes provided traders with spreadsheets as a benchmark for identifying the price of assets according to a particular theory. In a conventionalist context, the introduction of new practices corresponds to the introduction of new conventions, including new benchmarks, and in the latter case, a theoretical price generating new behaviours. Following Lewis' definition, we are able to derive three basic features of convention: (1) it is a classification; (2) it is a relative belief on how the world functions; and (3) it is a collective. This section will focus on the first two points: Lewis fails to pay them much attention, yet they are an essential part of our conventional approach to performativity. These characteristics will be the foundation of our definition of performativity, allowing an analysis of performative failures.

REGULATIVE CONVENTION AND CONSTITUTIVE CONVENTION: THE NEED FOR CLASSIFICATION

A convention is a classification insofar as it is a common representation of the game played by agents in order to recognise situations analogous to an original situation (*S*) in which the convention operates:

> [I]nstances of *S* do not have to be exactly alike. They merely have to be analogous, to fall under some common description that is natural enough to allow common knowledge of a propensity to extrapolate from some instances of *S* to others.
>
> (Lewis, 1969: 71)

This essential epistemic fact renders the convention both a choreographer indicating a point of coordination (Gintis, 2009), as well as a representation of the world which allows choice. This fact also incorporates a frame, bestowed with the name "decision frame" as result of the work of Tversky and Kahneman, which is a representation of the different possible choices associated with the results:

> We use the term "decision frame" to refer to the decision-maker's conception of the acts, outcomes, and contingencies associated with a particular choice. The frame that a decision-maker adopts is controlled partly by the formulation of the problem and partly by the norms, habits, and personal characteristics of the decision-maker.
>
> (Tversky and Kahneman, 1981: 453)

Performativity, as a convention, cannot be integrated with merely an informational influence (information is disclosed in such a way that agents did not have access to it), or by a simple application of economic policy (for example, a reduction in policy interest rates). Instead, it is the imposition of a new cognitive frame involving new habits of action.

Can one, for example, incorporate performativity in the classic case of applying an economic theory in the context of a monetary policy? One can thus ask, for example, whether a finance minister who wishes to stimulate demand and stabilise national income at a certain level by coupling a restrictive fiscal policy and an extensive monetary policy on the basis of the IS-LM model is performing the real world according to theory. An agent (a finance minister) applies a theory and changes the reality (moving from one national income to another, from one unemployment rate to another, etc.). Here, then, it could be asked: what is the difference between one such case and the introduction of Black, Scholes and Merton's equations in financial markets?

Since the intuitive definition put forward by Callon, the theory of performativity thus focuses on two elements. These elements are the role of objects and their abilities to make individuals behave in certain ways. The division between generic performativity and effective performativity has previously been discussed by MacKenzie (2006a: 31):

- *Generic performativity:* an element of economic theory which used by an agent acting in the economy.
- *Effective performativity:* the use of a theoretical element which consequently has a structural effect on the economy.

This partition makes it possible to separate performativity from simple theoretical application. On the one hand, as individuals, we apply theory during daily activities without changing our behaviour: the theory is used to discriminate several predefined actions. In the case of the IS-LM model, it serves as a decision-making tool that does not alter the structure of the choices available to agents who only react to a quantitative stimulus (interest rate, aggregate demand).[9] In the case of the financial markets and the Black-Scholes-Merton equations, the theory and the device on which it is based change the agents' behaviour by creating new arbitration practices based on new categories. The theory is performative in that it creates new classifications of the world (Roscoe, 2016) using new frames.

Tversky and Kahneman (1981) show through multiple experiments how participants' decisions are affected by the way a problem is presented. Tversky

Table 4.1 Game G

		B				
		x1	*x2*	*x3*	. . .	*xn*
A	*x1*	**1;1**	0;0	0;0	0;0	0;0
	x2	0;0	**1;1**	0;0	0;0	0;0
	x3	0;0	0;0	**1;1**	0;0	0;0
	. . .	0;0	0;0	0;0	**1;1**	0;0
	xn	0;0	0;0	0;0	0;0	**1;1**

and Kahneman use the term "decision frame" to refer to the way an individual conceives of the problem he is facing and what decisions are at his disposal.[10] Bacharach (2006) translates this idea into game theory by introducing the fundamental idea that players can frame the same objective game *G* in several ways, and therefore play a subjective game *G'k* (with $k = 1, \ldots, n$) as the *n* subjective games that players can frame. The concept of frames is based on the distinction between objects of choice and act-descriptions (Gold and Sugden, 2006: 10). The object is the real counterpart of what a predicate describes. Let us take an example from Schelling's (1960) famous study of matching games. Two individuals have lost themselves in a city that both do not know well. They do not have any means of communication, but using the city map, they can identify *xn* places to meet each other. We make the assumption that this interaction is a pure coordination game. The only thing that matters is that they agree on the same place to meet. Therefore, the interaction has the form of the objective game *G* shown in Table 4.1.

The *n* pure strategies equilibria are in bold. Note that there is also a mixed-strategy Nash equilibrium where each player plays each strategy with probability $1/n$. This objective game is not framed. However, from a constructivist perspective, any game is *de facto* framed by the players; an individual always plays a game through a frame determining a specific subjective or framed game. We can imagine here that one of the possible places is particularly salient because, say, the two players have first met there before. In this case, each player will use the frame $F = [F_{0,} F_1]$, where F_1 = [*where we first met*] is a family of only one predicate applying to only one of the *n* places. If both players have, in their respective frames, the family F_1 with probability $v\ (F_1) = 1$, then they will both play the framed game shown in Table 4.2.

Table 4.2 Game G'

		B	
		Choose where we first met	*Pick a place*
A	*Choose where we first met*	1;1	1/n ;1/n
	Pick a place	1/n ;1/n	1/n ;1/n

A player using the family F_0 cannot rationally choose a specific place to go. Therefore, he has to randomise and will choose each place with a probability $1/n$. If both players randomise, then the probability that they meet in one of the n places is $1/n$. This framed game has two Nash equilibria: [*Choose where we first met*; *Choose where we first met*] and [*Pick a place*; *Pick a place*]. However, the game now has only one strict Nash equilibrium. The framing process makes individuals play a different game than the objective game. Therefore, equilibria in the framed game (called by Bacharach *variable frame equilibria*) can differ from the Nash equilibria of the objective game. The notion of convention presupposes such an epistemic frame in the sense that one has to identify the different possible strategies (R or R'). A convention is therefore, at the same time, a frame of the decision-making problem and a solution to it. In other words, a convention is, at the same time, a constitutive epistemic device and a regulative one: "[Coordination problems] are situations in which, relative to some classification of actions, the agents have a common interest in all doing the same one of several alternative actions" (Lewis, 1969: 24); "[C]oordination may be rationally achieved with the aid of a system of concordant mutual expectations [. . .] about the agents' actions, preferences, and rationality" (Lewis, 1969: 33). It is possible to identify both the idea of a regulative convention (which indicates a particular strategy) and a constitutive convention (which defines the game) in Lewis' definition of convention. This latter concept is borrowed from Andrei Marmor, who defines a convention (as influenced by Searle) whose function is to define the framework of the game as constitutive. Marmor states that "their function is to define what counts as a winning and a loosing game, what are permissible and impermissible moves in the game, and so on" (Marmor, 2009: 36). In Part III, we shall explore the way in which economic theory has gradually provided a definition of rationality allowing the separation of rational behaviours from irrational behaviours (two constitutive conventions), thus creating the conditions of application of the convention of rationality (a regulative convention). Some economists have worked on the introduction of incentives for rational behaviour in the sense of economic theory, otherwise known as the theory of *nudges*.

Lewis attaches great importance to the idea that the convention also assumes an ability to recognise, by analogy, the problem of coordination to which the conventional solution is applied. Here, it is also interesting to note that he questions the fundamental ambiguity of any analogy that makes it possible to identify a problem of coordination: "There might be alternative analogies. If so, there is room for ambiguity about what would be following precedent and doing what did before" (Lewis, 1969: 37). Here it must be noted that the recognition of the problem of coordination presupposes a convention of selection of the analogy, simultaneously confirming the latter interpretation and backing up the use of Lewis' convention. The use of a regulative convention requires a constitutive convention which defines possible alternatives (the frame). When a theory performs the social world, it creates new classifications and new frames allowing new modalities of action. Such is the meaning of the

Searlian function assignment: X counts as Y, so I act with X as with Y. Now, if we return to Austin, we must explore the order of the illocutionary force of economic discourse. In producing a new economic theory, I am producing a new representation of the world. There is too much emphasis on summarising the illocution in Austin's examples of performative statements at the beginning of *How to Do Things with Words*, such as "I name this ship," and so on. In other words, there is too much of a tendency to reduce the illocutory to what Bourdieu calls "acts of institutions" (the mayor who opens a session, a notary who signs a document). Now, it is clear that for Austin every utterance carries an illocutionary force in that it is constitutive of something, a representation, which will produce effects:

CONVENTION AND MECHANISM

In addition to the need for an epistemic classification, allowing the development of conventional strategies, the notion of convention presupposes a certain belief regarding the ways in which the system functions. This imperative is built into condition (3) which is the belief that if a number of other individuals conform to *x*, it provides all other individuals with good reason to conform to *x*. If the framework of a pure coordination game renders this obvious, more complex social situations reveal the need for self-fulfilling prophecies. For example, an individual chooses a convention as a result of the knowledge that choosing it in solidarity with others will lead to an expected result. In this way, the use of the convention is also the recognition that the mechanisms governing the links between the categorised objects will render the expected result. This now calls for a move away from the illocutionary act to the perlocutionary act. The performative movement is hence to make people behave in a certain way by generating new representations (new frames) as well as new beliefs about the way the social world functions, namely the existence of a mechanism of self-fulfilling prophecies. Later, we will see that the clause of self-fulfilling prophecy is essential to our discussion from the moment the issue of performativity is addressed.

Performativity, illocutionary and perlocutionary forces

Uskali Mäki (2013) strongly criticised Donald MacKenzie's use of the concept of "[the] performative".[11] Mäki's critique focuses on Austin's definition of the performative, which is reduced to a constitutive speech act: when one declares two people united by the bonds of marriage, one's speech is constitutive of the conventional state that he or she produces. In other words, the formulation of the latter is constitutive of the act of language performed. It is not, however, conducive with what is discussed in the work of economic sociology. The discourse of economists is above all a convention that leads to beliefs that even they will become engaged with. Mäki comments that one must not confuse the illocutionary (performative) and the perlocutionary as they are two different ways, constitutive and causal, for language to have an effect on the external world. The contributions of Guala (2016) and Svetlova (2016) provide an argument contradictory to Mäki which I consider useful. Here I find myself in agreement with Mäki, since he attacks the way in which performative sociologists so often confidently apply the Austinian concept – they apply Austinian theory without giving his theory enough consideration. Nevertheless, I am more reluctant to follow him when he defends an original meaning of the term "performative" by settling on the concept of the illocutionary, then on the constitutive, as opposed to the causal.

It should first of all be recalled that Austin, in true *maïeutician* style, never expresses a definitive definition of the performative. He does, however, arrive at an analysis of its failures in the recognition of a particular type:

> Now we failed to find a grammatical criterion for performatives [. . .]. It is time to make a fresh start on the problem. We want to reconsider more generally the senses in which to say something may be to do something, or in saying something we do something (and also perhaps to consider the different case in which *by* saying something we do something).
>
> (Austin, 1962: 91)

Austin then adapts his vocabulary from "performative utterance" to the tripartite of locutionary, illocutionary and perlocutionary acts. It is important to specify that these acts are not mutually exclusive – Austin speaks about various "forces" – so that the same statement has a kind of performative thickness: it makes it possible to deploy all three forces. These three forces are closely entangled to such an extent that there is no such thing as a pure illocutionary speech act.

For Mäki, the Austinian definition of the illocutionary act rests on a constitutive relation, whereas the perlocutionary act relies on a causal relation. This distinction has been challenged, and it is well recognised that it is difficult to differentiate these acts (see Searle, 1995 and Millikan, 2014). In line with this, Guala (2016: 48) concludes that the institutional facts of which the acts of language are constitutive "are nothing but sets of actions and expectations about actions". For this reason, any act of language can *in fine* be defined as the creation or maintenance (enforcement) of a set of beliefs connected to expected behaviours following an utterance: a promise will count as a promise only if it *causes* expected effects. So how can we differentiate between the constitutive effect and the causal effect? Guala (2016: 47) uses the examples of the wedding and the wedding vows:

> Saying "I do" *brings about* a set of beliefs concerning the actions of your spouse and of third parties. Uttering "I promise to do *A*" *triggers* a set of expectations concerning your own actions and the actions that others will perform if you do not do it. But bringing about and triggering are causal relations, rather than relations of conceptual or ontological dependence.

The debate between Mäki and Guala (I will come back to Svetlova's article later) rests on the question of the dichotomy between causality and constitutivity which seems to be lacking in Austin's work, since to him illocutionary forces also produce causal effects. It is clear that for Austin all utterance carries an illocutionary force since even what seems to be a pure descriptive speech is constitutive of something (a representation) that will have causal effects. The illocutionary act has effects that stem from its institutional statute, and anticipation of the production of these effects is a felicity condition of the illocutionary force of the speech act (which chimes with Guala's view). To my view, what is at stake is no more the distinction between causal and constitutive effects, but rather the split between necessary effects and contingent effects: the fact that the statement "I do" implies that one regards me as administratively dependent on another individual is a necessary effect (illocutionary) of the speech act. Without these effects, we are not married. The fact that my close friends are horrified to see me marrying is a contingent and unnecessary effect (perlocutionary). Thus, the real debate is over the distinction between specific and necessary effects on the one hand, and contingent effects on the other – in other words, it is between institutionally or conventionally controlled effects and uncontrolled effects. The fact of saying "I do" causes a securing of my expectation over the behaviours of the other members of my community. It would seem more appropriate to separate the conventional and unconventional effects of the language than causal and constitutive relationship. In the first case, the effects are "normally" expected; in the second, nothing is normally expected. However, it seems also that not only can one speech have two types of effects simultaneously, but also that the effects of the speech can be regarded as conventional and non-conventional at the same time. A statement can fulfil some rules in order to take a certain stance implying a particular uptake, and simultaneously can make it possible institutionally to innovate with some room for freedom. This is the preoccupation in Svetlova's (2016) contribution, in which, following Butler (2010), the institutional dynamics must be understood through the prism of the perlocutionary force. Theories create new representations, new behaviours, which will lead to institutional changes. The consequence of such reasoning is that the frontier between illocutionary effects and perlocutionary effects is located historically, and thus is moving over time: perlocutionary effects can become illocutionary effects. This means that an unexpected effect can become an effect that must follow a felicitous speech act:

> If S's speech act is also an act of social and linguistic innovation which S nevertheless intends or at least hopes will be understood, the act must necessarily, and for that reason, take the form of an extension or criticism of some existing attitude or project which is already convention-governed and understood. It seems a necessary truth that unless the innovation either takes such a form, or can be reduced to it, it will stand no chance of being understood, and so can hardly count even as an intended act of communication.
>
> (Skinner, 1970: 135)

What follows is a very important point to which Mäki correctly directs us. The complex partition between illocution and perlocution possesses a sociological meaning, at least to the extent that certain fringes of social reality, rules and conventions are "taken for granted" (Schütz, 1954). The fact that any institution can be reduced to a set of behaviours does not imply that any institution has the same status for individuals. This is, I believe, a limitation of Guala's purely functionalist approach. To reduce institutions (the result of performative acts) to the anticipation of regularities of behaviour does not imply that any institution has the same status. For Austin, the effects produced by the illocutionary force of speech are more socially standardised than the effects produced by the perlocutionary force. This distinction ultimately allows a better understanding of both performative failures (since some effects contrary to expectations will be judged less important than others), but also aids an understanding of the margins of freedom of agents in terms of institutional innovation. What is at stake here is the question of the conditions for novelty. The perlocutionary effect is the other facet of the illocutionary act, while at the same time also necessary for any change in the institutional order to take place. It is evident at this stage that one must interrogate, as Mäki does, the original meaning of the concepts, which thus leads to questioning their use.

What is a theory?

Performativity is therefore the notion of "make to act" through the intervention of a convention resulting from economic theory. We must, however, now turn our attention to defining what is meant by "theory". Performativist literature remains relatively vague on this subject. The notion of convention will once again be integral to an interest in economic theories insofar as they can give rise to new social conventions. Our definition will therefore be oriented towards the following objective: to emphasise a homomorphism between social convention and theory so that it becomes possible that the second can take the form of the first.

We will explore the theory as the union of two closely interwoven elements, namely a model and a discourse. A model consists of an abstract world whose objects are classified, endowed with characteristics and are interrelated by relations allowing deductions to be made according to predicate logic. These relationships can take different forms (binary relation, equivalence, etc.). The most common of which is the functional relationship. Model is thus a matter of categorisation, assignment of relations and deduction. This is the essence of the hypothetico-deductive method, which in no way implies the content or use of what is inferred: this method is used to explain what is known (from a realist or instrumentalist point of view) or what is hidden (retrospective) to predict or to describe a desirable potential state or to refute the starting conditions (for example, through absurd reasoning). Thus, the pragmatics of a model is under-determined by its syntax. Sugden (2000a) appears to refer to models as "credible worlds". Let us now leave credibility aside and focus on the idea of a model as a world. Sugden uses George Akerlorf's esteemed example of the car market. Akerlof (1970) begins by defining a world containing:

- n automobiles of which the quality q (estimated in money) is a random variable in the range [0; 1] and its value is in terms of mathematical expectation 1/2;
- buyers whose reserve price is (3/2) q;
- sellers whose reserve price is q.

These different objects maintain the following relationships:

- Sellers and buyers are grouped into two different groups, each seeking to maximise an aggregate utility function.
- The quality of the cars is not visible to the buyers.
- It (the quality) is visible to the sellers.
- Buyers are risk-neutral.

From these relationships, Akerlof deduces a new world with the following characteristics:

- m cars whose quality q (estimated in money) is a random variable in the range [0 ; 3/4] and of mathematical expectation 3/8;
- all buyers are willing to pay up to 3/2 3/8 = 9/16.

He concludes that all the sellers of quality higher than 9/16 vehicles leave the market. This mechanism leads to the reduction of the quality of vehicles to 0, selling at a price of 0.

What does this model demonstrate? By itself, absolutely nothing. It solely describes a mathematical world in which conditions are correlated with characteristics ultimately contained in these original conditions. As such, Nancy Cartwright (2009) mentions a significant constraint of modelling: the model contains its environment, and the results that it reaches are included in its initial hypotheses. Cartwright considers that a model, an abstract experiment as a thought experiment, aims to isolate causal capacities – that is, to discover the powers which possess elements of a system producing specific results. She refers to the model as a "nomological machine", which is a device composed of factors, each possessing their own capacities, so that when placed in a stable environment, these factors give rise to regularities (Hédoin, 2012b). The major difficulty in capacity isolation is that a model is not an empirical experience – it is not placed in a stable environment; it does, however, contain its environment. If this does not seem to be a problem in physics (according to Cartwright), where the structural hypotheses of models (the laws of physics) are considered to have a very general scope, then it is quite different for economic modelling. Cartwright's argument emphasises the need to classify the functional links of a model. Consider a model composed of a set of variables linked together by a set of connections. This set of variables is split in two: some variables must explain, and others must be explained. Thus, we consider some variables and functional relations as given, an explanatory variable is varied and the changes of the system are attributed to this precise variable. This is the standard operation of the *ceteris paribus* clause, necessary for hypothetico-deductive reasoning. This clause, however, is only credible when something "being equal" takes the credible status of laws (sufficiently stable or unalterable). While this may not seem to be a problem when the theory of relativity is included in the *ceteris paribus* clause, its application regarding the Akerlof model is more complicated, for it is both the maximising behaviours and neutrality-facing risks that take on this particular status. The model is unable to assume its role as a nomological machine – that is, to release a particular causal capacity. As such, discourse surrounding a model must be included in a discourse likely to render the links that one wishes to highlight as "credible". This amounts to externally justifying the hierarchy of variables between the explanations and the model. The credibility of this hierarchy, and of the causal explanation it allows, will also rest on the credibility of two possible worlds: the world where the intervention on the explanatory variable exists, and the world where there is none. These two worlds must be credible enough to judge the effect of the intervention. In this case, Akerlof articulates a story in which a market system integrating asymmetries of information leads to the disappearance of the market by destroying the main benefits (equilibrium price, efficiency). This story, which is independent to the model, only makes sense when the two possible worlds and the mechanisms passing from one to the other are identifiable (optimal world, with market equilibrium and a suboptimal world, without market, a principle of rationality) and are considered credible by the interlocutor. The interlocutor considers that the model, although being a caricature of the real world (Gibbard and Varian, 1978), finds its value of truth in its representative relationship with the outside world (factually or counterfactually). We have already mentioned the syntax and the pragmatics of the model. The notion of causal discourse between entities refers here to its semantics (Walliser, 2011). It is now a question of establishing rules enabling correspondence between the elements of a reference system (as well as their causal capacities) and a semantically under-determined[12] model in order to ensure a cognitive meaning for the latter. This is the role of theoretical discourse. Its role is to justify links between a theoretical market composed of mathematical symbols and a second-hand car market in a city in the United States. The classifications internal to a model are thus expected to represent the common characteristics of singular real objects: from a vector, one can move on to a set of automobiles, then to all goods.

The question of credibility, namely the legitimising discourse of the formal model, refers directly to the conditions of felicity of scientific speech acts. Some procedures and contexts are socially accepted as indicators of the relevance of theories, including the refinement and robustness of modelling, falsificationism, the acceptance of the test procedure, the speaker's place in the scientific field and a number of elements directly involved in the immediate credibility of a theory (Brisset, 2018). Thus, we see here that a theory is not reducible to its formal content, nor is it is a closed system. It is inevitably open to a social context bestowing its explanatory power upon it. Ultimately, a theory consists of:

- i a classification (*ex ante*) of objects;
- ii relationships between these objects;
- iii a discourse (as well as its conditions of enunciation) proving that these links are assimilated to causal relations and that these theoretical objects possess referents;
- iv a classification (*ex post*) of credible worlds.

Here we find the formal characteristics of Lewis' convention. What will be demonstrated in the next section is that a scientific theory possessing a definition could become a social convention.

Homomorphism between convention and a definition of theory

The way in which this book has defined convention and theory suggests a homomorphism between the two entities. This has played an active role in the choice of using Lewis' definition of convention as opposed to, say, that of Keynes or Sugden. First, theory and convention are inevitably based on classifications of objects; these objects are, on the one hand, the components of an abstract world, yet on the other, they are a set of potential strategies. Secondly, these objects maintain relationships in both cases. Within the framework of theory, the *ex ante* classification is animated by a set of formal relationships so that the totality of this framework constitutes a credible world (or not). The conventional mechanism also works well for this purpose. A mechanism contained in Lewis' third condition is added to a starting classification: "This belief that others conform to *R* gives everyone a good reason to comply with *R*." If everyone complies with *R* and hopes to achieve a specific result, then that result is achieved – complying to the notion of a self-fulfilling prophecy as discussed earlier. The link between context *A* and the belief in *R* will also prove to be of importance. A polarisation of the beliefs following the behaviour *R*, given the mechanism of self-fulfilling prophecies, leads to the expected result by the agent who follows the convention. Context *A* proves that the follow-up of the convention is an element that carries out the credibility of a world where all individuals follow the *R* convention and where a compliance with *R* leads to an expected and desired result.

Finally, if a *k* actor considers by analogy (Lewis, 1969: 37–38) that the *ex ante* classification of theory *T* corresponds to context *A*, the actor thus possesses good reason to believe that the causal mechanism described in *T* will produce within *A* insofar as the actors composing *A* behave in the same way as the agents of the model (precisely because they have the same belief as *k*). Theory *T* is thus self-fulfilling and plays the role of a "fictive precedent" as defined by Lewis (1969: 39): "A fictive precedent would be as effective as an actual one in suggesting a course of action for us, and therefore as good a source of concordant mutual expectations enabling us to meet." Importantly, the world described by the theory (*ex post* classification) must be considered as desirable. Agents should have a preference for generalising the convention. It will serve as a convention within a population insofar as its members believe that *T* allows the possibility of identifying a desirable world. This normative clause will be discussed later.

Before concluding, I must state that the homomorphism between convention and theory which is identified here is above all an analytical construction that provides relevant theoretical tools in order to study performative failures. In this respect, any comparisons with epistemological conventionalism as explored by Poincaré or Popper must not be considered at this stage. Poincaré (1905 [1970]: 166) defines scientific convention as a tautological principle useful for scientific explanation. Popper, however, seeks the conventional component in the guiding principles of scientific research: critical rationalism, criteria dividing science and non-science and methodological rules of regulation for research practices (Bessis, 2004). The approach of this book is quite different, insofar as it roots itself in a sociological question as opposed to an epistemological one: why do some theories fail to become performative?

*

It has been shown in this section that the notion of convention complements the assignment of function insofar as it allows us: (1) to identify epistemic conditions for the monitoring of a social behaviour (common knowledge of modes of reasoning and framing); (2) to identify the reasons for the following behaviour (self-fulfilment); (3) to express a definition of theory; and (4) to understand the mechanism of performativity as an assimilation (whether through learning or through of making schemes) of theory as a credible precedent. These elements thus make it possible to attribute a certain number of conditions to performativity. This approach allows a better understanding of performativity by integrating the possibility of counterperformativity, defined as the failure of a theory to become a social convention.

It seems necessary, at first, to return to an important characteristic of the concept of convention, which is that it is an equivalent to equilibrium. A convention is a fixed point of representation according to what one finds in economic literature, thus its main fault is to misunderstand institutional change. This is highlighted by Bruno Amable and Stefano Palombarini (2005): similar to an approach from an orthodox form of Marxism, they state that the French economics of conventions:

> refuse to imagine an evolution in the time of the logic of the functioning of the institutions. [. . .] They are born to perform a function and live to fulfil that function. [. . .] Institutions cannot become autonomous in relation to the requirements of the justification that led to their birth.
>
> (Amable and Palombarini, 2005: 130; our translation)

If one only maintains the concept of convention, Amable and Palombarini are correct, and this is why the French theory of conventions supports the conceptual notion of "criticism" (Boltanski, 2011) as a reflexive capacity of social actors to take precedence over the structure, to question it, and to engage in "disputes". This model will thus allow one "to analyse the critical operations that people carry out when they want to show their disagreement without resorting to violence, and the ways they construct, display, and conclude more or less lasting agreements" (Boltanski and Thévenot, 2006: 25). This raises the question of the coherence between the idea of convention and that of the critique, in that convention is above all a concept of equilibrium. The conventionalist approach to performativity provides a theoretical basis in order to identify the conditions necessary for the performative phenomenon. Stating that a theory performs the social world is to say that it is implemented as a convention; thus Lewis' definition of convention allows one to shed light on the limits of this phenomenon. The theory of performativity first assumes that a theory will affect the social world if it possesses the formal characteristics of a convention. It also specifies that this convention must prevail in a world that is itself conventional. The conceptualisation provided by this book is not intended to tell the exact truth of the performative process, but instead to shed light on the scene's performativity. Where and how should one look for the failures of performativity? This is a key question. Now we must return to the work of Austin as a means of establishing an approach to performativity indicating the possibilities of its failure and the reasons for criticism on the part of the agents. A theory is rejected by agents as a convention when it does not go beyond the criticism they have of it. A critique can be considered in terms of the conditions that a theory must respect in order to be performative.

Three conditions for performativity

Condition of empiricity

Condition (5) of Lewis is paramount in that it is the reason for the existence of a convention. Take, for example, an individual who is faced with a large number of choices of equivalent coordination strategies and thus relies on social convention. In order to be effective, the individual, through the use of a constitutive dimension of convention, must be able to foresee the possibility of different behaviours (R and R'). Without this, it will not only be of no use to the actor, but the actor will not be able to understand it. Taking reference from Popper's work, we will now talk about the "empiricity condition". Similar to empirical theories, a convention must allow the identification of at least two classes of non-equivalent phenomena.[13] As stated by Lewis (1969: 90), to prefer something is to prefer it over something else; thus, in order to perform the social world, a theory must allow the differentiation of several possible behaviours to be made by the agent. It is only on this condition that a scientific concept (resulting from a theoretical classification) can act as a norm of representation. The notion of "concept" here refers to an element of theory affirming its role of a fictitious precedent as, once again, defined by Lewis: one identifies the classified objects of the theory (the concepts) to phenomena (in the phenomenological sense of the term) of the world. The philosophers Bernard Williams (1985) and Hilary Putnam (2002) define a class of concepts, called "thick concepts", that combine positive and normative considerations:

> The way these notions are applied is determined by what the world is like (for instance, by how someone has behave[d]), and yet, at the same time, their applications usually involves a certain valuation of the situation, of persons or actions.
>
> (Williams, 1985: 144)

The most frequently cited examples of this are notions of brutality, cruelty or courage. A thick concept is a bridge between the theoretical sphere and the social sphere. Normativity could therefore be considered at the core of the notion of performativity, insofar as it is an important modality of intervention of economic theory on the social world. Finally, we must ask here: is the theory of performativity not simply derived from the observation that there are normative economic theories? If, according to John Searle (1969), we define normativity with respect to commitments (such as promise) and their felicity conditions (definition of promise), then once an agent affirms "I must" on the basis of an economic statement, a normative framework is applied. Nevertheless, if the thesis of performativity is understood as the participation of economic theory in the construction of the social world, then the two terms refer to different realities. Indeed, what interests us here is precisely the construction of the institutional conditions of engagement and how an agent is made to act by mimicking economic theory. As such, the important thing to understand here is how a theoretical object can be used for normative purposes in the construction of the social world as well as the way in which it becomes a conventional norm from how one (normatively) perceives the real world. A set of theoretical statements must, in order to be performed, take on a form that allows it to be used both as a descriptive object and as a guide for action to be taken. This form can only be acquired by becoming empirical. It must also be able to serve the production of propositions relating to the outside world and propositions from which it is possible to identify a class of phenomena that do not conform to the statement in question. In other words, a scientific concept can serve as a guide for action within the social world if it reveals a classification of the social world to be comprehended by the agents (whether the latter are directly those who make the decisions, or those who build the technical devices they will use). Let us take the example of the category "rational", which will be studied further in Chapter 6. For an individual to consider himself rational, the concept of rationality must be defined in such a way that it can be employed in the production of empirical affirmations of the type: "x is rational". However, this requires the ability of an individual to distinguish between the "rational" and the "irrational". To say that "x is rational" amounts to saying, in the context of a simple classification into two subgroups, that "x is not irrational". It is obvious that this reasoning is based on the assumption that the theorists defining rationality and the social agents using the concept share the same interpretation of statements defining rationality. This hypothesis reveals, first, that the notion of convention presupposes (like any theory of the social) the existence of an epistemic community containing ordinary language as a background necessary for the process. Nevertheless, this hypothesis is weaker than it seems when we consider that a categorisation (that has been categorised as "rational") has an effect on our behaviour only insofar as it is integrated into devices (conventions and technical devices) imposing a common meaning. Take, for example, nudging devices put in place to promote rational behaviour (such devices will be studied later). It is thus important to note that the empirical form of a theoretical object is a necessary yet not sufficient condition for its performance. Thus, the reasoning developed here raises questions about the epistemological status of performed concepts: to become a social convention, a scientific concept must concern an empirical theoretical element, which is not the case for all the theoretical elements. This thesis will demonstrate that the concept of rationality has only had an influence on the social world (we will focus on the case of liberal paternalism) from the moment it has classified behaviours according to rational or irrational taxonomy. The theory of rationality has not always been permitted due to epistemological reasons; for example, in certain theoretical configurations, it was simply unnecessary to rationalise a concept allowing the articulation of empirical propositions. The criterion of empiricity is in essence a semantic criterion.

Conditions of self-fulfilment

Lewis' third condition designates the convention as a self-fulfilling belief: agents follow it because attains the expected result. If the condition of empiricity renders the possibility of choice to an agent by creating the possibility of a propositional content (I am doing R or R'), then agents still require good reason to act upon a choice of R or R'. A key factor in the success as well as in the failure of performativity must be its effectiveness in liaising between the agents' goals and the results of their actions. Merton (1948: 195) defines a self-fulfilling prophecy as follows: "The self-fulfilling prophecy is, in the beginning, a *false* definition of the situation evoking a new behaviour which makes the originally false conception come true." Merton's definition, however, contains no real criteria for judging truth and falseness. To remedy this, Isabelle This (1994: 185; our translation) provides another definition:

> We will say that a belief or an anticipation is self-fulfilling if it generates, because it has been adopted by individuals, a situation in which this belief is "true", or, at least "not invalidated", and in both cases considered as "confirmed" by individuals.

Considering self-fulfilling prophecies as the core of the notion of convention and *a fortiori* at the heart of the thesis's theory of performativity allows us to move performativity away from the reductive framework of coordination. In the case of Lewis' coordination, compliance with convention *R* is sufficient for the strategy to become self-fulfilling. What about the self-fulfilling capacity of *R* (*R* being inspired by a particular economic theory)? Is the fact that all agents conform to *R* sufficient for *R* to become self-fulfilling? If it is still a generalised coordination within the same strategy which is at stake, then the underlying mechanism of the self-fulfilling prophecy is not only the fact of coordination context as expressed in Lewis' game theory. Take, for example, the role of self-fulfilling strategies in the planning of urban space (Bourne, 1992; Staszak, 2000). Categorising certain geographic areas as economic and social disaster zones disincentivises investors and potential inhabitants, so that the reality gradually takes the form of the reality that is described. We are, indeed, discussing the case of a convention in the following terms:

(1) All agents conform to it.
(2) Similarly, all agents expect that almost everyone will also comply with it (this is, by definition, a disaster zone).
(3) Believing that others are complying provides agents with good reason to conform.
(4') Everyone prefers that the greatest number of agents conform to it: this clause is formulated by Lewis as it is part of a coordination framework. One could reformulate it as follows: *it is in conformity with the representations of each one that the greatest number conform to it.*
(5') Almost all agents would prefer that the greatest possible number of agents conform to another convention, provided that each or almost everyone conforms to it. The same consideration applies to the latter clause, which can be rephrased as follows: *if the largest number of agents adopted another new convention, then there would be good reason to comply with this new convention because of the mechanism of self-fulfilling prophecies.*

Although Lewis defends the idea that his definition of convention is able to free itself from the devices that have been used in its creation, it is clear that this is not the case: clauses (4) and (5) are in fact oriented towards coordination games. It is thus necessary to reformulate these clauses in order to be able to discuss conventions in the context of self-fulfilling prophecies, not only dependent on the coordination of the agents, but also mechanisms of aggregation of behaviours. A theory will retain its status as a convention only if it allows individuals to achieve the goals they have set for themselves, or at least that they believe that they have achieved this.

Bertrand Russell (1943 [2009]: 60–61) stated:

> Give me an adequate army, with power to provide it with more pay and better food than falls to the lot of the average man, and I will undertake, within thirty years, to make the majority of the population believe that two and two are three, that water freezes when it gets hot and boils when it gets cold, or any other nonsense that might seem to serve the interest of the State.

As Russell (1943 [2009]: 61) admits, it is highly unlikely that a belief can be imposed beyond compliance on speech alone when it is directly involved in everyday practices:

> Of course, even when these beliefs had been generated, people would not put the kettle in the refrigerator when they wanted it to boil. That cold makes water boil would be a Sunday truth, sacred and mystical, to be professed in awed tones, but not to be acted on in daily life.

This is precisely the dilemma faced by the Pope and the Inquisition when confronted with the Galilean theory in Bertolt Brecht's famous play, *Life of Galileo*: the characters must reject Heliocentrism in order to save the beliefs of the Christian tradition as well as allowing the merchant cities of northern Italy to integrate this new, practical theory into their maritime maps. The Inquisition concluded that: "The north Italian ship owners keep clamouring for Mr Galileo's star charts. We have had to yield to them, since material interests are involved" (Brecht, 1945 [1955]: 114; our translation).

The inertia of beliefs refuted by facts is certainly the most discussed theme of history and the philosophy of science. To note such a difficulty admits that a theory poses a problem of external validity. However, such a problem can be disguised *a posteriori* by an underlying ideology at the origin of a cognitive dissonance observed by Festinger et al. (1956) when they were ufologists and braced themselves all the more in their initial belief when faced with the failure of an eschatological prophecy. The very assumption of this type of phenomenon is the existence of a gap between facts and beliefs. In this respect, the problem of self-fulfilling prophecies is an additional step insofar as social beliefs carry the potential to call for their own corroboration. The existence of dissonance is thus based on the absence of self-fulfilling prophecies: the collective belief of a theory withheld by a whole population does not suffice for the latter to be confirmed as fact.

An external condition

In addition to the two first conditions, there exists an external condition: agents must have good reason to believe that the theoretical world coincides with the real world. If there is a proven incompatibility between the two worlds, the scientific convention cannot be established as a social convention. In Part III, we will study the attempt to set up market systems for organ transactions as proposed by Gary Becker and Julio Elìas (2007). In this context, the criterion of empiricity is respected insofar as the commodity is defined as what is traded on a market, rather than what is donated. To an extent, a self-fulfilling prophecy exists if everyone considers the organ as a commodity (a new classification redefining the framework of supply–demand coordination), and then a number of new individuals will respond to the market and become donors themselves, which will indeed reduce waiting lists. Nevertheless, in the theoretical world of Becker and Elìas, the organ is a commodity. This is not the case in the current social world. As a result, the social context is unable to indicate the convention of the market as a coordination focal point. However, the way in which the context is perceived (as a frame) is an inherent feature of the convention and a necessary condition for its follow-up. Lewis (1969: 80) provides the following example: suppose R, a convention, and R^* a consequence of R ("consequence" being understood as the fact that non-R^* would be a consequence of an alternative to R – that is, R'). R^* also constitutes as a convention. Suppose now, for example, that we have to meet each other alternately in cities T1 and T2. Each city offers three possible meeting places: P11, P12, P13 for T1 and P21, P22, P23 for T2. The convention R is as follows: when we meet in T1, we will meet in P11; in T2, we will meet in P21. Lewis concludes that a consequence R^* of R is that in T1, we meet in P11. Lewis' conclusion seems trivial, in that R^* is a part of R – but suppose the following case: let R be a convention of coordination through a market mechanism in the context of a kidney trade. If R^*: "as a commodity (a kidney) can be pledged against a credit". R^* is a consequence of R, and non-R^* may be a consequence of R' (for example, "coordinating on a gift mechanism"). Here, the market convention presupposes a classification involving another conventional mechanism, that of credit. Now, if one can accept R, it may be more complicated to accept the consequence R^*. If the kidney market itself can be considered acceptable by individuals, it will not be the same for the consequences it brings about.

This condition is the direct extension of Searle's metaphysical burden: social actors are born and live in a conventional world imposing on them. However, what remains, here as a point of inquiry is the fact that the social conventions that constrain the performative process can, at the same time, be the result of the individual representations and the macro-social entities imposing themselves on the agents. This justification will take the form, in the next chapter, of research that is both epistemological (showing the limits of individualist epistemology in general) and ontological (justifying the actual existence of conventions as emergent effects on individuals).

Conclusion: a conventionalist approach

Here, the analytical framework allows a reformulation of performativity as the setting up of a new convention, and, thus to identify conditions for this process. These theoretical tools refine the idea of performativity by enabling the failures of performativity to be understood, or more generally, an understanding of the influence of the social world, defined as a set of conventions on performative movement. Beyond this idea of failure, it is also as a result of cultural specificities that the latter is reintroduced. In a comparative study of the different cultural modes of output of economists, Marion Fourcade (2009) demonstrates that if the idea of performativity is, at once, elegant and heuristically interesting, it struggles to consider the national peculiarities of economic ideas. In fact, each nation, immersed in a particular cultural area, transfers to its professional economists cognitive categories that are directly constitutive to their intellectual products as well as the knowledge they assign themselves as economists. This is precisely related to the three limitations that have previously been highlighted.

First, let us revisit empiricism. A theoretical element can only be performed, to the extent that it provides a point of reference for social agents (who may be politicians). However, beyond this formal imperative, the choice of theoretical output which is to be elevated to the rank of empirical principle intended to be tested or applied to the economy can be explained in cultural terms corresponding to the vision of the world. The second limit relates to the self-fulfilment of the theory which has been performed. In order to understand performativity, one is required to grasp either the way in which theory serves as an effective reference for agents or what it is that masks the dissonance between social beliefs and social phenomena. The third limit, directly related to the cultural context of the output of economic knowledge, is the constraint of conventional coherence. The conventional set comprises a culture – that is, numerous categorisations accepted in a population.

These three conditions form a grid of analysis of performativity inspired by the Austinian approach, and here it is a question of defining performativity by its felicity conditions. Contrary to the approach of performativist sociology, this approach allows one to identify failures – namely the potential causes of failure to select a convention resulting from an economic theory in a particular social field. Thus, by considering performativity as a conventional process and by identifying certain characteristics that a theory must respect in order to perform the social world, we have been able to develop a critique by providing reasons why social actors can either accept or reject a theory. The conditions necessary for performativity that have been identified allow us to explain the potential reasons for the performative failure of various economic discourses and potential reasons for the emergence of a critique of theories wishing to rise to the rank of social convention.

The theoretical conclusions of this chapter will be illustrated in Part III. Before this, a significant element must be further explored – that of the ontological status given to conventions. The following question must be asked when considering macro-social categories, which has also been a topic in question since the birth of social sciences: how can one justify their use when we consider individuals as the obvious ontological basis of the social world? This question is paramount to the relevance of Searle's idea of "metaphysical burden" – the power of entities that emerge from interactions between individuals on those same individuals.

Notes

1 The philosopher Paul Boghossian posits the same theory. Whilst opposing the constructivism of the facts, he also asserts that "it is simply not true that a denial of description-independent facts is a generalization of the social relativity of descriptions" (Boghossian, 2006: 31).

2 Note here that the distinction made by Searle is far from evident. It is difficult to imagine that there can be an object devoid of any symbolic value. Nevertheless, it seems that we need to treat this classification using an ideal type method.

3 In reality, it is not the piece of paper that holds the power, but the person who owns it. Thus, at the assignment of status function "X, this piece of paper, is counted as Y, which is equal to a note worth 20 euros", which is equivalent to an acceptance of the type "S, the bearer of X, is enabled (S buys with X until the value of 20 euros is reached)" (Searle, 1995: 105).

4 Searle raises the problem of any attempt to reduce the social world to individuals alone (that is, methodological individualism). Reducing collective intentionality to individual intentionality poses a problem of infinite specularity. On this basis, collective intentionality would be defined as a set of individual intentionalities based on the belief that (the) *alter* will do X if he believes that (the) *ego* will also do X, if he thinks that (the) *alter*, and so on *ad infinitum*. Searle's solution is thus to substitute this deconstruction with a collective intentionality, namely the individual capacity to think in collective terms, a situation in which an individual's intention is only part of a collective.

5 This has been the subject of many debates (at the centre of which we find the famous problem of the private language of Wittgenstein). If language is an institution like others, how can one consider the emergence of language? For Searle, language is above all a pre-institutional fact and it is the condition of all human institutions. It is "a self-identifying category of institutional facts" (Searle, 1995: 73).

6 For more on this, see Brisset (2013).

7 Even if these characteristics are necessarily observable through our representations: the famous *theory-ladenness* issue.

8 The pressure of the socio-economic system on individuals who aspire to revolutionise their lifestyles has been theorised well beyond the present work by Christian Arnsperger under the term "existential trap" (Arnsperger, 2009; Brisset, 2012a).

9 This point is open to debate. See Pahl and Sparsam (2016).

10 This use of the notion of "frame" in the case of performativity is the product of a joint work with Cyril Hédoin. This idea is thus his as well as mine.

11 This section was first published in *Œconomia* (Brisset, 2017b). I deeply thank Jean-Sébastien Lenfant for help and comments.

12 The same formal model is applicable to several objects of study, so it can be interpreted (both from the point of view of reference and meaning) in many ways.

13 According to Popper, a theory is empirical if it is falsifiable – that is, it allows one to empirically identify at least two classes of phenomena: one that confirms the theory, and another that refutes it.

5 An ontological focus

The notion of convention is the entry point to this, the theoretical contribution of this book, as it reveals a simple mechanism: to become performative, a theory must be able to assume the status of institutional fact (in Searle's terms) as well as that of a function assignment accepted at the level of a community as a convention, and thus permeate a social world made of other institutional facts. It is precisely this kind of mechanism that the theory of performativity, as developed by "performativist sociologists", refuses to explore as a result of the ontology it has inherited from actor-network theory. The main objective of this chapter is to question the relevance of social ontology containing institutional facts (redefined as conventions as they have previously been defined by Lewis) as autonomous entities influencing the performative process. Earlier in book, it was noted that if the notion of a metaphysical burden was defined in a relatively vague way by Searle, then it could relate to the common notion of downward causation: a social entity, a convention, even though it is the result of a set of individual representations, acting upon the latter. This feedback system is constitutive of the third condition of felicity necessary for the performativity of a theory to occur – that is, to become a convention within an already constitutive world. Using the example of R from the previous chapter, we are able to consider that the consequences R^* of a convention R are incompatible with a third convention R' in place – R' slows down R only insofar as R' has an irreducible causal power over the representations of agents, even though it is the result of these same representations. Now, if the idea of convention renders it possible to better grasp social facts in their collective dimension, the idea of a metaphysical burden solely alludes to their restricted dimension. It is thus the task of this chapter to justify the existence of social entities, taking the form of conventions, irreducible to individual agents as well as imposing themselves on them (this is precisely what performativist sociology refuses to explore). This will be based on the epistemological and theoretical debates specific to the discipline of economics. Indeed, since the late 1970s, the importance of the role of macro-social entities in understanding economic phenomena has been widely accepted within the community of economists: through the new institutional economy, whose guarding figures are Oliver Williamson, Elinor Ostrom and Douglass North, with more recent contributions to game theory

(Sugden, 2000b; Aoki, 2001, 2007a; Greif, 2006; Gintis, 2009); as a result of the resurgence of the "old" American institutionalism (Hodgson, 2001, 2004); and in France, through the school of regulation (Boyer, 2004) and the French economics of conventions (Favereau, 1989; Batifoulier, 2001). The economics follows the sociological approach presented above, which, it will be remembered, is at the heart of recurrent criticisms of performativist theory. Although the notion of institution is now firmly rooted, a unanimous definition is still lacking. Nevertheless, on closer examination, the idea of institution refers to what Searle defines as institutional fact – a set of macro-social rules, formal or informal, structuring social interactions and allowing coordination between agents. Whilst, from an analytical point of view, the institution can thus be considered as a solution to the shortcomings of methodological individualism, from an ontological perspective it refers to a real entity with a clear causal status – that is, not reducible to the causal capacities of individuals alone. Although it is rare for economists to seriously commit themselves to the ontological status of their theoretical statements, it is common practice to justify the idea that institutions have a certain independence regarding individual actions by calling them emergent effects. In this context, one can usually identify a structural rule arising from the disorder of individual relations without being reducible to it. It is a question of irreducible feedback from emergent institutions to social agents' actions. It is common at this stage to discuss "downward causation", the central concept of the definition of emergence.

Although the rhetoric of emergence is often used in economics or sociology, it was left to Tony Lawson[1] to provide a systematic justification for it. According to Lawson (1997: 63, 2003: 43–44), a social level is defined as "emergent" if:

a it originates from interactions of a lower level (upward causation);
b only part of it remains dependent on the lower level;
c it does not depend entirely on this level; it acts in return on it (downward causation).

Here we find a first approximation of what can be added to Searle's idea of metaphysical burden. Lawson (2012: 348) explicitly places himself in line with Searle by integrating the notion of emergence (a point on which Searle nevertheless remains ambiguous):

> Whether or not it is built into the idea of emergence *per se* I additionally hold to the notion that although any higher level emergent entity and its properties are conditioned by and dependent upon lower level elements or components, they are nevertheless synchronically both causally and ontologically (and not merely taxonomically and epistemologically) irreducible to them. At first sight at least, Searle, as we will see, appears to reject this latter thesis of (synchronic) causal and ontological irreducibility. If this is indeed a difference between us, then it is a significant one.

> For it is the composite or stronger view additionally positing (synchronic) causal and ontological irreducibility (a conception which Searle terms 'emergence') that, when applied to social phenomena specifically, grounds most securely my assessment that a relatively autonomous social science is entirely feasible.

The notion of emergence was originally developed among philosophers of the mind through non-reductionist physicalism, having previously been criticised. Tony Lawson extensively revisits the non-reductionist physicalist definition of emergence. However, this definition poses a problem in that it does not justify the ontological leap between agents and social structures, a criticism of the notion of emergence that remains in contemporary literature. In our framework, it is necessary to justify the irreducibility of the causal power of an existing convention R' on the establishment of a convention R. The main shortcoming of Lawson's approach, regarding the approach adopted in this work, is the neglect of an intrinsic peculiarity of the social world insofar as the agents coordinate themselves by anticipating the actions of others. On the basis of this simple observation, we will attempt to show that we cannot reduce a theory of the social world to a strict and restrictive individualist theory, be it that of the agents of ANT or the individual rationality of mainstream economics. This chapter will demonstrate that this peculiarity is not limited to the theoretical framework alone, but constitutes an inherent characteristic of the social world – just like theoreticians, economic actors must inevitably consider certain collective rules as given and therefore as external to their own subjectivity. This point will be the foundation of downward causation in terms of the logical obligation for individuals to accept as given certain salient points of the social world such as conventions. As such, it is impossible to think of the social world as devoid of conventions shared by all the agents that compose it; it is not a question of laziness, but of a necessity that is both theoretical and ontological. The aim of this chapter is therefore to ontologically form the central concept of our approach: convention.[2]

We will first explore the origins of the concept of the emergent effect – that is, the irreducibility of macro entities to elements of a system, an idea that was originally proposed by Tony Lawson. This concept poses challenging issues at first glance. In order to preserve the process of emergence, an argument will be proposed justifying the thesis of descending causation. This idea will lead us to a new definition of downward causation, and *a fortiori*, of emergence in the specific context of the social sciences, a definition based on the notion of convention and justifying an alternative ontology to performativist sociology.

The origins of the concept of the emergent effect

The fundamental topic that is covered here is the reality of institutional facts as independent elements of the individuals forming a group. This research is by its nature ontological. The notion of ontology today mainly refers to two distinct meanings. First, ontology speculates on what really exists as opposed to what only appears to exist. A second meaning refers to the real-world assumptions underlying theory. This is the first perspective referred to in this context, while the second one was utilised when referring to the ontology of ANT. For a long time we have ignored, with a few famous exceptions, the question of the ontological commitment of theoretical statements in economics; this subject is today at the heart of the literature (Mäki, 1989; Hands, 2001; Lawson, 1997, 2003).

The question of the real existence of an entity is intimately linked to the causal power (actual or potential) it possesses over the entities that surround it. Proposing that institutional facts exist as independent entities inevitably supports the possibility that they possess a real and irreducible causal power over individual actions. As a result, it is also argued that a social entity that is not an individual can produce causal effects. This concept has previously been supported by Tony Lawson (1997, 2003, 2005, 2006). The social world is structured on different levels which simultaneously interact with each other through processes of ascending and descending causation; it is this very dual causation that is at the heart of the notion of emergence.[3]

Lawson applies an old definition of emergence to the social world, which was most frequently utilised in the field of philosophy of the mind during Scottish emergentism in the last quarter of the nineteenth century (McLaughlin, 1992). Although John Stuart Mill's idea of emergence is regularly cited, it was only with George Henry Lewes and his work *Problem of Life and Mind* (1874–1875) that the specific terminology appeared for the first time. He insists on the fundamental irreducibility of emergent effects as opposed to "resulting" effects:

> There are two classes of effects markedly distinguishable as resultant and emergent. Thus, although each effect is the resultant of its components, the product of its factors, we cannot always trace the steps of the process, as to see in the product the mode of operation of each factor. In this latter case, I propose to call the effect an emergent.
>
> (Lewes, 1874–1875: 412)

This notion is also found in the work of another Scottish theorist, Charlie Broad (1925: 59):

> [T]he characteristic behaviour of the whole could not, even in theory, be deduced from the most complete knowledge of the behaviour of its components, taken separately or in other combinations, and of their proportions and arrangements in this whole. This alternative [. . .] is what I understand by the "Theory of Emergence".

The ideas of emergence and downward causation constitute a possible solution to the problematic of the connection between body and mind, a problem that stems from the work of Descartes, for whom, if the body of a man is like that of the animal (an automaton), then it has the particular ability to incorporate a soul. This soul, located in the pineal gland, maintains contact with the "vital spirit" of the body so as to alter its movements, without the consequence of reciprocal actions between the body and the spirit. Thus, when one manipulates a musical instrument, the movements of one's body are of a physical nature, whereas one's will is a mental phenomenon. As result, an ambiguity of the conjunction of the movement and the absence of reciprocal actions is identified. This problem has been raised by a number of philosophers, opposing Descartes to reductionist positions like the ones found in La Mettrie (1747 [1981]): a man is similar to an animal, in that, he is simply a machine. The debates between the supporters of a (more or less relative) separation of the body and the mind manifested themselves in many forms up until the opposition between the Scottish emergence theorists, who adopted vitalist positions, and the mechanical philosophers. The idea of the emergence of the mind in the body is to be considered as a possible answer to the mechanical positions.

The notion of emergence was overshadowed and thus relegated to the rank of largely despised metaphysical curiosity during the decades that followed until it resurfaced in the 1970s with the renewal of discussions about the relationships between the mind and the underlying neurological processes (the problematic of the relationship between body and mind). This resurgence originated from physicalist reductionism, which was until this point a dominant theory, whose main pioneer was John Jamieson Carswell Smart (1959). The work on anomalous monism by Davidson (1980) and on multiple realisability by Putnam (1975) and Fodor (1982) was central to this turning point in theory. Anomalous anomism primarily states that there are no strict laws of the mind, and rejects the identity of mental and physical types. Putnam, later followed by Fodor, defended the idea that a psychological event can be physically realised in infinitely diverse ways, and that as such, the reduction of the macro to the micro is by its very nature impossible. These pivotal views open the door to a theory usually defined as non-reductive physicalism. Jaegwon Kim (2006) highlights a number of fundamental differences between classical emergentism and non-reductionist physicalism, yet he unites these two approaches surrounding three conditions, forming the definition of emergence: occurrence, irreducibility and downward causation.

(i) *Supervenience:* Kim (2006: 550) defines supervenience as follows: "If property M emerges from properties N_1, . . .,Nn, then M supervenes on N_1, . . .,N_n. That is to say, systems that are alike in respect of basal conditions, N_1, . . .,N_n must be alike in respect of their emergent properties." This indicates that the higher-level property M cannot differ in systems that have the same set of lower level properties. This is Lawson's point (b): there is an ontological dependence between the different strata of the social world: the sum of agents constitutes the institutions.

(ii) *Irreducibility:* The second condition for emergence is that an emergent property is not ontologically reducible to its micro-foundations (the lower level).

That is, even if it is ontologically constituted by its micro-foundations, an emergent property cannot be explained by them because of an ontological gap between the micro-foundations and the emergent property. Emergence is thus a *brute and unexplainable fact*: it is impossible to know on what kind of dependence the supervenience relation involved in emergence is founded (Kim, 2006: 556). This definition of irreducibility suffers from a lack of precision. What is the nature of the relationship between the macrostructure's properties and its micro-foundations? Stephan (2002) gives a useful definition of irreducibility divided in two characteristics. First, a systemic property M can be called irreducible if it cannot be deduced from the arrangement of its micro-foundations and the properties they have in isolation. Second, a systemic property M can be said to be irreducible if the parts' behaviours on which M supervenes are themselves irreducible: the behaviour of $N_1, \ldots, N_n$ cannot be deductively explained without taking M's behaviour into consideration (Stephan, 2002: 88–89). As an ontological statement, this second characteristic is essential because it leads to another one, which embodies the *brute* aspect of emergence: there seems to exist, in that case of irreducibility, a "downward causation" from the macro system to its parts.

(iii) *Downward causation:* The notion of downward causation is subject to sceptical claims in several fields. Hulswit (2006) shows that the use of this concept leads to some confusion since it is not even clear what we mean by "causing". In the case of social sciences, what is caused in downward causation is the behaviour of the agents in a social interaction. We will explore the notion of causation later. For the present step of the argumentation, we reduce this causal power to the fact that institutions make a difference in social interactions. Finally, it is possible to link downward causation to irreducibility: the behaviour of the microstructure cannot be reduced to its own causal power, and the causal power of the emergent property cannot be reduced to the causal power of its micro-foundations.

For the emergentists, the inexplicable and new character of an emergent effect is above all the result of an original ontological contribution – that is, of a downward causal power irreducible to the characteristics of the micro-foundations of the system. As such, the emergent is considered both an inexplicable fact (that is, irreducible) and authentic in that it possesses its own causal power independent of micro-foundations of the system. In the field of philosophy of the mind, the term "non-reductionist physicality" refers to upward determination (physicality) and downward causation (non-reductionism). Thus, according to this point of view, although mental and physical properties are properties of the same substance (the material constitution of individuals), the former are ontologically irreducible to the latter. The pain that amounts from wanting a drink of coffee as mental properties which exist in the world is constitutive as the physical substance on which they occur.

*

If the rhetoric of emergentism is now widespread in institutional economics, as in sociology,[4] it is thanks to Tony Lawson, who specifically justifies its use. First, he reworked the classical definition of emergence (combining supervenience, irreducibility and downward causation), as shown by the symmetry between its own definition and Kim's reconstruction. This justification focuses primarily on the independent causal status of institutional facts. Thus, Lawson's work is a justification for the following proposition: from an emergentist perspective, institutional facts deserve a proper causal status as they are emerging properties. The next section explores the rationale for this proposal by Lawson. We will then discuss the logical criticisms by which the concept of emergence can lead to spiritual philosophy. The question will thus be whether these criticisms also apply when social institutions are considered as emerging entities.

Criticism of the notion of emergence

The idea of a social world structured by emerging facts, as originally developed by Lawson, hinges on an argumentative method borrowed from what he claims to be the philosophical movement of critical realism.[5] This particular argument focuses on the transcendental argument, which finds its origin in Kantian philosophy, regarding a reverse deduction composed of what is necessary to justify facts established by experience. The transcendental argument stems from an observation (1) so *P*, before deducing (2) we cannot consider *P* without Q, it cannot be anything else; so that (3) we must think Q, and *in fine*, that (4) Q is necessarily true (Parthenay, 2008: 37). This mode of inference[6] is used by Lawson to reveal, beyond our direct empirical impressions, the fundamental ontological characteristics of the social world. In this case, Lawson starts from the empirical observation *P* of the effectiveness of human coordination, despite the complexity of the social world and the cultural differences faced by economic actors (Lawson, 2003: 35). However, it is impossible to think *P* without stating that human actions are intelligible and predictable for others because of pre-existing social rules (Q). These rules are then assimilated to common action procedures of the type: "If Y exists, under conditions of A, then X." It is essential to consider these social rules as real due to their very nature of being possible conditions of coordination:

> [B]ecause social structure is a precondition of social intentional human action and interaction, facilitating the exercise of human powers to which they are subject, then the properties of social structure cannot be reduced to, or explained completely in terms of, the capabilities of the human agent.
>
> (Lawson, 1997: 176)

> My own approach is multifaceted, but a central component has been to proceed by first identifying generalised features of experience concerning (aspects of) human interactions and then to question whether any of their preconditions (i.e. the conditions that must be in place for these experienced

> interactions and aspects to be possible) include those that are additionally irreducible outcomes of human actions (and if so to explore their natures, etc.). If such human-interaction-dependent features are so identified, then, being causally efficacious conditions of (further) human interaction they can be accepted as real and being products of human interaction they are seen additionally to be social.
>
> (Lawson, 2012: 347)

At this stage, two observations are available to us. The first concerns the notion of "structure". Structure refers to social elements that allow for social interactions – that is, institutional facts (in Searle's terms) that take on the status of a convention. Secondly, we find here a justification of supervenience (institutional rules are the fruit of human actions) and of downward causation (these same rules are the conditions of possibility of action in society). The transcendental argument is therefore the major justification for the double irreducibility inherent in emergentist thought. Institutional facts cannot be reduced to human behaviour in the same way that individual behaviour cannot be reduced to institutional facts. Thus, these facts are imposed on individuals even though they emerge from them.

The work of philosopher Jaegwon Kim pays particular attention to the justification of the classical definition of emergence. He stresses that if the principle of downward causation is at the heart of the concept of emergence, it is also its Achilles' heel. The very idea that emerging effects possess a new causal power is, for Kim, a logical absurdity. He asks: how can one defend that a macro-characteristic can supervene on a set of micro-characteristics, while considering that the latter require, in order to exist, the macro-characteristic itself? How could these higher-level properties be causally influencing and altering the conditions from which they arise? Other than these questions, Kim levels several types of criticisms (Kim, 1999, 2006). He focuses on a particular type of causality, which he calls synchronic. The typical case is as follows:

- A whole, composed of a set of micro-foundations $a_1, \ldots a_j$, has a certain emergent property M at moment t.
- In order for M to emerge at t, it is necessary that at least one micro-foundation, a_i, possesses a characteristic P at moment t.
- Property M emerging at t is the cause of the fact that a_i possesses P at t.

Thus, if a_i does not possess P, property M does not emerge, and without this property M, a_i does not possess P. This reasoning implies a causal circularity given the principle of effectiveness of the causal power: for an object to exert a causal power because of a certain characteristic, it must first possess this characteristic. Synchronous downward causation is thus, for Kim, an absurdity. Introducing a delay between upward and downward movements can, however, strengthen the notion. Kim proposes a second diachronic case, arriving at a more radical critique (Figure 5.1): suppose a causality moving from emergent effect *M* to another emergent effect M^*. As an emergent effect, M^* depends on a set of basic micro-properties, namely P^*. What follows is that M^* supervenes on P^*, thus discrediting *M* as the cause of M^*. The only way to maintain the proposition that *M* causes M^* is in the case of *M* causing P^*. To trigger the emergent phenomenon, it is necessary to provoke its basic conditions. It is at this stage that we find the principle of downward causation. However, as an emergent effect, *M* also occurs on a set of *P* micro-foundations. From this, it can be concluded that P is a sufficient condition to guarantee the existence of P^*. Moreover, *P* causes P^*, and downward causation is, in reality, superfluous. The principle of downward causation, being the central point of emergentism, led Kim to state that: "[i]f downward causation goes, so goes emergentism" (Kim, 2006: 558).

This ambiguity stems from the conjunction of assumptions of supervenience and irreducibility. This simultaneity implies a causal competition between mental properties and physical properties. Now, given the principle of supervenience, physical properties always provide a complete causal link (from *P* to P^*), so that the link at the level of mental properties is superfluous. A relationship between two emerging entities, such as the example of asking someone if she has seen Lars Von Trier's latest film, and she replies "no", can be reduced to a causal relationship at the level of neuronal attributes of both individuals.

Kim's criticism therefore gives rise to two different angles regarding the subject: whether the discourse on social ontology of emerging effects should be eliminated (the eliminative posture), or whether it should conserve them as purely explanatory concepts (the retentive posture). ANT and performativist sociology are clearly moving towards the former by removing any macro-social entity from its pattern of thought. However, as it has been shown above, the conjunction between upward and downward causation is an essential element

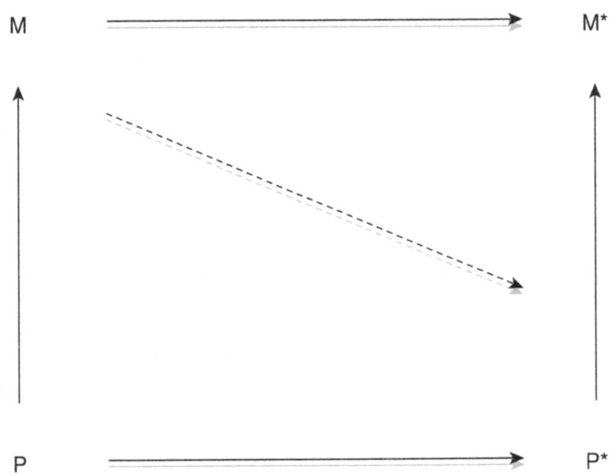

Figure 5.1 A diagram illustrating emerging causation

of Lawson's theory, as well as being central to the approach to performativity in this book. Individuals, as constitutive elements of the social world, are constrained by institutional facts – conventions – that are ontologically irreducible to them even though these institutional facts supervene on their interactions. Kim's argument, which condemns emergence to the status of a simple intellectual construction, is devastating for this type of perspective[7] – a social ontology combining supervenience and downward causation is simply incoherent.

*

Lawson deduces an ontological proposition from a purely epistemological position as follows: "It is impossible to understand the social world by excluding the notion of institutional structure." As such, institutions, as emerging effects, are reduced to epiphenomena (Pepper, 1926) which slowly disappear with the ever-growing progress of the social sciences – discovering the mechanisms of emergence results in its disappearance. This opinion is also shared by Joshua Epstein (1999: 54), one of the fathers of agent-based simulation (reductionist modelling by excellence), for whom "[i] n this strong classical usage, the term 'emerges' simply 'baptises our ignorance', to use Nagel's phrase". To regard institutions as emergent effects only makes sense within the framework of an epistemological limit regarding the reduction of all social facts to the characteristics of individuals. Thus, by pointing to the inconceivability of the notion of downward causation, we reduce emergence to the only problem of reductionism, a problem that is epistemological. To conclude, the notion of emergence enforces the methodological problematic of the relevance of a reductionist and individualist study of the social world. Since Kim's criticism is a formal criticism of principle, it tends *de facto* to be applied to any argument involving the notion of emergence. It is thus prevalent in the philosophy of mind and the social sciences, particularly in economics. As a result of its prevailing use in social disciplines, it has moved away from a reductionist perspective, namely through the bias of methodological individualism. Thus, the argument of supervenience reduces Lawson's argument to a retentive position as follows: emergence is a concept used to overcome the methodological limits of reductionism. These limitations will be addressed in the next section, and will serve as a basis when defending emergence.

Institutions and epistemological irreducibility: how to endogenise the rules

In contrast to the ontological perspective proposed by Lawson, institutional fact is generally considered (at least tacitly) as a simple analytical tool enabling a better understanding of the phenomena of coordination. Contemporary theorists claiming to be institutionalists, now numerous, agree on the role of institutions in making economic decisions. Hodgson (2007), who explored the "Folk theorem of institutionalism", states that any theoretical model has a conceptual obligation to mobilise a set of institutional facts, defined as rules of behaviour allowing for coordination to occur. As such, any theory of the social would, in essence, be irreducible to a theory of individual behaviour. The notion of reduction here refers to the classical concept of reductionism proposed by Ernest Nagel (1961). He stated that theory T_s is reducible to theory T_p if it is necessary and sufficient (1) to build for each concept proper to T_s a coextensive concept in T_p, namely a concept which relates to exactly the same entities in the world, and (2) to deduce the laws of T_s from the laws of T_p (Esfeld, 2009: 223). This goal develops and takes shape particularly in research on the micro-foundations for macroeconomics (namely by the New Classicalists). A conclusion that can be derived is as follows: a macroeconomic theory must be able to be reduced to a theory regarding behaviour of individuals. As we have seen, the performativist approach tacitly accepts this reductionist principle by reducing the social world to a set of singular agents. We will illustrate that such an approach is essentially impossible, in that explaining exchange requires at least one institution, and that it is to this epistemological constraint that Lawson's argument can be reduced, and therefore the same can be said for Searle's metaphysical burden.

The impossibility of an individualistic explanation of exchange, a fundamental economic fact, rests on the idea that any explanatory model is confronted with the imperative of respect for the rules of exchange (the contract). This has been articulated the most clearly by David Hume (1740 [1888]). For a mutually beneficial exchange to take place between two agents, the guarantee that the established terms of the exchange will be effectively respected is a fundamental condition. If it is not respected, a lack of an incentive to engage with others occurs. In this respect, Hume explores the respect of a promise in the exchange and the problems that occur as a result – "Why are individuals obliged to keep their promises?" – or, more importantly, "Why and how do agents convince each other that other agents will keep their promises?" These questions are explored in Hume's empiricism, according to which the verbal formula that the promise must, in order to be respected, be the expression of will. However, there is no guarantee that such will is consistently maintained over time. Hume (1740 [1888]: 517) states "[it is] certain we can naturally no longer change our own feelings, [than] the motions of the heavens". It is then with great difficulty that one imagines the very possibility of a deferred exchange in time or space enabling the transfer of property to be connected to physical transfer by the means of a purely verbal commitment: "One can not transfer the property of a particular house, twenty distant leagues; because the circumstance is required" (Hume, 1740 [1888]: 520). Jean-Pierre Dupuy (2014: 56) sums up the difficulty in the following way:[8]

> One agent must make the first move: he must hold out his hand in the hope that the other will respond in the same way. But what reason does he have to take the initiative in a world where, by hypothesis, no sense of obligation or duty – and therefore no sense of indebtedness – exists?

> There is nothing to stop the other agent from keeping what he freely offers without handing over anything in return. The first agent realizes this, and concludes that the best course of action from his point of view is to offer nothing. Even if the other agent were to promise to play his part in the transaction, there would be no reason to take him at his word: confidence is a futile gesture in the absence of elementary norms of responsibility and trustworthiness.

Understanding exchange therefore requires embedding it into a set of common rules, – institutions in the broad sense of the term, as given by Hodgson (2006: 17): "Institutions are systems of established and embedded social rules that structure social interaction." In this case, such rules will imply that "an agent knows that the other will keep his promise because of an institutional rule", and as a result, that the founding contract of this relationship will be respected. As in the case of Lawson, the institutional rule (or institution) can take the following form: "if Y, in conditions A, then X", where X corresponds to the respect of the contract by all, Y to the contract, and A to the particular social circumstances. The trust prevalent in the actions that follow the rule, including the compliance with the rule that follows from it, is much more than just a "lubricant of a social system" (Arrow, 1974: 23), it is a condition of existence.

If Hume, then later Dupuy, restrict the problem of respecting the rules of exchange to deferred exchanges in time or space, one can also consider that simultaneous exchange poses the same type of problem. For example, in order to engage in an exchange, it is necessary for agents to exclude the possibility of theft or the use of violence. As a result, the standard theory of general equilibrium calls for the hypothesis of voluntary exchange, according to which agents only trade if they wish. This assumption reduces all possible trades to mutually beneficial trading, ensuring that the price will be below the reserve price of agents. In other words, it guarantees among agents that the particular exchange is the only possible way of satisfying desires. Guerrien (1999: 29; our translation) thus points out: "the hypothesis of voluntary exchange imposes a condition on the relationships between individuals before they act. It cannot be the result of their actions [. . .] therefore, a project hinging on reducing everything to individual behaviour is logically impractical". In the same way, Davis (2003: 37) indicates that general equilibrium models "are reductionistic in only a qualified sense, because the existence proofs that underlie general equilibrium theory, and on which these models accordingly depend, make use of a number of 'global' assumptions that cannot be derived from individual behavior". As such, analysis cannot stem from a hypothetical state of nature from which social coordination emerges: the rules of exchange must be set before any exchange process can begin. The crucial question then pivots on the origin of the institutional rules guaranteeing respect for the rules of exchange.

From a more systematic point of view, if the exchange implicitly requires a third party to guarantee the application of the contracts, what guarantees that this third party will respect the contract with the traders?[9] Who controls the controller? In order to address the typical problem of the Aristotelian city, this question leads to an infinite regression. Hodgson (2002b: 114) points out:

> Attempts to explain each emergent layer of institutions always rely on previous institutions and rules [. . .]. Unless an institution-free state of nature can be formulated or discovered, then the idea of explaining all institutions in terms of individual interactions alone faces an infinite chain of links to be revealed.

Answering this question requires moving on from the defining institutional fact as a rule so that the reasons triggering the agent's belief in the effectiveness of the rule can be understood. Thus, for Aoki (2001: 185), "an institution is a self-sustaining system of shared beliefs about how the game is played". The problem of enforcement is therefore approached from an epistemic point of view as follows: for a rule to be followed, agents must have good reason to believe that others will follow it. The fundamental imperative of respect for contractual rules is thus to eliminate defection as a possible strategy, even though it seems to offer an advantage. The framework of the prisoner's dilemma, in which the agents must choose between respect for the contract (R) or defection (D) is relevant to this study (see Table 5.1).

If the strategy of mutual respect for the contract (R; R) is dominated then this socially optimal solution is replaced by mutual defection. This situation perfectly illustrates the difficulty of reducing transactions to mutually advantageous exchanges. Players 1 and 2 isolate themselves from each other, and trading is made impossible as a result of anticipating that this situation will be difficult to control. The question of the solubility of the dilemma when it is repeated on an infinite horizon has been and remains a subject of debate. Unlike a repeated finite game, where the perspective of a final period encourages defection and ultimately renders results similar to the classic prisoner's dilemma, the infinite horizon makes any threat of retaliation credible (that is, the end of cooperation). This would imply a net loss of future gains from cooperation. This perspective justifies a solution implying that all agents cooperate as long as others also cooperate. It is nevertheless known, with the aid of folk theorems, that all the outcomes of the game guaranteeing at least minimal utility (minimax) are potential Nash equilibria. An example of an equilibrium competing with what is proposed above is as follows: player 1 plays

Table 5.1 Prisoner's dilemma payoff matrix

		Player 2	
		R	*D*
Player 1	R	1 ; 1	-1 ; 2
	D	2 ; -1	0 ; 0

successively R, D, R, D . . . as long as player 2 alternates inversely D, R, D, R . . . (Bowles and Gintis, 2011: 81–92). An alternative solution is the use of mixed strategies – randomise the set of actions. Nevertheless, if I know that the other party is randomising his set of strategies, all the rational strategies at my disposal remain valid and undifferentiable. For coordination on the rule to be followed, it is necessary that the agents have compatible representations of the future – that is, they anticipate mutually advantageous strategic patterns – and this is therefore self-fulfilling. However, if there are a multitude of possible coordination equilibria, nothing that can be found in a theory of purely individual rationality (and reductionism) can decide the outcome of the game, and therefore the very existence of the exchange. We thus face, once again, a game problem as studied by Lewis, one he solves by introducing the notion of convention. It is therefore possible to illustrate that this convention is irreducible to the theory of individual rationality (Hédoin, 2012a), in that there are an infinity of potential conventions. The existence of multiple equilibria thus remains an insoluble problem in an individualistic framework.[10] This argument is a central point of the French theory of conventions (Orléan, 1989, 2002; Dupuy, 1989; Batifoulier, 2001). On the one hand, a convention refers to the existence of an epistemic community indicating social projections essential to coordination (and therefore to social life). On the other hand, this salience is inevitably posited *a priori* because of the impossibility of inferring its existence from individual behaviours, without falling back on the problem of multiple equilibria leading to cases of incalculability. This incalculability is, in the final analysis, the result of self-referentiality linked to the choice of one of the equilibria of social coordination. For example, I choose the convention (thus the equilibrium) x because I know that the other agent will choose it too. I know that the other agent also acts knowing that I am going to choose it, and I know that the acting agent knows that I know he will choose it, *ad infinitum*. Thus, an agent α, defined as a simple algorithm, would be unable to stop his decision process before another agent β, in that the decisions of β are integrated into the reaction function of α, and vice versa (Rosser, 2004; Koppl, 2008a, 2008b).

In Figure 5.2, there is no Nash equilibrium in pure strategies, but one in mixed strategies where Holmes and Moriarty assign a probability weight of 1/2 to each pure strategy. However, the concept of equilibrium in mixed strategies is problematic from the perspective of computability because it is one of the properties of this equilibrium that if one believes that others will play their mixed strategy, then one has no reason to also play their mixed strategy; indeed, any pure strategy which has a positive probability of being played at the mixed strategies equilibrium will give the same utility. Binmore (1987) goes further by arguing that even games with (multiple) equilibria in pure strategies can be non-computable. On the one hand, this means that the analyst is unable to understand players' choices, and on the other hand, it is impossible for the players to make a rational choice. We fall into an infinite regress of "I expect that you expect that I expect", and so on *ad infinitum*, so no certain decision can be made. In this game, best-reply strategies are not computable even for perfectly rational agents. In the social world, if an actor has to make a decision

		Moriarty	
		Dover	Canterbury
Holmes	Dover	0 ; 1	1 ; 0
	Canterbury	1 ; 0	0 ; 1

Figure 5.2 Holmes–Moriarty game payoff matrix

depending on expectations about others' expectations, he cannot do it by a pure act of knowledge he may have of others, but by perceiving an exogenous feature as a given. As a consequence, this feature is given a certain independence from his personal expectations. This exogenous feature is an emergent property. From this point of view, infinite regression as we find it in the Holmes–Moriarty problem is an epistemological problem for the economist who wants to discover why Holmes finally decided to get off the train at Dover or Canterbury. Consequently, as long as our approach does not consider any superior entity introducing *a priori* a choice procedure – a convention – then the possibility of understanding social coordination is eliminated. Therefore, all explanatory models inevitably stem from a set of exogenous conventions (theoretically common conventions indicating a body of social saliences necessary for coordination) which cannot be reduced to behavioural theories The institutional fact, approached as a convention, is considered here as a pure conceptual object. Thus, on an epistemological level, the use of convention is the result of the stalemate of pure methodological individualism.

This development makes it possible to reinstate Tony Lawson's argument in a purely epistemological perspective. The transcendental argument is based on the idea that the concept of convention is necessary for the development of knowledge regarding coordination that exists in the real world. As such, nothing is stated here about the connection between the concept of convention and the real world. The position of economists regarding institutional facts is retentive (as defined by Kim), and the first element of these facts is convention, thus allowing coordination.

The idea that institutional facts lead to coordination by indicating specific cooperative behaviour to individuals reoccurs throughout the history of economic thought. As a result, there are multiple definitions of the concept of institution in economics. In Lawson's work, we have seen that the institutional fact is defined as a rule indicating behaviour. Nevertheless, and in accordance with the above discussion, it is necessary to establish a definition of institutional fact incorporating the idea that a formal rule will be respected only if it is "believed" by individuals. This condition is essential for the rule to be self-enforcing. The notion of convention, as we have seen, can fulfil this criterion by abrogating the infinite possibilities of the mirror game into which a purely reductionist (individualistic) theory of social phenomena will fall. On the one hand, it allows the economist to think about the possibility of social coordination as a result of external mediation (Orléan, 2011). On the other hand, it indicates a common world of the interpretation of the rule which must be followed by all (an epistemic community). Here, we will explore, once again, the principle of downward causation, from supra-individual conventions to agents. The notion of cause here refers to the antecedent allowing coordination to reproduce. Causal explanation is assimilated to deductive reasoning: a convention is a necessary premise for the explanation of human behaviour in society.

If we have seen that it is always necessary to set up a pre-existing social framework for human actions, proponents of ontological individualism nonetheless consider this framework as a purely analytical tool, making it possible to provide good explanations and predictions. This compromise between ontological individualism and methodological institutionalism seems to be accepted today in the form of social phenomena which are considered as ontologically reducible to individual behaviour. What follows is a point of view entirely consistent with Kim's critique of emergence, which further underlines the intrinsic limits of Lawson's transcendental argument. The gap between the empirical finding of successful coordination of agents and the impossibility of a deductive explanation of this coordination on the basis of purely individualistic theories is not a relevant justification for the actual existence of institutional facts or of conventions as causal structures underlying social phenomena. At best, this discrepancy reveals a methodological weakness of the reductionist approach and justifies migration to other explanatory models (which Lawson proposes). The reasoning developed here is very much consistent with ANT's criticism formulated in Chapter 3. We cannot consider actors who are disembedded in the face of technical objects. Hume, Lewis and Wittgenstein point out the same problem, namely the incompleteness of the rules, including the rules of exchange, in Hume, those of language in Wittgenstein, and those of coordination according to Lewis.

The objective of what follows is to develop an approach beyond Kim's criticisms in order to provide a new theoretical foundation for the emergence of the social world. Thus, as a concept, the institutional fact, possessing the status of convention, exists in the event of downward causation rendering it possible to think about the coordination of actions.

From epistemological emergence to ontological emergence

Despite Kim's criticism, this chapter argues that the social sciences possess additional arguments[11] in favour of an ontological view of institutional facts as emerging effects. Indeed, if the biological level of emergence refers to the material reduction evoked by Kim, the social world is not without its own peculiarities. It is because the social actor is not able to understand the mechanisms from individual representations to institutional facts necessary for its coordination with others that he submits himself to these institutional facts. Therefore, it defines institutional facts as exogenous in character. Moreover, these facts put pressure on individuals: it is difficult to break away from the rules in place around us, as agents, as a result of an anticipated social cost, thus negating what Giddens (1984: 50) states to be our ontological security: "Ordinary day-to-day life – in greater or less degree according to context and the vagaries of individual personality – involves an ontological security expressing an autonomy of bodily control within predictable routines." As a result of institutional fact, an agent is given a sense of security when acting. Given the information gathered so far, it is appropriate now to develop the notion of a burden evoked by Searle by demonstrating that the social actors themselves (not only the theoretician) have no choice but to consider institutions as given and external.

The argument of this chapter asserts that the problem of reductionism concerns both the theorist of the social world and the social world itself. Within this, problems of knowledge and ontology merge: the social actor is part of the system he studies, his epistemological limits are indeed a characteristic of social ontology. It is therefore possible to extend by parallel the epistemological conclusions concerning the limits of the scientific explanation in terms of human knowledge. The women and men of which the social world is composed cannot rèduce their own beliefs about the world in which they live to those relating only to their peers taken individually. Similar to theorists, individuals must consider institutional facts as external and defined as conventions embodied within socio-technical devices. In the final analysis, this idea brings us back to the problem of methodological individualism – this time, common to both the economist and the economic agent:

- *On an epistemological and theoretical level:* we cannot consider social interactions outside any pre-existing conventional architecture, due to the risk of infinite regression preventing the understanding of decision-making in society. We have seen that a convention represents an inference specific to a community of agents, thus salience indicates a common social behaviour in a given situation.
- *In terms of individual actions within the social world:* it is impossible for each agent to understand why other agents implement a particular strategy without considering the existence of a conventional rule of a higher level that is imposed on them, and as a result, they are unable to deduct the exact nature, origin nor the evolution of it through pure deductive and individualistic reasoning. Social actors have no other choice – because of the impossibility of using deductive and individualistic inference – than to regard the other as an *ego*, endowed with the same epistemic characteristics and common coordinating points of cooperation. Note here that we are talking about choices in a completely indeterminate way. These do not in themselves assume intentionality; rather, they enter the pre-intentional sphere necessary for generic social life.

It is clear that a parallel exists between social actors and social scientists, in that the problem of coordination is common to both. As part of the implementation of contracts, a convention is the result of human actions as well as a means of allowing agents to overcome the problem of coordination by establishing a principle of ontological security. For example, an agent knows that another agent will respect his promise in this given institutional context, a context that imposes itself on both the agent and his peers. In this respect, the coexistence between supervenience and downward causation, which posed a problem in the context of the hard sciences, is here altered in that the epistemological character of the notion of emergence evoked by Kim becomes an ontological characteristic of a social world subject to coordination problems. Institutional facts supervene on all individuals (they are ontologically subjective, as defined by Searle: without individuals, no institutional facts). Moreover, they cannot be reduced to them because of a logical impossibility (the problem of incomputability linked to respect for the exchange rule) converted into an ontological jump (parallel between agent and theorist).[12]

It is thus possible to adapt the conceptual definition of the institutional fact (a device serving the coordination of agents) developed above to an ontological perspective by utilising the principle of parallelism between the economist and the social agents. According to Boschetti and Gray (2007), who defend a similar reasoning for the emergence in mind, we can consider the emergent properties that are institutional facts as social tools allowing access to a superior computational capacity and thus able to overcome the problems of self-referentiality. The common knowledge of a convention considered as exogenous is the solution to the problem of coordination, and allows the convergence of the agents towards a precise strategy confirming the effectiveness of the convention itself. As such, as well as being catalysts for mere decision-making, conventions and actions are interdependent:

- There can be no social action without institutional facts, in that the foundation of economic action in society (respect for contracts) is linked to self-referentiality. In itself, self-referentiality entails the need for common inferences for cooperation. For example, one must consider social rules as given before entering the social game. These rules guarantee one's ontological security as much as they constrain one's actions by the social cost that would result from not respecting them.
- Convention acts through the agents themselves. This avoids both the error of ontological individualism and the reification of institutional facts (which this time would render the individual himself an epiphenomenon) by considering institutional facts not as efficient causes, but as material causes in the Aristotelian sense (Vandenberghe, 2007: 512). For example, a convention is a necessary but not sufficient condition of human actions in society (the sufficient condition being the socialised actor). We are thus faced with a particular type of causation – a constitutive causation. In contrast, the standard representation, such as that applied by Kim, is diachronic and asymmetrical (that is, the cause precedes the effect). The constitutive relation is both synchronic and symmetrical: the individual behaviour is a cause of the social as much as the social is a cause of the individual behaviour.

Convention renders social life possible by guaranteeing respect for its rules. The social problems of indecisiveness dissolve in the cognitive capacity attributing beliefs to the collective. Thus, the transcendental argument, according to Lawson, is elevated to the level of the social actors themselves, emphasising the necessity for both the economist and the social agent to depart from an institutional state considered as a given (accepted as an exogenous object). The overlap between epistemological and ontological perspectives of emergence justifies the ontologically emergent character of institutional facts and the impossibility of ontological individualism because of the interdependence between actions and conventions. Institutions can thus be defined as incarnations, within socio-technical devices, of conventions generating in a population a set of coherent (self-fulfilling) beliefs. This allows the ability to discriminate various equivalent solutions of coordination when it is impossible to form (whether by the theoretician or the actors) an explanation of the social on the only computational capacities of the actors. Thus, the coordination convention is based on deeper conventions relating to the cognitive framework constituting a worldview (common priors involved in the identification of social contexts justifying following a convention) and on formal rules (for example, the legal system) constantly updating the justification of the convention. This conventional three-stage device constitutes institutional fact.

To conclude, it is now possible to provide a definition of the emergent phenomenon in the strict framework of the social world:

(i') *Social supervenience:* the convention is an ontologically subjective entity – it only exists due to individuals treating it and believing it as given.
(ii') *Irreducibility:* as a result of the limitations of methodological individualism, it is logically impossible to consider a convention on the basis of purely individualistic theories.
(iii') *Social downward causation:* convention operates from the outside by converging beliefs towards the respect of rules necessary for social life. This exteriority is the result of a logical constraint imposed on the social actor to consider conventions as given in that their function solves a fundamental problem of incomputability (related to irreducibility) affecting an essential element of economic and social life, namely respect for the rules.

This definition has the advantage of being specific to institutional facts as emerging objects, beyond the simple analogy stemming from philosophy of mind. Contrary to Lawson's work, this definition moves beyond Kim's criticism by reconciling supervenience and downward causation utilising the argument of parallelism between the social scientist and the agent. It turns out that we are entitled to consider conventions as emerging effects exerting pressure on individuals. Contrary to what Callon asserts, a common world does indeed exist.

The theoretical developments of this chapter have justified both the importance and necessity of a structured ontology. The social world contains emerging institutional facts taking the form of conventions (as defined by Lewis) and a concept that strengthens the idea of a pressure of institutional facts on the performative movement. Now, how can we link these elements more explicitly to the idea of an external limit to performativity? Here, we must exploit the incompatibility between different conventions: for example, if a conventional consequence R^* of a convention R contradicts a third convention R' already existing (emergent), then R' provides good reason in favour of the agents rejecting R. Previously, organ donation was utilised as an illustration of this mechanism. This subject, which studies in depth in Chapter 8, renders it possible to develop the definition of convention evoked so far. As such, we can recall that a convention is a classification carried by the agents who anticipate the mechanism of coordination. The agents thus perceive the world through these classifications (constitutive conventions) and social earmarks which indicate advisable actions to take in a given situation (regulatory conventions).

Emergent effects and performativity

The role of conventions can be illustrated by the notion of social earmarking, borrowed from American sociologist Viviana Zelizer (1979, 1985, 1997, 2005, 2011). This concept refers to the idea that actors orient their practices and their relationships towards the objects that surround them according to socially constructed links that they accept as given (even if Zelizer theorises the evolution of these conventional devices).

Zelizer has produced a large number of works regarding social status transformations of different types of objects, such as money, children or romantic relationships. For Zelizer, the use and social place of an element are determined by its earmarking, precisely defined as a cognitive phenomenon of classification. Zelizer's ambition is to qualify two important ideologies in economic sociology as well as in economics. On the one hand, there is the ideology of "separate spheres", regarding the economic and other social spheres as separate. The economic sphere relates to cold rationality and the social, of solidarity and sentiment. This ideology leads to the "hostile worlds" thesis: any intrusion of the social sphere into the economic sphere ruins any possibility of rational action; conversely, the economy would inevitably corrupt the solidarity of the social sphere. The other ideology is defined by Zelizer as "nothing but", which leads economists to consider the social world as entirely governed by market mechanisms, and sociologists to consider economics as systematically embedded in the social sphere. Zelizer articulates an alternative approach, which she calls "differentiated ties". She considers social earmarking as the essential, though evolving, element of social practices such as actors orienting their practices and their behaviours regarding the objects that surround them according to socially constructed links:

> In the broadest terms, people create connected lives by differentiating their multiple social ties from each other, marking boundaries between those different ties by means of everyday practices, sustaining those ties through joint activities (including economic activities), but constantly negotiating the exact content of important social ties.
>
> (Zelizer, 2005: 32)

Rejecting the myth of the corruption of the social by the economy, Zelizer considers the confrontations between the different types of social markings. There is no longer any economic sphere or social sphere as such, there are only markings linked to organisations of life in a community: the importance is not the corruption of the social world by the economic sphere or the reduction of the social sphere to that of the economic, but the maintenance of "good matches" between earmarked objects and social devices.

Zelizer (1985) illustrates this with the example of a child who was considered as a source of income, a labour unit, and gradually acquired a status moving away from economic earmarking. This process redefined actions considered as normal regarding his offspring. As a cognitive element of classification, earmarking is a convention:

> [R]epresentations and practices combine to establish social boundaries between different kinds of social relations. As people erect and enforce such boundaries, they generate three simultaneous effects: First, the boundaries separate social relations whose distinction matters greatly for routine social life. Second, they reinforce the proper matching of meanings, monetary media, and economic transactions within each social relation thus distinguished. Finally, they define the right and obligations of third parties with respect to each sort of social relation.
>
> (Zelizer, 2011: 85)

Markings enable the discrimination of objects and reduce the fundamental uncertainty related to the social world by orienting them towards a socially accepted practice: "In most such relations, institutional supports, widely shared definitions, and coaching by third parties reduce uncertainty and negotiation; few people, for example, have much trouble working out how to behave as student and teacher" (Zelizer, 2005: 33–34). Beyond a purely cognitive aspect, earmarking can also be applied to legal devices such as the outright prohibition of organ trade or the regulation of potential markets. Zelizer (2005: 62) thus derives a plethora of legal questions:

- What kind of relationship is it?
- What types of rights and obligations are associated with this type of relationship?
- Has one of these rights or obligations been violated by one of the protagonists?
- Which legal sanction should be applied?

Earmarking is clearly of conventional form: it is a classification orienting towards habits of action, it imposes itself on individual practices, and it is what has been called an emerging effect necessary for coordination. An example, once again from the work of Zelizer, will help to better understand the crux of the third limit to performativity, which is: in order to become a convention a theory must be adapted to a conventional set constitutive to the social world. One of Zelizer's best-known topics of study is her work on the social marking of money (Zelizer, 1997). Opposing the reductive vision of money as a pure economic object, Zelizer defends the idea that money is inevitably socially marked and differentiated. For example, Zelizer refers to the way in which the origin of money determines how it is spent. Take the famous example of prostitutes. Prostitutes tend to spend money earned from prostitution ("dirty money") on leisure, and any money received from the state is carefully budgeted and put towards the education of their children. Thus, earmarking allows the study of social conflicts. At the beginning of the nineteenth century, the management of poverty in the United States underwent extensive campaigns in order to rationalise domestic practices. For example, legislation agreed to help the poor financially to the extent that a financial gift can educate those in financial difficulty with the aim to teach them how to better and independently manage the benefits they receive. One of the great misunderstandings of philanthropists was the habit of those in economic difficulty of subscribing to very expensive life insurance policies. They were unable to change some principles of domestic management imbued with the idea of what a "good death" should be, accompanied by a proper funeral. Thus, the categories of philanthropists simply did not correspond with the idea of a good death. Here, we are faced with a problem of classification: good death or bad death; money well spent or badly spent. In a conventional system, a type of income goes to a type of expense. Such will be the way in which one will apprehend the friction during performative phenomena: if the theory R, which pretends to perform the social world, supposes a social marking R^* in strong contradiction with the conventions (classification) in place R', it may "fail" if it does not review its content. This is what is found in market resistance, also studied by Zelizer:

> When new forms of economic activity arise, how do ordinary people integrate them into their existing webs of meaning and solidarity?
>
> (Zelizer, 2011: 1)

> It may well "corrupt" values into numbers, but values and sentiment reciprocally corrupt money by investing it with moral, social, and religious meaning [. . .]. My hypothesis is that cultural resistance to including certain items in the social order – namely those related to human life, death, and emotions – into a market-type of exchange introduces structural sources of strain and ambivalence into their marketing.
>
> (Zelizer, 2011: 19–20)

What is apparent here is that the convention acts as an earmarking device: it is essential to social life as well as for the purpose of constraining the implementation of new social norms. The social world is not malleable at will, and a theory must adapt to become performative. As will be demonstrated in Chapter 8, as a conventionally non-market organisation, human organs are removed from market mechanisms, forcing economists to invent new modes of matching (finding a good match) the social representation of the organ.

Thus, social marking can be a hindrance to performative processes, depending on the different contexts in which they take place. The fact that institutional facts are taken into account does not preclude the consideration of institutional particularities (Herrmann-Pillath, 2013, 2016).

Notes

1 It may be noted that the idea of emerging orders with the claim of systematicity originated from the work of Hayek (1973 [1912]). The emerging order is, according to him, a set of rules between the natural order (*physei*) and the conventional order (*nomô*). It is a spontaneous order emanating from practices (*kosmos*), and cannot be reduced to an order arranged by human design (*taxis*). It will not be possible to delve further into the details of Hayek's justification here.

2 See Whittle and Spicer (2008) for more information on the ontology of ANT.

3 Here, the debates typical to holism and individualism are ignored; instead, specific details of more contemporary economic analysis are explored. Social facts' existence is, according to Durkheim, proof of scientific reasoning behind these facts, namely sociology. Regarding the connection between institutionalism and holism, see Hodgson (2001) and Davis (2003). These authors consider that the dividing line between holism and institutionalism is the insistence on the conjunction of ascending and descending causalities imperative to the creation of emergence (as we will see below). Please note, however, that there are emergentist readings of Durkheim (Cherkaoui, 1998). On this subject, see also Douglas (1986) or Bourdieu (2012).

4 Today, the notion of emergence is at the heart of the theories of complex systems (Simon, 1996), whether in physics (Gell-Mann, 1995), biology (Kauffman, 1995) or in social sciences (Elder-Vass, 2010). Applied to the social world, this perspective considers institutions, groups and social norms as inexplicable regarding individual behaviours, and as a force imposing on individuals as external facts (downward causation) even though they are the fruit of human behaviour (occurrence). Emergentist rhetoric is now widely utilised in economics (Gintis, 2009; Hodgson, 2000a, 2004; Hodgson and Knudsen, 2006a, 2006b).

5 Following the work of Roy Bhaskar (1989), the proponents of Critical Realism (Archer, 1995) attempt to introduce (or reintroduce) ontological reflections within the social and natural sciences. For more on critical realism, see Vandenberghe (2007); for a presentation on the emergence of social structures, see Elder-Vass (2010).

6 In his work *Critique of Pure Reason*, Kant (1781 [1998]: 176) defines transcendental exposition as "the explanation of a concept as a principle of which insight into the possibility of other synthetic *a priori* cognitions can be gained". His work aims to justify synthetic *a priori* concepts, such as that of cause, as necessary conditions for knowledge. If we consider that all perception requires judgement based on concepts, then these concepts cannot be the result of experience. These concepts are inevitably *a priori*, and cannot be considered as mere habits of thought based on everyday experience (a concept defended by David Hume). This reading of Kant by Strawson (1966) has provoked a great philosophical debate (see Parthenay and Thomas-Fogiel, 2005).

7 A similar criticism is made by Deichsel (2011).

8 See also Hardin (2003, 2006).

9 In game theory, for example, we seek to understand the emergence and transformation of institutional structures. However, to make an institution emerge from a game requires that this game is set up (payoff, implementation of exchanges) (Aoki, 2001: 14–16).

It is therefore necessary to search for the origin of this basic structure in areas outside the explained domain (the legal system, a meta-game in which the agents choose the rules of the game). Now, the same problem resurfaces when one wishes to endogenise these domains to a purely individualistic explanation.

10 This conclusion has, for example, led to a particularly rich programme of refinement of the main concepts of classical game theory (Gold and Sugden, 2006).

11 The problem with Lawson's (1997: 175–177) approach is that he employs the same argument when discussing the emergence of the mind over physical characteristics as well as the emergence of social structures over individualities: "I have accepted that, because it is necessary for certain definite states of the physical world, determining the conditions of applicability of the physical laws to physical principles. Human agency cannot be reformulated simply in terms of physical laws. Previously discussed in the same way that the social structure is a precondition of intentional human powers to which they are subject, then the properties of social structure cannot be reduced to, or explained completely in terms of, the capabilities of the human agent" (Lawson, 1997: 176). The same idea is present in Lawson (2012).

12 Thus, following the demand of Van de Vijver (1997), we intend to specify the concept of emergence within the precise framework of the social sciences.

Conclusion to Part II

From the assignment of function to social earmarking, Part II offered a new definition of performativity as a process of setting up a new convention involving new social practices (to be executed) according to a marking principle. At the same time, this definition addresses Austin's theorisation of performative failures as well as establishing a structured social ontology contrasting with the performativist one. The three limits to the performative movement which have been identified are: a limit of empiricity, a limit of self-realisation and finally a limit of coherence with the conventions in place. Economists and sociologists are therefore invited to look at three elements when they study performativity:

- How does a performed theory gain an empirical status necessary for its performance?
- How does the theory in question auto-realise in the eyes of social actors?
- How was it rendered compatible with conventions structuring the social environment?

These questions provide a basis for analysis of the failure of performativity as well as the success of performative movement. The next part provides an opportunity to apply the already developed concepts to different scenes of performativity.

Part III

Three scenes of performativity

Introduction to Part III

The first two parts of this book have been devoted to presentation and criticism, as well as to the proposition of a complementary alternative performativist approach. This alternative is based on the need to acquire certain analytical tools when one apprehends a scene of performativity. These tools, social conventions, raise three questions:

- How did the theory acquire an empirical status necessary for its performance?
- How did the theory in question become self-fulfilling in the eyes of social actors?
- How did the theory become compatible with the conventions structuring the social environment?

In an Austinian fashion, these questions refer to what could be described as some conditions of felicity. They allow us to take a fresh look at the performativity scenes by considering the friction of the performative process, which is slowed down (or even blocked) so that it becomes necessary for theories to adapt to the social world. Thus, the objective here is not only to underline the complete failures of performativity, but to consider both the alterations of reality and those of theories. Ultimately, this approach allows us to better consider the continuum from generic performativity to Barnesian performativity (see Chapter 3). It will be illustrated that it also has the advantage of allowing the identification within the theories of precise performative factors.

It is now time to ask these questions in the context of three case studies, three scenes of performativity, borrowed from the performativist literature or developed for this book. Each case questions one of the three conditions of felicity, and was chosen because it helps illustrate a particular difficulty a theory has to overcome in order to perform the social world.

The first question concerns the idea of a formal limit to performativity: to have the capacity to penetrate the social world by taking the status of a convention, it is still necessary for a theory to take the empirical form of a convention. In other words, it must make it possible to discriminate between different choices available to social actors, and it must allow the construction of a decision-frame common to the whole population. Chapter 6 will raise this question in the framework of the setting up by experimental economics of technical devices orienting the choice of actors towards more rational decisions on the meaning of economic theory. What we well know as *nudges*, linked to liberal paternalism, as we shall see, lead to a definition of an empirically charged rationality – that is, a definition allowing us to separate the set of potential actions into two classes: the rational actions class and the irrational actions class. It will be shown that understanding the performativity of rationality requires diving into the theoretical and epistemological mutations of the principle of rationality in economics: in the reflections of the classical thinkers of the eighteenth century, rationality above all was the animating principle of thought experiments, and lacks a clear distinction between rationality and irrationality. Only when this distinction has been clearly stated, especially with the emergence of revealed preference theory, has rationality has been able to serve as a touchstone for some public policies. It is the illocutionary part of the speech act of economists: to create a distinction in the real world. Bringing about in agents a reaction involving effects on the social world constitutes the second condition. This is the self-realisation of the theory that will serve to move the social agent from the state of understanding to that of action. Two things should be distinguished here: on the one hand, the agent's awareness of a self-fulfilling mechanism for achieving his goals, and on the other the effectiveness of this mechanism.

It is essentially on the second point that we will focus in Chapter 7, as part of a canonical example of the performativist literature: the construction of financial reality by the Black-Scholes-Merton equations on the Chicago stock exchange in the 1970s. If it is commonly accepted that this example indicates the fertility of the performativity thesis, we will show that nothing is less obvious. The model has never really sculpted the world in its image, so it comes up against a financial phenomenon imposing changes: the financial crash of 1987.

Finally, if the theory can stumble on the validity of a mechanism, we will also see the way in which existing conventional facts can block performative phenomena. One example that has already been mentioned several times, the attempt to establish markets for organs, will be studied in Chapter 8, exploring the constitutive convention of a representation of the organ which calls into question the establishment of the market as a matching structure.

6 Performativity and empiricity

Rationality and liberal paternalism

This chapter intends to examine the first of our conditions of felicity, namely the condition of empiricity.[1] This condition, which refers to the form a theoretical element must take to become performative, seems to constitute a blind spot for performativist studies – a desertion of scientific discourse that takes root in the theoretical origins of ANT. One of ANT's goals has been to understand the development of the social as an assembly of heterogeneous agents, including both humans and non-humans, with a focus on technical devices. As such, performative sociology tends to abandon the theoretical discourse of economists. The objective of this chapter is to study a more complex chain, introducing both the scientific discourse as such and the social conventions to which it gives birth through technical devices: *theoretical convention – (social convention – technical device) – shaping of the social world.*

To understand that a theoretical element can become a convention is to understand its integration within a social device constituting a new action framework. To this end, it must first be empirically armed so it can allow the articulation of empirical proposals offering new strategies to individuals. We will study the concrete example of a central concept of economic theory: rationality. In fact, the concept of rationality is both a scientific convention within the community of economists and a benchmark serving a number of rationalising public policies. If the idea of rationalisation of the world is common in sociology (at least since Weber's work), studies often do not take into account how this concept is thought of within the economic discipline itself – an essential element in understanding how it is integrated within political devices to promote more rational behaviour on the part of the actors.[2] This task is at the centre of this chapter, focusing on a particular performativity scene. In recent years, liberal paternalism has been an important field of study in normative economics. This corpus is built around a simple idea: individuals are often irrational; they are regularly led to regret their past decisions. Hence the idea that it is possible, without depriving them of their freedom of choice, to influence them so that they make decisions that conform to rationality as defined by economic theory. This influence takes the form of what are called *nudges* – technical devices influencing the social actors without depriving them of the right to choose. Here we encounter the concept of frame, which is constitutive of the Lewisian definition of convention: redefining the set of strategies agents can adopt. Let us take a famous example. In a canteen, presenting plates of healthy foods in front of plates judged less healthy, in conformity with ideas about good food, encourages people to choose the healthy options. The performative scope of this case lies in the identification of a principle of rationality to justify such measures (it is more rational to choose to eat well). However, to be operative, this principle of rationality must be discriminating, it must make it possible to identify irrational behaviours (Why is eating fries irrational?) and therefore become empirical in the sense given above: it must indicate several possible behaviours for the individuals, rational behaviours, and irrational behaviours (a new frame). Behavioural economics has chosen to try to define rational and irrational behaviours in a systematic way. Shaping the concept of rationality is part of a double movement: first, and contrary to many older theories, it becomes an empirical concept in the sense previously defined; secondly, its epistemological status changes. Indeed, while rationality has most of the time been an animating principle of economic models, a principle that was not tested (unlike the models themselves), it became, with decision theory and behavioural economics, the element one seeks to confirm empirically. Hence, there is a need to define rationality empirically: to test the rationality of an agent, it is necessary to define what would be irrational behaviour. This is the consistency of revealed preferences which acts as a definition: agents are rational when they show consistency in their choices; conversely, they are not rational when their behaviours reveal inconsistency. This chapter will begin by showing that the definition of rationality has not always been consistent with this requirement of empiricity, and that behavioural hypotheses have often not been intended to be tested, but to animate economic reasoning. As such, rationality has not often been defined for itself, for example among classical economists, but it has also taken tautological forms, impossible to test (irrefutable), for example for Mises or Becker. Thus, the identification of irrational behaviour was secondary, even impossible. The change came in two stages: with the theory of revealed preferences, which offers a stable definition of rationality, as well as with experimental economics, which places irrationality at the heart of its debate. The section "Liberal paternalism" will show how, once an empirical definition of rationality has been established, it has been seized by liberal paternalism in order to set up technical devices for individuals to act rationally. Without deciding on the complete performativity of the theory of rationality, the idea will be mainly to underline that the form of the concept is a prerequisite necessary to the performative will.

Performing by rationality

Rationality is a key concept of economic analysis, which offers many examples of the performative process of theoretical statements. On the one hand, as a theoretical concept, it constitutes a central element of economic modelling. On the other hand, it is often considered as a value enabling the proper functioning of social systems. As Arrow (1974: 16) clearly points out: "[A]n economist by training thinks of himself as the guardian of rationality, the ascriber of rationality to others, and the prescriber of rationality to the social world." Marschak (1950: 111) also observed: "The theory of rational behaviour is a set of propositions that can be regarded either as idealized approximations to the actual behaviour of men or as recommendations to be followed." If these authors were aware that the principle of rationality could be considered both as a tool for describing behaviour and as a guide for action, it is with the project of liberal paternalism, embodied in the economics of nudges (Sunstein and Thaler, 2008), that this idea really took shape. As a first approximation, a nudge can be defined as a technical device whose objective is to inspire actors to make a rational decision. A true political project, liberal paternalism is the perfect example of an attempt to perform an economic concept. In accordance with what has been explained in Part II, we will show that the performativity of rationality (the fact that it becomes a convention) cannot be explained solely by setting up technical devices whose elaboration has been informed by an economic theory. Indeed, the performativity of rationality has required that this concept take a particular shape to define irrationality in the face of rationality. This implementation went hand in hand with a change in the epistemological status of rationality within economic reasoning. To become performative, a theoretical concept must necessarily adopt the form of a thick concept in Williams' sense: to have at the same time a positive and normative charge, the concept must be able to describe as much as to prescribe a particular behaviour. As far as rationality is concerned, the fundamental milestone on this journey was a change in its epistemological status: the principle of rationality, over time, has become an empirically charged concept – a concept that makes it possible to discriminate a class of irrational behaviour. Because it has become a theory in itself, it should be tested. Defining irrationality has been an important direction of economic theory, and more particularly of behavioural economics. This result has subsequently served as a basis for the construction of performative tools that disseminate the theory of rationality in the social world. The objective of this section is to show how a scientific concept belonging to a particular language has gradually been transformed in order to become practical by acquiring an empirical scope.

From classical rationality to rationality-consistency

Maurice Lagueux (2010) considers David Hume's essay *Of the Balance of Trade* (1752c [1994]) as one of the first uses of the idea of rationality within economic reasoning. Its famous *price specie flow mechanism* is a theoretical description of how the money supply of a national economy is readjusted automatically following an exogenous increase: soaring prices act in favour of a deficit in the balance of trade, and therefore for an exit of currencies from the national territory:

> Suppose four-fifths of all the money in Britain to be annihilated in one night, and the nation reduced to the same condition, with regard to specie, as in the reigns of the Harrys and Edwards, what would be the consequence? Must not the price of all labour and commodities sink in proportion, and everything be sold as cheap as they were in those ages? What nation could then dispute with us in any foreign market, or pretend to navigate or to sell manufactures at the same price, which to us would afford sufficient profit? In how little time, therefore, must this bring back the money which we had lost, and raise us to the level of all the neighbouring nations? Where, after we have arrived, we immediately lose the advantage of the cheapness of labour and commodities; and the farther flowing in of money is stopped by our fulness and repletion.
>
> (Hume, 1752c [1994]: 138)

This mechanism is ultimately based on the ability of economic agents to arbitrate between the assets of different countries. The principle of rationality here plays the role of the main causal explanation of the underlying economic mechanism: it is the factor by which the system adjusts to an advantageous shock. For Lagueux, this mode of reasoning is one of the major contributions of classical economists, who, in reaction to the mercantilist thesis, intend to prove that *laissez-faire* is not a *laissez-aller*. The notion of rationality is obviously not cited as such. In the eighteenth century, we are more likely to read of the deliberative and calculative virtue of reason, as opposed to the impulse of passions (Boudon, 2009). In this text and in others (Hume 1752b [1994], 1758 [1994]), Hume expresses his fear of the spirit of jealous emulation leading Great Britain into several wars at the expense of its interests: "Thus human nature checks itself in its airy elevations: Thus ambition blindly labours for the destruction of the conqueror, of his family, and of everything near and dear to him" (Hume, 1752b [1994]: 160). According to Hume, it is this same jealousy, violent and impulsive passion, which impels the refusal of free trade in spite of its advantages. If the fight between reason and passions was particularly discussed in the eighteenth century, Hume (1740 [1888]) nevertheless firmly attacked this opposition in order to consider it as a simple analytical distinction. Reason and passion are simply two non-contradictory, distinct elements of the individual decision-making process. If the passions refer to states (anger, happiness, etc.) leading volition, reason is, according to Hume, only a case of being aware of the links maintained between the different elements of the world. Knowing that an apple has a taste that pleases me is like making the connection between an external physical object and a passion. As such, reason may deceive the individual in the case of an error of belief relating to the end appreciation:

> The moment we perceive the falsehood of any supposition, or the insufficiency of any means our passions yield to our reason without any opposition. I may desire any fruit as of an excellent relish; but whenever you convince me of my mistake, my longing ceases.
>
> (Hume, 1740 [1888]: 416–417)

The principle of rationality engaged in economic reasoning is not reason as such, but a condition of its expression. Hume opposes violent passions, which ruin all use of reason in the process of deliberation, as they cause the agent to make decisions that are obviously contrary to his desires (it is therefore not a question of reason). It is obviously a reconstruction of Humean thought, which in his economic and political essays does not focus as much on the passions of human beings in general as on the passions of princes or rulers. According to Hume, these lead systematically to a pathological arrangement between the political and the economic: by bringing together the logic of trade and that of war (symbolised by a Machiavellian "reason of state"), the princes of the eighteenth century yield to their violent passions and drive commercial societies to ruin (Hont, 2005). We find in Hume's work an important distinction between reason and the principle of rationality, the latter approaching what today would be called a "reasonable" character of action: a state of mind leading to good use of reason. Thus, the principle of rationality used by Hume does not allow a clear distinction between rational action and irrational action in modern theory because it does not commit itself to the ends of action, of which Hume (1752a [1994]) theorises about dynamics. As Picavet (1996: 69; our translation) rightly writes:

> The Humian approach to the question obviously does not allow sharing between rational and irrational actions. At most we can notice that certain passions are more "calm" than others, and can therefore appear more easily "reasonable" in the eyes of the world.

The price specie flow mechanism, Adam Smith's principle of gravity or even the equalisation of the profit rates of David Ricardo – all of these reasonings rest on a simple idea: people are not so "stupid" as to fail to choose what appears clearly advantageous to their personal interests conditioned by their tastes (Lagueux, 2010). This is what Lagueux means by the principle of rationality, the pertinent feature of which is considered, since Weber, as an instrumental conception of rationality: the individual tries to determine the means which seem to him the best in order to attain his goals. This is the case with arbitration in the monetary mechanism mentioned above: if the objective is to get rich, then it is advisable to arbitrate in the sense described by Hume. Among classical economists, the principle of rationality has the primary objective of making sense by identifying the origin of economic fluctuations. For David Ricardo (1809: 102), this element is the very condition of the construction of an economic theory allowing prediction: "It is self-interest which regulates all the speculations of trade, and where that can be clearly and satisfactorily ascertained, we should not know where to stop if we admitted any other rule of action." This principle of rationality has undergone major changes throughout the history of economic thought.[3] The main effect of these has been to give rationality scientific substance by allowing its formalisation. Lagueux identifies two milestones in this analytical incarnation: marginalism, which opens the door to the concept of maximisation under constraint, and rationality-consistency, which he identifies as originating with Paul Samuelson's revealed preferences. These two steps follow a logical sequence:

> (1) being rational is to maximize in the sense of reaching the highest degree in preference satisfaction, (2) preferences cannot be observed and measured without consistency, and (3) "to maximize" in a way that cannot be observed and measured is not to maximize at all.
>
> (Lagueux, 2010: 49)

Lagueux endeavours to demonstrate that redefined, rationality is much more restrictive than the principle of rationality engaged in the reasoning of classical economists. The author focuses particularly on the fundamental axioms that today constitute the heart of standard microeconomic theory. These axioms are well known: an agent is rational if his preferences respect the conditions of completeness, reflexivity and transitivity. It is on these conditions that a relation of preference constitutes a *total pre-order.* This representation, which prohibits changes in tastes, returns such an idea to the field of irrationality, something unthinkable in the light of the principle of rationality associated with classical authors. Indeed, if by agent we generally mean a subject acting in accordance with his beliefs and desires, the definition given above takes us away from this intuitive idea in favour of a vision in terms of necessary reactions provoked once desires and beliefs are set.[4]

This binding also presupposes the omniscience of agents concerning past, present and future world states: if they do not change their beliefs, it is because they already know the course of history. Contrary to the classical view, in which the principle of rationality leaves the door open to a process of adaptation of tastes to the judgements of reason, rationality-consistency starts from a fixed state of preferences whose internal consistency is considered. The decision-making process is therefore determined in a specific context, something that does not guarantee the Humian perspective (Picavet, 1996). This perspective is supported by the standard theory of expected utility, which appeared in Von Neumann and Morgenstern's (1947) work and was popularised by Samuelson (1952). Decision-making in an uncertain environment involves choosing one action rather than another by evaluating the probability of achieving potential states of the world: $x = x_1, \ldots, x_n$, with a probability function $p(x)$ associated with each state. The result of an action *æ* depends on the future state of the world *f (x, æ)*. Deciding to adopt *æ* rather than another possible action, one anticipates a utility *u(f (x, æ))* obtained in the state of the world *x*. The expected utility of the action *æ* is then:

$$U(æ) = \sum_{x \in X} p(x)u(f(x,æ))$$

In this representation, the agents' evaluations of the probabilities and states of the world are given objectively.

A change of epistemological status

The central point of the transformation from the rationality principle to its now-standard definition can be seen as a change in its epistemological status. In the case of a principle of broad rationality, rationality is subjective. This vision finds its culmination in Mises' praxeology. As an *a priori* conception of rationality, it aims to lead to an apodictic insight by way of its irrefutable nature. In accordance with the Austrian tradition, rationality is defined in a purely subjective way:

> It is a fact that human reason is not infallible and that man very often errs in selecting and applying means. An action unsuited to the end sought falls short of expectation. It is contrary to purpose, but it is rational, i.e., the outcome of a reasonable – although faulty – deliberation and an attempt – although an ineffectual attempt – to attain a definite goal. The doctors who a hundred years ago employed certain methods for the treatment of cancer which our contemporary doctors reject were – from the point of view of present-day pathology – badly instructed and therefore inefficient. But they did not act irrationally; they did their best. It is probable that in a hundred years more doctors will have more efficient methods at hand for the treatment of this disease. They will be more efficient but not more rational than our physicians.
>
> (Mises, 1949 [1996]: 20)

In this view, the impossibility of opposing the rational to the irrational makes any statement exclusively based on this concept irrefutable: there is no crucial experience to test the rationality of an individual. The work of Gary Becker (1968) on the rational explanation of crime has the same characteristic: all criminal behaviour can be reduced to rational behaviour, excluding the discriminating character of the principle of rationality and the definition of crime. Walliser (2011) speaks of a sub-explanatory model. Without going to the extreme, the principle of rationality mobilised by classical economists was simply not intended to identify rationality (and therefore irrationality) in itself.[5] The ambition was to understand the behaviour of theoretical economic systems as a whole. This is the case, for example, of macroeconomic reflections:

rationality is defined insofar as it makes it possible to understand the system's dynamics, hence the numerous debates relating to the necessity of realism of the hypothesis of rationality. The rational agent is, ultimately, only the support for general economic behaviour, and is never envisaged for himself. The framework of rationality-consistency offers a completely different perspective. By endowing the principle of rationality with a consequent empirical load, the theory of rational choice produces an opposition between the rational and the irrational and makes possible its testability. The path from subjective rationality to empirical rationality allows this concept to potentially assume two different epistemological statuses.[6] On the one hand, it is possible to see the principle of rationality as what drives a model to be tested. On the other hand, rationality can itself be considered as the theory subjected to the test. This duality of epistemological status has been particularly studied in the philosophy of economics since the short article by Karl Popper (1967) on the explanation and the place of the principle of rationality in the social sciences.

In this work, Popper intended to adapt the standard model of scientific explanation, the deductive-nomological (D-N) model,[7] to explanation in social science. In this context, the D-N model is renamed situational analysis (SA). The explanatory structure of the D-N model, developed by both Hempel and Oppenheim (Hempel, 1942; Hempel and Oppenheim, 1948) and by Popper (in Adorno and Popper, 1979), consists essentially in deducing a particular event from a set of explanans containing at least one universal law and a set of initial conditions: "The essential logical schema of any explanation therefore consists of a deductive logical inference, of which the premises consist of the initial theory and conditions, and whose conclusion is the explicandum" (Popper, in Adorno and Popper, 1979). The logical structures of the D-N and SA models can take the forms shown in Table 6.1.

Hempel and Oppenheim (1948; Lallement, 2007) interpret four conditions for the operation of this model:

- i The explanandum must be a logical consequence of the explanans.
- ii The explanans must contain at least one general law.
- iii The explanans must have a testable empirical content.
- iv The elements of the explanans must be true.

Table 6.1 The logical structures of the D-N and SA models

D-N model	*SA model*
Explanans	*Explanans*
– Initial conditions – General law (theory)	– Model (theory) – Principle of rationality
Explanandum	*Explanandum*
– Events	– Behaviour

The main idea is to test the theory, materialised by a general law (covering law), with the help of a forecast. Although the two modes of explanation are at first sight symmetrical (Nadeau, 1993: 37; Mongin, 2002b), situational analysis differs structurally from the D-N model since, if it is the principle of rationality that plays the nomological role, the theory (the model) should be tested: "A good methodological practice consists in not declaring responsible the principle of rationality, but the rest of the theory, that is to say the model" (Popper, 1967: 146; our translation). Although this interpretation is not unanimous among Popper's readers (Nadeau, 1993; Lallement, 1987; Koertge, 1979), it highlights the transformation of the principle of rationality cited above. By removing its status as a universal premise from the classics or from Mises, the principle of rationality has been placed at the heart of the empirical test. For Mises, as for the classics, the principle of rationality is what Popper calls an "animating principle" of the model: the rational agent is an element that allows us to study the functioning of a model we wish to test.[8] It is on this specific point that a major change in the use of the principle of rationality in behavioural economics depends: now this aspect of economic theory is considered for itself. It allows the production of empirical statements (testables), identifying a new class of phenomena: irrational behaviour. The important point is that rationality is defined this time independently of the context in which the individual is immersed, for example by the consistency of the preferences revealed by the choices. If, as we shall see, behavioural economics describes irrationality as a gap between the subjective representations of agents and the objective world, the big difference is that the starting point which allows this observation of irrationality is the observation of behaviours for themselves (inconsistency of preferences), and not insofar as they do not correspond to the objective reality of the world. By producing a partition of individual behaviours between rational and irrational, the empirical definition of rationality can form the basis of a choice between two types of behaviour. Let us take an example:

> *The principle of rationality:* with equivalent qualities, if there is indifference between several goods, a rational actor will buy the cheapest good.
>
> *Observation:* we observe that this is not always the case.
>
> *Conclusion:* agents are not always rational.

By giving an empirical content to the principle of rationality and by defining rationality as a particular behaviour that can be unfollowed, we allow the identification of a type of behaviour considered irrational: not to determine choice with respect to the price. The definition of irrationality in terms of consistency, as well as the change in the epistemological status of the principle of rationality observed in many areas of economics (mainly decision theory), lends an empirical significance to rationality. It is nevertheless necessary to clarify things on this point. Strictly speaking, the notion of consistency remains difficult to falsify. Amartya Sen (1993) shows that in the case of the inconsistency of an agent faced with different alternatives, the problem can be reformulated to restore the coherence of the choice. Sen's example is as follows: at a social event, a guest is given a fruit basket containing two pears and an apple. The guest chooses to take a pear. However, if there had been two pears and two apples, then he would have picked an apple. The individual may at first glance be considered irrational in that his preferences seem inconsistent. More precisely, the example violates the weak axiom of revealed preferences. This states that if the choice of an individual reveals that he prefers A to B, then he will choose A whenever it is available alongside B. Nevertheless, redefining the set of choices by including, for example, a social norm of the type "it is impolite to pick the last fruit" (in this case, to pick the last apple) makes it possible to restore the coherence of the behaviour. Indeed, "choosing the only apple remaining in the basket" and "choosing an apple among others in a basket" become different choices, and we restore the consistency of preferences.[9] Empiricity, namely the possibility of testing the rationality of agents, is here largely nuanced. Yet it is clear that the ambition to form an empirical theory of rationality is present. In the tradition of a general movement of emancipation from psychology, but also from the influence of logical positivism, the theory of revealed preferences considers only observable phenomena with the capacity to refute theories. If Sen is right in his criticism, the fact remains that economists regularly identify in their research practices behaviours that they describe as irrational within the meaning of this theory. The next sub-section will therefore address the other side of the question, the definition of irrationality. This work of definition has been mainly the object of experimental economics.

Defining irrationality

As seen previously, the notion of rationality is defined essentially according to two criteria: (i) the preferences must be consistent and stable, (ii) the weight of the utilities of the various alternatives must be weighted by the objective probabilities of the realisation of the events. A definition of irrationality is established from the lack of this definition. This work has mainly been done by behavioural economics. In a series of founding articles, Daniel Kahneman and Amos Tversky attempt to show, using a set of experiments, that reality is indeed much more complex than the standard theory of rationality assumes. We will focus here on the behavioural fringe of experimental economy.

The most famous behavioural experiment (Tversky and Kahneman, 1981: 453), repeated several times, is as follows.

The government must put in place a programme to fight a serious epidemic. The number of deaths following this epidemic is estimated at 600. The choice between two competing immunisation campaigns is offered to a sample of 152 people:

Programme A: 200 people will be saved.

Programme B: There is 1/3 probability that 600 people will be saved, and 2/3 probability that no people will be saved.

In this experiment, 72% of people choose solution A. The authors then repeat the experiment on another sample of 155 people, with the following propositions:

Programme A': 400 people will die.

Programme B': There is 1/3 probability that nobody will die, and 2/3 probability that 600 people die.

This time, it is the second programme which gains support (78%). This leads to two remarks. First, in terms of expected utility, the programmes are identical two by two (A is identical to B, and A' to B'), so there is no justification for choosing one rather than the other. Secondly, propositions A and A' (respectively B and B') are strictly equivalent. This experiment clearly calls into question both the hypothesis of coherence of preferences, since A is preferred to B, then B is preferred to A, and the theory of expected utility, since there is discrimination between choices implying the same. It would be possible to "save" the theory of revealed preferences by stating that choices A and A' are simply different, therefore the axiom of transitivity remains unimpaired. This approach is not the one chosen by the authors we will follow. Taking these phenomena into account, prospect theory (Tversky and Kahneman, 1979) leads to a refinement of revealed preference theory. On the one hand, it will lead to considering context (c) as a perquisite element of choice; on the other hand, the probabilities are subjectivised by a nonlinear transformation function $\pi(.)$ weighting the objective probabilities:

$$U(æ,c) = \sum_{x \in X} \pi(p(x))u(f(x,æ),c)$$

Behavioural economics generally distinguishes three explanations for the nonlinear transformation of probabilities and the role of context:

i *The framing effect:* the different ways of presenting an alternative influence the agent's reasoning. In the example above, the formulation is the reversal of the preferences' factor.

ii Faced with the multiplication of decision-making, the agent often relies on heuristic ones to avoid an excessive choice procedure. For example, Tversky and Kahneman (1974) evoke the heuristic of availability: the probability of an event is estimated by the ease with which such an event comes to mind. In another context, Ariely et al. (2003: 84) emphasise that the evaluation of agents is highly sensitive to the context of choice.

The authors show, for example, that if the last two digits of an agent's social security number are successively requested and then the price of any good is evaluated, there will be a strong correlation between the answers to these two questions. This is called the anchoring heuristic

iii *Cognitive bias:* here the inclination is no longer the result of an external element, but of interpretations specific to the agent or to the community to which he belongs. The most commonly evoked bias in the literature is the *status quo* one: the agent tends to overstate the utility of the current situation and underestimate the utility of potential situations. Another well-known disposition is the preference for the present: a risk of loss is felt more strongly than an objectively equivalent expectation of gain (aversion to loss).

The extensive lesson of behavioural economics is therefore that the structure of preferences cannot be considered as a simple parameter. It always depends on the context of choice. Kahneman (2011) defends that the standard micro-economic representation of utility function preferences neutralises the effect of the environment on preferences revealed by choice. Mainly, the notion of an indifference curve would stipulate very precisely that there is indifference between the baskets of goods. On the contrary, according to prospect theory, the fact that one of these baskets is different on one particular point may justify its choice at the expense of the others. He develops the following example (Kahneman, 2011: 291): two employees, Albert and Ben, work for the same company, have the same position and equivalent preferences on the division of their time between work and leisure. The company offers them a promotion. This can take two forms: an annual increase of $10,000 or an additional day's holiday per month. The employees must then decide who will access which option, knowing that each brings the same gain in utility. Equipped with equivalent preferences, a draw is required. A few months later, we propose to Albert and Ben that they swap their situations. The alternatives available to them are as follows:

- no gain, no loss (maintain the current contract);
- a loss of 12 days' vacation against a salary gain of $10,000, and vice versa (exchange contracts).

According to Kahneman, the standard theory considers an independence of individual choices concerning all reference points, for example initial endowments. This perspective leads to the conclusion that in this particular case, both employees will be indifferent to change. Prospect theory, however, holds that everyone will prefer to stay in the initial position because of an endowment effect (Knetsch, 1989). In general, it will be considered that the initial position as well as the manner in which an individual is brought to an end position are essential elements of the evaluation process of the different alternatives.

The view that behavioural economics is a critical feature in the standard conception of rationality can nevertheless be nuanced. Indeed, rather than questioning the notion of rationality, the tendency is to keep it as a benchmark of what is a rational individual. In other words, rationality-consistency retains its conventional role. The rhetoric of dual-self models is exemplary of this perspective: behavioural economists often consider that individual decisions are the result of the cross-influence of two decision-making processes,[10] one respecting the standard assumptions of rationality, the other falling under the yoke of the subjective processes mentioned above. As Ferey (2011: 245; our translation) points out: "The individual's unity is lost in favour of a representation of the agent as hosting different types of processes leading to the decision." Behind a positive appearance – the questioning of the standard theory of rational choice – lies a normative aim that is no less obvious (Berg and Gigerenzer, 2010): the tendency is to identify a normal and a pathological pole defined by a deviation from the standard theory. For example, Kahneman (2011: 378) claims: "A decision maker who pays different amounts to achieve the same gain of experienced utility (or be spared the same loss) is making a mistake." In other words, it is often found that among the authors belonging to this theoretical field, the standard axioms of rationality must remain a norm. Some of them are little discussed, for example monotony or continuity. If, in the case of monotony, Tversky and Kahnemman (1986) showed that its probabilistic version, namely first-order stochastic dominance, could be violated, they tended rather to modify their own theory (in this case, the type of nonlinear transformation of probabilities) in order to maintain dominance. The continuity is much less debated, undoubtedly because it constitutes above all a technical hypothesis taking meaning only in the framework of reflections not referring directly to the rationality of the agent, but more in the conditions necessary to the work of modelling of an economic system as a whole.

*

The essential point here is that, in accordance with Lewis' definition, rationality now has a form needed for the penetration of the social world as a convention. It makes it possible to empirically identify an adverse convention, that of irrationality. This characteristic comes from two important changes. First, the principle of consistency of preferences makes it possible to identify rational and irrational behaviours for themselves. Secondly, part of economic theory has favoured focusing solely on the theory of choice, allowing the identification of cognitive biases explaining irrationality. Whereas economic theory most often considers the principle of rationality as an animating element of models, it is now considered for itself as an empirical principle that should be tested.

Liberal paternalism

The normative scope of the behavioural research programme is accentuated all the more because it now claims to be at the service of public policies (Ferey et al., 2013). This movement takes shape within a liberal ideology considering that only a rational agent is able to make good decisions. This dogma is embodied in what has become known as liberal paternalism. If we have concentrated on the formal aspect of the theoretical elements by illustrating the constraint of empiricity as a technical constraint, we should not be mistaken about the social and cultural aspects that underlie this constraint. The choice to look at rationality stems, in a manner consistent with the methodological conventions of reductionism and individualism, from the way economists are produced in different national cultures. From this last point follows a consideration of economists' role in the public space as well as the direction of their work. We will focus on the work of Marion Fourcade, *Economists and Societies* (2009), whose primary ambition is to understand, through a comparative study, the societal conditions for the production of economic and social knowledge and the crystallisation of the economist's role within the city. Through this work, for example, the author draws the major demarcations between three different institutional systems: France, the United States and the United Kingdom. In France, economists, due to its technocratic origin inherited from a centralising state tradition, direct their expertise towards state action. Conversely, practical skills, their market performance, guide the selection of economists in the United States. Considered as an expert, the American economist is formed within a culture that values the effectiveness of market competition as the supreme principle of governance. These principles of neo-liberal governance shape a cognitive framework that significantly guides the theoretical contents themselves. There is no doubt that this framework is particularly conducive to valuing the principle of rationality as the central concept of economic science, as well as leading to the emergence of liberal paternalism. In this way, if one concentrates mainly on the formal aspect (the cultural aspect will be studied in Chapter 8), our approach is perfectly compatible with work directed towards a contextual approach of the economic governance.

General principles of liberal paternalism

Assuming the main behavioural results mentioned above, mainly underdetermination (linked to the framing effect) of choices with respect to preferences, supporters of liberal paternalism argue that any choice inevitably takes place within a context that is the result of decisions made by third parties. As such, individual choices are necessarily influenced by *others*, an agent or an institution that has decided (even in spite of itself) the "architecture of choice", the way in which the different alternatives are presented. The existence of this architect of choice is inherently inevitable given the social character of our environment. This is what Sunstein and Thaler, who are the main representatives of liberal paternalism in economics, claim: "There is, in those situations, no alternative to a kind of paternalism – at least in the form of an intervention that affects what people choose" (Sunstein and Thaler, 2003: 1164). In other words, the idea of a context of neutral choice and of total freedom, in the negative sense of an absence of constraint, is for these authors nonsense. In accordance with the Kahnmanian roots of liberal paternalism, the context tends to modify the structure of choice of individuals by moving them away from the main virtue of freedom, the standard of rationality-consistency. Failing to be able to make their choices completely free, it is enough to impose on the agents a context that makes it possible to reach a decision similar to the one that would have been taken in a situation of total freedom: a rational decision. In this logic, freedom is mimicked by behaviour consistent with rationality, which is ultimately considered the only desired consequence of freedom. Nevertheless, and in a manner consistent with liberal precepts, in no case should the individual be forced to choose one alternative over another. On the contrary, it must be oriented towards the right choice: "A good system of choice architect helps people to improve their ability to map and hence to select options that will make them better off" (Sunstein and Thaler, 2008: 101). The *better off* is assimilated to a rapprochement with the classical axioms of rationality-consistency. In the perspective of dual-self models, Sunstein and Thaler oppose an automatic, intuitive, irresponsible and irrational system, a reflexive system which is deliberate and rational. Sunstein and Thaler also oppose the image of a perfectly rational individual, the *Econs*, systematically taking his decisions in a rational and reflexive way, the normal social actor, whose automatic system takes precedence over the rational system. The principal ambition of liberal paternalists is not to render people rational, but to bring about choices built on the basis of the automatic system of decisions made on the basis of the rational system: "If people can rely on their Automatic Systems without getting into trouble, their lives should be easier, better and longer" (Sunstein and Thaler, 2008: 24).

The project of liberal paternalism is particularly exemplary in the nudges policy project initiated by Sunstein and Thaler in their iconic book *Nudge: Improving Decisions about Health, Wealth and Happiness* (2008). A nudge can be defined as a technical device influencing the choice of individuals so that they do not regret it *ex post*. The notion of *ex post* regret becomes, in the context of liberal paternalism, the empirical touchstone of irrationality, as well as the normative justification for intervention. *Ex-post* regret is for many the true marker of irrationality (Gilboa, 2009). It is precisely this point that differentiates the permanent violation from the rationality model – found, for example, in Allais (1953) – of temporary violations linked to the contexts of choice. We thus arrive at a normative definition of rationality apparently close to that given by Savage (1954), who latter insists that a theory of rationality is normatively acceptable if, as soon as it is violated by a subject, the fact of pointing it out will imply a change in behaviour. However, the idea of personalities' multiplicity allows the alternative position to persist in a behaviour that does not conform to the theory of expected utility, even though the individual may *ex post* regret an act. It is this actuality, this point, which justifies *nudging*, simple learning being insufficient. Consequently, beyond the problem raised by Sen, the criterion of *non-regret ex post* completes the definition of rationality in terms of coherence, in order to seek a real empirical scope. The canonical example in the United States results from defined-contribution savings plans which in the early 1980s replaced defined-benefit plans. In a country where life risk insurance is largely dependent on private savings choices through 401(k) plans,[11] there is frequently *ex post* regret about a low level of savings. This result is often considered as an underestimation of the utility linked to a saved amount in the future compared to immediate availability of the sum. Thus, when a company offers a set of savings plans to its employees, two issues arise: on the one hand, the participation rate is often low; on the other hand, the savings plans chosen are often of little importance. Sunstein and Thaler (2008) now propose to overcome this preference bias with another bias, that of the *status quo*. As a first step, the traditional system of voluntary registration for savings plans (opt-in) needs to be replaced by an automatic plan enrolment system from which employees must unsubscribe if they wish (opt-out). In a study by Madrian and Shea (2001), automatic enrolment leads the participation rate in savings programmes to increase from 20% to 90%.

Then comes the question of the level of savings. Here again, the default choice remains the preferred tool: one chooses to automatically enrol employees in a large savings plan, and if an individual desires a plan he deems best, then he must deviate from the default choice. One of the lessons of behavioural economics is, as previously observed, that an individual tends to prefer the present situation to any other potential situation. Thanks to choice by default, one influences the individual's choice so that he will not regret his choice *a posteriori*. This principle can be paired with a gradual increase in the savings rate linked to wage increases (Thaler and Benartzi, 2004). Therefore the nudge[12] tends to restore the temporal coherence of the preferences constituting the classical definition of rationality. This device is quite representative of the Foucauldian definition (Foucault, 2004; Fridman, 2010) of neo-liberalism as a mode of governmentality – creating the conditions for establishing an order mimicking the liberal ideal without interfering directly in the choice of agents. The focus is mainly on the use of Kahnmanian behavioural economics. Another approach, generally represented by Alvin Roth and Charles Plott, sees experimentation as a powerful tool for institutional change. Francesco Guala (2007) emphasises the disciplinary dominance of this branch of experimentation. For him, this dominance is explained by the fact that it allows one to "do things", which is unlike behavioural economics, which would be content to test existing theories. The example of nudges deeply nuances this point of view: the economy of nudges establishes examples of performativity by economic discipline.

First, it is based on a set of technical arrangements that serve the individual in his decision-making. Secondly, these technical arrangements are created in order to conform the behaviour of agents to the economic theory of rationality. Christian Licoppe (2010) identifies two different performative registers. On the one hand, the technical device can be set up so that it produces directly in the world a set of behaviours consistent with a particular economic theory.

In this context, the tool whose construction has been informed by economic theory is a constituent element of the social world – for example, accounting rules or financial instruments for calculating the prices of financial securities. Another performative register is that of the production of a choice context influencing (without directly making the decision) the choice of social actors in the sense prescribed by economic theory. It is clearly in this second register that the nudge can be brought back.

An application: redefining poverty

Once clearly translated into a general political corpus, the empirical definition of rationality can be used in more narrow contexts.[13] This has been the case in development economics, where some who are on the fringe have grasped the principle of nudging. This penetration of behavioural economics into development economics has not only been an opportunity to implement a new type of control mechanism which was meant to settle major political debates, in particular between William Easterly and Jeffrey Sachs about massive aid, but also to provide a new definition of poverty in terms of irrationality. Banerjee and Duflo (2011) proposed, first, to redefine aid as an incentive, and secondly, to systematically test the various potential incentive modalities using randomised trials. The starting point for this paradigmatic overrun is a behavioural definition of poverty: poverty is rooted in the psychological phenomena of deviation from ideal-typical rational behaviour, one of the major deviations being time inconsistency:

> In the present, we are impulsive, governed in large part by emotions and immediate desire: small losses of time (standing in line to get child immunized) or petty discomforts (glutes that need to be woken up) that have to be endured right now feel much more unpleasant in the moment than when we think about them without a sense of immediacy (say, after a Christmas meal that was heavy enough to rule out all thoughts of immediate exercise). The reverse, of course, goes for small 'rewards' (candy, a cigarette) that we really crave in the present; when we plan for the future, the pleasure from these treats seems less important.
>
> (Banerjee and Duflo, 2011: 64–65)

For example, Michael Kremer et al. (2011) mention the problem of water treatment with chlorine in countries without running water: even whether there is systematic availability of chlorine doses, it is observed that all too often people do not use them. The authors attribute this fact to time inconsistency. As we have seen, nudging devices are considered as means for combating this type of phenomenon. Banerjee and Duflo (2011) explicitly refer to the work of Thaler and Sunstein. In the same vein, a technical device called *one turn* has been tested, consisting of a chlorine dispenser installed in the immediate vicinity of the village water source. This leads to less effort, which encourages many people to directly treat the water on site. The points of rapprochement between the work of Banerjee and Duflo as well as Thaler and Sunstein are on the one hand the focus on the psychological mechanisms constituting a hiatus between real and rational behaviours, and on the other the way to remedy this as the problem lies in the establishment of local systems of incentives playing on cognitive bias. This second point positions authors on the margins of the standard approaches of the fight against poverty by focusing not on the general problems of governance (INSTITUTIONS in capital letters), but on small-scale social devices (institutions in lower case): "To really understand the effect of institutions on the lives of the poor, what is needed is a shift of perspective from INSTITUTIONS in capital letters to institutions in lower case – the 'view from below'" (Banerjee and Duflo, 2011: 243).

Establishing a strong bond between Banerjee and Duflo and liberal paternalism may seem a little premature when one can apprehend that time inconsistency is far from the only reason for the deficient use of interventions in the fight against poverty. In particular, they argue that while time inconsistency may be a good way to explain the low attendance at health clinics to vaccinate children, it does not explain why parents repeatedly postpone vaccination. For Banerjee and Duflo, the additional explanation is the underestimation of profits. Experiments have also tested the underestimation of benefits and showed that promoting the awareness of benefits via a subsidy when first used actually resulted in an increase in the use of a device. Here, contrary to the case cited above, the incentive allows learning about the benefits. If experience thus confirms Banerjee and Duflo's intuition that underestimation is an important parameter, it is not enough to remove their perspective from liberal paternalism. Indeed, more than time inconsistency in the strict sense (hyperbolic discounting), we have seen that liberal paternalism considers, above all, the criterion of *a posteriori* regret as the sign of a dynamic of utility functions. Faced with complex choices (Sunstein and Thaler, 2008: 103), agents use diverse decision heuristics. These choices reveal to the theorist, at a time t, the preferences associated with probabilities of the associated events' realisations. Nevertheless, in future, the agents regret their choice: "If I had known, I would have vaccinated my children." The agents would then revisit their choice if they had the opportunity. This regret leads the theorist to re-evaluate the agent's preferences. However, this mechanism is compatible with the behaviours put forward by Banerjee and Duflo, and those considered by Sunstein and Thaler. The conciliation between Banerjee and Duflo and liberal paternalism does not seem problematic from an analytical point of view (Davis, 2013). The fight against malaria is a paradigmatic example in this area. One way to effectively fight the spread of malaria is the use of mosquito nets. Jeffrey Sachs (2005) therefore proposed massive assistance to provide mosquito nets free of charge to populations at risk. In the "anti-aid" camp, William Easterly (2006) judged such a proposal counterproductive, since the aid is systematically diverted into circles of the parallel economy where people tend not to use nets and where massive aid tends to perpetuate a relationship of domination between North and South. In accordance with the presuppositions of liberal paternalism, Duflo and Banerjee consider that the main explanation for the non-use of nets is a behavioural problem (time inconsistency/underestimation of actual benefits). They advocate a nudging device: an incentive system should be put in place to re-evaluate the anticipated benefits of the nets. In this case, Banerjee and Duflo play on another behavioural bias mentioned previously: the *status quo* bias. The idea is that once they have bought a mosquito net at a very low price, people are afterwards more willing to buy and use it, even at a higher price. This is a pure and simple case of nudging.

Banerjee and Duflo derive a new definition of poverty centred on remoteness *vis-à-vis* rational action. In this perspective, the hiatus between the rational and the irrational finds its origin in psychological parameters and in contexts: the first are activated by the second. In other words, and according to prospect theory, the context of choice activates cognitive biases leading behaviour to conform more or less to the definition of rationality as it is envisaged by economists. We can therefore understand the normative and performative power of the theory of rationality-consistency when we assign it to a specific classification by combining poverty and irrationality. From then on, the fight against poverty is transformed by metonymy into a search for rational action. It should be noted that the assimilation between irrationality and poverty is not new, and that the debate on helping the poor in the United States in the early twentieth century was similar in terms of organising aid to encourage the poor to adopt behaviours that were considered responsible and rational (Zelizer, 2011). At the time, economists were also involved, but it was then a question of applying good accounting principles.

Conclusion

This chapter illustrated the analytical interest of the condition of empiricity. Thus, the form of a concept plays on its performativity. It is on this condition that the theory becomes "performable", capable of taking the form of a benchmark on which social actors can rely. We have studied the chain from rationality theory to nudging as a performative device through a shaping of the concept of rationality necessary for its performativity. This condition has been the result of a change in both the form and the epistemological status of the principle of rationality throughout the history of economic thought. In the state, our reflection shows that it is vain to oppose performativity by the idea or by the technique. Indeed, if the technical device, here a nudge, is a crucial link in the performative process, the form of the concept to perform is just as important. Without an empirical definition of rationality, there is no nudging, therefore no performativity.

Notes

1 This chapter was first published in *Revue de philosophie économique* (Brisset, 2014a).
2 In a brilliant article with the evocative title "A new mentality for a new economy: performing the homo economicus in Argentina (1976–83)", Daniel Fridman (2010) studies how the military junta in Argentina between 1976 and 1983 was able to use neo-liberal theories in order to establish control over the population. This control mainly involved the performativity, through learning, of the rational behaviours related to consumer and producer theories. Fridman's perspective is clearly not to consider economics as it is in a scientific setting, but to focus on the practices of state economists in setting up a form of science governmentality through political market devices. However, it is essential, to understand in greater depth the idea of performativity of the concepts and to consider them in their use within the scientific fields.
3 On the incompatibility between classical rationality and rationality consistency, see Sugden (2005).
4 The history of the concept of rationality is complex. The link between revealed preference theory, developed by Samuelson (1938) and Houthakker (1950), and the notion of consistency of ordinal preferences is complex and controversial. On this point, see Mongin (2000) and Giocoli (2003).
5 The choice to make the individual the basic unit of social explanation has been challenged in many ways. It is conceivable, as indicated above, to consider organisational structures as *sui generis* entities, but the reverse path is also possible by considering entities of lower scales. In this respect, we can cite the work of Ken Binmor (1987, 1988), who considers the agent as an interacting meta-program using programs in the form of decision heuristics overcoming the problems of computability. From the same perspective, there is the work of Richard Dawkins (1976) and the notion of the meme. A meme is defined as the unit of cultural evolution, resembling the gene in biology. In both cases, decision heuristics and memes are lower units of scale than agents, expressing themselves through them while maintaining a certain autonomy.
6 To adopt the words of Jon Elster (1983): to move from a narrow conception of rationality (that of Mises and the classics) to a broad conception. On this point, see Lagueux (1993).
7 The formulation of the D-N model has been the subject of critical discussions, both in the philosophy of science in general and in economic epistemology. For more on this, see Mongin (2002a) or Lallement (2007).
8 In the context of the hard sciences, Popper identifies Newton's laws as principles animating an initial situation. For example the planets of the solar system explain eclipses.
9 For a more general point of view on the issue, see Bhattacharyya et al. (2011).
10 The idea of a duality of psychological processes is not new in itself. It has mainly been developed in cognitive psychology (although one regularly goes back to the work of William James). For an overview of these theories, see Chaiken and Trope (1999).
11 This is a funded retirement savings plan, widely used in the United States since the 1980s. Its name derives from Section 401(k) of the US tax code.
12 We are only dealing here with a specific aspect of liberal paternalism and nudging – that is, as a means of performing the world. For a critique, see Berg and Gigerenzer (2010).
13 This section follows the reflections initiated by Judith Favereau (Brisset and Favereau, 2013; Favereau, 2014).

7 Performativity and self-fulfilment

The case of the Black-Scholes-Merton equations

This chapter attempts to illustrate the heuristic contribution from our second condition of performativity, namely self-fulfilment.[1] It will be devoted to the study of a standard case in the performativist literature: the influence of the Black-Scholes-Merton equations on the financial markets. It will be shown that if these equations have indeed played an important role in the construction of the financial world, considering the mechanism of self-fulfilment can also show that they failed to conform the financial world to the model on a particular point: the shape of price movements. The financial markets are a privileged object of study of economic sociology in general, and of performativist sociology in particular. The study by Donald MacKenzie and Yuval Millo, "Constructing a market, performing theory: the historical sociology of a financial derivatives exchange" (2003), which highlights the crucial role of financial theories in the constitution of financial markets, can be regarded as the foundation of this series of works. On the one hand, this survey has generated a vast literature, both from the authors themselves (MacKenzie, 2004, 2006a, 2006b, 2007, 2010) and from commentators (Boldyrev and Svetlova, 2016a; Steiner, 2016). On the other hand, it is often considered as the first study demonstrating the relevance of the performativist approach (Muniesa and Callon, 2009: 291), to the extent that most commentators, especially English-speaking ones, consider it the key reference in the field.

The arguments of the authors will be revisited before shedding new light on them: yes, the equations have had an influence on market practices, but they have nevertheless failed to modify important features of financial phenomena, to such an extent that they were partially questioned during the stock market crash of 1987. According to MacKenzie, this event is a reversal: a performative phase is followed by a counter-performative phase – a time for the performative; a time for the opposite movement. It will be shown here that this was not the case, and that the crash was above all a sign of the model's performative incapacity. Some details of the model will be used to identify what is problematic in the MacKenzie and Millo study. The idea of BSM performativity is based on MacKenzie and Millo's finding that a central assumption of the model becomes true as traders use BSM in their valuations: all options on the same underlying asset with the same expiry date and with different strike prices have the same implied volatility. This is a relationship that ceases to exist after 1987, hence the idea of a "counterperformativity": reality ceases to conform to the model. In fact, this reversal is characterised by the appearance of what has been called the *smile* of volatility: options corresponding to greater variations are exchanged at higher prices, which denotes a great fear of extreme variations. However, the defence here will be that the argument is based on a misunderstanding of the implied volatility status, which, far from indicating the level of actual volatility, is above all an indicator of how agents view risk. In other words, it indicates a polarisation on a level of volatility, and not the actual volatility of the underlying assets. MacKenzie and Millo's reasoning assumes that as long as the set of individual representations follows this particular representation of price variations, then financial phenomena will conform to this representation. But this is true only if we assume the self-realisation of the representation in question. What is far from obvious is that it is not enough that the entire population of options traders follow a convention of representation for the social reality to conform to it. To take this line of thought will require going deeper into the theoretical foundations of the BSM model, and mainly from the theory of constancy of implied volatility *vis-à-vis* the strike price. Such an assumption is based on a Brownian conception of stock market movements: an exponential Brownian motion. Briefly, the Brownian representation of risk falls squarely within both the hypotheses of an efficient market and rational expectations: markets are efficient and expectations rational, prices are de-correlated and variations can only stem from the appearance of new information. They therefore reflect the fundamentals of the economy, which justifies a relatively calm vision of price movements, embodied in the log-normal law, since we consider that the events of the real economy also fall under this probabilistic law. If the implied volatility–strike price relationship assumed by BSM corresponds directly to the idea that the price changes follow a normal distribution, then the integration of the smile from 1987 indicates a probability distribution that accepts more extreme events. We then speak of leptokurticity: more peaked and fat-tailed (the Greek *kurtosis* meaning curvature, *lepto* meaning thin). The question is therefore the following: does the integration of leptokurticity indicate that the financial phenomenon has changed, or that the BSM model has never shaped the social world, in the sense that it has never self-realised on this point? I tend to favour the second proposition. There are two reasons for this. First, it is has been well documented that implied volatility is only a poor indicator of real volatility. There is therefore no reason to go from adopting a representation of the risk included in BSM to a self-realisation of this representation. Secondly, a vast literature has devoted itself to the theorisation of financial bubbles in the presence of rational expectations, an assumption which we will see often justifies the use of Brownian motion. A Brownian representation does not dispose of the existence of the internal dynamics of the markets leading to a large price motion and therefore to leptokurticity. This is a phenomenon which has always existed, even when MacKenzie and Millo evoke the so-called performativity of the financial world by BSM.

Financial phenomena and performativity: the Black-Scholes-Merton case

This first section reviews the main features of MacKenzie and Millo's work. As seen previously, the authors envisage a chronology of events in two stages. In the first period, the option pricing model dramatically changed the financial markets. By using it in their arbitrage activities, traders tended to bring reality closer to the theoretical. These arbitrages were then based on a new coordination benchmark, namely the options' implied volatility, calculated from BSM. MacKenzie and Millo's reasoning is entirely based on this fact: implied volatility tends to respect a central hypothesis of the model, that all options on the same underlying asset, with the same expiry date, must have the same implied volatility, regardless of the option strike price. This is what is observed in the first historical phase. The second period began with the crash of 1987. From this point on, we observe that the stable relationship between implied volatility and the strike price ended. MacKenzie and Millo conclude that it resulted in a movement of "counterperformativity".

Redefining options, performing financial markets

The MacKenzie and Millo inquiry looks back from a theoretical and a practical point of view at a founding event in the financial markets. It is devoted to the development by Fisher Black and Myron Scholes (1973) then Robert Merton (1973) of an option pricing model and its application on the Chicago Board Options Exchange (CBOE), one of the leading modern derivatives markets. This model was initially widely disseminated within the trading community before being integrated into the technical market device: in 1986, the BSM equations were implemented in the automated quotation software, Autoquot, of the CBOE. This story is an important milestone in financial engineering, so much so that in 1997 Robert Merton and Myron Scholes (Fisher Black deceased in 1995) received the Swedish National Bank's Prize in Economic Science in Memory of Alfred Nobel. The importance of this work comes essentially from the fact that the scope of the famous Black-Scholes-Merton equations go far beyond the simple options framework. Indeed, following their dazzling success, the equations were implemented in order to generate the prices of the underlying assets compatible with the prices of the options. Thus, BSM came to incorporate the first general theoretical framework of market finance. MacKenzie and Millo (2003: 9) therefore question the unprecedented success of the equations:

> Why was option pricing theory so successful empirically? Was it because of the discovery of preexisting price regularities? Or did the theory succeed empirically because participants used it to set option prices? Did it make itself true? As will be seen, the answer is broadly compatible with Callon's analysis.

The authors explain this success by the massive use of the BSM model in the actual evaluation of the "normal" prices of the options, causing real prices to conform to the theoretical prices.

Let us start by describing the model in question briefly. The core idea of the model is that if a reduced number of hypotheses are respected, option prices will depend only on the underlying stock price and the variables that are taken as constant. As a consequence, it is possible to generate a hedged position, consisting of a long position in stock and a short position in options whose value will depend not only on time, but also on the values of known constants. These hypotheses are:

a The short-term interest rate is known and constant.
b The stock price follows an exponential Brownian motion.
c The stock pays no dividends.
d There are no transaction costs.
e It is possible to borrow any fraction of the price of a security to buy or to hold at the short-term interest rate.
f There are no penalties to short selling.

If conditions a–f are fulfilled, it is possible to build and to continuously adjust a portfolio containing underlying stocks and government bonds (or cash) which replicates the payoffs of the option. So the payoffs options (including the option price) and those of the portfolio should be the same, since arbitragers will buy the cheaper options and sell the more expensive ones. The history of this revolutionary reasoning has been discussed in-depth by historians of finance (Bernstein, 1995, 2005, 2007; MacKenzie, 2006b; Mehrling, 2012). Option pricing theory is also the result of several controversies related to general pricing theory since Markowitz (1952) and then Modigliani and Miller (1958) linked together expected gain and risk. This led to the so-called Capital Asset Pricing Model (CAPM) (Treynor, 1962; Sharpe, 1964; Lintner, 1965; Mossin, 1966), based on the seminal contribution of James Tobin (1958) on which Black and Scholes drew to propose their first model.[2] Merton disrupted these developments when he proposed the ideas of portfolio dynamic and continuous arbitrage (including Ito's lemma) which constitute the grounds for the BSM model. This major development culminated in the famous BSM equations, where V is the price of the option, S is the price of the stock, t is the time, σ is the volatility of the stock, and r is the riskless rate of interest:

$$\frac{\partial V}{\partial t} + \frac{1}{2}\sigma^2 S^2 \frac{\partial^2 V}{\partial S^2} + rS\frac{\partial V}{\partial S} - rV = 0$$

MacKenzie and Millo (2003: 9) explain the central place of BSM in modern finance as due to a "performative" mechanism *à la* Callon rather than its descriptive accuracy. There is no clear definition of the notion of performativity in MacKenzie and Millo's first article. However, MacKenzie (2006b: 31, 2007: 55) distinguishes two kinds of performativity:

> *generic performativity:* "an aspect of economics (a theory, model, concept, procedure, data-set, etc.) is used by participants in economic processes, regulators, etc.";
>
> *effective performativity:* "the practical use of an aspect of economics has an effect on economic processes".

MacKenzie considers generic performativity as not in itself of particular interest, and sees only effective performativity as inspiring. He also defined two subclasses of effective performativity:

> *Barnesian performativity:* "practical use of an aspect of economics makes economic processes more like their depiction by economics";
>
> *counterperformativity:* "practical use of an aspect of economics makes economic processes less like their depiction by economics".

The Barnesian definition of performativity evokes the self-fulfilling mechanism described by Robert K. Merton (1948: 195): "The self-fulfilling prophecy is, in the beginning, a *false* definition of the situation evoking a new behaviour which makes the originally false conception come true." Economics shapes the economy in its own image when agents use it as a benchmark to choose how to behave, which makes the economic theory at least partly true – that is, when economics become self-fulfilling. As mentioned in Chapter 5, Merton does not provide a clear definition of "truth". By true, I mean the Popperian understanding of "not falsified by facts" (or "corroborated"). This mechanism, which is the heart of MacKenzie and Millo's study of the performativity of the BSM model, moves away from the Callonian definition of performativity. Indeed, Callon clearly defends a generic definition of performativity, and explicitly rejects the concept of a self-fulfilling prophecy (Callon, 2007: 321).

Let us summarise MacKenzie and Millo's argumentation. With the exception of volatility, all the parameters of the BSM model are easily observable. So the use of BSM is particularly straightforward since traders calculate the volatility of the underlying asset price which returns a theoretical value fitting the current market price of the option. This so-called implied volatility in the BSM model is supposed to be the same for all the options for the same underlying asset with the same expiry date and different strike prices. The graph of implied volatility against strike prices is a flat line (Figure 7.1).

This linear relation (the "flat line") became a central element for MacKenzie and Millo: spreaders used this "normal" level of implied volatility as a way of profiting from price discrepancies. They used it to identify relatively cheap options to buy (A in Figure 7.1) and relatively expensive options to sell (B).

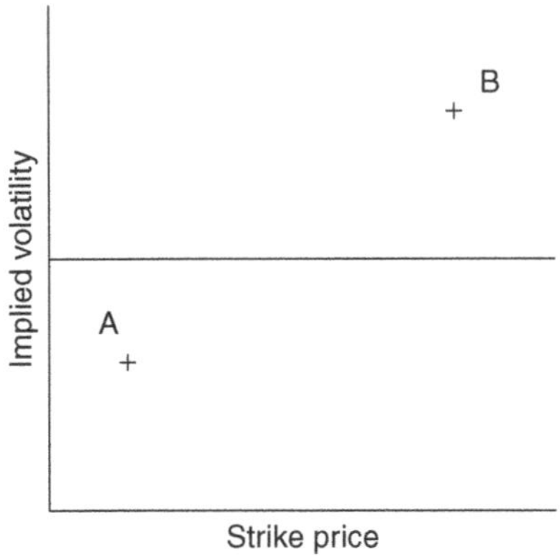

Figure 7.1 The flat line of implied volatility
Source: MacKenzie (2007: 68).

If implied volatility of A is under the mean implied volatility, A is undervalued since there is a positive correlation between implied volatility and the price of options. For MacKenzie and Millo, this process is a typical case of performativity: the theory brings a new definition of the option by creating a new tool to apprehend reality, namely implied volatility: "Gradually, what was being bought and sold in an options market was reconceptualized: it was the Black-Scholes-Merton model's key parameter, volatility. If stock volatility increased, options became more valuable; if it decreased, they became cheaper" (MacKenzie and Millo, 2003: 125). As discussed in the previous chapter, the theory identifies two types of options: a normal and an overvalued or undervalued type. Thus, the theory of financial markets related to the BSM equations responds well to our first criterion, that of empiricity.

At this stage, this is a generic case of performativity. However, such trading is a central mechanism in the way BSM performs financial phenomena within a Barnesian perspective: traders effectively flatten the line. Thus, self-fulfilling through the spread on volatility levels is a central element in MacKenzie and Millo's thesis of performativity. It is important to stress that BSM explicitly provides what Mehrling (2012: 132) views as a normative theory of rational option pricing. This point is particularly clear in the case of Fischer Black. In 1972, at the Center for Research in Security Prices Seminar, Black showed his hostility to the creation of the CBOE, to the point of comparing it to a gambling house. However, once it was established, he did what he could to ensure that the market reached an efficient equilibrium. For instance, he sold printed tables based on the BSM model which allowed a quick evaluation of the implied volatility of options in order to facilitate efficient trade-offs. If market investors exploited the profit opportunities correctly using the BSM price-sheets, the market reached the efficiency indicated by the BSM model. Note that Black had coauthored with Jack Treynor guidelines for security analysts (Treynor and Black, 1973). However, Black, MacKenzie and Millo were in agreement that the BSM model had been adopted because it implied profit opportunities for traders. The only point of difference was that Black saw the BSM model as channelling effective laws of the system (opportunities come from a trend away from the real values), while MacKenzie and Millo emphasised a self-fulfilling process: "The suggestion that the Black-Scholes-Merton model may have been performative in the Barnesian sense is the conjecture that the use of the model was part of the chain by which its referential character – its fit to "reality" – was secured" (MacKenzie, 2007: 67). Of course, MacKenzie and Millo's argument goes beyond the simple mechanism of self-fulfilment. Performativity necessitates a few felicitous conditions to be respected. First, options were considered "unknown beasts" by most of the trader community, traumatised by the 1929 Wall Street crash. Secondly, BSM was seen as a fair way to trade. MacKenzie and Millo provide a fascinating description of the social pressure against the use of Black's sheets:

> [Traders] would laugh at you and try to intimidate you out of the pit, saying, "You're not a man if you're using those theoretical value sheets." They'd take your sheets and throw them down on the floor and say, "Be a man. Trade like a man. . . . You shouldn't be here. You're not a trader. You can't trade without those."
>
> (Hull interview, in MacKenzie and Millo, 2003: 124)

It took some time for the idea of "secure" and "rational" hedging to penetrate the ethos of the trading floor. This moral obstacle nevertheless jumped at the chance of a stock market crisis. In 1978, a sudden rise in stock prices led to significant losses. This event was decisive in the valuation and acceptance of hedging activity as well as the "rational" management of assets:

> Gradually, the CBOE market makers began to develop a distinct self-identity in which careful pricing and hedging were important. On the agricultural exchanges, the stereotypical belief was "I got the trade 'cos I'm faster than you, buddy." In New York, it was "I got the trade 'cos I'm here," because I am the designated specialist. In the CBOE's growing self perception, it was "I got the trade 'cos I thought it out."
>
> (Doherty interview, in MacKenzie and Millo, 2003: 124–125)

Thirdly, market regulation needed to correspond with the BSM hypothesis. For instance, Regulation T, which governs the extension of credit by security brokers and dealers by holding a margin requirement for stock purchases, became less restrictive. So the *e.* condition became a reality. The felicity condition is an important and necessary but not a sufficient condition for the self-fulfilling mechanism emphasised above.[3] When felicity conditions are held in the absence of a self-fulfilling motion, MacKenzie calls this *generic performativity*, which is of little interest. BSM changed the world by changing the way people looked at it. This is an important point which historians of economic thought have noted (Mehrling, 2012; Bernstein, 2005). MacKenzie and Millo tried to go beyond this by exploring how the changing perspective on the options market changed the market itself.

The financial crash and counterperformativity

In the October 1987 stock market crash, the BSM model failed in fitting the social world to economic theory. On Black Monday, the Dow Jones lost 22.8% of its value, and S&P 500 lost 20%. Jackwerth and Rubinstein (1996: 1612) demonstrated that under the log-normal hypothesis, such deviation corresponds to the probability 10^{-160}, "which is virtually impossible". The October 1987 event led the flat line to assume the famous volatility skew: volatility decreases as the strike price increases. The question emerging from this fact is simple: why did the BSM model seem to fulfil all of the conditions of performativity only until the 1987 crash? We have discussed how the BSM model provides a representation of a specific good, the option, and allows identification of different options regarding a normal volatility. However, is this collective convention equivalent to the move in real prices? If the BSM model was self-fulfilling, our answer would be positive: the fact that people adhere to the BSM model implies that it becomes true. Before 1987, the observed implied volatility followed the BSM model: the flat line on the graph of implied volatility against the strike prices was observable. However, the October 1987 crash changed this: the graph of implied volatility against strike prices now tends to slope downwards. This is the famous *volatility smile*: price options which correspond to large fluctuations (c1 and c2 in Figure 7.2) are traded at a higher price.

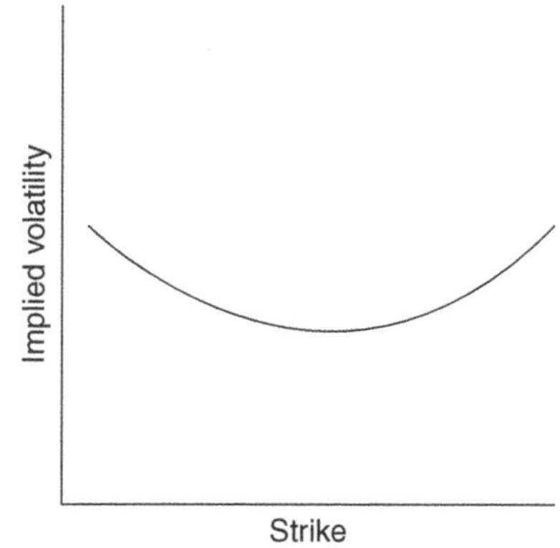

Figure 7.2 The volatility smile

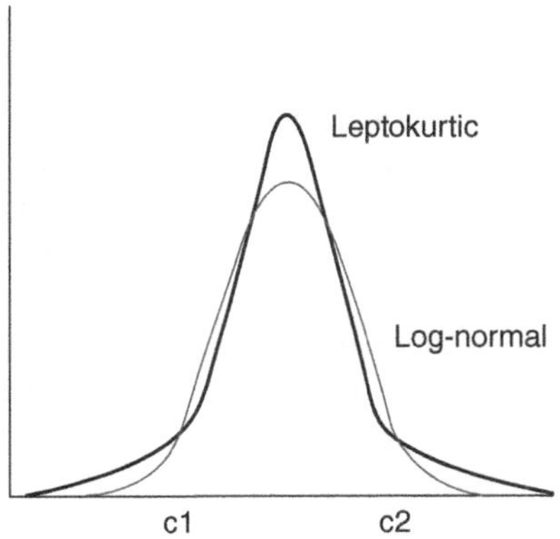

Figure 7.3 Log-normal and leptokurtic distributions

Unlike the BSM probabilistic hypothesis, the smile no longer corresponds to a log-normal distribution which excludes large depreciations and appreciations, but fits with a leptokurtic distribution function: more peaked and fat-tailed (Figure 7.3).

For MacKenzie (2006b, 2007),[4] the existence of the smile since 1987 reveals the historical contingency of performativity of the BSM model: price patterns followed the model up to 1987. Then an external shock changed this convergence world/model towards the smile: one time for performativity, one time for "counterperformativity". This is the point where we disagree. The fact that implied volatility fits the BSM model (that is, the fact that investors coordinate their representations on the flat line) teaches us nothing about the real world except that a subjective vision of the world (BSM's flat line) fits with another subjective vision (implied volatility) without any real outcome. Indeed, the implied volatility by construction is a level of volatility compatible with actual option prices given the BSM assumptions. Financial phenomena which are actual stock volatility have never been implied in the reasoning. The 1987 crash might indicate that financial phenomena can resist the theory precisely because the risk representation involved in BSM is not self-fulfilling. Arguing for the *performativity twist* which took place in 1987 from performativity to counterperformativity is to overlook the fact that the risk representation of the BSM model can be contradicted by the objectivity of the financial phenomena: the price motions. It has been well documented that implied volatility does not track actual volatility. Fortune (1996) shows that implied volatility is not an optimal forecast of actual volatility in the sense that implied volatility is a biased forecast of actual volatility. Instead of a performativity twist (performativity and counterperformativity), it could be suggested that the BSM model never fits with real price fluctuations, and that traders realised this in 1987. The smile is the result of this awareness. For the sake of completeness, MacKenzie and Millo emphasised option market overlearning: to explain observed index option prices requires every four years adding an artificial crash to the 1987 observed stock prices series. The authors explain this as due to the traumatic character of the 1987 crash. The smile is reduced to a kind of collective trauma. Nevertheless, to say that a collective representation is overlearning is not to say that the previous representation (the flat line) was correct. Although the smile is over-pronounced, it might be a better representation than the simple flat line.

We have shown that the flat line was linked directly to the log-normal distribution. In the next section, we will explore this representation of price fluctuations in order to understand what is supposed to be "performative" in MacKenzie and Millo's work, and why it is not.

*

For the moment, we have mainly emphasised the fact that implied volatility is primarily linked to a representation of risk, and does not tell us much about financial phenomena. As such, the reversal which MacKenzie is talking about can be interpreted as a direct confrontation between a set of false representations and a financial phenomenon (price variations). There is still a need to characterise the gap between these two entities. We have seen that the flat line hypothesis was directly linked to log-normal distribution. The section "Leptokurticity as a limit for performativity" will be devoted to the theoretical foundations of these representations of price variations. The history of thought is important here to understand the interweaving between this representation and its theoretical justifications, namely the ideas of random walks, informational efficiency and rational expectations. These concepts structure a calm vision of price variations, a view consistent with log-normal distribution. However, many works have questioned this vision: the leptokurticity which the traders become aware of following the 1987 event is a normal state of price variations – a state of bubbles and reversals, which, as we know today with the theorisation of rational bubbles, is not incompatible with the idea of rational expectations. Whereas in the reconstruction of MacKenzie and Millo the BSM model is victim of a reversal of reality, I will defend the idea that it was simply false and non-performative, not self-fulfilling: there was indeed mimetic polarisation on the use of BSM, but not self-realisation, so that the model was partly amended by the introduction of the smile.

Stochastic norm and resistance of financial phenomena

We are challenging that in the case of price fluctuations, representation and phenomena should not be confused. The French sociologist Éric Brian is clear on this point: randomness and uncertainty come before the calculation, not after (Brian, 2009: 5). The BSM model is supported by such an act of representation when it assumes that the stock price follows an exponential Brownian motion. The Brownian representation of risk consists of two intertwined sets of ideas. First, that the increments of the random variable of the continuous random walk are independent and identically distributed (i.i.d.). A stochastic process with independent and stationary increments defines a Lévy process, named after the French mathematician Paul Lévy. Such a stochastic process is characterised as memoryless: a Markov first-order chain. This implies that the expected speculative gain is equal to zero: the best forecast of tomorrow's course is today's course. In addition to the characterisation of the law of probability as a log-normal law, this hypothesis reduces the continuous random walk to a particular case of the Lévy process: a Brownian motion.

These sets of ideas are intertwined in the sense that defining the market as a memoryless process leaves aside the risk of financial self-maintaining booms or crashes – a risk that is incompatible with the normal distribution which is characterised by the idea of some small variations around the mean. This twofold conception can be traced back to the work of Jules Regnault and his 1863 work *Calcul des chances et philosophie de la Bourse*, in which he compares speculation to fair gambling where each bet is independent of any other: as in a coin-toss, there is no way systematically to beat the market in making bets on short-term movements in prices since the probabilities of upward and downward movements are equal. In other words: there is no benefit in knowing past prices. Regnault also maintains that traders' errors follow a normal distribution. This representation found support in Louis Bachelier's seminal article "Théorie de la speculation" (1900). If S_t is the stock course:

$$E_t\left(S_{t+1} - S_t\right) = 0 \text{ and } E_t\left(S_{t+1}\right) = S_t$$

This probabilistic schema can be extended to the entire market process. The Brownian representation of the risk is constitutive of the BSM model. The flat line of volatility corresponds to the implied log-normal probability distribution which was a common frame for options traders before 1987.[5]

Random walk, market efficiency and rational expectations

Karl Pearson (1905) first used the term "random walk". This notion, as we have seen, implies that past values are of no utility for predicting future values. The early history of finance can be reduced to disagreement over whether market courses follow random walks (Stabile, 2005; Walter, 2013). While advocates of technical analysis, following the so-called Dow Theory (for instance, Schabacker, 1930), defend the existence of market trends, Alfred Cowles III tried to show empirically that market forecasters cannot forecast anything (Cowles, 1933). This last position complies with the idea of a random walk. Following the seminal contribution from Working (1934), Maurice Kendall (1953: 18) tested this hypothesis on stock markets in 1953 and concluded that:

> Such serial correlation as is present in these series is so weak as to dispose at once of any possibility of being able to use them for prediction. The Stock Exchange, it would appear, has a memory lasting less than a week.

Although Brownian motion was first proposed (after Bachelier) by Osborne (1959), it was not until the mid-1960s that the concept was given a theoretically base. In the different "old" approaches, the absence of correlation of successive prices is explained by the idea that investors' decisions concerning a stock are independent from one transaction to another, which seems scarcely plausible to the modern reader. Roberts (1959) was one of the first to indicate the lack of theoretical foundation for the random character of stock price fluctuations (Jovanovic, 2008, 2009). He proposed the famous arbitrage proof argument, which same argument was used by Samuelson to provide the missing theoretical justifications for Kendall's observations of random processes:

> Perhaps it is a lucky accident, a boon from Mother Nature so to speak, that so many actual price time series do behave like uncorrelated or quasi-random walks. [. . .] Perhaps it is true that prices depend on a summation of so many small and somewhat independent sources of variation that the result is like a random walk. But there is no necessity for this. And the fact, if it is one, is not particularly related to perfect competition or market anticipations. [. . .] I shall deduce a fairly sweeping theorem in which next-period's price differences are shown to be uncorrelated with (if not completely independent of) previous period's price differences.
>
> (Samuelson, 1965b: 42)

Samuelson (1965a, 1965b, 1973) shows how, under certain conditions, new information unpredictability leads stock prices to follow a stochastic process sequence where expectation of the next value in the sequence is equal to the present observed value given knowledge of all previous values: this is a *martingale*.[6] Samuelson linked randomness, anticipation and speculation closely using the martingale model: traders' arbitrages would balance out prices around a value corresponding to the present stock of information. The title of his paper is explicit – "Proof that properly anticipated prices fluctuate randomly" – and his conclusion was that: "If one could be sure that a price will rise, it would have already risen" (Samuelson, 1965b: 41).

This is a major twist in economic thinking. Economists were rather sceptical about the idea of a random walk since they were committed to the idea of a correlation between stock prices and expected future returns.[7] LeRoy (1989: 1588) explains it thus:

> If stock prices had nothing to do with preferences and technology, what about the prices of the machines that firms use? What about the wheat the farmer produces and the baker uses, but which is also traded on organized exchanges just like stock? Where does the Marshall's *Principles* stop and the random walk start?

Samuelson links randomness, information about fundamentals, and capital market efficiency since it is precisely the exploitation of the information concerning the fundamentals which justifies the idea of randomness.[8] This reasoning was founded theoretically on Fama's (1965c, 1970) efficient market hypothesis: a market is said to be efficient if it fully reflects the available information (Φ_t) As a consequence, the martingale model constitutes a possible test for the efficient market theory:[9] expected profit has to be null.

Entanglement between discounted cash flow and efficiency is closely ingrained in the notion of rational expectations. In Fama (1965c), there are some "superior chart readers" able to approximate the intrinsic value. In his 1970 paper, all available information Φ_t is costlessly available to all market participants, and all these participants are agreed on "the implications of current information for the current price and distribution of future prices of each security" (Fama, 1970: 387). Of course, Fama did not use the rational expectation hypothesis directly, although Muth's famous paper had been published in 1961. Nevertheless, in Fama's definition of market efficiency, the idea that agents know the relevant system describing the economy is clear. Moreover, Lucas (1978) considers that expectations are rational if prices fully reflect all the available information. If the asset price respects this characteristic, it is said to be efficient – it efficiently integrates all the pertinent information in the price. If expectations are rational and the market is efficient, the best forecast of tomorrow's price is today's price, because it reflects all of the information:

$$\mathrm{E}\left(S_{t+1} \mid \Phi_t\right) = S_t$$

In Fama's view, efficiency[10] and randomness justify one another: if markets are efficient, then it follows that future returns are unpredictable, and if we observe that future returns are unpredictable, then this proves that markets are efficient.[11]

While there is a clear distinction to make between continuous random walks and martingales (LeRoy, 1989), we also draw close links between efficiency and randomness in general which justifies the use of the Lévy process in financial formalisation. This is the case of the BSM model.

The normal representation of asset fluctuations

The next major step is to associate a probabilistic law with the stochastic process. We have shown that the essence of the Brownian motion is the normal law. The story of the normal law has been studied widely (Bernstein, 1995). This representation generally does not take account of extreme events, in the sense that it recognises only small, calculable variations around a central mean. Thus, Benoît Mandelbrot (1963) suggested replacing it with a Lévy α-stable distribution with infinite marginal variance – that is, some strongly leptokurtic distributions. In the French newspaper *Le Monde*, Mandelbrot declared:

> Individuals use an inapplicable theory – the Merton, Black and Scholes one, which comes from Bachelier's 1900 works – which made no sense. I claimed it since 1960. This theory does not take into consideration prices' instantaneous variations, which is biasing the means. This theory argues that it leads to the taking of tiny risks, which is wrong. It was unavoidable that terrible events would happen. Financial catastrophes are often due to evident phenomena experts did not want to see. They swept the bomb under the carpet!
>
> (Mandelbrot, 2009; our translation)

This claim is reminiscent of Stephen Stigler's (1990: 3) comment in his history of statistics:

> Much of the material presented in modern courses on statistical methods for social sciences is superficially similar to texts available by 1830, and yet the adoption of these methods for the different purposes of the social scientists were so glacially slow that it amounted to a reinvention.

So now we have a vision of what is supposed to be performative in the BSM model's flat line hypothesis: an efficient market, memoryless, without risk of a large crash. It justifies the use of the normal distribution, precisely what was challenged in 1987 with the introduction of the volatility smile.

Leptokurticity as a limit for performativity

The performative power of the BSM option pricing model ran up against a strong counter-phenomenon: asset prices did not follow the standard representation emphasised in the previous section. The nub of my argumentation is that the quoted market prices exhibited a leptokurtic distribution long before the introduction of the BSM model on the CBOE. Hence, the BSM model never performed (in a Barnesian understanding) the economy which led to the emergence of the volatility smile in 1987. This is the way that MacKenzie and Millo use the concept of performativity. They consider the rapprochement between theoretical and empirical implied volatility as a case of Barnesian performativity, which refers to the fact that the practical use of an aspect of economics makes economic processes more like their depiction by economics. To them, the "aspect of economics" is the BSM model, and implied volatility is the "economic process", which becomes more like its depiction by the BSM model. My claim is that to understand the "counter-performativity" of 1987, it is necessary to go beyond implied volatility when considering volatility, since I consider the flat line of volatility to be an aspect of economics, and stock volatility the economic process. Leptokurticity was recorded long before 1987 (Walter, 2013: 279–285). The French sociologist Éric Brian (2009) pointed to the constant gap between the actual and the log-normal distribution from 1830 to 2009. That is sufficient reason to doubt the plasticity of financial phenomena in the story of MacKenzie and Millo. What we want to show is that leptokurticity is linked closely to the nature of financial phenomena. It is difficult to change Nature.

Explaining leptokurticity: nuancing performativity

Beyond the question of price fluctuations – that is, about the proper repartitioning function, and to say that the Brownian representation of the risk is hardly self-fulfilling – it is necessary to spell out the origins of leptokurticity and to prove that a normal representation is not sufficient to create a normal world. The relevance of the log-normal distribution rests mainly on the central limit theorem: the sum of a large number of independent variables converge toward a normal distribution. This shows the existence of a finite variance. Yet Paul Lévy proposed that the normal distribution was a special case of a larger family of what he called α-stable distributions which gather all laws with downward tails (MacKenzie, 2006b; Sent, 1999). The main characteristic of these distributions is stability. This is *in fine* a generalisation of the central limit theorem: the sum of the variables exhibiting distributions with decreasing tails approaches a stable distribution controlled by four parameters: stability (α), skewness (β), scale (c) and mean.

Two kinds of stable laws can be identified according to their variance calculability. On the one hand, the Laplace-Gauss distribution ($\alpha = 2$) shows a finite and calculable variance. On the other hand, there are some stable distributions with infinite variance ($0<\alpha<2$), such as the Cauchy law ($\alpha = 1$) and the Lévy law ($\alpha = 1/2$). Yet, the latter exhibit a distribution which corresponds much more closely to the leptokurtic course fluctuations observable throughout history. Christian Walter (2010) observed that the market remains quiet except when it moves a lot.

There are two kinds of explanations for leptokurticity: exogenous and endogenous. Let us begin with the exogenous ones. First, it is possible to assign responsibility for market leptokurticity to the non-normality of exogenous phenomena. This is what Mandelbrot (1973) describes as the *Noah Effect*, when a large amount of information provokes some large isolated price movements, and Mirowski (1989) describes as the *Joseph Effect*, when the prices see-saw. The latter effect focuses on how agents interpret the information flow. As a result, a small piece of information such as a tender offer announcement could have a great effect. Nevertheless, it has been shown that considering one specific piece of information as the primary cause of a huge price fluctuation most of the time is an *ex-post* reconstruction. Shortly after the 1987 crash, Robert Shiller (2000: 121) questioned some investors about the impact on their behaviours of ten pieces of information which appeared in the press in the days preceding the crash. There were an American strike targeting an Iranian oilfield and a massive sale of shares held by the stock market guru Robert Prechter. The only one which they took note of was the price decreases that occurred immediately before the nineteenth century. However, this information was directly related to the crash. Shiller concludes by underlining the importance of the deviation of investors' attention from certain events. In the case of Black Monday, Shiller gives the example of an article published in the *Wall Street Journal* on that day which compared the Dow Jones charts preceding 1987 and 1929. The article emphasised the verisimilitude of both. Shiller (2000: 94) concludes:

> When the big price declines on the morning of October 19, 1987, began, the archetype that was the 1929 crash encouraged many people to question whether "it" was happening again [. . .]. The mental image of the biggest crash in history possibly happening on that very day had potential to enhance the feedback from initial price declines to later price declines.

Here we should highlight a first mechanism limiting the self-fulfilment of the BSM model's efficient market hypothesis: the conflict of representations. One could argue that if all traders shared the same Brownian representation, there would be no possibility of a crash since no one would take the possibility of hyperinflation or deflation of stocks prices seriously. Nevertheless, there are several concurrent representations in the marketplace. For instance, the way a previous crash might influence investors suggests to me that they will behave *as if* the price will fall. MacKenzie and Millo, in line with several economists, argue that the smile of the implied volatility from 1987 exhibits a shared fear of price shifts among options traders. However, these kinds of fears might have been present before 1987. So there is a dissonance between two conventions (the BSM model on the one hand, the volatility smile on the other) – a dissonance which makes the BSM model unable to perform the financial world. This point reveals the importance of historical contingency. The next section considers endogenous mechanisms leading to leptokurticity.

The main reason why the BSM model was accepted on the CBOE is that investors saw opportunities for profits in trading off against anomalies that seemed to contradict the BSM model. This is how Black envisioned the way the BSM model had to work: the more traders expected to make a profit, the more they used the BSM model, the more the market became efficient, the better the BSM model worked. However, there are some technical reasons which led Brownian motion to be retained as a benchmark despite it being well known from the 1970s that the normal distribution implied in Brownian motion does not describe real security returns (Teichmoeller, 1971; Hagerman, 1978). Merton (1976) was aware of the limits of normal distribution when he updated the BSM model by designing what today is known as the *jump-diffusion model* (following Press, 1967). The two basic elements of this model are Brownian motion (diffusion part) and the Poisson process (the jump part). Merton (1976: 127) assumes that while the "normal vibrations in price" are due to new information about the entire market, the "abnormal vibrations in price" are specific to the firm (uncorrelated to the market). It was shown later that the jump risk is not diversifiable (Jarrow and Rosenfeld, 1984), which makes the central mechanism of the BSM model (riskless hedging) impossible.

For Walter (2013: 328), this impossibility constituted an obstacle to the diffusion of the jump-diffusion model in applied finance. More generally, the loss of the second moment (infinite variance) was synonymous with the loss of all the statistical tools available. When Mandelbrot tried to promote the vision of "wild" randomness (using the Lévy α-stable distribution), he was labelled a doomsayer.[12] Even Fama (1976a: 33–35), who paid great attention to Mandelbrot's propositions, concluded that:

> [T]he cost of rejecting normality for securities returns in favor of non-normal distributions are substantial [. . .] statistical tools for handling data from non-normal [. . .] distributions are primitive relative to the tools that are available to handle data from normal distribution.

Mandelbrot's hypothesis was dropped because in everyone's view it was considered an unruly monster (MacKenzie, 2006a: 105–118) which did not allow statistical and econometric tests. By the end of the 1970s, most references to the Mandelbrot program had disappeared (Mirowski, 1995). Jovanovic and Schinckus (2013a: 339) point to four possible explanations for the resilience of the Gaussian framework: (1) path dependency due to the historical development of financial economics, (2) simplicity (the simple use of mean and variance), (3) the link between normality and equilibrium, and (4) the central-limit theorem.

Rational bubbles and leptokurticity

The kind of framing effect stressed by Shiller might explain a sudden fall in prices. There is an extensive literature on the possibility of bubbles even in the case of rational expectations which is the central justification of market efficiency and Brownian motion. In a context of informational efficiency, the stock price depends on both the fundamental value of the stock (which is the actualisation of future dividends) and a subjective element: the resale price of the stock. If one defines the price by the spread between itself and the fundamental value, the focus is on the subjective part:

$$S_t = \frac{1}{1+x} E_t\left(S_{t+1}\right)$$

This equation is consistent with the efficiency paradigm: there is no way to release a speculative surplus. This is the so-called "no arbitrage" condition. Standard financial theory ignores these speculative parts of the price determination by invoking the transversality condition (which states that the expected stock resale price tends towards zero). In their seminal model, Blanchard and Watson (1984) do not consider this hypothesis. The stock price now is composed of a fundamental value and a speculative bubble, and there is an infinity of prices which respect the no arbitrage condition. Thus, it is possible to achieve endogenous price movements producing bubbles. In conclusion, rational expectations do not necessarily guarantee that the price will fit the fundamental value: there are several self-confirming beliefs that the asset price depends on information which includes variables or parameters that are not part of market fundamentals. Blanchard and Watson (1982: 20) provide a model of such dynamics:

> If bubbles grow for a while and then crash, the innovations in the bubble will tend to be of the same sign while the bubble continues, then reverse signs when a crash occurs. The runs for the bubble innovation will then tend to be longer than for a purely random sequence, making the total number of runs over the sample smaller. Crashes will produce large outliers so that the distribution of innovations will have fat tails (i.e. the distribution will be leptokurtic).

The endogenous dynamics of the price seems to limit the idea that a theory will be self-fulfilling. The fact that some agents' representations correspond to the efficient market hypothesis is not a guarantee that this representation can make the market more efficient. Rational bubble theory proves the possibility of big market shifts. The origin of price variations could be different. Nevertheless, this fact rests on a process which directly calls into question the transversality condition: hyperinflation of stock resale prices. The momentum effect is a perfect example: the empirically observed tendency for rising stocks to rise further, and falling stocks to keep falling (Jegadeesh and Titman, 1993). This observation gave birth to a simple strategy: buying rising stocks and selling falling ones, which enhances the original tendency through a mimetic process, and contests the rational expectations hypothesis.

A market, in essence, is a place for conventional equilibriums, or in other words, mimetic behaviours. If market agents do not consider the fundamental value of a stock, but rather the majority opinion of it, any further information is able to provoke a conventional switch which could lead to a crash. Here, we are in the typical Keynesian beauty contest world (Keynes, 1936 [2013]). In Keynes' beauty contest, agents are led to infinite regressive thinking since they have to choose the model which they think others will also choose. Agents base their decisions on conventions which can collapse suddenly. The foundations of the BSM model do not avoid that kind of process. The expectation of dividends rests also on an endless regression, since nobody can know the future. Here again, a common evaluation of the future is *per se* an intersubjective tacit agreement about the future states of the economy and the way these discount fluxes can be calculated. Beyond this common representation of the future, the rational expectation and market efficiency hypotheses rest on another strong hypothesis: the existence of a fundamental value reflecting the conditions in the market for the underlying asset (an existence that has been long discussed[13]). Yet, like financial markets, real markets depend on the polarisation of goods and capital values (Orléan, 2011). This is a strong argument for the intrinsic strong volatility of the financial market through the volatility of the conventions in the real economy.

So aside from empirical proofs of the leptokurtic nature of the market prices, there is a strong theoretical foundation for suggesting that the BSM model cannot perform stock prices in order to confirm the flat line of implied volatility.

Nuancing performativity

MacKenzie and Millo's history can be challenged about the same point: the BSM model is not really self-fulfilling. First, we could consider the conflict of representations. Of course, if we consider only the argument of performativity in the strict market of options, we cannot help but notice a convergence between the BSM model flat line hypothesis and the actual implied volatility in the period 1976–1987 (Rubinstein, 1985). Options traders shared the same representation through their use of the BSM model as a benchmark. Thus, the implied volatility (which is a subjective level of volatility) came to fit with the flat line. Such a representation excludes the possibility of a violent crash. Nevertheless, in the stock market, any small piece of information is able to produce violent price fluctuations, as described in the *Wall Street Journal* article cited by Shiller. Thus, to say that the linear relation between implied volatility and strike prices is confirmed in the options market is not to imply that the historical volatility corresponds to the log-normal distribution in the stock market. Black Monday contradicts this representation. It is possible also to stress that the performativity thesis overlooks the important role of exogenous information in the stock market. To say that the BSM model can become true if it becomes a coordination convention is to ignore the impact of real markets on financial markets, or to suppose that the BSM model is true in hypothesising a Gaussian economy (without, for instance, earthquakes or tsunamis).

Finally, MacKenzie and Millo seem to accept the BSM model's representation of the world by ignoring the intrinsic financial market fluctuations *à la* Keynes. Even when retaining the rational expectation hypothesis, it is possible theoretically to exhibit the possibility of bubbles and crashes: financial markets are *per se* conventional arenas. This is somewhat reminiscent of how Poincaré urged caution about Bachelier's thesis, applying the natural trait in human nature to a herd like Panurge's sheep.

Thus, leptokurticity can be seen as both an exogenous element and an endogenous dynamic. The so-called volatility smile is not a sudden shift from self-fulfilment to self-destruction, from a log-normal to a leptokurtic world; it is a sudden awareness by the investor of an important characteristic of the financial world: leptokurticity. The hypothesis corresponding to the flat line, the log-normal distribution, never became true. As a consequence, 1987 was a powerful shock for theoretical innovation and brought renewed interest in the parametric use of the BSM model (Jackwerth, 1999) and a rise in econophysics (Jovanovic and Schinckus, 2013a, 2013b).

Fisher Black (1975) was clearly aware of the fact that the BSM model was based on empirically wrong assumptions. Nevertheless, as we have shown above, the objective of the BSM model was not necessarily to describe the world, but to help traders "to understand how change in the underlying assumptions would cause a change in the calculated option price" (Mehrling, 2012: 245). This objective is clear in Black's 1989 article "How to use the holes in Black-Scholes". The smile is clearly a sign of the BSM model's adaptability: practical and easy to use and adapt, the BSM model remains the theoretical foundation of most of the models elaborated after 1987. My claim is that to provide insights into the reasons for the evolutions in the use of the BSM model, the idea of performativity should be inseparable from the idea of counterperformativity, and counterperformativity should be linked closely to the concept of self-fulfilment. There is still work to be done.

Conclusion

This chapter illustrated the way in which the theoretical condition of self-fulfilment, participating in our conventionalist definition of performativity, makes it possible to better understand performativity in different contexts. In this case, it has been shown that one of the founding works of performativist literature lacks a crucial aspect when it does not take this element seriously. Faced with the emergence of a belief to amend the Black-Scholes-Merton model, namely the smile of volatility, MacKenzie and Millo conclude with a reversal of the performative phenomenon: the financial representation phenomenon that supports a particular theory succeeds a phase of "counterperformativity". This way of seeing things helps to preserve the initial idea by assuming a transformation of the financial world. There is, however, another interpretation, largely supported by academic work: the BSM model has simply never performed the world, in that it never self-realised. Black Monday is not a sign of a change in/of social reality following a performative moment, but a sign that reality has never conformed to the model. It is clear that the elements of the financial phenomenon have forced an amendment of the standard Gaussian representation.

Notes

1 An earlier version of this chapter was published in *Journal of the History of Economic Thought* (Brisset, 2017a).
2 Black and Scholes participated actively in the development of the CAPM (Black et al., 1972).
3 The idea that Regulation T places an important legal limitation on the volume of corrective margin switching, which investors can generate, was at the heart of the David Durand's critique of the realisticness of the model of Modigliani and Miller (Durand, 1959).
4 The second bias we observe is a volatility skew on the left. This characteristic is linked to an implicit distribution off-centre on the left. For Jackwerth and Rubinstein (1996), this discrepancy is clearly the result of greater risk aversion since the crash of 1987: decreases are more likely than extreme rises in the prices of the underlying assets.

5 The history of the normative foundations of probabilities exhibits an interesting imbrication between the fair and the rational. While the criterion of fairness can be seen as the result of study of games (the famous problem of points set by Pascal), the criterion of rationality seems to be used in gambling (for example, Pascal's Wager).
6 Similar results are presented in Mandelbrot (1966).
7 The correlations between market prices and what might be called "intrinsic value" were among the principal items of theoretical finance long before Samuelson and Fama. For a historical perspective, see Stabile (2005).
8 On the link between the near-randomness of price changes and the economic fundamentals within the efficient market hypothesis, see Delcey (2017).
9 Although Samuelson and Fama came to similar conclusions, their positions towards the market were different. While Fama does not hide his faith in free markets, Samuelson (1965b: 48) claims: "One should not read too much into the established theorem. It does not prove that actual competitive markets work well. It does not say that speculation is a good thing or that randomness of price changes would be a good thing. It does not prove that anyone who makes money in speculation is ipso facto deserving of the gain or even that he has accomplished something good for society or for anyone but himself. All or none of these may be true, but that would require a different investigation." See Jovanovic (2008).
10 The evolution of the definition of efficiency is a separate topic. Recall that Fama provides three definitions. In Fama (1965c), he defines an efficient market as one where prices are the best estimates of intrinsic values given all the available information. The third definition (Fama, 1976b) introduces the notion of rational expectations (the agents know the model and the values of the parameters). LeRoy (1976, 1989) points to the tautological nature of Fama's 1970 definition of efficiency (see also Fama, 1976a). After Fama, Jensen (1978) proposed his own definition: a market is said to be efficient if it is impossible to beat the market by investing in a portfolio based on available information. There are numerous other definitions (Beaver, 1981; Malkiel, 1989; Long, 1990). An important tipping point in the history of this notion was the seminal work of Harrison and Kreps (1979) and Harrison and Pliska (1981), who linked no-arbitrage theory and equivalent martingale measures closely.
11 Samuelson (1973) clearly nuanced this link between randomness and efficiency by showing that randomness is not incompatible with the existence of a set of investors who can systematically do better than others. On the debate about the link between efficiency and randomness, see Jovanovic (2009).
12 "Mandelbrot, like Prime Minister Winston Churchill before him, promises us not utopia but blood, sweat, toil, and tears. If he was right, almost all of our statistical tools are obsolete – least squares, spectral analysis, workable maximum likelihood solutions, all our established sample theory, closed distribution functions. Almost without exception, prior econometric work would be meaningless. Surely, before consigning centuries of work to the trash pile, we should seek some assurance that our work is truly useless" (Cootner, 1964: 337).
13 "We must recognize, however, that intrinsic value is an elusive concept. In general terms, it is understood to be that value which is justified by the facts [...]. But it is a great mistake to imagine that intrinsic value is as definite and determinable as market price" (Graham and Dodd, 1934: 17).

8 A conventional limit to performativity

The example of organ trade

> The only gift is a portion of thyself.
>
> (Ralph Waldo Emerson, *Gifts: An Essay*)

This chapter focuses on social conventions' pressure on the performative process. To perform and then to become a convention itself, a theory must be compatible with a set of conventions in place. This is an element we have already encountered during the examination of performativity scenes in the previous two chapters. Both the implementation of nudging policies and the use of the Black-Scholes-Merton equations revealed the importance of the normative elements: to accept (or to ensure public acceptance of) a new mode of governmentality on the one hand, and to admit the use of BSM calculation sheets on the other. In accordance with our conventionalist approach, this type of limit to the performativity of a theory depends on the compatibility between the classifications carried by the performed theory and those of the social world (we discussed frame: see Chapter 4). As we saw in the first part of this book, the reduction of the performativist problematic to devices prevents apprehension of the influence of the social on the performative process.

We will study here the case of the performativity of theoretical markets in the context of organ trade.[1] The establishment of a market for inter-vivo organs has from the outset given rise to strong criticism (Radcliffe-Richards et al., 1998). From a purely economic point of view, the prohibition of organ trade appears for many to be inefficient. In itself, the market solution to the problem of the distribution of organs between demanders and suppliers is justified by economists in a generic way: as in any market, and in line with the welfare economics, decentralised exchange is supposed to lead to a situation of maximising social welfare. This is what Kaserman and Barnett (1991), as well as Becker and Elìas (2007), argue. The history of organ commerce is, in the broad sense (beyond market exchange), instructive on this point (see the section "Transplantation and organ commerce"). The principle of transplantation has required a classification of the organ among legally transferable objects (objectivation). This point has in the past struck (and continues to conflict with) the way of formulating the body in systems of representation: the body as a representative of a deceased person as part of post-mortem removal, the body as support for the person in a general setting. The objectivation of the organ required, on a medical level, a redefinition of death as encephalic death, and on a legal level, that we frame social commerce in organs in the generic sense of the term. In France, the Caillavet law regulates post-mortem donation by the principle of presumed consent, and organ donation between living beings is strictly limited to the restricted family circle. This objectivation has not been a smooth process, and some devices still pose major problems. It is on this undermined ground that economists take up the question of the establishment of markets (see the section "Performativity and the organ market"). The organ is a thing. It is now a question of transforming it into a market thing. Merchandising is largely forbidden today by way of two types of argument: a technical argument (the market is inefficient within the framework of the organ) and a moral argument (the market implies a relationship of domination between the donor and the demander). Both aspects seem to have a common cause, a socially accepted way of considering organs as non-market objects: organs are not commodities, they cannot be managed by the market (see the section "Conventional incompatibility"). This is a social convention in the sense that it has been defined: a mode of classification orienting the agents on a particular coordination strategy, namely focusing on non-commercial trade. We will discuss, as in Chapter 4, social earmarking in the sense of Zelizer. By classifying the organ as a commodity, economic theories damage social representations (classifications) in such a way that, first, organ trade is prohibited by law, and secondly, the establishment of a market for the organs does not guarantee that the actors participate in this market (hence the problem of efficiency). In both cases, it is the inappropriate aspect of the market exchange which poses a problem: it is forbidden collectively in the first case, and one decides individually not to use it in the second. Hence performativity fails. We will see that the rejection of commodification has had the effect of forcing economists to think of alternative matching modes to the market. The theoretical tools developed by the Nobel Prize winner Alvin Roth, whose use and performativity result precisely from the fact that they carry representations compatible with the way the organ is socially envisaged, will be examined in particular.

Transplantation and organ commerce

Organ transplant is one of the major medical revolutions of the twentieth century. Although it affects a large number of organs today (heart, lung, liver, pancreas), renal transplant is the emblem of this practice because of its widespread practice and its effectiveness. The medical transplant procedure, inter-vivo or post-mortem, cannot be thought of separately from a set of representations and social activities in which it has hardly taken place. Beyond its technical possibility, which will be presented below, organ transplant has required an evolution of social representations. Two important changes are to be considered: that of the social definition of death, and that of the body. This is what we will see in the sub-section "The problem of the production and distribution of organs". It is only once the technique is mastered, once the principle of transplant has been more sustainably inscribed in the representations of the world, that economic considerations appear (see sub-section "The problem of the production and distribution of organs"). Philippe Steiner, in his reference work, *La transplantation d'organes. Un commerce nouveau entre les êtres humains* (2010b), thinks of transplantation as the alliance of medical technologies and social technologies: on the one hand the technical possibility, on the other hand the social possibility, conditioned by the introduction of a new definition of death: encephalic death. In order to set the context for the emergence of the issue of markets for organs we will explore this further, as it reveals strong axiological tensions.

Technical possibility

The technical history of organ harvesting as well as transplantation is, like any other, made up of trial and error, more or less controlled procedures, frustrating failures and hazardous successes. On this point, this discussion makes no claim to completeness or originality, but it seems necessary, in order to approach the economic problems of transplants, to describe the main features of this history. Claire Boileau (2002) goes back to 1749, when the French naturalist Henri Louis Duhamel du Monceau grafted the spurs of a chicken onto the head of another chicken. The success of the operation led to an important movement of experiments on animals, including the first attempts at skin transplants. In 1804, the Italian scientist Giuseppe Boronio tried skin grafts on sheep, cows and horses. The attempts at transplantation extended to human beings with the experiments of Berger in 1822, then of Jacques Louis Reverdin at the Collège de France in 1869. In 1906, Lyon doctor Mathieu Jaboulay unsuccessfully attempted to transplant a pig kidney, then a goat kidney, to the folds of the elbows of two women. These multiple experiments make it possible to uncover some essential elements in the realisation of organ transplants: the importance of developing a technique of vascular suture and surgical anastomoses,[2] the role of refrigeration in graft preservation, and the importance of genetic relatedness between donor and recipient. Tissue compatibility between donor and recipient organisms is also necessary (Boileau, 2002: 33). This aspect was mainly studied by the Russian surgeon Yurii Voronoy, who proved that the phenomenon of rejection is immunological in nature. This period of experimentation of all kinds faded with the crisis of 1929, before the end of the Second World War marked the return of research, with a focus on homografting. In 1947, in Boston, a surgeon attempted to transplant a kidney from a corpse to a woman whose abortion had caused transient renal failure. This operation was carried out clandestinely in the middle of the night, as authorisation to attempt the operation had been refused by the hospital administration. If the transplant was rejected, it would have served its function by the time the kidneys of the patient recovered. Thus, this operation was a first success in transplantation if we consider that the objective here was not to replace the patent's organ. In 1951, the first kidney transplant was attempted in Paris from a living donor (sentenced to death). The receiver survived 17 days. Then, in 1952, the whole of France was moved by a story which still has a central symbolic place within surgical mythology. Marius Renard, a 16-year-old carpenter, fell from some scaffolding, damaging his only kidney. As a last resort, his mother offered to give him one of her kidneys. The dramatic aspect of the situation impelled Jean Hamburger, who at the time ran the nephrology department at Necker Hospital, to attempt the operation. The transplant took place on Christmas Eve, which only adds to the drama of this story. The operation was at first considered a success. However, Marius died after 21 days. The first total kidney transplant success came in Boston, in 1954, when a team led by three surgeons, Joseph Murray, Artwell Harrison and John Murray, performed an operation on twins. This success encouraged the identification of relevant immune factors. In this field, a decisive step was taken in 1956 by Jean Dausset, who noticed that despite ABO compatibility (compatibility of blood type[3]), following a large blood transfusion a patient may suffer from fever. Dausset also discovered that the body produces antibodies against exogenous white blood cells. This leukocyte system was named HLA (human leucocyte antigen). This blood group equivalent for tissues constitutes a defence system against transplanted organs. To identify a problem is not to solve it, and it would take more than ten years for Jean-François Borel to isolate from a mushroom taken in Norway a molecule with the property of inhibiting immune reactions. In 1980, cyclosporine was synthesised, and transplantation could move into a new era. It was no longer an operation of despair, but a surgical act requiring the supply and distribution of scarce resources: organs (Steiner, 2010a). Once the technology was under control and immunosuppressors developed, social and economic considerations came to light. This is what we will see in the subsection "The problem of the production and distribution of organs" and the section "Performativity and the organ market".

Moving the borders: the body, the person, death

The very idea of transplantation collides with a number of socially established representations. These relate to the body, to death and to mortuary rites. Before coming to the economics of transplantation, it is necessary to briefly discuss how it fits into society. In fact, market resistance is directly linked to the problem of adjustments between technical possibilities and social conventions, adjustments that mark the history of transplants. Once the border of the skin is crossed, both the organ and the body (as part of post-mortem harvesting) become things whose trade in the broad sense of the term is regulated by law. This tries to answer the following questions: When does the body cease to be the support of a person and become a thing? Who does this body and the organs in it belong to? In the context of inter-vivo organ trade, who has the right to transfer the organ? Under what conditions? It will be seen, moreover, that the answers given by the law are not always followed by effects, and social representations are strongly resistant. The proposal of some economists to transform organs into a commodity is clearly part of the problem of the objectivation of organs. Transplantation results in the transformation of an organ into a resource (Steiner, 2010b). As such, the organ is given the status of something that can be produced, distributed and consumed. We thus return to the sphere of economy in the substantive sense of the term. The economic aspect of the social management of organs will be covered later. We will focus here rather on the social difficulties posed by their reification. Jean-Pierre Baud (1993) reports an anecdote illustrating the difficulty. It concerns a man, incarcerated at the prison of Avignon, who unintentionally severed a finger, which was placed in a jar. What to do with this finger? It was initially retained by the prison authorities contrary to the claims of its "owner" and his lawyer. This led to a claim that it was an abusive confiscation in that it was a part of the person's body. The judge in charge of the case decided against them by considering the finger as a simple object, like the jar in which it was placed. The legal dilemma here is directly related to the blind spot in which organs are located *vis-à-vis* Western legal thought, rooted in Roman law. By dividing the world exclusively between things and the person, this school of law does not make it possible to directly apprehend the status of an organ or part of the human body. There is no intermediate category between person and thing. As far as organ donation is concerned, the law has therefore had to rule outside any pre-existing framework. To whom do the organs of a deceased person belong? The first major French law on transplantation, the Caillavet law, established the principle of presumption of consent in the context of post-mortem transplantation. This principle was renewed by the most recent bioethics laws (1994 and 2004) via the principle of "exemption from explicit consent". In this perspective, death is synonymous with transferability. The recipient of the body part is designated by the person to whom it belongs, except in the case where there is no pronouncement. Nevertheless, it is clear that the practices are far from being in line with the law. Beyond the desire of the deceased and presumed consent, it is usually the family who make the decision about donation. All this is in a context of mourning, a symbolically and emotionally charged event. For families, the organ can never really be considered as something easily transferable. Here we touch on the sacredness of the corpse. It is one thing, but not just anything: it is destined to take an important place within the ritual (burial or cremation) which goes beyond the temporality of the ceremony (the symbolic importance of the grave). The history of the legal status of the body is part of the management of the status of the external thing that acquires the organ, beyond the body, because of the advance of medical technologies. As the boundary of the body is broken, it is a question of constructing a new one: when does the organ become a transferable and appropriable thing, and cease to be the support of the person?

Two cases here must be discriminated: live harvesting and post-mortem harvesting. If the two types are mobilised by economists in the theoretical construction of the markets for organs, it is mainly the case of the inter-vivo exchange which provokes debate. Nevertheless, these debates are rooted in a representation of the organ that can only be grasped by returning to the symbolic violence represented by post-mortem harvesting. With discussions raised by the new definition of death necessary for this type of levy, one becomes aware of violence. Indeed, the new definition of death gradually imposing itself from the late 1960s, passing from the cardio-respiratory criterion to that of a complete and irreversible loss of brain activity, is directly related to the shortage of transplant material the medical community has been facing since the widespread practice of transplantation began. In 1968, at Harvard Medical School, an ad hoc committee chaired by Henry Beecher was formed. This committee presented a report that opened as follows:

> Our primary purpose is to define irreversible coma as a new criterion for death. There are two reasons why there is need for a definition: (1) Improvements in resuscitative and supportive measures have led to increased efforts to save those who are desperately injured. Sometimes these efforts have only partial success so that the result is an individual whose heart continues to beat but whose brain is irreversibly damaged. The burden is great on patients who suffer permanent loss of intellect, on their families, on the hospitals, and on those in need of hospital beds already occupied by these comatose patients. (2) Obsolete criteria for the definition of death can lead to controversy in obtaining organs for transplantation.
>
> (Harvard Ad Hoc Committee, 1968: 337)

It is striking that the notion of irreversible coma is directly justified by the possibility of organ harvesting this new definition of death would allow. This criterion, called the "Harvard criterion", began to spark discussions of technical issues (Bossi, 2012: 36). It must indeed give it substance, both medically and legally. In the first perspective, the report retains the notion of encephalic death (total absence of brain activity) versus neocortical death (absence of "superior" brain function: consciousness, cognitive function). This choice was mainly motivated by the refusal to consider as dead patients still able to breathe independently. Once this criterion was established, it was still necessary to define a legal procedure authorising the finding of death. In France, it was the Conseil d'État which, in 2006, defined the conditions for the declaration of death: absence of consciousness, spontaneous activity, reflexes of the brainstem and spontaneous ventilation. This definition is compatible with the cardiorespiratory criterion, where the patient is given mechanical ventilation. In this case, the legislation specified either the completion of two electroencephalograms revealing a flat trace, or an angiogram indicating that the brain was no longer receiving a blood supply. Although the Harvard criterion seems now to be accepted, especially because it appears in legal texts, it reveals a profound ambivalence, which is embodied in the clash between this criterion and the well-established historical and social criterion of cardiopulmonary arrest. This confrontation is already evident in daily medical practices. The large number of testimonies collected in France by Claire Boileau (2002) reveals how cardiac arrest remains the dominant symbolic border of death for patients, but also for doctors. This duality between "medical" death and "symbolic" death is all the more complex as the body in a state of encephalic death retains other signs of life such as heat, respiration (even assisted) and reflexes. Boileau (2002: 82–83; our translation) reports the words of a woman whose father was in a brain-dead state: "He had his thumb moving a lot. You know, like when you crush a spider, it moves again. There it was the same [. . .] I asked a nurse [. . .]. She told me it's normal." Another testimony, from a nurse, reveals this ambiguity among the medical profession: "When there is no heart harvesting, when the heart is no good, the urologists – it happened twice – ask, "You are sure he is dead?" But after a cardiac arrest, they do not ask themselves that kind of question" (Boileau, 2002: 77; our translation). For the author, this problem of definition is attributable to two elements. First, in a systemic vision of death inherited from the Middle Ages, the heart is considered as the source of physical and spiritual life. Secondly, if cardiorespiratory arrest is observable to the naked eye by the layman, encephalic death imposes between the dead person and close family members a technical frontier, an expert system which the family member must resign themselves to believe. This last fact is not unique to the family. Boileau (2002: 84–86; our translation) reports the testimony of a transplant surgeon:

> – I seize the electrocauteriser to trace the incision. At first contact with the skin, the donor's body jerks vigorously. Instantly, I stop my action, seized by fear.
>
> "He is moving!" I say to the anaesthesiologist, implying by this, and most concisely, that I am afraid he is still alive, that we are committing the irreparable, [. . .] perpetrating a real murder.
>
> "It can happen," he answers calmly. It is only the medullary reflex arches that persist. We will increase the dose of curare. You know, we always use it before harvesting.
>
> Well, no, I did not know that! Or rather, to this day, I had not realised that spinal reflexes persisted and that a subject in an irreversible coma remained motionless because of curarisation. What sort of death is this that it must be tranquillised so that it does not move?

So despite the legal institutionalisation of encephalic death, cardiac arrest death remains a symbolic barrier impeding organ donation when hospital coordinating nurses approach families to seek authorisation to harvest organs from a patient: in the traditional representation of death, to allow this taking is to let go.

Beyond the inertia of practices and representations, virulent philosophical critiques of the Harvard definition have emerged (Bossi, 2012). Hans Jonas (1974) was one of the first and fiercest critics of the criterion of encephalic death, accusing it of being purely pragmatic, depriving the human being of death in favour of an external end: the removal and transplant of organs. Here we are faced with a utilitarian definition of death, contrary to the oath of Hippocrates ("Into whatsoever houses I enter, I will enter to help the sick, and I will abstain from all intentional wrong-doing and harm, especially from woman and woman, bond or free") and opening the door to excesses. Bossi gives the example of a very ethically problematic case. In 2008, in Denver, the hearts of three children with serious neurological damage were removed after cardiac arrests ranging from 1.25 to 3 minutes. However, according to specialists, despite major lesions, cardiac resuscitation would have been possible. The question then arises: to what extent can we end the lives of some to save others? The answer depends on the definition of death that is adopted. We will see that the same question resonates in the context of inter-vivo trade, although on a different level: is the organ a thing that gives itself, or something that sells itself? From the person/body border (where the body is precisely the support of the person and the definition of death the central issue), one passes on to the border between a thing that can be the object of trade (*res in commercio*) and one whose trade is prohibited (*res extra commercium*), between thing that can be given and thing that can be marketed. By breaking the barrier of the skin, the organs have been transformed into things that can be extracted. It remains to define this thing, to distinguish the modalities of trade. Today, French law allows the donation of organs within a restricted circle: father, mother, brother, sister, spouse, son, daughter, grandparents, uncles, aunts, first cousins, spouses of the father and from the mother. We talk about "emotional donation". To extend this circle by making the organ a commodity like any others is the object of the commodification proposed by certain economists.

The purpose of these few lines has been to show how the possibility of transplant has disrupted a continuum of conventions ranging from law to representations related to the body and death. It is in this undermined terrain that the economic problem exists: that of the "production" and distribution of organs (Steiner, 2010b: 37).

The problem of the production and distribution of organs

The improvement of transplant techniques has transformed the organ into a resource for both medical professionals and recipients. It thence becomes an economic good in the substantive sense of the term – intended to be produced, distributed, appropriated. Until the 1970s, transplantation remained a last-ditch operation, with costs and distribution issues not being fundamental problems. Philippe Steiner (2010b: 132) writes about "coordination by hope": uncertainty concerned only the efficiency of the medical act, the failure rate being extremely high. From the 1970s, the increasing mastery of medical techniques has raised the question of the optimal use of the rare resource that is the organ, especially since we see in many countries severe deficits. Economic coordination replaces coordination by hope. The growing shortage contrasts with real technical possibilities and entails a need for rationalisation:

> The production of the scarce resource therefore involves important political work to establish the conditions for the transfer of a resource that is created in the very movement that makes it possible to transfer it from one body to another.
>
> (Steiner, 2010b: 146; our translation)

The issue of scarcity then penetrated the medical sphere, illustrated by Becker and Elìas (2007) with the extension of waiting lists in the United States. Although the economy of transplantation relies on a large number of organisational technologies, we focus here on the question of the matching technology between transplants and patients, and more particularly on the pairing of transplants taken from the living. This is where the market becomes a potential answer to the problem: "Medicine and the market, the body and the rational decision of the economic agent were linked to the occasion of this advanced medical technique" (Steiner, 2010b: 46; our translation). In France, awareness of an organ shortage emerged in the early 1990s. The market solution was immediately rejected in 1994 with the revision of the bioethics law, which set the first legal framework for the economic management of the organ economy by introducing the principle of non-patrimoniality of the human body. This prohibits its sale.

Performativity and the organ market

Scarcity has led to the problem of the production and distribution of organs. At this stage, the performative power of economic theories becomes thick: in the mode of social engineering, economists have tried to set up incentive market systems in order to increase the availability of organs. Market solutions have been systematically confronted with strong social resistance. This section discusses both attempts for commercial applications to organ trade and their criticisms. These criticisms will be linked to conventional pressure in the next section.

The market solution

Faced with growing shortages and longer waiting lists, some economists advocate a so-called market solution. While several types of trading architectures have been proposed, very few of them relate to a real "over-the-counter" market. This is particularly the case with Kaserman and Barnett's model (1991). Becker and Elìas (2007) diverge from the pure market model. We will return to these two models, which adopt the same starting point: "When an economist sees a persistent gap between demand and supply – as in the demand for and supply of organs for transplants – the next step is usually to look for obstacles to equilibrating that market" (Becker and Elìas, 2007: 3). Kaserman and Barnett's approach is part of a post-mortem organ offer, but nevertheless applies very well to inter-vivo trading, given the lack of specifications for the donor (Sambuc, 2013). In effect, the authors simply apply the standard framework of market theory: the supply of organs increases with price, the movement is reversed for demand. As Figure 8.1 shows, in a simple donation system, the level of supply (a) is insufficient to satisfy demand, whereas the integration of a market price as an adjustment variable increases the quantity available by passing the offer at level f. The surface 0ifa represents the total surplus. The introduction of a price implies a transfer of surplus from the receivers to the donors (0aed), in that the free organs in a donation system now have a price. Collective welfare increases, an increase represented here by the triangle afg. This surplus of welfare breaks down into a quantitative surplus (gef) for the demanders, and a financial surplus (efa) for the suppliers.

Kaserman and Barnett apply here standard market theory, ignoring the specifics of organ trading. Thus, we simply move from a non-market situation to a market situation, and we evaluate this change through a comparative analysis of welfare surplus. The emergence of a price of equilibrium theoretically clears the market, and the market solution seems appropriate.

For their part, Becker and Elìas (2007) tried to integrate into their model some constraints due to transplant logistics. They envisaged a more credible, monopsonistic system in which the health system is on the demand side, offering individuals the opportunity to purchase an organ. In the current state of the inter-vivo kidney trade – a system operating only though unpaid donations – demand far exceeds supply. This is illustrated in Figure 8.2, in which SS and DD respectively represent supply and demand. It goes without saying that this reasoning will only hold if we ultimately consider as many markets as organ

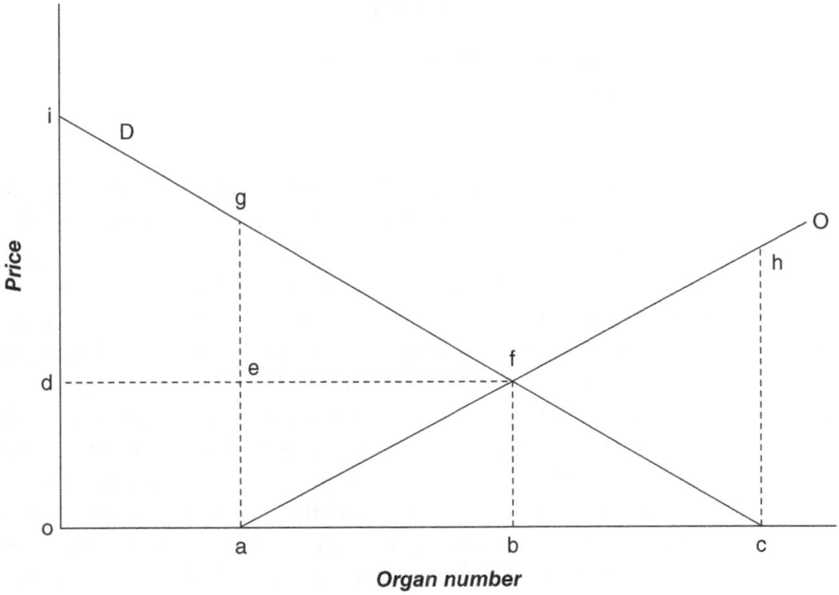

Figure 8.1 Introduction of the market and increase of collective well-being

Source: Kaserman and Barnett (1991).

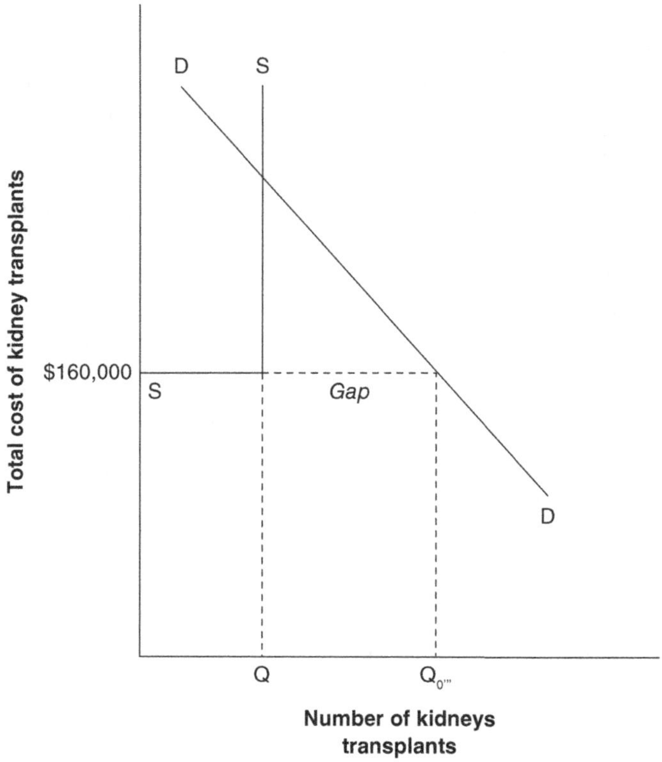

Figure 8.2 Kidney market without financial incentive
Source: Becker and Elias (2007: 8).

types and HLA types. On the ordinate, the unit cost of organs is capped by the willingness to repay insurance (private or public). The authors estimated this cost at $160,000 in 2007.

In the case of a donation, the offer is completely inelastic regarding cost, and is therefore an inverted L. The demand is also of a special nature. Unlike an over-the-counter market, it is a third party, the doctor, who decides to put the patient on the waiting list. Thus, according to Becker and Elìas, we arrive at a paradoxical situation: the more the progress of medicine makes it possible to reduce the cost of transplants, the more operating techniques progress, the more demand increases, and so does the gap between a fixed offer and a variable demand. To mitigate the lack of supply, and thus to arrive at a situation of market equilibrium, Becker and Elìas advocate the establishment of a financial incentive. The calculation of this financial incentive includes three components: (i) the risk of death during the transplant, (ii) the duration of convalescence and (iii) the decrease in the quality of life following the operation. Let us limit ourselves to the main principles of this calculation:

(i) Putting a price on the fatal risk implies giving a price to human life. Becker and Elìas set the latter at $5,000,000 for an average person with an annual income of $35,000. Considering the risk of death following a kidney removal at 0.1%, the compensation on this risk is set at $5000.
(ii) The compensation due in the convalescence period, four weeks for a kidney, is fixed at $2500 on the basis of an annual salary of $35,000.
(iii) The authors affirm that kidney removal does not imply any deterioration in the quality of life, but: "For now, we arbitrarily add a generous $7500 to measure the quality-of-life component of the price" (Becker and Elìas, 2007: 10–11).

That gives a total price of $15,000, which, in addition to the $160,000 cost of the transplant, gives a unit cost of $175,000. Note that the incentive is here thought of only as compensation, and not as a price adjusting supply and demand. Its introduction would have two major effects. On the one hand, inelastic supply would become completely elastic, because the number of available organs was very large (S*S * in Figure 8.3). On the other hand,

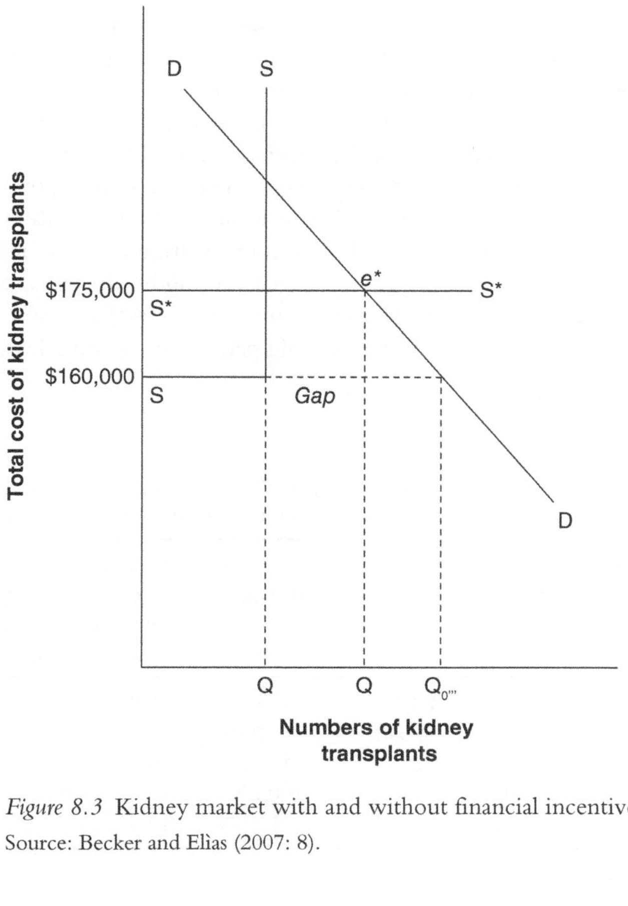

Figure 8.3 Kidney market with and without financial incentive

Source: Becker and Elìas (2007: 8).

with the increase in cost, the demand for organs decreases: if one considers a reimbursement as public or private, or even an individual financing his own care, the increase of the cost decreases access to care. Thus, we reach the equilibrium quantity Q1, and the market is completely cleared. If a -1 demand elasticity is applied, then the cost increase will reduce demand by 9.5% (15,500/160,000).

Estimating the quantity demanded at 21,500 transplants in 2005, this decrease would correspond to 2040 people. On the other side, kidney transplants would increase from 13,500 to 19,460 (+44%). The authors believe that this reasoning is sufficient to justify the implementation of an organ pseudo-market. The demonstration is of course dependent on the level of the chosen parameters (essentially the value of the statistical life and the evaluation of the loss of quality of life). In Table 8.1, Becker and Elìas studied different cases of setting these parameters. Quality of life was calculated via a rate, QALY (quality-adjusted life year), weighting the value of statistical life in view of individual specificities, including the weight of different disadvantages. We can then estimate the loss of quality of life following a change of condition. Culter and Richardson (1997: 246) estimate, for example, that an amputee's QALY in the United States in 1990 is 0.89 (compared with 0.87 in 1970). Becker and Elìas remain unclear on this point, but they estimate a loss of QALY of 0.15 in case of complications following a kidney removal, against a loss of zero otherwise.

For the authors, Table 8.1 clearly argues for the establishment of an inter-vivo organ market. The introduction of the incentive allows both an increase in supply and a reduction in demand, hence the decline in the number of transplants with the increase in remuneration. There is an additional positive element to this procedure: it makes it possible to reduce waiting time. When we know that the unemployment rate of a patient on a waiting list for transplant is 15% higher than normal, and that the long-term mortality rate of a person who received a transplant is 50–80% lower than among patients on waiting lists, this element becomes extremely significant.

Table 8.1 Estimate of an organ's price and the impact on the total number of kidneys transplanted under different assumptions about the value of statistical life.

Value of statistical life	*Risk of death component*	*Quality of life component*	*Time value*	*Total price of a kidney*	*Induced price variation (%)*	*Variation in number of transplants (%)*
$2,000,000	$2000	$2997	$2692	$7689	4.8	52
$3,000.000	$3000	$4496	$2692	$10,188	6.4	49
$5,000,000	$5000	$7493	$2692	$15,185	9.5	44
$7,000,000	$7000	$10,490	$2692	$20,677	17.3	39
$10,000,000	$10,000	$14,985	$2692	$27,677	17.3	32

Source: Becker and Elìas (2007: 15).

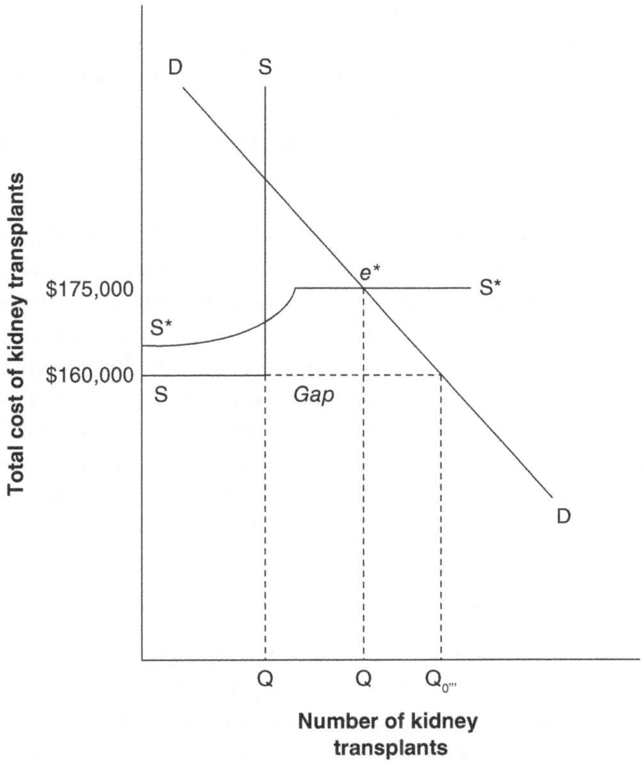

Figure 8.4 Kidney market with live and post-mortem harvesting

Source: Becker and Elìas (2007: 19).

Becker and Elìas' proposal is then substantiated to integrate a post-mortem market in which the financial incentive would be paid to the donor's heirs. Other systems have been considered, including a "futures market" (Hansmann, 1989) in which the donor today sells the possibility of removal of his organs in case of a "good death" (encephalic death). In this case, the remuneration may be financial, or take the form of priority on the waiting list in case of future need of a transplant.[4] Hansmann refers in this case to a post-mortem agreement: the arrangement with an insurance company of a right to organs which it can subsequently bring to the market, allowing a reduction in one's health insurance premium. Since post-mortem harvesting is generally less expensive, the combination of the two systems would have the advantage of combining the flexibility of inter-vivo transplants and the lower cost of post-mortem transplants.[5] This is what we can observe in Figure 8.4: up to a cost of $175,000, organs can come from cadaveric organ donation, then the inter-vivo market takes over to fully clear the market.

The main argument in favour of establishing a market for organs is therefore the reduction of waiting lists through two mechanisms: increase in supply and a drop in demand. There are of course other justifications (Morelon, 2003):

- The sale of an organ would represent an income allowing families in need to live for several months or even years.
- The purchase (here by the institution) of an organ confers a value, encouraging a sense of responsibility on the part of the recipient, who will more willingly take immunosuppressive treatment.
- The removal of an organ is a substantial operation, so it is legitimate to compensate for it by remuneration.

To what extent can we qualify the demand as well as the theoretical justification for setting up an organ market of performative movement? If we again take the theoretical elements put forward in Part II of this study, one notes initially that the establishment of a market for organs rests on a new classification: the organ is not only considered as one thing (the fruit of the development of transplant techniques), but as a rare resource, and *a fortiori* as a commodity. This classification becomes a convention to the extent that the agents follow it, moving it to the market and abandoning the organ to a market mechanism that is said to be able to reduce waiting lists. It is thus a question of "make to act" on the basis of a new classification of the objects of the world.

The limits of the market solution

The objective of this chapter is to consider the rejection of the market solution by considering it from the point of view of incompatibility between the organ market theory and the classification, the social earmarking, that exists in the majority of contemporary societies. To do this, once the economists' proposals have been put forward, we can begin by bringing to light the most commonly criticised claims of commodification, before bringing them back to the idea of conventional incompatibility in the section "Conventional incompatibility". Three reasons for the rejection of the market solution have been identified. The first relates to the particular structure of organ markets. A second reason relates to what the market is likely to exercise *vis-à-vis* the donated organ. The third and final criticism raises the moral problem of encouraging members of vulnerable populations to sell their organs.

The structure of the markets

The focus here is on debates about the efficiency of a potential organ market. We will rely on the work of Cléa Sambuc (2012), which provides a survey of this issue. It seems that we can identify two types of problem related to the establishment of a market for organs: the structure of traffic patterns and the negative externalities that would imply the establishment of such a market. The particular market structure implied by a physical characteristic of the organ, namely its rapid degradation, provides a first point of criticism of the market approach. If we talk about organs harvested post-mortem (taken into account in the models studied above), then the cold ischemia time – the time during which the organ retains its functional qualities – necessitates an efficient transport network for the conservation centres as well as excellent coordination with potential recipients. These constraints imply relatively heavy fixed costs, which are synonymous with strong scale economies. As a result, a competitive and decentralised situation would almost automatically lead to a concentration of transplant activity around organ transport and preservation activities. This concentration is nevertheless limited by the degradation of the organs It therefore inevitably leads to a set of geographical monopolies (Sambuc, 2012: 56), as in the famous case of the iceberg described by Krugman (1991, 1998).[6] As pointed out by Arrow (1972), decentralisation can ultimately lead to a set of geographic monopolies, undermining the supposed benefits of the market proposed by Kaserman and Barnett:

> In the case of organs, if each centre transplants only those it has harvested itself, the chances of a perfect match between supply and demand diminish. A national network for information-sharing and centralised management appear, from this point of view, more efficient.
>
> (Sambuc, 2012: 56; our translation)

Now we will address the demand side. It has already been pointed out that in the case of a non-homogeneous good such as an organ, there are ultimately as many markets as there are HLA types and ABO groups, so one has to evaluate the impact of this heterogeneity on the implicit hypothesis of the model of perfect competition, namely atomicity, that justifies the fundamental assumption of price-taking. This assumes that no agent will have real market power, especially since HLA type and blood group are not the only variables. To be precise, there are as many markets as HLA types, ABO groups, dates and conditions of availability. As Garban and Barro (2003) point out, the probability of finding a matched donor in a non-related family is 1/40,000e. As such, Sambuc (2012: 57) prefers to speak of a "bilateral oligopoly" rather than a potentially competitive market. However, if we remain within the framework of the standard theory of markets, this questioning of the competitive structure can only raise the price above the theoretical price. This challenges the reasoning of Kaserman and Barnett.

The second point limiting the impact of the market solution is the appearance of negative externalities questioning the effectiveness of the market process. In this case, a widespread criticism is that the introduction of remuneration would lead to a decline in the quality of the product traded. Two reasons are given: first, the remuneration is likely to attract populations at risk; second, donors might hide any defects. These points were highlighted by Richard Titmuss (1970) during the debate on blood remuneration in the 1970s. Here we are confronted with a typical case of information asymmetry between the donor and the recipient (Arrow, 1972). Although the criticism is commonly accepted, Cooper and Culyer (1973) as well as Ireland and Koch (1973) set out to counter it. For the former, the market would, on the contrary, improve the quality of the products because of competition between the harvesting organisations. For Sambuc, the factual test renders this argument difficult, in that the data clearly show that the risk of contamination following a blood transfusion has increased in the United States with the introduction of remuneration. Ireland and Koch claim that this increase, rather than the establishment of a market, is the result of too much regulation providing no sanctions in a case of contamination. Market mechanisms of sanctions are impeded by state intervention, and the state itself takes no action. To this, Sambuc answers, rightly, that the argument cannot be tenable for the organs, as the small scale of supply makes the effects of reputation difficult to gauge. It should be added that a recipient's need for an organ in an emergency will lead him to be less demanding in the quality of the good. Here we come to a characteristic of organ trade: it is a distress trade.

Motivation and the crowding-out effect

A recurring criticism of the introduction of organ markets concerns the perverse effects of compensation beyond quality decline. This debate begins with the work of Titmuss (1970), who supported a relatively common position in economic sociology. Viviana Zelizer (for example, in Zelizer, 2011) qualified this position as a "hostile worlds" theory: the social world is divided into two types of incompatible arrangements – on the one hand that of solidarity and the social bond, on the other hand selfishness and market activities. According to this vision, no combination of the two arrangements is possible: any intrusion of commercial rationalism would corrupt the mechanisms of social solidarity. Conversely, the intrusion of the irrationality of solidarity into market mechanisms would lead to the inefficiency of the latter. For Zelizer, Titmuss' works are exemplary of this vision of the world: "[B]lood as a living tissue may now constitute in Western societies one of the ultimate tests of where the "social" begins and the "economic" ends" (Titmuss, 1970: 219). Titmuss (1970: 220) questions the growing demands at that time for a blood market system. He reacted primarily to a publication by the Institute of Economic Affairs in London in which two economists, Cooper and Culyer (1968), argued that the introduction of market incentives would increase the supply of blood while contesting the "monopoly of altruism". The logic is similar to that proposed by Becker and Elìas for organs. Titmuss' argument is based on a comparative study of the American paid system and the English donation system. This comparison proved the inefficiency of the trading system, essentially due to its disastrous effects on the altruistic donation system. The main effect of the market would be to convert a gift into remuneration: the introduction of monetary remuneration would erode the feeling of duty towards others. It is here that an antagonistic view of the market and altruism is conveyed.

Titmuss' book provoked reactions from two economists: Robert Solow (1971) and Kenneth Arrow (1972). Both of these critics make it clear that Titmuss' argument is hardly convincing to them: "Formal philanthropy has always been a prominent element of all economic systems and has shown no signs of diminution" (Arrow, 1972: 345); [I]f to a voluntary blood donor system we add the possibility of selling blood, we have only expanded the individual's range of alternatives" (Arrow, 1972: 350). What Arrow is asking for is a theoretical analysis of why the creation of a market for blood would reduce altruistic donation, seeking a justification for the thesis of hostile worlds. As Steiner (2001a) highlights, Titmuss' reasoning was supported much later by the experimental economist Bruno Frey (1997; Frey and Oberholzer-Gee, 1997). The famous reasoning developed by Frey is based on a refinement of rational choice theory. Not being able to directly observe the agents' preferences, training and evolution, the standard investigation method is to find explanatory factors external to individuals, the most important in our discipline being monetary remuneration fixed by price. Frey shows that in the face of this kind of extrinsic motivation that constitutes the price effect, human behaviour can be directed by other types of incentives, called "intrinsic", stemming from the personal satisfaction derived from the activity as such. Frey uses here a conceptual distinction from psychology, more specifically the work of Edward L. Deci (1971, 1972):

> It is possible to distinguish between two broad classes of motivation to perform an activity: intrinsic motivation and extrinsic motivation. A person is intrinsically motivated if he performs an activity for no apparent reward except the activity itself [. . .]. Extrinsic motivation, on the other hand, refers to the performance of an activity because it leads to external rewards (e.g., status, approval, or passing grades).
>
> (Deci, 1972: 113)

Frey's work therefore attempted to consider the conjunction of the two types of motivations. The main result was to emphasise the negative effect extrinsic motivations may have on intrinsic motivations. This has been called the "hidden cost of reward": offering remuneration may decrease supply, since extrinsic utility is replaced by intrinsic utility, and the loss of intrinsic utility is not offset by the gain in extrinsic utility. Frey and Oberholzer-Gee (1997) attempted to prove the relevance of this concept during an experiment relating to the implementation of local projects of general interest which the nearest residents were likely to oppose. This effect is known in English as NIMBY ("Not In My Back Yard").[7] The most emblematic examples relate to nuclear energy: nuclear power plants or radioactive waste storage centres. It is precisely in this latter case that the authors tried to validate the idea of an eviction effect between intrinsic and extrinsic motivation. In an experiment in Switzerland, they collected answers to two questions:

> *Question 1:* "Suppose that the National Cooperative Company for the Storage of Radioactive Waste, after drilling, proposes to build a radioactive waste storage center in your municipality. The federal experts are examining this proposal and the federal parliament decides to build this center. During a meeting at your town hall, would you accept or refuse this proposal?"

> *Question 2:* "Suppose that the National Cooperative Society for the Storage of Radioactive Waste, after drilling, proposes to build a radioactive waste storage center in your municipality. The federal experts are examining this proposal and the federal parliament decides to build this center. In addition, the parliament decides to compensate all residents in the amount of 5,000 francs per year and per person. Your family will receive xxx francs a year. These compensations will be financed by Swiss taxpayers. During a meeting at your town hall, would you accept or refuse this proposal?"

When the first question was asked, 50.8% of the agents voted for the project, 44.9% opposed it and 4.3% did not offer an opinion. For the second question, the acceptance rate dropped to 24.6%. This gap can be explained in many ways, the most credible for Frey and Oberholzer-Gee being that the integration of financial incentives destroys the altruism of the agents, their dedication to civil society. Applied to the donation of blood, and even more so to organ donation, this reasoning tends to indicate that the setting up of market mechanisms can potentially lead to a reduction in donations because of altruism in favour of an increase in the supply of organs for pecuniary reasons, without the two effects offsetting each other. Thus, this analysis directly contradicts the arguments of Arrow and Solow, showing not only that money cannot buy everything, but that money can even result in a lower supply. This was summarised by Frey and Jegen (2001: 590):

> Arguably, the "crowding-out effect" [. . .] is one of the most important anomalies in economics, as it suggest the opposite of the most fundamental economic "law", that raising monetary incentives increases supply. If the crowding effect holds, raising monetary incentives reduces, rather than increases, supply.

The category "intrinsic motivation" remains empty, in that it is simply opposed to that of "extrinsic motivation". However, in my opinion it is possible to give it more substance by means of a preponderant concept in sociology: "axiological rationality". Raymond Boudon (2009: 77–100, 2011) defines axiological rationality as follows: a compatible system of Q arguments containing at least one normative proposition N. We will be rational from an axiological point of view when we accept N if no system of arguments Q' preferable to Q and leading to prefer N' is available. Boudon extracts an example from the *Wealth of Nations* where Smith questions why the English consider it normal and legitimate that soldiers are paid less than miners. The argument system is as follows:

> [T]he salary is the remuneration of a service rendered. Equivalent service, wages must be equivalent. In the value of a service come various elements: in particular the duration of the apprenticeship that it implies and the risks to which it exposes the one that renders.
>
> (Boudon, 2009: 80–81; our translation)

Soldiers and miners experience similar lengths of training, and both risk their lives. Nevertheless, given the promise of symbolic remuneration conferred by a military career, the principle of equal remuneration requires compensation for the miner. This compensation can be pecuniary. We go from intrinsic motivation to symbolic remuneration. This type of reasoning can be applied to the results of Frey and Oberholzer-Gee. In the context of the first question, we can consider the following reasoning:

- i All citizens should equally enjoy a tax-financed public facility.
- ii To agree to sacrifice a part of one's well-being in the name of greater collective well-being is a characteristic of the good citizen.
- iii The public facility, a nuclear waste treatment centre, poses a risk of radiation to some citizens. The negative externality provoked by this centre comes to tinge the enjoyment the local residents gain from this installation.
- iv The acceptance of the establishment of such a centre near a citizen's home therefore deserves compensation.
- v This compensation can be intrinsic: the feeling of being recognised as a good citizen.

This reasoning is entirely related to the fact that an individual who is asked to accept the construction of a nuclear waste centre feels considered as a citizen, which triggers a type of axiological rationality based on a symbolic remuneration. What the swaying of opinions as soon as a pecuniary remuneration is proposed shows is that the monetary exchange extracts the individuals from this mode of reasoning by eliminating premises (i) and (ii). Thus, the relationship between the polluter and the local resident is no longer assimilated to a relationship between the individual and the community, the intrinsic remuneration disappearing, which makes the individual wonder whether the sum proposed is enough to accept taking a risk. In the case evoked by Boudon, if the symbolic remuneration of a soldier disappeared with an increase in his remuneration, turning him into a mercenary, then this remuneration must be at least at the level of that of the miner. Applied to the donation of blood or organs, this reasoning leads to an understanding of why intrinsic symbolic remuneration for the donation may be more important than pecuniary remuneration, and that the latter may exclude the "supplier" of organs from a donor role so that he will refuse to give even if it is still possible to do so. This way of theorising the crowding-out effect is based on the agent's perception of his environment and the task he is being asked to perform.[8]

Distress trade and donor freedom

The last set of criticisms that will be discussed is to some extent related to an important hypothesis of the market model: the hypothesis of voluntary exchange, according to which the agents only exchange if they wish to. If, technically, this assumption guarantees that the price will be between the reserve prices of the agents, it also contains an argument regularly invoked by defenders of the market solution: the actors will remain free in whether or not to enter the organs market. However, detractors of organ market trading say that remuneration tends to corrupt the autonomy of choice of donors who sell an organ for the purpose of receiving an income, and people not advocating themselves as suppliers. The anthropologist Lawrence Cohen (2003) argued, for example, that the generalisation of the kidney market in a poor country where the population is heavily indebted limits freedom of choice by turning the kidney into widespread credit collateral. As a final resort, the body is the human being's last possession. There is then a strong negative externality to the kidney trade: either it forces individuals to pledge a kidney to access credit, or it raises interest rates for people not willing to pledge. These considerations are true limits to market logic (Satz, 2008). Titmuss (1970: 277) had already signalled that remuneration for blood donation could imply this type of mechanism:

> [T]he commercialization of blood and donor relationships [. . .] places immense costs on those least able to bear them – the poor, the sick and the inept – increases the danger of unethical behavior in various sectors of medical science and practice, and results in situations in which proportionately more blood is supplied by the poor, the unskilled (and) the unemployed [. . .] Redistribution [. . .] of blood and blood products from the poor to the rich appears to be one of the dominant effects of the American blood banking systems.

Philippe Steiner (2010b: 288–300) deepened and systematised this criticism on the basis that this is the nature of freedom facing the commercial contract at stake. The argument used by Arrow, Becker and Elìas to justify the implementation of the market solution – an argument according to which every individual is free to put himself on the market, refers to a negative conception of freedom, as theorised by Isaiah Berlin. In his famous essay *Two Concepts of Liberty*, Berlin (1958: 7) defines freedom as the absence of wilful interferences: "I am normally said to be free to the degree to which no man or body of men interferes with my activity." Individuals are not, in the context of this definition, hindered in their desire to enter or leave the market. To contest this, Steiner summons a republican definition of freedom. From this perspective, mainly driven by the work of Philip Pettit (1997, 2006), freedom is defined not by the absence of interference, but by the arbitrary control exercised by others on my person. In other words, freedom is defined by the absence of domination:

> [S]omeone has dominating power over another, someone dominates or subjugates another, to the extent that: 1. they have the capacity to interfere; 2. On an arbitrary basis; 3. In certain choices that the other is in a position to make.
>
> (Pettit, 1997: 52)

Freedom is therefore understood as the position enjoyed by an individual when he lives in the presence of other persons who, by virtue of a social apparatus, refrain from exercising over others a power of domination. Steiner emphasises that if the hypothesis of voluntary exchange guarantees the compatibility of the market mechanism with both negative freedom and republican freedom, then this is only valid as long as we consider the market and only the market as place of coordination of offers and suppliers. As soon as one moves upstream of the market, the arbitrary domination described by Pettit resumes its validity:

> The market is not in itself the place of formation of a relation of domination, but it can be a powerful vector of diffusion by ratifying, by means of freely agreed exchanges, situations of inequality whose consequence is the domination endured by those who are not able to access other options because of their social and economic conditions.
>
> (Steiner, 2010b: 296; our translation)

Exchange neutrality, which ensures that the conditions of initial justice (initial distribution or freedom to exchange) are not questioned by the exchange is also at the heart of Léon Walras' theory: the criterion justice cannot be judged within the market, the latter only legitimising the final distribution in the name of its own neutrality *vis-à-vis* the initial conditions (Bourdeau, 2005). Steiner proposes as an example a figure central to republicanism: the slave. The negative definition of freedom makes it difficult to understand the domination of the good master over the slave (Bourdeau, 2012), where "good" means "not interfering in the actions of the slave". However, for Pettit, the relationship of domination inherent in the institution of slavery need not be updated to be tangible as long as the "good treatment" depends solely on the master's own arbitrary will. As a result, the arbitrariness of the master's behaviour locks the slave into a servile attitude towards him: "In short, the slave does not enjoy a social status that allows him to look right in the master's eyes"[9] (Bourdeau, 2012: 7–8; our translation). Thus, if the possibility is given to him, and even if he is free (in the negative sense of the term) to choose to sell his organs on the markets, an individual too poorly endowed with economic capital to live and support his family is forced to take this path, the only one available to him. His situation is comparable to that of the slave, in that as long as a sufficient proportion of the population of which he is a part decides to accept the principle of organ market trade, he will have no choice but to endure it, especially if the mechanism described by Cohen is realised. In the latter case, the market does not augment the number of choices available to him nor guarantee an organ as an assurance of a debt, but obliges him to commit an organ to the extent that the free market increases the interest rate. To quote the famous formula of Henri-Dominique Lacordaire (1872: 494; our translation), taken from the 51st Conference of Notre-Dame: "Between the strong and the weak, between the rich and the poor, between the master and the servant, it is freedom that oppresses and the law that liberates."[10] Freedom to sell becomes a necessity to make part of one's body available. It turns economic distress into partial slavery. A more detailed analysis of the potential consequences of the market for freedom (mainly of people in difficulty) then calls into question a basic principle of the market perspective itself, that of the sovereignty of the individual.[11]

Conventional incompatibility

Apart from the question of market structures, the criticisms of the market solution identified in the previous section lead us to consider the special status of organs in our conventional systems of representation. Indeed, I would like to argue that both the technical critique of the crowding-out effect and the moral criticism of distress trade rely on a particular representation of the organ as fundamentally non-marketable, in that not only is it not conventionally classified as such, but its commodification breaks with the very legitimacy of the market order. This legitimacy, as conceived here, is based on the idea of remuneration, as opposed to the mechanism of mere incentive: on the one hand fair remuneration for a good, on the other hand the practice of illegitimate power over others; on the one hand what is due, on the other the handling of people in distress. Now, the frontier between these two categories seems to me to rest above all on an element of conventional type – that is, on a classification of the merchant and the non-merchant.

Conventions, earmarking and incentives

Here we touch on the importance of social earmarking: as a non-market object, the organ cannot be assigned to a market system. This marking appears as soon as we question the points of view of Titmuss and Cohen (systematised by Steiner thanks to the notion of republican freedom), which is what Becker and Elìas do. To prohibit the trade of organs should lead to the prohibition of any professional dangerous activity; it could even forbid some professional activities, since it can always be considered that one is alienated because of reduced freedom of choice. Trade should also be prohibited in general, since any sales action may be considered from the point of view of economic necessity and of distress weakening the republican freedom of the term: "Should poor individuals be deprived of revenue that could be highly useful to them, especially when their organs might save the lives of persons who desperately need to replace their defective organs?" (Becker and Elìas, 2007: 21). It is the lack of objective and transcendent reasons for the disqualification of the organ as a commodity which underlies the argument of Becker and Elìas. If the criticisms suggested by Sambuc relate to a brute fact in the sense of Searle – that the organ is extremely fragile and deteriorates rapidly – the explanation of the rejection of the market is practically never to be sought in an intrinsic characteristic of the organ, but in a social representation *vis-à-vis* the latter. Technical criticisms, relating to the efficiency of market matching, reveal a similar mechanism: if remuneration for organs can potentially have a negative effect on supply, the reason is precisely a particular earmarking: the organ is not a commodity, the order of remuneration must not be monetary, and the gift is the symbolically appropriate distribution system. Therefore, nothing pushes me to go on a market where this remuneration will be less because it is assimilated to a deviation *vis-à-vis* the convention in place (selling an organ earns me less than donating it). This deviation leads market remuneration for organs into a grey zone, between the legitimacy of market trade and non-market trade: the remuneration is illegitimate to the extent that a non-market good is subject to a mode of distribution that does not suit it. The (illegitimate) market remuneration for a non-market good becomes an incentive, as described by the American philosopher Ruth Grant. In her illuminating work of 2012 (see also Grant, 2015), Grant defines an incentive as an offer that has the following characteristics:

- It is an extrinsic profit whilst not being the logical consequence of a system of remuneration: it is neither an income nor compensation. For example, for Becker and Elìas, an amount of money was transferred to the donor in the name of quality of life, even though the author considers that there is no decline in the quality of life.
- It is set up in order to lead to a particular action.
- It is set up in order to deviate from the *status quo* by motivating a person to choose a different course than he would have chosen without this incentive.

For Grant, as a means of directing behaviour, incentive must be seen as a political modality of exercise of power, alongside strength and persuasion, when defining power as the ability to divert the actions of others in order to achieve goals other than their own. It is then understandable that the real problem of the market for organs is not the market system *per se*, but the power relation that any monetary system assumes, since it is perceived as an incentive and not remuneration.[12] It is also in some cases non-market remuneration that may be considered illegitimate as falling into the grey area of incentives. In accordance with Zelizer's criticism, we do not descend into caricature of hostile worlds here: it is not an incompatibility between the market and the non-market, but a conflict of representation that is being highlighted – in other words, a problem of complementarity between a conventional system in place and a constitutive classification of an economic theory. To use the notation used previously, R is an agreement to coordinate through a market mechanism in the context of kidney trade. Let R^* be "as a commodity, a kidney that can be pledged against a credit". R^* is a consequence of R, and non-R^* may be a consequence of R' (for example, "coordinate by a donation mechanism"). Convention R produces here another conventional mechanism that is related to commodification: the possibility of using an organ as financial collateral, a possibility considered illegitimate in that it is a power relationship, and not free consent. This point has, for example, been widely debated in the context of paid clinical trials: when is it considered that remuneration for participating in clinical trials raises the problem of the power of a part of society, which enjoys the introduction of new drugs, over another part of the population by making its members take risks because of economic difficulties? The concept of "free consent" is essentially empty. It can only be challenged by the invocation of conventional illegitimacy, namely to qualify the monetary counterpart of a transplant not as remuneration (legitimate within the market order), but as an incentive within Grant's meaning. Importantly, the power relationship can also be reversed: asking for a financial reward from a family member is considered illegitimate in that one would benefit from the distress (medical in this instance) of others. Recall the definition of marking given by Zelizer (2005: 32):

> In the broadest terms, people create connected lives by differentiating their multiple social ties from each other, marking boundaries between those different ties by means of everyday practices, sustaining those ties through joint activities (including economic activities), but constantly negotiating the exact content of important social ties.

Market earmarking, by introducing the organ in a generalised commensurability (Radin, 1996), leads to a report of power considered improper.[13]

On the basis of this observation, economists will attempt to build a space of legitimacy with the aim of removing the trade in organs from the grey area of incentives by implementing a social system of distribution in accordance with the marking of the organ. In an article that entered into the Pantheon of economic thought, after receiving the Nobel Memorial Prize in Economic Sciences, Alvin Roth (2007) returned to the difficulty posed by "repugnant markets" in market design. A market is said to be repugnant when the existence of supply and demand does not allow the establishment of a system of exchange by the market because of its repulsive aspect for the population: "[E]ven where there may be willing suppliers and demanders of certain transactions, aversion to those transactions by others may constrain or even prevent the transactions" (Roth, 2007: 40). Roth gives a large number of examples of this type of property, whose merchant nature has been rejected: money (loan interest), prostitution, slavery, organs, sperm and eggs, life insurance, etc. Two cases must be distinguished: if a market is deemed repugnant by the suppliers and the demanders themselves, there is no supply and demand because the institutional structure of allocation of a good can be considered as a characteristic of this good. Nevertheless, if it is neither the suppliers nor the demanders who prevent a market from being set up, but a group of third parties, then we can consider that it is society that reduces the contractual freedom of individuals. Such a definition of repugnance relies entirely on the weight social conventions place on the constitution of markets: the illegitimacy of the insertion of a symbolically marked good into a distribution system that does not correspond to it, creating the grey zone of incentive as illegitimate manipulation. As such, and to avoid the principle of hostile worlds Zelizer denounced, it would be more accurate to speak of a repugnance of the market *vis-à-vis* the organ. It is this repugnance, constituting a conventional border between the merchant and the non-merchant, which prevents the performativity of markets for organs and compels economists to design alternative matching systems that do not involve any monetary transfer.

The non-market solution: building a space of legitimacy

The large number of critics of the organ business justifies the prohibition of market exchange as part of the law. In France, the Law of Bioethics no. 94-654, 29 July 1994, stipulates that "no payment, whatever its form, can be allocated to the one which lends itself to the collection of elements of its body, or in the collection of its products", thus reinforcing a ban dating from 1976. In the United States, the National Organ Transplant Act legislates in the same direction: "It shall be unlawful for any person to knowingly acquire, receive, or otherwise transfer any human organ for valuable consideration for use in human transplantation if the transfer affects interstate commerce." The almost universal prohibition (only Iran allows monetary remuneration for organs) defeats the performativity of organ markets, and has led economists to envisage alternative modes of pairing. The organ is labelled as non-market within the framework of historically established social conventions; the economist must therefore set up a system of legitimate, non-market matching. According to Alvin Roth (2007), the economic design must make it possible to circumvent the refusal of the market solution. For some years, market design has been a central part of the discipline; the Nobel Prize has been awarded to several of its specialists, such as Vernon Smith, Leonid Hurwicz and Alvin Roth. It is a direct branch of experimental economics, principally through works by Charles Plott and Vernon Smith. In contrast to the behavioural approach discussed in the previous section, the experimental economics which inspires economic design was primarily aimed at understanding the institutional rules that can lead to results comparable to those described in economic modelling. The central point is no longer the rationality of the agents, whose behaviour becomes dependent on the institutional rules, but the institutional rules themselves. It is therefore from game theory, the filed of economics that studies the rules of the game (Roth, 2002: 1342), that one can derive a great deal, especially its theoretical tools. A canonical example (discussed in Chapter 3), also studied in performativist literature, is the design of a bidding system for the distribution of the radio spectrum set up by the US Federal Communication Commission in 1994 (Guala, 2001; Muniesa and Callon, 2007; Mirowski and Nik-Khah, 2007). A second canonical case of economic engineering is the reform of the matching of physicians to hospitals in the United States in 1995. Whereas in 1950 the authorities had decided to set up a national clearing house to ensure the best possible respect for student choices, this system was called into question at the end of the 1980s. This challenge is mainly the result of socio-cultural evolution leading to the instability of the device. Indeed, the ever-increasing proportion of couples wishing to be posted to jobs in the same cities was not taken into account in the procedure used. The result was great instability: young doctors quickly changed institutions after their first assignment – a damaging situation for both doctors and hospitals. Alvin Roth was responsible for providing an alternative system (Roth and Peranson, 1999). He used a matching algorithm to integrate this new data. The interest of this case is precisely that the solution put in place was not a market one, but a centralised matching mode without price. However, in the case of kidneys taken from living donors, Alvin Roth notes that the substitution of a system of exchange between donor/recipient pairs with a simple market allows the acceptance of non-market trade of organs. This type of system was first suggested by Felix Rapaport (1986), and realised for the first time in South Korea in 1991, then in Switzerland in 1999, and was inherited by Alvin Roth and his team, who theorised fine mechanisms, principles and operating conditions, as well as testing their effectiveness. As we have seen, the market solution is, with the exception of Iran, rejected as a mode of organ matching. Mainly two mechanisms remain available: (1) registration on a waiting list for post-mortem donation, (2) direct donation within a compatible pair. These two mechanisms would be at the heart of a set of research aimed at implementing the most efficient allocation procedures possible. This research, which is part of market design studies, relates to what the Roth calls the matching market. The starting point for this research programme was the shortage of post-mortem donations, resulting in longer waiting lists (Roth et al., 2004, 2005).

In 2003, 8665 kidney transplants involving cadaveric removals took place in the United States for 60,000 patients on the waiting list. In the same year, 3436 patients died while waiting for a kidney. For the author, there is a need to palliate this deficiency by the mixture of the two mechanisms mentioned within procedures that are more complex and more effective on two levels: first, in terms of the number of transplants; secondly, in terms of compatibility between donor and recipient. In order to simplify the details of the various strategies proposed, only blood compatibility will be considered here, on the basis of the ABO system

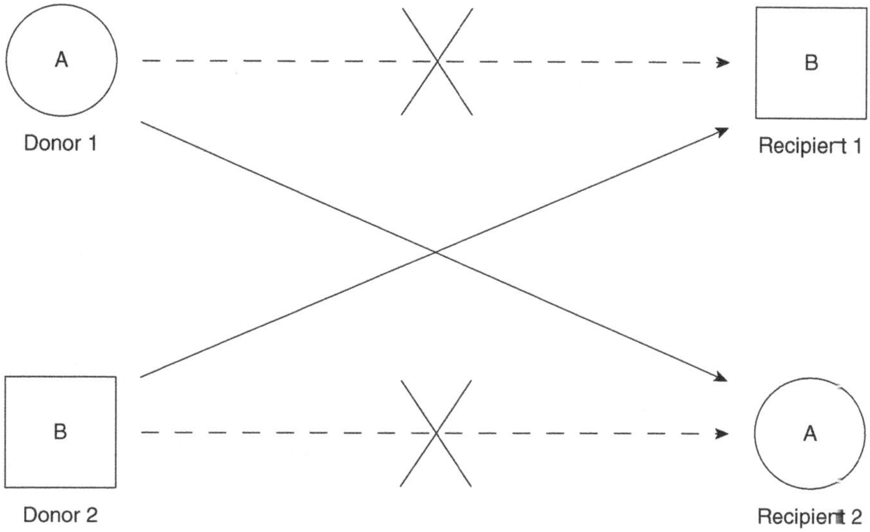

Figure 8.5 Two-way exchange

(Wallis et al., 2011). In this context, the basic principle of the matching market is the identification of donor/receiver pairs (kidney paired donation), incompatible through the simple mechanism of two-way exchange. Imagine that a person in need of an organ knows someone willing to give him one, for example his spouse, but there is blood incompatibility between them. The main idea is to match this first pair with another pair of people in a similar situation, but whose donor and recipient are respectively compatible with the recipient and the donor of the first pair. So the exchange does not take place between individuals, but between pairs of donors/recipients. In Figure 8.5, Donor 1, incompatible with the second member of his pair (Recipient 1), gives a kidney to Recipient 2, belonging to another pair and with whom it is compatible. At the same time, Donor 2 provides a kidney to Recipient 1. This simple mechanism is the basic structure of Alvin Roth et al.'s market design, in that it allows for multiple enhancements.

The main limitation of this simple structure is that it is hard to apply when certain pairs have difficulties not only in finding compatible donors, but also in finding a compatible donor from whom an incompatible recipient can receive an organ. This is particularly the case for people with the O blood group. The solution to this problem is to expand the structure to a three-way exchange, as shown in Figure 8.6.

This structure overcomes the problem of group O, in that it avoids the imperative of reciprocity between pairs. This principle can, of course, be extended to a larger number of pairs. It is also possible to support these mechanisms by adding other sources of organs, including waiting lists. In Figure 8.7, Donor A provides an organ to Recipient A on the waiting list for post-mortem donation. In exchange, Receiver O gains priority position on this same waiting list.

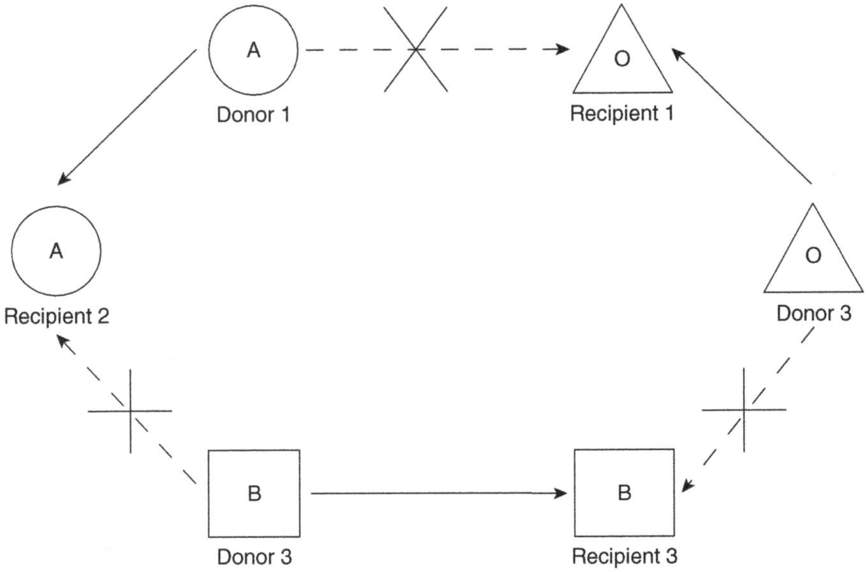

Figure 8.6 Three-way exchange

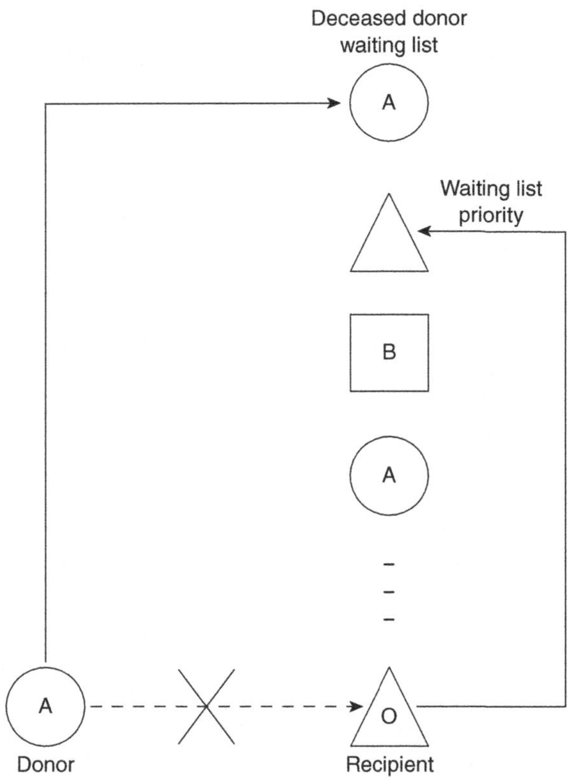

Figure 8.7 Exchange within a list

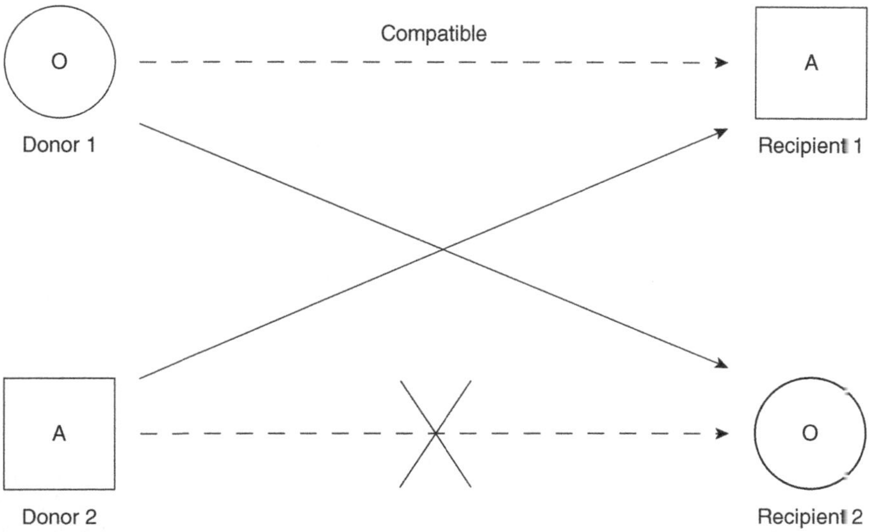

Figure 8.8 Two-way exchange with compatible pairs

One element that should not be overlooked is that in these procedures, increasing the number of committed pairs increases the chances of finding a compatible donor. Therefore, increasing the number in the group to whom the allocation procedures of compatible bidder and applicant pairs are applied may be relevant if we consider universal donors, such as those with blood group O, as in the case shown in Figure 8.8.

Incorporating purely altruistic and not directed gifts into the reasoning has expanded the potential sources of organs, as well as the mechanisms available for institutional design. The primary virtue of altruistic giving is to allow the development of previously unattainable chains by creating domino effects, as shown in Figure 8.9. The chain, called NEAD (Nonsimultaneous Extend Altruistic Donor), includes an altruistic donor and a time gap between two simultaneous chains. In this case, the last donor in the first chain, who normally should have provided his organ to a patient on a waiting list, allows a delayed start to a new chain (a "bridge donor"). The device therefore addresses the problem of the rapid deterioration of organs after harvesting, which can reduce supply.

Having considered a set of mechanisms, it remains to evaluate their effectiveness. This work was done by Roth et al. (2004, 2005), as well as by Saidman et al. (2005). The first in the series of works involving Roth will be of particular interest. Using the principle of simulation, they aim to study the hypothesis according to which not only does the matching market make it possible to offer an opportunity to people on waiting lists, but also the size of the group to which an algorithm of distribution of the organs is applied is an essential element: the more important it is, the greater the connection between donors and suppliers. Moreover, this study tends to show that efficiency increases with the mixing of the mechanisms addressed above. In the model developed by Roth et al. (2004, 2005), each

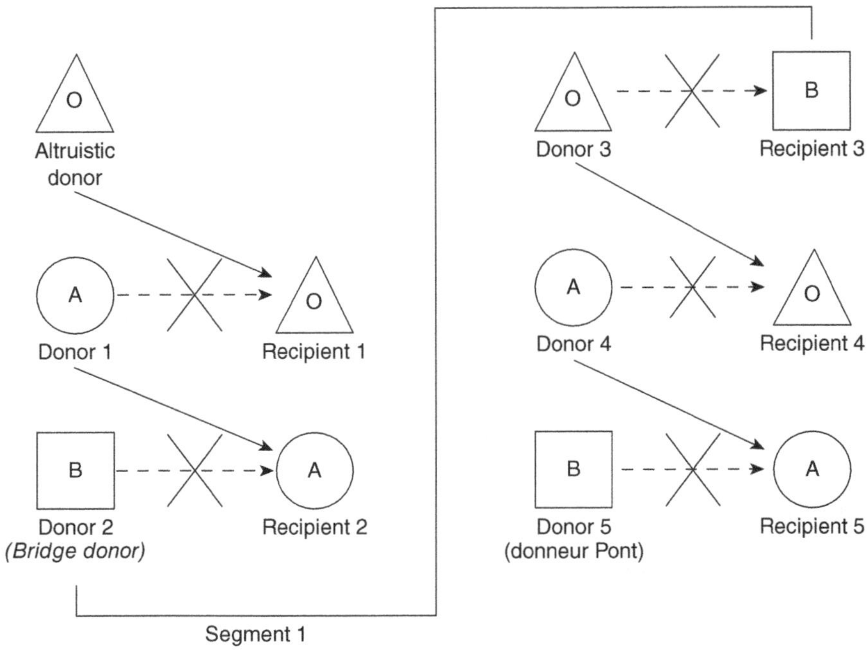

Figure 8.9 Altruistic donor and non-simultaneity

patient requiring an organ and presenting himself with an incompatible donor provides strict preferences (based on blood compatibility, donor age and tissue compatibility) for different donors, as well as the possibility of taking priority on the deceased donor waiting list. Roth et al. showed that the quantity of transplants depends on the following parameters:

i the size of the group;
ii the presence of the alternative "waiting list";
iii the maximum number of transplants that can be performed at the same time – in other words: the maximum size of the chain;
iv the presence in the group of compatible pairs.

In the case without waiting list alternatives, authors use the standard top trading cycle (TTC) algorithms developed by Shapley and Scarf (1974): if each agent (pair) has preferences over all the pairs, there exists at least one chain of pairs (a_1, a_2, . . . a_n) in which each pair chooses the following, and a_n chooses a_1. In each chain, the organs are allocated and the process continues until no pair remains. If the possibility of choosing the waiting list is allowed, Shapley and Scarf use an alternative algorithm, top trading cycles and chains (TTCC), in which a_n dictates the waiting list priority. The results of the simulation run by Roth et al. (2005) are conclusive: the more participants there are, the greater the group of choices, and the more efficient the matching process. These results are convincing for Shapley and Scarf: the size of the group, the widening of all types of pairs and the complexification of the l-chains make the matching mechanisms more efficient, which legitimises a concrete design whose implementation mechanism of couples' relationship would follow an algorithm similar to the one tested. Finally, the organs are harvested at the same time (here we exclude the mechanism of Figure 8.9).

Gift-giving and the limit of performativity

Let us focus on three salient features of the matching market *à la* Roth: first, we abandon the monetary relationship between donor and recipient. The pattern of matching means that the recipient is matched, within a pair, with a donor who agrees to sacrifice a kidney (which will be exchanged). Secondly, the exchange takes place between two pairs, and the receiver is first matched with a member of what Steiner (2010a, 2010b) calls his emotional community. Finally, the structure of the pairing (the organ harvesting taking place at the same time) minimises the fear of opportunistic behaviour in terms of refusing to donate a kidney once the family member has received a transplant.

We can therefore conclude that a technical device has been used as a tool for the shaping of reality, in that the system devised by Roth makes it possible to bridge the gap between economic theory and the social world. Here, the conventional resistance to the performativity of a mode of pairing has forced the economist to design a system that conforms to the non-market vision of the organ. According to Steiner, this system is relatively close to the category of gift-giving developed by Marcel Mauss. Despite the classic rhetoric of donation ("organ donation"), the system promoted by Roth is certainly the first to be really related to a system of Maussian gift-giving, characterised by the triple obligation to give, receive and reciprocate. Nothing is less true with regard to post-mortem donation, for which there is simply no direct link between donor and recipient (even considering the family as the donor), so no obligation to give back. In this particular context, organ donation is first and foremost a dialogue maintained within an emotional community about what the deceased would have liked, or what seems right from the point of view of the mortuary rite. The problem is quite different in the context of transplantation within the emotional community of the recipient. The conditions are linked, so that we can potentially speak of a gift. In their reference book, Fox and Swazey (2013: 32) warn against the misuse of the gift rhetoric adopted by the medical authorities, a rhetoric that values altruistic giving as a true gift of life. As Steiner (2010b: 85–86) also underlines, the Maussian gift is only apparently a matter of altruism and disinterestedness (Brisset, 2017c). Mauss (1923–1924 [2007]: 142; our translation) particularly insists on the power relationship and the agonistic escalation that often underlies the gift: "Some of the most expensive houses are burned, we throw into the water, to crush, to "flatten" our rival. Not only does one make progress, but one also moves one's family up the social ladder." This is the meaning of the triple obligation when it is never closed. Fox and Swazey emphasise greatly the different pressures, from the family as well as from the medical profession, on the potential donor. This is so even though the gift of an organ can be followed, with difficulty, by a counter-gift, which is what distances us from the Maussian gift. The authors speak of more than one sacrifice as a gift, or even a "tyranny of the gift". It is not uncommon for the medical team to be prepared to offer a compatible person a medical alibi so that they can legitimately refuse to donate. This tyranny affects both the donor and the recipient, locked into the impossibility of paying back an overwhelming debt – an overwhelming aspect taking both material and immaterial form, as Godbout (2008: 421) observes, for example, in the context of the post-mortem gift, the fear of being led to embody the donor. The author relates the case of a donor's wife wishing to put her head on the chest of the receiver to hear her husband's heart beating. The liquidation of the debt passes here into a loss of identity.

In this case, we have to deal with an abusively negative view of debt (Godbout, 2008), perhaps inherited from the Maussian perspective. Effectively, "owing something to someone" can be a positive experience ("I owe him so much"), the reward for which is eternal gratitude (Schwerin, 1998). Nevertheless, whether in its negative or positive sense, the concept of non-repayable debt breaks with the structure of the Maussian gift, so that one can legitimately say that it has never actually been practised in the context of organ trade before Roth's work. It is indeed with these that the relationship seems to have taken the shape of gift-giving. It is not between two people, but between two emotional communities (two pairs), mediated by socio-technical equipment consisting of medical teams and the matching system.[14] The obligation of reciprocation (an organ for an organ) is inscribed, for the first time, at the heart of the economic pairing. It is the condition of existence that is guaranteed by the simultaneity of surgical procedures. The exchange is essentially considered fair if it involves two pairs and two equivalent bodies. This avoids introducing the organ into the system of generalised commensurability of market goods. It is no longer an unfair remuneration, which is an incentive to express the power of one individual over another – at least according to the American law which authorises such a system, and in the eyes of many detractors of the market solution, ready to follow Roth.

The pressure of social conventions on the performed economic theory then brings out a new system of gift-giving that is compatible with the non-market representation of the organ. Roth's theory is performative (Steiner, 2010a), unlike that of Becker and Elìas. The agents are ready to coordinate their use because of a conventional complementarity to the non-market earmarking of the organ, synonymous with donation. Roth's gift-giving system is accepted when it is a refinement of the simple gift system already established.

Conclusion

In this chapter, the effectiveness of the tool "convention" in understanding the social pressures undergone by the performative phenomenon was revealed. This is a felicity condition: to shape the world in the image of a theory, although it is necessary that this modelling is socially accepted. The performativity of markets in the context of organ trade fails for a simple reason: the organ is considered a non-market good within the conventional categories of the social world. Thus, the market as a matching procedure is set aside because of moral considerations. The exchange of an organ for money is considered improper because of the power relationship between the donor and the recipient. Here, financial remuneration is often equated with an incentive to deviate from the will of others to achieve one's own ends – a step that must not be taken in a case of extreme distress, both for the donor and the benefactor: how can we blame a person on the waiting list for doing everything possible to get an organ? As such, the organ is a loathsome commodity – a commodity whose merchantability is not recognised – and economists wanting to address the problem of organ shortage through the rationalisation of matching procedures are forced to abandon the market solution in favour of an alternative system. The particularly interesting point is that in the end, the construction of the social world by economist theorists leads to a system that remains completely new whilst still compatible with the non-market convention. It is getting closer to the Maussian gift-counter-gift, which paradoxically, was not the case with the so-called "donation" systems set up around the world. The economist is therefore confronted with a resistant social world, subjectively objective in the sense of Searle, that constrains its performative capacity (see Chapter 5).

Notes

1 Although I will rely on a relatively large literature, Philippe Steiner's (2010b) work will be the starting point.
2 A reconnection of blood vessels, which differentiates grafts from transplants.
3 The blood group of an individual depends on the type of antigen (A or B) present on the surface of his red blood cells. It can be of group A, B, AB (if both antigens are present) or O (in case of absence of antigens).
4 For an overview, see Howard (2007).
5 Sambuc (2013) nevertheless emphasises that remuneration linked to a futures contract and calculated on an actuarial basis would necessarily be modest given the low probability of dying under conditions allowing transplant. It would then be necessary to increase insurance premium reductions to make them effective incentives. Such a measure would have the perverse effect of increasing the price of organs on the market. Cohen (1989) proposes a futures market system in which it is no longer the donor, but his heirs who receive a premium for the organ actually taken. The incentive is therefore biased to the possibility of leaving a larger inheritance.
6 The idea of "iceberg cost" is regularly attributed to Samuelson (1954), although it seems that the first to have evoked the idea was Johann Heinrich von Thünen. It consists of considering that the cost of transporting a good is paid for with the good itself.

7 For a political critique of this notion, see Camille (2013).

8 This remains relatively consistent with the standard economic theory of rationality in terms of stability of preferences; it is sufficient to explain intrinsic motivation variations by changes in the agent's perception of his environment, or even of the environment itself (Frey and Jegen, 2001: 592).

9 Just like the son who, under Roman law, enjoys a situation close to the slave: even having acquired adulthood, he remains at the mercy of his father. This surely explains the important role of parricide in ancient literature.

10 The complete quotation is as follows: "Know therefore those who do not know it, know the enemies of God and of the human race, whatever name they take, that between the strong and the weak, between the rich and the poor, between the master and the servant are liberty that oppresses, and the law that liberates. Law is the sword of the great, duty is the shield of the small ones". It concerns the sacred dominical rule. Lacordaire thus opposes the law of God, immutable and universal, to that of men, fluctuating and serving the powerful.

11 For further reflections on this point, see Brisset (2017c).

12 On this point, see Friedman and Friedman (2006).

13 Roman law enshrines this principle by stipulating that the body of a free man cannot be the subject of any estimate.

14 This element is not contradictory, contrary to what Fox and Swazey seem to say, of the Maussian gift. Indeed, the latter also requires an underlying social device, the principle of symmetry that Karl Ponalyi writes about at great length.

Conclusion to Part III

The second part of this book showed the theoretical interest of developing a theory of performativity considering felicity conditions – namely, conditions to be met so that a perfect performativity can be put in place. This third part allowed us to demonstrate the heuristic relevance of this perspective by analysing three case studies. Each of the studies focused on a condition of felicity (empiricity, self-fulfilment and conventional compatibility). The general idea is not to define performativity in so rigorous a sense that it would simply be impossible to identify it. There is no such thing as perfect performativity, bringing together all the underlined conditions. Each time, there is a progressive adjustment, more or less powerful, between the theoretical and the real. This book's approach is precisely to point out these frictions, where performativity fails, where the theory adapts to a reality that resists it: the theory of rationality must become empirical to allow the establishment of policies of rationalisation, the BSM model had to adapt to real financial movements, economists had to set up matching systems in accordance with the social representations of the organ.

General conclusion

This work has adopted a particular posture. Written by an economist, it ventured into poorly known lands for someone who has been trained in this discipline, those of sociology and philosophy. This multidisciplinarity is not justified for its own sake, but because it was the most effective way to answer a specific question resulting from a reconstruction of the theory of performativity: how to explain the conditions necessary for performativity, which means how to think of the reasons for performative failures. In its Callonian sense, the notion of performativity is now well established in the field of social sciences. This is evidenced by the debates it provokes. A largely overestimated gimmick for some, it was a way to renew the approach of the social for others; the least we can say is that the approach does not leave one indifferent – so much so that its use is increasingly a function of the rhetorical process. A number of philosophers have not been particularly enthusiastic about the particular use of the Austinian concept by Michel Callon's continuators. Compared to Austinian theory, considered rigorous, systematic and taking care to explore the conditions necessary for the realisation of speech acts, Callonian performativity is seen as a distortion that struggles to convince philosophers accustomed to Austinian pedagogy. This story is not new. Judith Butler, who also takes up the idea of performativity in the context of gender studies, has also been subject to this type of attack. This is the fate of any conceptual hijacking. This is the price of novelty. This does not mean, however, that the critics in question, who some people will hastily call conservatives, have missed their target.

In a way, the approach of this book falls between these two limits: conservative because it poses to the Callonian theory of performativity a permanent question, stemming from the philosophy of language, that of the conditions of felicity of the performative act exerted by economic theory; creative as it uses a concept that also comes from the philosophy of language, that of convention, to try to shed new light on the contours of performativity. This is a vast programme that no single book could exhaust. This one is only a first step, with all of its theoretical imperfections and shortcuts. I hope I can extend my work by deepening its sociological and philosophical dimensions.[1]

At the end of this theoretical journey, it is time to return to its main stages. This work consists of four major milestones: to define and resituate the theory of the performativity of economic theories; to explore, systematise and develop criticism; to propose analytical tools that would overcome these criticisms; and finally, to implement these tools. The first stage, consisting of Chapters 1 and 2, led to the discovery of a fundamental characteristic of the theory of performativity: the desire to break with those Bruno Latour called "sociologists of the social" – namely, those who accept the takeover of social actors by macro-social entities. In the context of economic sociology, it is more particularly the concept of embeddedness that is rejected by the school of Michel Callon. There is no common world: the social environment is constantly being constructed and redefined as a network uniting humans and non-humans, agents and techniques. This social ontology is the direct legacy of actor-network theory. From this perspective, economic theories perform in the social world when they fit into devices that make people do things that conform to the theory. These technical devices are multiple, diffused, heterogeneous: price-sheets available to arbitrageurs on the financial markets, rating software, nudges, matching algorithms – many cases that have been widely discussed. The technicist vision of the social world of which the theory of performativity is a carrier has attracted a large number of critics. Considering the social as a vast and highly malleable technical network, it abandons the traditionally critical posture of economic sociology *vis-à-vis* economic theories. Michel Callon is explicit about this: there is no point in placing oneself as a competitor with economists in the heuristics of the social world; it is better to consider them as part of the world in whose construction they participate. Exploring the criticisms of performativity allowed us, in a second step, to identify the deep point of disagreement, the original theoretical weakness: the difficulty of addressing performative failures. One of the major reasons for this deficiency is the fact of not considering performativity as a social process taking place in a world made up of macro-social entities. This posture leads to an extremely loose vision of performativity, a position that largely explains today's increasingly rhetorical use of the notion. This brings us to the third step: redefining performativity so that performative failures can be thought about. In this respect, the concept of convention is the central axis of our theoretical reconstruction: a theory transforms the social world when it becomes a social convention which is an element considered as a coordination marker within a population. This work allowed us to define more precisely what we understood by "theory" in the performativist viewpoint, but also, and above all, to identify the conditions necessary for performativity to put in place a new convention. These three conditions are empiricity, self-fulfilment and compatibility between the conventions translating the theory and existing conventions. The fourth step was to apply the analytical tools to "scenes of performativity" in order to prove their analytical relevance, as well as showing how they illuminated these scenes in a new way. To think of failure as we have done is to point out in performative movements places of friction. There is no such thing as a perfect performativity. Every performative process encounters resistances, and this work has identified them.

Note

1 See, for instance, Brisset (2018).

Bibliography

Adorno, T., & Popper, K. (1979). *De Vienne à Francfort. La querelle allemande des sciences sociales*. Brussels: Complexes.

Akerlof, G. (1970). The market for "lemons": quality uncertainty and the market mechanism. *Quarterly Journal of Economics*, *84*, 488–500.

Akrich, M. (2006a). La construction d'un système socio-technique. Esquisse pour une anthropologie des techniques. In M. Akrich, M. Callon, & B. Latour (Eds), *Sociologie de la traduction: textes fondateurs* (pp. 109–134). Paris: Mines Paris.

Akrich, M. (2006b). La description des objets techniques. In M. Akrich, M. Callon, & B. Latour (Eds), *Sociologie de la traduction: textes fondateurs* (pp. 159–178). Paris: Mines Paris.

Akrich, M. (2006c). Les objets techniques et leurs utilisations. De la conception à l'action. In M. Akrich, M. Callon, & B. Latour (Eds), *Sociologie de la traduction: textes fondateurs* (pp. 179–199). Paris: Mines Paris.

Allais, M. (1953). Le comportement de l'homme rationnel devant le risque: une critique des postulats de l'école américaine. *Econometrica*, *21*, 503–546.

Amable, B., & Palombarani, S. (2005). *L'économie politique n'est pas une science morale (Raisons d'agir)*. Paris: Raison d'agir.

Ambroise, B. (2008). *Qu'est-ce qu'un acte de parole?* Paris: Vrin.

Ambroise, B. (2015). À propos de Fabian Muniesa. The provoked economy: economic reality and the performative turn. *L'homme et la société*, *197*(3), 204–215.

Ambroise, B., Salle, G., & Sobel, R. (2015). L'économie entre performativité, idéologie et pouvoir symbolique. *L'homme et la société*, *197*(3), 13–30.

Aoki, M. (2001). *Toward a Comparative Institutional Analysis*. Cambridge, MA: MIT Press.

Aoki, M. (2007a). Endogenizing institutions and institutional changes. *Journal of Institutional Economics*, *3*(1), 1–33.

Aoki, M. (2007b). *Linking Economic and Social-exchange Games: From the Community Norm to CSR*. SIEPR Discussion Paper No. 07-18. https://siepr.stanford.edu/sites/default/files/publications/07-18_0.pdf.

Archer, M. (1995). *Realist Social Theory: The Morphogenetic Approach*. Cambridge: Cambridge University Press.

Ariely, D. (2009). *Predictably Irrational, Revised and Expanded Edition*. New York: HarperCollins.

Ariely, D., Loewenstein, G., & Prelec, D. (2003). "Coherence arbitrariness": stable demand curves without stable preferences. *Quarterly Journal of Economics*, *118*(1), 73–106.

Aristotle. (2015). *On Interpretation*, Trans. E. M. Edghill. Adelaide: University of Adelaide. https://ebooks.adelaide.edu.au/a/aristotle/interpretation/.

Arnsperger, C. (2009). *Éthique de l'existence post-capitaliste*. Paris: Cerf.

Arrow, K. J. (1951). *Social Choice and Individual Values*. New York: Wiley.

Arrow, K. J. (1972). Gifts and exchanges. *Philosophy and Public Affairs*, *1*(4), 343–362.

Arrow, K. J. (1974). *The Limits of Organization*. New York: Norton.

Aspers, P. (2007). Theory, reality, and performativity in markets. *American Journal of Economics and Sociology*, *66*(2), 379–400.

Aumann, R. (1976). Agreeing to disagree. *Annals of Statistics*, *4*(6), 1236–1239.

Austin, J. L. (1962). *How to Do Things with Words*. Cambridge, MA: Harvard University Press.

Austin, J. L. (1979). Performative utterances. In J. O. Urmson & G. J. Warnock (Eds), *Philosophical Papers* (pp. 233–252). New York: Oxford University Press.

Azariadis, C. (1981). Self-fulfilling prophecies. *Journal of Economic Theory*, *25*(3), 380–396.

Azariadis, C., & Guesnerie, R. (1982). Prophéties créatrices et persistance des théories. *Revue économique*, *33*(5), 787–806.

Bacharach, M. (2006). *Beyond Individual Choice: Teams and Frames in Game Theory*. Princeton, NJ: Princeton University Press.

Bachelard, G. (1949). *La psychanalyse du feu*. Paris: Gallimard.

Bachelard, G. (1971). Actualité de l'histoire des sciences. In J.-F. Braunstein (Ed.), *L'histoire des sciences* (pp. 159–174). Paris: Vrin.

Bachelier, L. (1900). Théorie de la spéculation. *Annales de l'École Normale Supérieure*, *3*(27), 21–86.

Backhouse, R., & Medema, S. (2009). On the definition of economics. *Journal of Economic Perspectives*, *23*(1), 221–233.

Banerjee, A., & Duflo, E. (2011). *Poor Economics: A Radical Rethinking of the Way to Fight Global Poverty*. Boston, MA: Public Affairs.

Baranzini, R. (2006). Nature et statut épistémologique des lois économiques dans l'oeuvre de Léon Walras. *Economie et société, Série "Histoire de la pensée économique"*, *40*(12), 1671–1691.

Baranzini, R., Diemer, A., & Mouchot, C. (Eds). (2005). *Études walrassiennes*. Paris: L'Harmattan.

Baranzini, R., Legris, A., & Ragni, L. (Eds). (2011). *Léon Walras et l'équilibre économique général – recherches récentes*. Paris: Economica.

Barber, B. (1995). All economies are "embedded": the career of a concept, and beyond. *Social Research*, *62*(2), 387–414.

Barnes, B. (1983). Social life as bootstrapped induction. *Sociology*, *17*(4), 524–545.

Barnes, B. (2011). Relativism as completion of the scientific project. In R. Schantz & M. Seidel (Eds), *The Problem of Relativism in the Sociology of (Scientific) Knowledge* (pp. 23–39). Frankfurt: Ontos verlag.

Batifoulier, P. (Ed.). (2001). *Théorie des conventions*. Paris: Economica.

Batifoulier, P., & Thévenon, O. (2001). Interprétation et fondement conventionnel des règles. In P. Batifoulier (Ed.), *Théorie des conventions* (pp. 219–252). Paris: Economica.

Baud, J.-P. (1993). *L'affaire de la main volée. Une histoire juridique du corps humain*. Paris: Seuil.

Beaver, W. (1981). Market efficiency. *Accounting Review*, *56*, 23–37.

Becker, G. S. (1968). Crime and punishment: an economic approach. *Journal of Political Economy*, *76*, 169–217.

Becker, G. S., & Elìas, J. J. (2007). Introducing incentives in the market for live and cadaveric organ donations. *Journal of Economic Perspectives, 21*(3), 3–24.

Beckert, J. (2011). Where do prices come from? Sociological approaches to price formation. *Socio-economic Review, 9*(4), 757–786.

Berg, N., & Gigerenzer, G. (2010). As-if behavioral economics: neoclassical economics in disguise. *History of Economic Ideas, 18*(1), 133–165.

Berger, P., & Luckman, T. (1966). *The Social Construction of Reality*. London: Penguin Books.

Berlin, I. (1958). *Two Concepts of Liberty*. Oxford: Oxford University Press.

Bernstein, P. L. (1995). *Against the Gods*. Hoboken, NJ: Wiley.

Bernstein, P. L. (2005). *Capital Ideas: The Improbable Origins of Modern Wall Street*. Hoboken, NJ: Wiley.

Bernstein, P. L. (2007). *Capital Ideas Evolving*. Hoboken, NJ: Wiley.

Bessis, F. (2004). *Karl Popper et la dynamique des conventions*. Document de travail capitalisme(s) et démocratie(s). http://docplayer.fr/43806770-Karl-popper-et-la-dynamique-des-conventions-1.html.

Bhaskar, R. (1989). *The Possibility of Naturalism: A Philosophic Critique of the Contemporary Human Sciences*. Brighton: Harvester.

Bhattacharyya, A., Pattanaik, P., & Xu, Y. (2011). Choice, internal consistency and rationality. *Economics and Philosophy, 27*(1), 123–149.

Binmore, K. (1987). Modeling rational players, Part 1. *Economics and Philosophy, 3*(2), 179–214.

Binmore, K. (1988). Modeling rational players, Part 2. *Economics and Philosophy, 4*(1), 9–55.

Binmore, K., & Klemperer, P. (2002). The biggest auction ever: the sale of the British 3G telecom licences. *Economic Journal, 112*(478), C74–C96.

Black, F. (1989). How to use the holes in Black-Scholes. *Journal of Applied Corporate Finance, 1*(4), 67–73.

Black, F., & Scholes, M. (1973). The pricing of options and corporate liabilities. *Journal of Political Economy, 81*(3), 637–654.

Black, F., Jensen, M. C., & Scholes, M. (1972). The Capital Asset Pricing Model: some empirical tests. In M. Jensen (Ed.), *Studies in the Theory of Capital Markets* (pp. 79–121). New York: Praeger.

Blanchard, O., & Watson, M. (1984). Bulles, anticipations rationnelles et marchés financiers. *Annales de l'INSEE, 54*, 79–100.

Blaug, M. (1972). Was there a marginal revolution? *History of Political Economy, 4*(2), 269–280.

Block, F. (2003). Karl Polanyi and the writing of *The Great Transformation*. *Theory and Society, 32*(3), 275–306.

Bloor, D. (1976). *Knowledge and Social Imagery*. London: Routledge.

Bloor, D. (1997). *Wittgenstein, Rules and Institutions*. London: Routledge.

Bloor, D. (1999). Anti-Latour. *Studies in History and Philosophy of Science, 30*(1), 81–112.

Boghossian, P. (2006). *Fear of Knowledge: Against Relativism and Constructivism*. Oxford: Clarendon Press.

Böhme, J. (2016). "Doing" laboratory experiments: an ethnomethodological study of the performative practice in behavioral economic research. In I. Boldyrev & E. Svetlova (Eds), *Enacting the Dismal Science: New Perspectives on the Performativity of Economics* (pp. 87–108). New York: Palgrave Macmillan.

Boileau, C. (2002). *Dans le dédale du don d'organe. Le cheminement de l'ethnologue*. Paris: Éditions des archives contemporaines.
Boldyrev, I., & Svetlova, E. (2016a). After the turn: how the performativity of economics matters. In I. Boldyrev & E. Svetlova (Eds), *Enacting the Dismal Science: New Perspectives on the Performativity of Economics* (pp. 1–27). New York: Palgrave Macmillan.
Boldyrev, I., & Svetlova, E. (Eds). (2016b). *Enacting the Dismal Science: New Perspectives on the Performativity of Economics*. New York: Palgrave Macmillan.
Boltanski, L. (2011). *On Critique: A Sociology of Emancipation*. Cambridge: Polity Press.
Boltanski, L. (2012). *Love and Justice as Competences: Three Essays on the Sociology of Action*. Cambridge: Polity Press.
Boltanski, L., & Thévenot, L. (2006). *On Justification: Economies of Worth*. Princeton, NJ: Princeton University Press.
Bonnay, D., & Laugier, S. (2003). La logique sauvage de Quine à Lévi-Strauss. *Archives de philosophie, 66*(1), 49–66.
Boschetti, F., & Gray, R. (2007). Emergence and computability. *Emergence: Complexity and Organization, 3*(1/2), 120–130.
Bossi, L. (2012). *Les frontières de la mort*. Paris: Manuels Payot.
Boudon, R. (2009). *La rationalité*. Paris: Presses Universitaires de France.
Boudon, R. (2011). Ordinary rationality: the core of analytical sociology. In P. Demeulenaere (Ed.), *Analytical Sociology and Social Mechanisms* (pp. 33–49). Cambridge: Cambridge University Press.
Boulding, K. E. (1966). The economics of knowledge and the knowledge of economics. *American Economic Review, 56*(2), 1–13.
Boumans, M. (2005). *How Economists Model the World into Numbers*. London: Routledge.
Bourdeau, V. (2005). *L'économie politique républicaine de Léon Walras*. Université de Franche-Comté, Besançon.
Bourdeau, V. (2012). Le marché des égaux: un aspect socialiste de l'échange républicain. *Revue de philosophie économique, 13*(2), 3–24.
Bourdieu, P. (1981). Décrire et prescrire. Note sur les conditions de possibilité et les limites de l'efficacité politique. *Actes de la recherche en sciences sociales, 38*(1), 69–73.
Bourdieu, P. (1991). *Language and Symbolic Power*. Cambridge: Polity Press.
Bourdieu, P. (1994). *Raisons pratiques. Sur la théorie de l'action*. Paris: Seuil.
Bourdieu, P. (1997 [2000]). *Pascalian Meditations*. Stanford, CA: Stanford University Press.
Bourdieu, P. (2001). *Science de la science et réflexivité*. Paris: Raison d'agir.
Bourdieu, P. (2012). *Sur l'état*. Paris: Seuil.
Bourne, L. S. (1992). Self-fulfilling prophecies? Decentralization, inner city decline, and the quality of urban life. *Journal of the American Planning Association, 58*, 509–513.
Bowles, S., & Gintis, H. (2011). *A Cooperative Species*. Princeton, NJ: Princeton University Press.
Boyer, A. (1994). *Introduction à la lecture de Karl Popper*. Paris: Presses de l'École Normale Supérieur.
Boyer, R. (2004). *Théorie de la régulation: les fondamentaux*. Paris: La Découverte.
Brecht, B. (1945 [1955]). *La vie de Galilée*. Paris: L'Arche.
Breton, Y., & Klotz, G. (Eds). (2009). *Jules Dupuit. Œuvres économiques complètes, 1*. Paris: Economica.
Brian, É. (2009). *Comment tremble la main invisible. Incertitude et marchés*. Paris: Springer.

Brian, É. (2010). Aléas, normes sociales et limites de la performativité. In C. Walter (Ed.), *Nouvelles normes financières* (pp. 191–219). Paris: Springer.
Bridel, P. (2008). Bortkiewicz et Walras. Notes sur une collaboration intellectuelle avortée. *Revue d'économie politique, 118*(5), 711–742.
Brisset, N. (2010). Compte-rendu de l'ouvrage de Claude Parthenay: vers une refondation de la science économique? Economie et argument transcendantal. *Economie et société, Série "Histoire de la pensée économique", 49*(2), 116–120.
Brisset, N. (2011). Les limites de la performativité des énoncés en économie: les apports de John Searle. *Œconomia, 1*(4), 557–588.
Brisset, N. (2012a). Compte-rendu de l'ouvrage de Christian Arnsperger: éthique de l'existence post-capitaliste. *Œconomia. History/Methodology/Philosophy, 2*(1), 116–120.
Brisset, N. (2012b). Deux approches de l'influence du discours économique sur les phénomènes sociaux. *Revue de philosophie économique, 13*(2), 25–62.
Brisset, N. (2012c). Retour sur le désencastrement: Polanyi ou la science économique vue comme une institution influençant l'évolution des systèmes économiques. *Revue européenne des sciences sociales, 50*(1), 7–39.
Brisset, N. (2013). Discours économique et évolution institutionnelle: les apports de J.R. Commons. *Economie et société, Série "Histoire de la pensée économique", 49*(10), 1777–1802.
Brisset, N. (2014a). D'une convention à une autre: quand la rationalité performe le réel. *Revue de philosophie économique, 15*(2), 69–108.
Brisset, N. (2014b). *Performativité des énoncés de la théorie économique: une approche conventionnaliste.* Université de Lausanne – Université de Paris 1 Panthéon Sorbonne, Paris.
Brisset, N. (2014c). Performer par le dispositif? Un retour critique sur la théorie de la performativité. *L'année sociologique, 64*(1), 217–246.
Brisset, N. (2015a). Comment (et pourquoi) repenser la performativité des énoncés théoriques. *L'homme et la société, 197*(3), 31–63.
Brisset, N. (2015b). La construction de la finance contemporaine. *Cités. Philosophie, politique, histoire, 64*(4), 39–51.
Brisset, N. (2015c). Les institutions comme objets émergents: une perspective ontologique. *Revue économique, 66*(3), 615–644.
Brisset, N. (2016a). Economics is not always performative: some limits for performativity. *Journal of Economic Methodology, 23*(2), 160–184.
Brisset, N. (2016b). Performativité et autoréalisation: le cas de la finance. *Revue européenne des sciences sociales, 54*(1), 37–73.
Brisset, N. (2016c). Un marché sans marchandise? Répugnance et matching market. *Revue d'économie politique, 126*(2), 125–153.
Brisset, N. (2017a). On performativity: option theory and the resistance of financial phenomena. *Journal of the History of Economic Thought, 39*(4), 549–569.
Brisset, N. (2017b). The future of performativity. *Œconomia. History/Methodology/Philosophy,* 7(3), 439–452.
Brisset, N. (2017c). *What Do We Learn from Market Design?* GREDEG Working Paper. www.gredeg.cnrs.fr/working-papers/GREDEG-WP-2017-03.pdf.
Brisset, N. (2018). Models as speech acts: the telling case of financial models. *Journal of Economic Methodology, 25*(1), 21–41.
Brisset, N., & Favereau, J. (2013). *Randomization of What? Moving from Libertarian to "Democratic Paternalism".* GREDEG Working Papers 2016-34. Nice: GREDEG

CNRS, University of Nice Sophia Antipolis. https://ideas.repec.org/p/gre/wpaper/2016-34.html.
Broad, C. D. (1925). *The Mind and Its Place in Nature*. London: Kegan Paul, Trench, Trubner & Co.
Burt, R. (1992). *Structural Holes: The Social Structure of Competition*. Cambridge, MA: Harvard University Press.
Burt, R. (2005). *Brokerage and Closure: An Introduction to Social Capital*. Oxford: Oxford University Press.
Butler, J. (2010). Performing agency. *Journal of Cultural Economy*, *3*(2), 147–161.
Callon, M. (1986a). Eléments pour une sociologie de la traduction. La domestication de coquilles Saints-Jacques et des marins-pêcheurs dans la bais de Saint-Brieuc. *L'année sociologique*, *36*, 169–208.
Callon, M. (1986b). Some elements of a sociology of translation: domestication of the scallops and the fishermen of St Brieuc Bay. In J. Law (Ed.), *Power, Action and Belief: A New Sociology of Knowledge?* pp. 196–223). London: Routledge.
Callon, M. (1998a). The embeddedness of economic markets in economics. In M. Callon (Ed.), *The Laws of the Markets* (pp. 1–57). Oxford: Plon.
Callon, M. (Ed.). (1998b). *The Laws of the Markets*. Oxford: Blackwell.
Callon, M. (1999). Ni intellectuel engagé, ni intellectuel dégagé: la double stratégie de l'attachement et du détachement. *Sociologie du travail*, *41*, 65–78.
Callon, M. (2002). Pour en finir avec les incertitudes? *Sociologie du travail*, *44*, 255–287.
Callon, M. (2005). Why virtualism paves the way to political impotence: Callon replies to Miller. *Economic Sociology European Electronic Newsletter*, *6*(2), 3–20.
Callon, M. (2006a). La performativité de l'économie. *Le libellio d'AEGIS*, *2*(3), 21–28.
Callon, M. (2006b). Sociologie de l'acteur réseau. In M. Akrich, M. Callon, & B. Latour (Eds), *Sociologie de la traduction: textes fondateurs* (pp. 267–276). Paris: Mines Paris.
Callon, M. (2007). What does it mean to say that economics is performative? In D. MacKenzie, F. Muniesa, & L. Siu (Eds), *Do Economists Make Markets?* (pp. 311–357). Princeton, NJ: Princeton University Press.
Callon, M. (Ed.). (2013). *Sociologie des agencements marchands*. Paris: Mines Paris.
Callon, M., & Ferrary, M. (2006). Les réseaux à l'aune de la théorie de l'acteur-réseau. *Sociologies pratiques*, *13*(2), 37–44.
Callon, M., & Latour, B. (1981). Unscrewing the big leviathan; or how actors macrostructure reality, and how sociologists help them to do so. In K. Knorr & A. Cicourel (Eds), *Advances in Social Theory and Methodology* (pp. 277–303). London: Routledge and Kegan Paul.
Callon, M., & Latour, B. (1992). Don't throw the baby out with the Bath school! A reply to Collins and Yearley. In A. Pickering (Ed.), *Science as Practice and Culture* (pp. 343–368). Chicago, IL: Chicago University Press.
Callon, M., & Latour, B. (2006). Le grand léviathan s'apprivoise-t-il? In M. Akrich, M. Callon, & B. Latour (Eds), *Sociologie de la traduction: textes fondateurs* (pp. 11–32). Paris: Mines Paris.
Callon, M., & Latour, B. (2013). "Tu ne calculera pas!" – ou comment symétriser le don et le capital. In M. Callon (Ed.), *Sociologie des agencements marchands* (pp. 9–41). Paris: Mines Paris.
Callon, M., & Muniesa, F. (2005). Economic markets as calculative collective devices. *Organization Studies*, *28*(8), 1229–1250.

Callon, M., Barry, A., & Slater, D. (2002). Technology, politics and the market: an interview with Michel Callon. *Economy and Society, 31*(2), 285–306.

Callon, M., Lascoumes, P., & Barthe, Y. (2001). *Agir dans un monde incertain. Essai sur la démocratie technique*. Paris: Seuil.

Callon, M., Méadel, C., & Rabeharisoa, V. (2000). L'économie des qualités. *Politix, 13*(52), 211–239.

Callon, M., Millo, Y., & Muniesa, F. (Eds). (2007). *Market Devices*. Norwich: Blackwell.

Camille. (2013). *Le petit livre noir des grands projets inutiles*. Paris: Le passager clandestin.

Carrier, J. G., & Miller, D. (Eds). (1998). *Virtualism*. New York: Berg.

Cartwright, N. (2009). If no capacities then no credible worlds. But can models reveal capacities? *Erkenntnis, 70*, 45–58.

Cavell, S. (1969). *Must We Mean What We Say?* New York: Scribner.

Chaiken, S., & Trope, Y. (Eds). (1999). *Dual-process Theories in Social Psychology*. New York: Guilford Press.

Cherkaoui, M. (1998). *Naissance d'une science sociale: la sociologie selon Durkheim*. Geneva: Droz.

Chiappori, P.-A. (2004). Anticipations rationnelles et conventions. In A. Orléan (Ed.), *Analyse économique des conventions* (pp. 102–117). Paris: Presses Universitaires de France.

Cohen, L. (1989). Increasing the supply of transplant organs: the virtues of the future market. *George Washington Law Review, 58*(1), 1–51.

Cohen, L. (2003). Where it hurts: Indian material for an ethics of organ transplantation. *Zyogon, 38*(3), 663–688.

Collins, H., & Yearley, S. (1992a). Epistemological chicken. In A. Pickering (Ed.), *Science as Practice and Culture* (pp. 301–326). Chicago, IL: Chicago University Press.

Collins, H., & Yearley, S. (1992b). Journey into space. In A. Pickering (Ed.), *Science as Practice and Culture* (pp. 369–389). Chicago, IL: Chicago University Press.

Commons, J. R. (1924). *Legal Foundations of Capitalism*. New York: Augustus M. Kelley.

Commons, J. R. (1925). Law and economics. In M. Rutherford & W. J. Samuels (Eds), *John R. Commons Selected Essays, II* (pp. 331–342). London: Routledge.

Commons, J. R. (1934 [2005]). *Institutional Economics: Its Place in Political Economy*. London: Transaction.

Commons, J. R. (1935). The place of economics in social philosophy. In M. Rutherford & W. J. Samuels (Eds), *John R. Commons Selected Essays, II* (pp. 474–486). London: Routledge.

Commons, J. R. (1970). *The Economics of Collective Action*. Madison, WI: University of Wisconsin Press.

Commons, J. R. (2005). *Institutional Economics. Its Place in Political Economy*. London: Transaction.

Cooper, M. H., & Culyer, A. J. (1968). *The Price of Blood*. London: Institute of Economic Affairs.

Cooper, M. H., & Culyer, A. J. (1973). The economics of giving and selling blood. In A. Alchian & W. Allen (Eds), *The Economics of Charity* (pp. 109–123). London: Institute of Economic Affairs.

Cootner, P. H. (1964). *The Random Character of Stock Market Prices*. Cambridge, MA: MIT Press.

Cowles, A. (1933). Can stock market forecasters forecast? *Econometrica, 1*(2), 309–324.

Culter, D. M., & Richardson, E. (1997). Measuring the health of the U.S. population. *Brookings Papers on Economic Activity. Microeconomics, 1997*, 217–282.

Davidson, D. (1980). *Essays on Actions and Events*. Oxford: Clarendon Press.

Davis, J. (2003). *The Theory of Individual in Economics*. London: Routledge.

Davis, J. (2013). Economics imperialism under the impact of psychology: the case of behavioral development economics. *Œconomia, 4*(2), 119–138.

Dawkins, R. (1976). *The Selfish Gene*. Oxford: Oxford University Press.

Debreu, G., & Scarf, H. (1963). A limit on the core of an economy. *International Economic Review, 4*(3), 235–246.

Deci, E. L. (1971). Effects of externally mediated rewards on intrinsic motivation. *Journal of Personality and Social Psychology, 18*(1), 105–115.

Deci, E. L. (1972). Intrinsic motivation, extrinsic reinforcement, and inequity. *Journal of Personality and Social Psychology, 22*(1), 113–120.

Deichsel, S. (2011). Against the pragmatic justification for realism in economic methodology. *Erasmus Journal for Philosophy and Economics, 4*(1), 23–41.

Delcey, T. (2017). *Efficient Market Hypothesis, Eugene Fama and Paul Samuelson: A Reevaluation*. https://hal.archives-ouvertes.fr/hal-01618347.

Deleuze, G. (1989). Qu'est-ce qu'un dispositif? In Association pour le Centre Michel Foucault (Ed.), *Michel Foucault philosophe. Rencontre internationale Paris 9, 10, 11 janvier 1988* (pp. 186–195). Paris: Seuil.

Dequech, D. (2008). Book review of Donald MacKenzie, Fabian Muniesa and Lucy Siu (Eds), *Do Economists Make Markets? On the Performativity of Economics*. *Journal of Economic Issues, 42*(4), 1175–1176.

Desgranges, G., & Negroni, G. (2001). Apprentissage et équilibres à taches solaires. Un point de vue divinatoire. *Revue économique, 52*(3), 583–593.

DiMaggio, P. (1990). Cultural aspects of economic action and organization. In R. Friedland & A. F. Robertson (Eds), *Beyond the Marketplace: Rethinking Economy and Society* (pp. 113–136). New York: Aldine de Gruyter.

Dimand, R. W. (2009). The Cowles Commission and foundation on the functioning of financial markets from Irving Fisher And Alfred Cowles to Harry Markowitz and James Tobin. *Revue d'histoire des sciences humaines, 20*(1), 79–100.

Douglas, M. (1966). *Purity and Danger: An Analysis of the Concepts of Pollution and Taboo*. London: Routledge and Kegan Paul.

Douglas, M. (1986). *How Institutions Think*. Syracuse, NY: Syracuse University Press.

Dubois, M. (2005). L'action scientifique: modèles interprétatifs et explicatifs en sociologie des sciences. *L'année sociologique, 55*(1), 103–125.

Dubois, M. (2007). La construction métaphorique du collectif: dimensions implicites du prêt-à-penser constructiviste et théorie de l'acteur-réseau. *L'année sociologique, 57*(1), 127–150.

Dumez, H. (2014). Le tournant performatif. À propos de *The Provoked Economy* de Fabien Muniesa. *Le libellio d'AEGIS, 10*(4), 61–66.

Dumez, H., & Jeunemaître, A. (2010a). Michel Callon, Michel Foucault and the "dispotitif". When economics fails to be performative: a case study. *Le libellio d'AEGIS, 6*(4), 27–37.

Dumez, H., & Jeunemaître, A. (2010b). Quand l'économie échoue à être performative. Une étude de cas. In M. Akrich, Y. Barth, F. Muniesa, & P. Mustar (Eds), *Débordements: mélanges offerts à Michel Callon* (pp. 129–141). Paris: Mines.

Dumont, L. (1971). *Homo hierarchicus. Essai sur le système des castes*. Paris: Gallimard.

Dumont, L. (1985). *Homo aequalis*. Paris: Gallimard.

Dupuit, J. (1844). De la mesure de l'utilité des travaux publics. In Y. Breton & G. Klotz (Eds), *Jules Dupuit. Œuvres économiques complètes, 1* (pp. 203–241). Paris: Economica.

Dupuit, J. (1849). De l'influence des péages sur l'utilité des voies de communication. In Y. Breton & G. Klotz (Eds), *Jules Dupuit. Œuvres économiques complètes, 1* (pp. 203–241). Paris: Economica.

Dupuy, J.-P. (1989). Convention et common knowledge. *Revue économique, 40*(2), 361–400.

Dupuy, J.-P. (1992). *Introduction aux sciences sociales*. Paris: Ellipse.

Dupuy, J.-P. (2014). *Economy and the Future*. East Lansing, MI: Michigan State University Press.

Durand, D. (1957). Growth stocks and the Petersburg Paradox. *Journal of Finance, 12*(3), 348–363.

Durand, D. (1959). The cost of capital, corporation finance, and the theory of investment: comment. *American Economic Review, 49*(4), 639–655.

Durkheim, É. (1893 [1930]). *De la division du travail social*. Paris: Presses Universitaires de France.

Durkheim, É. (1895 [1930]). *Les règles de la méthode sociologique*. Paris: Flammarion.

Durkheim, É. (1908 [1975]). *Éléments d'une théorie sociale*. Paris: Les éditions de minuit.

Durkheim, É. (1912 [1960]). *Les formes élémentaires de la vie religieuse. Le système totémique en Australie*. Paris: Presses Universitaires de France.

Easterly, W. (2006). *The White Man's Burden*. New York: Penguin Press.

Ekelund, R., & Hebert, R. (1999). *Secret Origins of Modern Microeconomics: Dupuit and the Engineers*. Chicago, IL: University of Chicago Press.

Elder-Vass, D. (2010). *The Causal Power of Social Structures*. Cambridge: Cambridge University Press.

Elster, J. (1983). *Sour Grapes: Studies in the Subversion of Rationality*. Cambridge: Cambridge University Press.

Epstein, J. M. (1999). Agent-based computational models and generative social science. *Complexity, 4*(5), 41–60.

Esfeld, M. (2009). *Philosophie des sciences*. Lausanne: Presses polytechniques et universitaires romandes.

Etner, F. (1987). *Histoire du calcul économique en France*. Paris: Economica.

Eymard-Duvernay, F. (1989). Conventions de qualité et formes de coordination. *Revue économique, 40*(2), 329–360.

Eymard-Duvernay, F. (2002). Les qualifications des biens. *Sociologie du travail, 44*, 255–287.

Fama, E. (1963). Mandelbrot and the stable Paretian Hypothesis. *Journal of Business, 36*(4), 420–429.

Fama, E. (1965a). Portfolio analysis in a stable Paretian market. *Management Sciences, 11*(3), 404–419.

Fama, E. (1965b). Random walks in stock market prices. *Financial Analysts Journal, 21*(5), 55–59.

Fama, E. (1965c). The behavior of stock-market prices. *Journal of Business, 38*(1), 34–105.

Fama, E. (1970). Efficient capital markets: a review of the theory and empirical work. *Journal of Finance, 25*(2), 383–417.

Fama, E. (1976a). *Foundations of Finance*. London: Basic Books.

Fama, E. (1976b). Reply. *Journal of Finance, 31*(1), 143–145.

Fama, E. (1991). Efficient capital markets II. *Journal of Finance, 46*(5), 1575–1617.

Favereau, J. (2014). *L'approche expérimentale du J-PAL en économie du développement: un tournant épistémologique?* Université de Paris 1, Paris.

Favereau, O. (1989). Marchés interne, marchés externes. *Revue économique, 53*(2), 325–336.

Favereau, O. (2008). The unconventional, but conventionalist, legacy of Lewis's "convention". *Topoi, 27*(1–2), 115–126.

Felin, T., & Foss, N. (2009a). Performativity of theory, arbitrary conventions, and possible worlds: a reality check. *Organization Science, 20*(3), 676–678.

Felin, T., & Foss, N. (2009b). Social reality, the boundaries of self-fulfilling prophecy, and economics. *Organization Science, 20*(3), 654–668.

Ferey, S. (2011). Paternalisme libéral et pluralité du moi. *Revue économique, 62*(4), 737–750.

Ferey, S., Gabuthy, Y., & Jacquemet, N. (2013). L'apport de l'économie expérimentale dans l'élaboration des politiques publiques. *Revue française d'économie, 28*(2), 155–194.

Ferraro, F., Pfeffer, J., & Sutton, R. (2005). Economics language and assumptions: how theories can become self-fulfilling. *Academy of Management Review, 30*(1), 1–24.

Ferraro, F., Pfeffer, J., & Sutton, R. (2009). How and why theories matter: a comment on Felin and Foss. *Organization Science, 20*(3), 669–675.

Festinger, L., Riecken, H., & Schachter, S. (1956). *When Prophecy Fails.* New York: Harper Torchbooks.

Feyerabend, P. (1970). *Against Method: Outline of an Anarchist Theory of Knowledge.* Minneapolis, MN: University of Minnesota Press.

Fine, B. (1998). The triumph of economics; or, "rationality" can be dangerous to your reasoning. In J. G. Carrier & D. Miller (Eds), *Virtualism* (pp. 49–73). New York: Berg.

Fine, B. (2003). Callonistics: a disentanglement. *Economy and Society, 32*(3), 478–484.

Fine, B. (2005). From actor-network theory to political economy. *Capitalism Nature Socialism, 16*(4), 91–108.

Fodor, J. A. (1982). *Representations.* Cambridge, MA: MIT Press.

Fortune, P. (1996). Anomalies in option pricing: the Black-Scholes model revisited. *New England Economic Review* (March–April), 17–40.

Foucault, M. (2004). *Naissance de la biopolitique.* Paris: Gallimard-Seuil.

Fourcade, M. (2009). *Economists and Societies.* Princeton, NJ: Princeton University Press.

Fox, R. C., & Swazey, J. P. (2013). *Spare Parts: Organ Replacement in American Society.* London: Transaction.

Fraenkel, B. (2008). Le signature: du signe à l'acte. *Sociétés et représentations, 25,* 13–23.

François, P. (2008). *Sociologie des marchés.* Paris: Armand Colin.

Frank, R. H., Gilovich, T., & Regan, D. T. (1993). Does studying economics inhibit cooperation? *Journal of Economic Perspectives,* 7(2), 159–171.

Frege, G. (1948). Sense and reference. *Philosophical Review, 57*(3), 209–230.

Frege, G. (1956). The thought: a logical inquiry. *Mind,* new series, *65*(259), 289–311.

Frey, B. S. (1997). *Not Just for the Money.* Cheltenham: Edward Elgar.

Frey, B. S., & Jegen, R. (2001). Motivation crowding theory. *Journal of Economic Surveys, 15*(5), 589–611.

Frey, B. S., & Oberholzer-Gee, F. (1997). The cost of price incentives: an empirical analysis of motivation crowding-out. *American Economic Review, 87*(4), 746–755.

Fridman, D. (2010). A new mentality for a new economy: performing the homo economicus in Argentina (1976–83). *Economy and Society*, *39*(2), 271–302.
Friedman, E. A., & Friedman, A. L. (2006). Payment for donor kidneys: pros and cons. *Kidney International*, *69*, 960–962.
Gale, D., & Shapley, L. S. (1962). College admissions and the stability of marriage. *American Mathematical Monthly*, *69*(1), 9–15.
Garban, F., & Barro, C. (2003). *Guide pratique de l'hématologie*. Paris: Elsevier Masson.
Garcia-Parpet, M.-F. (1986). La construction sociale d'un marché parfait: le marché au cadran de Fontaines-en-Sologne. *Actes de la recherche en sciences sociales*, *65*, 2–13.
Garcia-Parpet, M.-F. (2007). The social construction of a perfect market: the strawberry auction at Fontaines-en-Sologne. In D. MacKenzie, F. Muniesa, & L. Siu (Eds). *Do Economists Make Markets?* (pp. 20–53). Princeton, NJ: Princeton University Press.
Garcia-Parpet, M.-F. (2014). Marché, rationalité et faits sociaux totaux: Pierre Bourdieu et l'économie. *Revue française de socio-économie*, *13*(1), 107–127.
Garfinkel, H. (1967). *Studies in Ethnomethodology*. Englewood Cliffs, NJ: Prentice Hall.
Gay, P. du. (2010). Performativities: Butler, Callon and the moment of theory. *Journal of Cultural Economy*, *3*(2), 171–179.
Gell-Mann, M. (1995). *The Quarks and the Jaguar*. London: Abacus.
Gibbard, A., & Varian, H. R. (1978). Economic modes. *Journal of Philosophy*, *75*(11), 664–677.
Giddens, A. (1984). *The Constitution of Society: Outline of the Theory of Structuration*. Cambridge: Polity Press.
Giddens, A. (1990). *The Consequences of Modernity*. Oxford: Polity Press.
Gilboa, I. (2009). *Theory of Decision under Uncertainty*. Cambridge: Cambridge University Press.
Gintis, H. (2009). *The Bounds of Reason*. Princeton, NJ: Princeton University Press.
Giocoli, N. (2003). *Modeling Rational Agents*. Cheltenham: Edward Elgar.
Godbout, J. T. (2008). De la dette à l'identité: le don d'organes et de sang. In P. Chanial (Ed.), *La société vue du don* (pp. 418–428). Paris: La Découverte.
Gold, N., & Sugden, R. (2006). Introduction. In M. Bacharach, *Beyond Individual Choice: Teams and Frames in Game Theory* (pp. 1–34). Princeton, NJ: Princeton University Press.
Graham, B., & Dodd, D. L. (1934). *Security Analysis*. New York: Whittlesey House.
Granovetter, M. (1973). The strength of weak ties. *American Journal of Sociology*, *78*(6), 1360–1380.
Granovetter, M. (1974). *Getting a Job: A Study of Contacts and Careers*. Cambridge: Cambridge University Press.
Granovetter, M. (1985). Economic action and social structure: the problem of embeddedness. *American Journal of Sociology*, *91*(3), 485–510.
Grant, R. W. (2012). *Strings Attached*. Princeton, NJ: Princeton University Press.
Grant, R. W. (2015). Rethinking the ethics of incentives. *Journal of Economic Methodology*, *22*(3), 354–372.
Greif, A. (2006). *Institutions and the Path to the Modern Economy: Lessons from Medieval Trade*. Cambridge: Cambridge University Press.
Grunberg, E. (1978). "Complexity" and "open systems" in economic discourse. *Journal of Economic Issues*, *12*(3), 541–560.
Grunberg, E. (1986). Predictability and reflexivity. *Journal of Economics and Sociology*, *45*(4), 475–488.

Grunberg, E., & Modigliani, F. (1954). The predictability of social events. *Journal of Political Economy*, *62*(6), 465–478.

Grunberg, E., & Modigliani, F. (1965). Discussion: reflexive prediction. *Philosophy of Science*, *32*(2), 173–174.

Guala, F. (2001). Building economic machines: the FCC auctions. *Studies in History and Philosophy of Science*, *32*(3), 453–477.

Guala, F. (2005). Talking about structures: the "transcendantal" argument. *Revue de philosophie économique*, *12*(2), 3–17.

Guala, F. (2007). How to do things with experimental economics. In D. MacKenzie, F. Muniesa, & L. Siu (Eds), *Do Economists Make Markets?* (pp. 128–162). Princeton, NJ: Princeton University Press.

Guala, F. (2016). Performativity rationalized. In I. Boldyrev & E. Svetlova (Eds), *Enacting the Dismal Science: New Perspectives on the Performativity of Economics* (pp. 29–52). New York: Palgrave Macmillan.

Guerrien, B. (1999). *La théorie économique néoclassique, 1. Microéconomie*. Paris: La Découverte.

Hacking, I. (2001). Philosophie et histoire des concepts scientifique: façonner les gens I. Lecture at Collège de France 2001–2002. https://www.college-de-france.fr/media/ian-hacking/UPL7997567846150782232_Hacking2001_2002.pdf.

Hacking, I. (2004). Philosophie et histoire des concepts scientifique: façonner les gens II. Lecture at Collège de France 2004–2005. https://www.college-de-france.fr/media/professeurs-honoraires/UPL46353_UPL35833_hackingres0405.pdf.

Hagerman, R. (1978). More evidence of the distribution of security returns. *Journal of Finance*, *33*(4), 1213–1221.

Hands, W. (1990). Grunberg and Modigliani, public predictions and the new classical macroeconomics. *Research in the History of Economic Thought and Methodology*, 7, 207–223.

Hands, W. (2001). *Refection without Rules: Economic Methodology and Contemporary Science Theory*. Cambridge: Cambridge University Press.

Hansmann, H. (1989). The economics and ethics of markets for human organs. *Journal of Health Politics, Policy and Law*, *14*(1), 57–85.

Hardin, R. (2003). *Indeterminacy and Society*. Princeton, NJ: Princeton University Press.

Hardin, R. (2006). *Trust*. Cambridge: Polity Press.

Harrison, M., & Kreps, D. (1979). Martingales and arbitrage in multiperiod securities markets. *Journal of Economic Theory*, *20*, 381–408.

Harrison, M., & Pliska, S. (1981). Martingales and stochastic integrals in the theory of continuous trading. *Stochastic Processes and Applications*, *11*, 215–260.

Harvard Ad Hoc Committee. (1968). A definition of irreversible coma. *Journal of the American Medical Association*, *205*(6), 337–340.

Hayek, F. A. (1973 [2012]). *Law, Legislation and Liberty*. Chicago, IL: Chicago University Press.

Heap, S. H., & Varoufakis, Y. (2004). *Game Theory: A Critical Text*. London: Routledge.

Hédoin, C. (2012a). Linking institutions to economic performance: the role of macro-structures in micro-explanations. *Journal of Institutional Economics* (April), 1–23.

Hédoin, C. (2012b). Models in economics are not (always) nomological machines: a pragmatic approach to economists' modeling practices. *Philosophy of the Social Sciences*, *20*(10), 424–459.

Hédoin, C. (2012c). Veblen et son actualité: sélection multi-niveaux et darwinisme généralisé. *Œconomia*, *2*(2), 179–207.

Hempel, C. (1942). General laws in history. *Journal of Philosophy, 39*, 35–48.

Hempel, C., & Oppenheim, P. (1948). Studies in the logic of explanation. *Philosophy of Science, 15*(2), 135–175.

Herrmann-Pillath, C. (2010). A neurolinguistic approach to performativity in economics. *Journal of Economic Methodology, 17*(3), 241–260.

Herrmann-Pillath, C. (2012). Institutions, distributed cognition and agency: rule-following as performative action. *Journal of Economic Methodology, 19*(1), 21–42.

Herrmann-Pillath, C. (2013). Performativity of economic systems: approach and implications for taxonomy. *Journal of Economic Methodology, 20*(2), 139–163.

Herrmann-Pillath, C. (2016). Performative mechanisms. In I. Boldyrev and E. Svetlova (Eds), *Enacting the Dismal Science: New Perspectives on the Performativity of Economics* (pp. 53–86). New York: Palgrave Macmillan.

Herrmann-Pillath, C., & Boldyrev, I. (2014). *Hegel, Institutions and Economics: Performing the Social.* New York: Routledge.

Hinchliffe, S. (1996). Technology, power and space – the means and ends of geographies of technology. *Environment and Planning D: Society and Space, 14*(6), 659–682.

Hirschman, D. (2015). Has performativity lost its punch? *European Journal of Sociology, 56*(3), 531–534.

Hodgson, G. M. (2000a). The concept of emergence in social science: its history and importance. *Emergence, 2*(4), 65–77.

Hodgson, G. M. (2000b). What is the essence of institutional economics? *Journal of Economic Issues, 34*(2), 317–329.

Hodgson, G. M. (2001). *How Economics Forgot History*. London: Routledge.

Hodgson, G. M. (2002a). Darwinism, causality and the social sciences. *Journal of Economic Methodology, 11*(2), 175–194.

Hodgson, G. M. (2002b). The evolution of institutions: an agenda for future theoretical research. *Constitutional Political Economy, 13*(2), 111–127.

Hodgson, G. M. (2004). *The Evolution of Institutional Economics*. London: Routledge.

Hodgson, G. M. (2006). What are institutions? *Journal of Economic Issues, 40*(1), 1–25.

Hodgson, G. M. (2007). Meanings of methodological individualism. *Journal of Economic Methodology, 14*(2), 211–226.

Hodgson, G. M. (2009). *Donald MacKenzie. An Engine Not a Camera: How Financial Models Shape Markets.* Cambridge, MA MIT Press, 2006; *Material Markets: How Economic Agents are Constructed.* Oxford, Oxford University Press, 2009 [reviews]. *Socio-Economic Review, 8*, 399–310.

Hodgson, G. M., & Knudsen, T. (2006a). The nature and units of selection. *Journal of Evolutionary Economics, 16*(5), 477–489.

Hodgson, G. M., & Knudsen, T. (2006b). Why we need a generalized Darwinism, and why generalized Darwinism is not enough. *Journal of Economic Behavior and Organization, 61*(1), 1–19.

Hodgson, G. M., & Knudsen, T. (2008). The emergence of property rights enforcement in early trade: a behavioral model without reputational effects. *Journal of Economic Behavior and Organization, 68*(1), 48–62.

Holm, P. (2007). Which way is up on Callon? In D. MacKenzie, F. Muniesa, & L. Siu (Eds), *Do Economists Make Markets?* (pp. 225–243). Princeton, NJ: Princeton University Press.

Holmes, O. W. (1885). The law. In O. W. Holmes (Ed.), *The Essential Holmes* (pp. 221–224). Chicago, IL: University of Chicago Press.

Holmes, O. W. (1895). Learning and science. In O. W. Holmes (Ed.), *Law in Science and Science in Law* (pp. 184–185). Chicago, IL: University of Chicago Press.

Holmes, O. W. (1899a). Law in science and science in law. In O. W. Holmes (Ed.), *The Essential Holmes* (pp. 185–200). Chicago, IL: University of Chicago Press.

Holmes, O. W. (1899b). The theory of legal interpretation. In O. W. Holmes (Ed.), *The Essential Holmes* (pp. 296–300). Chicago, IL: University of Chicago Press.

Holmes, O. W. (1990). *The Common Law*. Boston, MA: Little, Brown.

Holmes, O. W. (1992). *The Essential Holmes: Selections from the Letters, Speeches, Judicial Opinions, and Other Writings of Oliver Wendell Holmes, Jr.* Chicago, IL: University of Chicago Press.

Hont, I. (2005). *Jealousy of Trade: International Competition and the Nation State in Historical Perspective*. Cambridge, MA: Belknap Press.

Houthakker, H. (1950). Revealed preference and utility function. *Economica, 17*, 159–174.

Howard, D. H. (2007). Producing organ donors. *Journal of Economic Perspectives, 21*(3), 25–36.

Hull, J. (2011). *Options, futures et autres actifs dérivés*. Upper Saddle River, NJ: Pearson.

Hulswit, M. (2006). How causal is downward causation? *Journal for General Philosophy of Science, 36*(2), 261–287.

Hume, D. (1740 [1888]). *A Treatise of Human Nature*. Oxford: Oxford University Press.

Hume, D. (1752a [1994]). Of refinement in the arts. In K. Haakonssen (Ed.), *Political Essays* (pp. 105–114). Cambridge: Cambridge University Press.

Hume, D. (1752b [1994]). Of the balance of power. In K. Haakonssen (Ed.), *Political Essays* (pp. 150–160). Cambridge: Cambridge University Press.

Hume, D. (1752c [1994]). Of the balance of trade. In K. Haakonssen (Ed.), *Political Essays* (pp. 136–149). Cambridge: Cambridge University Press.

Hume, D. (1758 [1994]). Of the jealousy of trade. In K. Haakonssen (Ed.), *Political Essays* (pp. 150–153). Cambridge: Cambridge University Press.

Ireland, T. R., & Koch, J. (1973). Blood and American social attitudes. In A. Alchian & W. Allen (Eds), *The Economics of Charity* (pp. 161–174). London: Institute of Economic Affairs

Jackwerth, J. C. (1999). Option implied risk-neutral distributions and implied binomial trees: a literature review. *Journal of Derivatives*, 7(2), 66–82.

Jackwerth, J. C., & Rubinstein, M. (1996). Recovering probability distributions from option prices. *Journal of Finance, 51*(5), 1611–1631.

Jaffé, W. (1976). Menger, Jevons, and Walras de-homogenized. *Economic Inquiry, 14*, 511–524.

Jarrow, R. A., & Rosenfeld, E. R. (1984). Jump risks and the intertemporal capital asset pricing model. *Journal of Business, 57*(3), 337–351.

Jegadeesh, N., & Titman, S. (1993). Returns to buying winners and selling losers: implications for stock market efficiency. *Journal of Finance, 48*(1), 65–91.

Jensen, M. (1968). The performance of mutual funds in the period 1945–1964. *Journal of Finance, 23*(2), 389–416.

Jensen, M. (1978). Some anomalous evidence regarding market efficiency. *Journal of Financial Economics, 6*(2/3), 95–101.

Jonas, H. (1974). *Philosophical Essays. From Ancient Creed to Technological Man*. Chicago, IL: Chicago University Press.

Jovanovic, F. (2008). The construction of the canonial history of financial economics. *History of Political Economy, 40*(2), 213–242.

Jovanovic, F. (2009). L'institutionnalisation de l'économie financière: perspectives historiques. *Revue d'histoire des sciences humaines*, *20*(1), 3–9.

Jovanovic, F., & Schinckus, C. (2013a). Econophysics: a new challenge for financial economics? *Journal of the History of Economic Thought*, *35*(3), 319–352.

Jovanovic, F., & Schinckus, C. (2013b). The emergence of econophysics: a new approach in modern financial theory. *History of Political Economy*, *45*(3), 443–474.

Kahneman, D. (2011). *Thinking Fast and Slow*. London: Penguin Books.

Kahneman, D., & Tversky, A. (1979). An analysis of decision under risk. *Econometrica*, *47*(2), 263–292.

Kant, I. (1781 [1998]). *Critique of Pure Reason*. Cambridge: Cambridge University Press.

Karpik, L. (1989). L'économie de la qualité. *Revue française de sociologie*, *30*(2), 187–210.

Karpik, L. (2010). *Valuing the Unique: The Economics of Singularities*. Princeton, NJ: Princeton University Press.

Kaserman, D. L., & Barnett, A. H. (1991). An economic analysis of transplant organs: a comment and extension. *Atlantic Economic Journal*, *19*(2), 12–20.

Kauffman, S. (1995). *At Home in the Universe: The Search for Laws of Self-organization and Complexity*. London: Viking.

Kendall, M. G. (1953). The analysis of economic time-series, Part I: prices. *Journal of the Royal Statistical Society. Series A*, *116*(1), 11–34.

Keucheyan, R. (2007). *Le constructivisme: des origines à nos jours*. Paris: Hermann.

Keynes, J. M. (1936 [2013]). *The General Theory of Employment, Interest and Money*. Cambridge: Cambridge University Press.

Kim, J. (1999). Making sense of emergence. *Philosophical Studies*, *95*, 3–36.

Kim, J. (2006). Emergence: core ideas and issues. *Synthèse*, *151*, 547–559.

Kim, J., Kjellberg, H., & Helgesson, C.-F. (2006). Multiple versions of markets: multiplicity and performativity in market practice. *Industrial Marketing Management*, *35*, 839–855.

Kjellberg, H., & Helgesson, C.-F. (2006). Multiple versions of markets: multiplicity and performativity in market practice. *Industrial Marketing Management*, *35*, 839–855.

Knetsch, J. (1989). The endowment effect and evidence of non-reversible indifference curves. *American Economic Review*, *79*(5), 1277–1284.

Knorr-Cetina, K. (1981). *The Manufacture of Knowledge*. Oxford: Pergamon Press.

Koertge, N. (1979). The methodological status of Popper's rationality principle. *Theory and Decision*, *10*(1/4), 83–95.

Koppl, R. (2008a). Computable entrepreneurship. *Entrepreneurship Theory and Practice*, *32*(5), 919–926.

Koppl, R. (2008b). Thinking impossible things: a review essay. *Journal of Economic Behavior and Organization*, *66*(3–4), 837–847.

Koppl, R., & Rosser, B. (2002). All that I have to say has already crossed your mind. *Metroeconomica*, *53*(4), 339–360.

Kremer, M., Shea, D., Miguel, E., & Zwane, A. P. (2011). Spring cleaning: rural water impacts, valuation, and property right institutions. *Quarterly Journal of Economics*, *126*, 154–205.

Krugman, P. (1991). Increasing returns and economic geography. *Journal of Political Economy*, *99*(3), 483–499.

Krugman, P. (1998). Space: the final frontier. *Journal of Economic Perspectives*, *12*(2), 161–174.

La Mettrie, J. (1747 [1981]). *L'homme-machine*. Paris: Folio.

Lacordaire, H.-D. (1972). *Conférence de Notre-Dame de Paris*, Vol. *3*. Paris: Libraire Poussielgue Frères.

Lagueux, M. (1993). Analyse économique et principe de rationalité. *Revue de synthèse*, *114*(1), 9–31.

Lagueux, M. (2005). L'agent économique: rationalité maximale ou minimale? *Cahiers d'économie politique*, *49*, 143–158.

Lagueux, M. (2010). *Rationality and Explanation in Economics*. London and New York: Routledge.

Lagueux, M. (2012). A reply to Paul Dumouchel. *Œconomia*, *2*(2), 247–251.

Lakatos, I. (1976). *Proofs and Refutations*. Cambridge: Cambridge University Press.

Lallement, J. (1987). Popper et le principe de rationalité. *Économie et société, Série PE*, *21*(2), 25–40.

Lallement, J. (2007). Le modèle déductif-nomologique et l'explication en économie. In A. Leroux & P. Livet (Eds), *Leçons de philosophie économique. Tome III: science économique et philosophie des sciences* (pp. 183–209). Paris: Economica.

Latour, B. (1987). *Science in Action: How to Follow Scientists and Engineers through Society*. Cambridge, MA: Harvard University Press.

Latour, B. (1989). *La science en action*. Paris: La Découverte.

Latour, B. (1991). *Nous n'avons jamais été modernes: essai d'anthropologie symétrique*. Paris: La Découverte.

Latour, B. (1992). One more turn after the social turn. easing science studies into the non-modern world. In E. M. Mullin (Ed.), *The Social Dimensions of Science* (pp. 272–292). Notre Dame, IN: Notre Dame University Press.

Latour, B. (1993a). *Amaris ou l'amour des techniques*. Paris: La Découverte.

Latour, B. (1993b). *The Pasteurization of France*. Cambridge, MA: Harvard University Press.

Latour, B. (1996). *Petites leçons de sociologie des sciences*. Paris: La Découverte.

Latour, B. (1999). For David Bloor . . . and beyond: a reply to David Bloor's "Anti-Latour". *Studies in History and Philosophy of Science*, *30*(1), 113–129.

Latour, B. (2005). *Reassembling the Social*. Oxford: Oxford University Press.

Latour, B. (2011). Il n'y a pas de monde commun: il faut le composer. *Multitudes*, *45*(2), 38–41.

Latour, B. (2012). *Enquête sur les modes d'existence*. Paris: La Découverte.

Latour, B., Jensen, P., Venturini, T., Grauwin, S., & Boullier, D. (2012). "The whole is always smaller than its parts" – a digital test of Gabriel Tardes' monads. *British Journal of Sociology*, *63*(4), 590–615.

Laugier, S. (1992). *L'anthropologie logique de Quine*. Paris: Vrin.

Laugier, S. (2013). *Why We Need Ordinary Language Philosophy*. Chicago, IL: Chicago University Press.

Lawson, T. (1997). *Economics and Reality*. London: Routledge.

Lawson, T. (2003). *Reorienting Economics*. New York: Routledge.

Lawson, T. (2005). The nature of institutional economics. *Evolutionary and Institutional Economic Review*, *2*(1), 7–20.

Lawson, T. (2006). The nature of heterodox economics. *Cambridge Journal of Economics*, *30*(4), 483–505.

Lawson, T. (2012). Ontology and the study of social reality: emergence, organisation, community, power, social relations, corporations, artefacts and money. *Cambridge Journal of Economics*, *36*(2), 345–385.

Lawson, T. (2013). Emergence and social causation. In J. Greco & R. Groff (Eds), *Powers and Capacities in Philosophy* (pp. 285–307). London: Routledge.

Le Jallé, E. (2012). La convention: ce que Lewis doit (ou non) à Hume. *Klesis*, *24*, 239–271.

Le Velly, R. (2007). Le problème du désencastrement. *La revue du Mauss*, *29*, 181–196.

Le Velly, R. (2012). *Sociologie du marché*. Paris: La Découverte.

Le Velly, R., & Bréchet, J.-P. (2011). Le marché comme rencontre d'activités de régulation: initiatives et innovations dans l'approvisionnement bio et local de la restauration collective. *Sociologie du travail*, *53*, 478–492.

Lebaron, F. (2000). *La croyance économique, les économistes entre science et politique*. Paris: Seuil.

Lebaron, F. (2010). *La crise de la croyance économique*. Paris: Editions du croquant.

Lehmann-Waffenschmidt, M. (1990). Predictability of economic processes and the Morgenstern Paradox. *Schweizer Zeitschrift für Volkswirtschaft und Statistik*, *2*, 147–161.

Lehmann-Waffenschmidt, M., & Sandri, S. (2007). Recursivity and self-referentiality of economic theories and their implications for bounded rational actors. *Dresden Discussion Papers in Economics*, 03/07.

Leland, H., & Rubinstein, M. (1976). The evolution of portfolio insurance. In D. Luskin (Ed.), *Portfolio Insurance: A Guide to Dynamic Hedging*. Hoboken, NJ: John Wiley.

LeRoy, S. (1976). Efficient capital market: a comment. *Journal of Finance*, *31*(1), 139–141.

LeRoy, S. (1989). Efficient capital markets and martingales. *Journal of Economic Literature*, *27*(4), 1583–1621.

Lewes, G. H. (1874–1875). *Problems of Life and Mind, First Series: The Foundation of a Creed*. London: Trübner.

Lewis, D. (1969). *Convention*. Oxford: Blackwell.

Lewis, D. (1972 [1983]). Languages and language. In *Philosophical Papers*, Vol. *1* (pp. 163–188). Oxford: Oxford University Press.

Licoppe, C. (2010). Michel Callon et le "tournant performatif" de la théorie de l'acteur-réseau. Vers une anthropologie des objets techniques en situation. In M. Akrich, Y. Barth, F. Muniesa, & P. Mustar (Eds), *Débordemement. Mélange offerts à Michel Callon* (pp. 291–298). Paris: Mines Paris.

Lintner, J. (1965). The valuation of risk assets and the selection of risky investments in stock portfolios and capital budgets. *Review of Economics and Statistics*, *47*(1), 13–37.

Locke, J. (1689 [2015]). *An Essay Concerning Human Understanding*. Adelaide: University of Adelaide. https://ebooks.adelaide.edu.au/l/locke/john/l81u/index.html.

Long, J. B. (1990). The numeraire portfolio. *Journal of Financial Economics*, *26*, 29–69.

Lucas, R. E. (1976). Econometric policy evaluation: a critique. Carnegie-Rochester Conference Series on Public Policy, *1*, 19–46.

Lucas, R. E. (1978). Asset prices in an exchange economy. *Econometrica*, *46*, 1429–1445.

MacKenzie, D. (2003). An equation and its worlds: bricolage, exemplars, disunity and performativity in financial economics. *Social Studies of Science*, *33*, 831–868.

MacKenzie, D. (2004). The big, bad wolf and the rational market: portfolio insurance, the 1987 crash and the performativity of economics. *Economy and Society*, *33*(3), 303–334.

MacKenzie, D. (2006a). *An Engine, Not a Camera*. Cambridge, MA: MIT Press.

MacKenzie, D. (2006b). Is economics performative? Option theory and the construction of derivatives markets. *Journal of the History of Economic Thought*, *28*(1), 29–55.

MacKenzie, D. (2007). Is economics performative? Option theory and the construction of derivatives markets. In D. MacKenzie, F. Muniesa, & L. Siu (Eds), *Do Economists Make Markets?* (pp. 54–86). Princeton, NJ: Princeton University Press.

MacKenzie, D. (2009). *Material Markets: How Economic Agents Are Constructed*. New York: Oxford University Press.

MacKenzie, D. (2010). Models as coordination devices. In M. Akrich, Y. Barth, F. Muniesa, & P. Mustar (Eds), *Débordements: mélanges offerts à Michel Callon* (pp. 299–302). Paris: Mines Paris.

MacKenzie, D., & Millo, Y. (2003). Constructing a market, performing theory: the historical sociology of a financial derivatives exchange. *American Journal of Sociology, 109*, 107–145.

MacKenzie, D., & Spears, T. (2014). 'The formula that killed Wall Street': the Gaussian copula and modelling practices in investment banking. *Social Studies of Science, 44*, 393–417.

MacKenzie, D., Muniesa, F., & Siu, L. (Eds). (2007a). *Do Economists Make Markets?* Princeton, NJ: Princeton University Press.

MacKenzie, D., Muniesa, F., & Siu, L. (2007b). Introduction. In D. MacKenzie, F. Muniesa, & L. Siu (Eds), *Do Economists Make Markets?* (pp. 1–19). Princeton, NJ: Princeton University Press.

Madrian, B. C., & Shea, D. F. (2001). The power of suggestion: inertia in 401(k) participation and savings behavior. *Quarterly Journal of Economics, 116*(4), 1179–1187.

Mäki, U. (1989). On the problem of realism in economics. *Richerce economiche, 43*, 176–198.

Mäki, U. (2013). Performativity: saving Austin from MacKenzie. In V. Karakostas & D. Dieks (Eds), *EPSA11 Perspectives and Foundational Problems in Philosophy of Science* (pp. 443–453). Dordrecht: Springer.

Malinowski, B. (1922). *Argonauts of the Western Pacific: An Account of Native Enterprise and Adventure in the Archipelagoes of Melanesian New Guinea*. London: Routledge and Kegan Paul.

Malkiel, B. (1989). Is the stock market efficient? *Science, 243*, 1313–1318.

Mandelbrot, B. (1963). The variation of certain speculative prices. *Journal of Business, 36*(4), 394–419.

Mandelbrot, B. (1966). Forecasts of future prices, unbiased markets, and "martingale" models. *Journal of Business, 39*(1), 242–255.

Mandelbrot, B. (1973). Le syndrôme de la variance infinie et ses rapports avec la discontinuité des prix. *Économie appliquée, 26*, 321–348.

Mandelbrot, B. (2009). Il était inévitable que des choses très graves se produisent. *Le Monde*, 18 October.

Mannheim, K. (1936). *Ideology and Utopia: An Introduction to the Sociology of Knowledge*. London: Routledge.

Marget, A. W. (1929). Morgenstern on the methodology of economic forecasting. *Journal of Political Economy, 37*(3), 312–339.

Markowitz, H. M. (1952). Portfolio selection. *Journal of Finance*, 7, 77–91.

Markowitz, H. M. (1959). *Porfolio Selection: Efficient Diversification of Investments*. New York: John Wiley.

Markowitz, H. M. (1991). Autobiography. In T. Frängsmyr (Ed.), *Les Prix Nobel: The Nobel Prizes 1990*. Stockholm: Nobel Foundation.

Markowitz, H. M. (1999). The early history of portfolio theory: 1600–1960. *Financial Analysts Journal, 55*(4), 6–16.

Marmor, A. (2009). *Social Conventions: From Language to Law*. Princeton, NJ: Princeton University Press.

Marschak, J. (1950). Rational behavior, uncertain prospects, and measurable utility. *Econometrica, 18*(2), 111–141.

Marx, K. (1844 [2007]). *Economic and Philosophic Manuscripts of 1844*. New York: Dover Publications.

Maucourant, J. (2005). *Avez-vous lu Polanyi?* Paris: La Dispute.

Maucourant, J., & Plociniczak, S. (2009). L'institution selon Karl Polanyi. Fondements et mise en perspective contemporaine. *Tracés, 17*(2), 143–156.

Maucourant, J., & Plociniczak, S. (2013). The institution, the economy and the market: Karl Polanyi's institutional thought for economists. *Review of Political Economy, 25*(3), 512–531.

Mauss, M. (1902–1938 [2006]). *Sociologie et anthropologie*. Paris: Presses Universitaires de France.

Mauss, M. (1923–1924 [2007]). *Essai sur le don*. Paris: Presses Universitaires de France.

McLaughlin, B. P. (1992). The rise and fall of British emergentism. In N. Beckermann, H. Flohr, & J. Kim (Eds), *Emergence or Reduction?* (pp. 49–93). Berlin: Walter de Gruyter.

Mehrling, P. (2012). *Fischer Black and the Revolutionary Idea of Finance*. Hoboken, NJ: Wiley.

Meiksins Wood, E. (2002). *The Origin of Capitalism: A Longer View*. London: Verso

Merton, R. C. (1973). Theory of rational option pricing. *Bell Journal of Economics and Management Science, 4*(1), 141–183.

Merton, R. C. (1976). Optimal pricing when underlying stock returns are discontinuous. *Journal of Financial Economics, 3*, 125–144.

Merton, R. C., Simons, R. V., & Wilkie, A. D. (1994). Influence of mathematical models in finance on practice: past, present and future. *Philosophical Transactions: Physical Sciences and Engineering, 347*(1684), 451–463.

Merton, R. K. (1948). The self-fulfilling prophecy. *Antioch Review, 8*(2), 193–210.

Merton, R. K. (1996). *On Social Structure and Science*. Chicago, IL: University of Chicago Press.

Meyer, J. W., & Rowan, B. (1977). Institutionalized organizations: formal structure as myth and ceremony. *American Journal of Sociology, 83*(2), 340–363.

Miller, D. (1986). Exchange and alienation in the "Jajmani" system. *Journal of Anthropological Research, 42*(4), 535–556.

Miller, D. (2002). Turning Callon the right way up. *Economy and Society, 32*(2), 218–233.

Miller, D. (2005). Reply to Michel Callon. *Economic Sociology European Electronic Newsletter, 6*(3), 3–13.

Millikan, R. G. (2014). Deflating socially constructed objects: what thoughts do to the world. In M. Gallotti & J. Michael (Eds), *Perspectives on Social Ontology and Social Cognition* (pp. 27–39). New York: Springer.

Millo, Y. (2007). Making things deliverable: the origins of index-based derivatives. In M. Callon, Y. Millo, & F. Muniesa (Eds), *Market Devices* (pp. 196–214). Oxford: Blackwell.

Mirowski, P. (1989). 'Tis a pity econometrics isn't an empirical endeavor: Mandelbrot, chaos and the Noah and Joseph Effects. *Ricerche economiche, 43*, 76–99.

Mirowski, P. (1990). From Mandelbrot to chaos in economic theory. *Southern Economic Journal, 57*(2), 289–307.

Mirowski, P. (1995). Mandelbrot's economics after a quarter century. *Fractals, 3*, 581–600.

Mirowski, P. (2007). Markets come to bits: evolution, computation and markomata in economic science. *Journal of Economic Behavior and Organization, 63*(2), 209–242.

Mirowski, P. (2013). "Facebook teaches you to be a neoliberal agent". *An interview with Philip Mirowski*. https://estudiosdelaeconomia.wordpress.com/2013/07/22/facebook-teaches-you-how-to-be-a-neoliberal-agent-an-interview-with-philip-mirowski/.

Mirowski, P. (2015). Review of *The Economics of Economists: Institutional Setting, Individual Incentives, and Future Prospects*, edited by Alessandro Lanteri and Jack Vromen. *Erasmus Journal for Philosophy and Economics, 8*(1), 105–109.

Mirowski, P., & Nik-Khah, E. (2007). Markets made flesh: performativity, and a problem in science studies, augmentation with consideration of the FCC auctions. In D. MacKenzie, F. Muniesa, & L. Siu (Eds), *Do Economists Make Markets?* (pp. 190–224). Princeton, NJ: Princeton University Press.

Mises, L. (1949 [1996]). *Human Action*. San Francisco, CA: Fox and Wilkes.

Modigliani, F., & Miller, M. H. (1958). The cost of capital, corporation finance and the theory of investment. *American Economic Review, 48*, 655–669.

Mongin, P. (2000). Les préférences révélées et la formation de la théorie du consommateur. *Revue économique, 51*(5), 1125–1152.

Mongin, P. (2002a). La conception déductive de l'explication scientifique et économique. *Social Science Information, 41*(2), 139–165.

Mongin, P. (2002b). Le principe de rationalité et l'unité des sciences sociales. *Revue économique, 53*(2), 301–323.

Morelon, E. (2003). Pourquoi développer la pratique du "donneur vivant"? *Laennec, 51*(2), 10–20.

Morgan, M. (2012). *The World in the Model*. Cambridge: Cambridge University Press.

Morgan, M. S., & Morrison, M. (Eds). (1999). *Models as Mediators: Perspectives on Natural and Social Science*. Cambridge: Cambridge University Press.

Morgenstern, O. (1928). *Wirtschaftsprognose. Eine Untersuchung ihrer Voraussetzungen und Möglichkeiten*. Vienna: Springer.

Morgenstern, O. (1935a). Perfect foresight and economic equilibrium. In A. Schotter (Ed.), *Selected Economic Writings of Oskar Morgenstern* (pp. 169–183). New York: New York University Press.

Morgenstern, O. (1935b). Vollkommene Voraussicht und wirtschaftliches Gleichgewicht. *Zeitschrift für Nationalökonomie, 6*, 337–357.

Morgenstern, O. (1972). Descriptive, predictive and normative theory. *Kyklos, 25*, 699–714.

Morrison, M., & Morgan, M. S. (1999). Models as mediating instruments. In M. Morrison & M. S. Morgan (Eds), *Models as Mediators* (pp. 10–37). Cambridge: Cambridge University Press.

Mossin, J. (1966). Equilibrium in a capital asset market. *Econometrica, 34*(4), 768–783.

Muniesa, F. (2000). Un robot walrasien. Cotation électronique et justesse de la découverte des prix. *Politix, 13*(52), 121–154.

Muniesa, F. (2003). *Des marchés comme algorithmes: sociologie de la cotation électronique à la Bourse de Paris*. Paris: École national supérieur des mines de Paris.

Muniesa, F. (2005). Contenir le marché: la transition de la criée à la cotation électronique à la Bourse de Paris. *Sociologie du travail, 47*, 485–501.

Muniesa, F. (2011). Comment la Bourse fait ses prix. Ethnographie d'un cours d'action boursière. In S. Houdart & O. Thiery (Eds), *Humains non humains* (pp. 176–190). Paris: La Découverte.

Muniesa, F. (2014). *The Provoked Economy*. New York: Routledge.

Muniesa, F. (2016). Performative mechanisms. In I. Boldyrev & E. Svetlova (Eds), *The Problem with Economics: Naturalism, Critique and Performativity* (pp. 109–129). New York: Palgrave.

Muniesa, F., & Callon, M. (2003). Les marchés économiques comme dispositifs collectifs du calcul. *Réseaux*, *122*, 189–233.

Muniesa, F., & Callon, M. (2007). Economic experiments and the construction of market. In D. MacKenzie, F. Muniesa, & L. Siu (Eds), *Do Economists Make Markets?* (pp. 163–189). Princeton, NJ: Princeton University Press.

Muniesa, F., & Callon, M. (2009). La preformativité des sciences économiques. In P. Steiner & F. Vatin (Eds), *Traité de sociologie économique* (pp. 289–324). Paris: Presses Universitaires de France.

Muniesa, F., & Teil, G. (2006). Donner un prix: observations à partir d'un dispositif d'économie expérimentale. *Terrains & travaux*, *11*(2), 222–244.

Musselin, C., & Paradeise, C. (2002). Le concept de qualité: où en sommes-nous. *Sociologie du travail*, *44*, 256–260.

Muth, J. (1961). Rational expectation and the theory of price movements. *Econometrica*, *29*(3), 315–335.

Nadeau, R. (1993). Confuting Popper on the rationality principle. *Philosophy of the Social Sciences*, *23*(4), 446–467.

Nagel, E. (1961). *The Structure of Science: Problems in the Logic of Scientific Explanation*. London: Routledge.

Nik-Khah, E. (2006). What FCC auctions can tell us about the performativity thesis. *Economic Sociology European Electronic Newsletter*, 7(2), 15–21.

Orléan, A. (1989). Pour une approche cognitive des conventions économiques. *Revue économique*, *40*(2), 241–272.

Orléan, A. (2002). Le tournant cognitif en économie. *Revue d'économie politique*, *112*(5), 717–738.

Orléan, A. (Ed.). (2004a). *Analyse économique des conventions*. Paris: Presses Universitaires de France.

Orléan, A. (2004b). L'économie des conventions: définitions et résultats. In A. Orléan (Ed.), *Analyse économique des conventions* (pp. 9–48). Paris: Presses Universitaires de France.

Orléan, A. (2011). *L'empire de la valeur*. Paris: Seuil.

Osborne, M. F. M. (1959). Brownian motion in the stock market. *Operations Research*, 7, 145–173.

Ossandon, J., & Pallesen, T. (2016). Testing the provoked economy. *Journal of Cultural Economy*, *9*(3), 310–315.

Pahl, H., & Sparsam, J. (2016). The IS-LMization of the general theory and the construction of hydraulic governability in postwar Keynesian macroeconomics. In I. Boldyrev & E. Svetlova (Eds), *Enacting the Dismal Science: New Perspectives on the Performativity of Economics* (pp. 151–181). New York: Palgrave Macmillan.

Pareto, V. (1917 [1968]). *Traité de sociologie générale*. Geneva: Droz.

Parthenay, C. (2008). *Vers une refondation de la science économique?Economie et argument transcendantal*. Paris: Cerf.

Parthenay, C., & Thomas-Fogiel, I. (2005). Science économique et philosophie des sciences: la question de l'argument transcendantal. *Revue de méthaphysique et de morale*, *3*, 428–456.

Pearson, K. (1905). The problem of the random walk. *Nature*, *72*(1867), 294–342.

Peirce, C. S. (1868). Some consequences of four incapacities. In C. Hartshorne & P. Weiss (Eds), *The Collected Papers of Charles Sanders Peirce*, Vol. *5* (pp. 156–189). Cambridge, MA: Belknap Press.

Peirce, C. S. (1878a). How to make our ideas clear. In N. Houser & C. Kloesel (Eds), *The Essential Peirce*, Vol. *1* (pp. 124–141). Bloomington, IN: Indiana University Press.

Peirce, C. S. (1878b). The fixation of belief. In C. Hartshorne & P. Weiss (Eds), *The Collected Papers of Charles Sanders Peirce*, Vol. *5* (pp. 223–227). Cambridge, MA: Belknap Press.

Pepper, S. C. (1926). Emergence. *Journal of Philosophy*, *23*, 241–245.

Pestre, D. (2006). *Introduction aux science studies*. Paris: La Découverte.

Pettit, P. (1997). *Republicanism: A Theory of Freedom and Government*. Oxford: Oxford University Press.

Pettit, P. (2006). Freedom in the market. *Politics, Philosophy and Economics*, *5*(2), 131–149.

Picavet, E. (1995). *Approches du concret*. Paris: Ellipses.

Picavet, E. (1996). *Choix rationnel et vie public*. Paris: Presses Universitaires de France.

Poincaré, H. (1905 [1970]). *La valeur de la science*. Paris: Flammarion.

Polanyi, K. (1944 [2001]). *The Great Transformation: The Political and Economic Origins of Our Time*. Boston, MA: Beacon Press.

Polanyi, K. (1947a). On belief in economic determinism. *Sociological Review*, *39*(2), 96–112.

Polanyi, K. (1947b). Our obsolete market mentality. *Commentary*, *3*(1), 109–117.

Polanyi, K. (1957). The economy as instituted process. In K. Polany, C. M. Arensberg, & H. W. Pearson (Eds), *Trade and Market in the Early Empires: Economies in History and Theory* (pp. 243–270). Chicago, IL: Henry Regnery.

Polanyi, K. (1977a). The economistic fallacy. *Review (Fernand Braudel Center)*, *1*(1), 9–18.

Polanyi, K. (1977b). *The Livelihood of Man*. New York: Academic Press.

Popper, K. (1935 [2005]). *The Logic of Scientific Discovery*. London: Routledge.

Popper, K. (1944). *The Poverty of Historicism*. London: ARK Paperbacks.

Popper, K. (1967). La rationalité et le statut du principe de rationalité. In E. Claassen (Ed.), *Les fondements philosophiques des systèmes économiques* (pp. 142–150). Paris: Payot.

Press, S. J. (1967). A compound events model for security prices. *Journal of Business*, *40*(3), 317–335.

Putnam, H. (1975). The meaning of "meaning." In K. Gunderson (Ed.), *Minnesota Studies in the Philosophy of Science, Volume VII: Language, Mind, and Knowledge* (pp. 131–193). Minneapolis, MN: University of Minnesota Press.

Putnam, H. (2002). *The Collapse of the Fact/value Dichotomy*. Cambridge, MA: Harvard University Press.

Quine, W. V. O. (1951). Two dogmas of empiricism. *Philosophical Review*, *60*, 20–43.

Quine, W. V. O. (1958). La mythe de la signification. In B. Ambroise & S. Laugier (Eds), *Philosophie du langage. Signification, vérité et réalité* (pp. 147–194). Paris.

Quine, W. V. O. (1960). *Word and Object*. Cambridge, MA: MIT Press.

Quine, W. V. O. (1963). *From a Logical Point of View*. New York: Harper Torchbooks.

Quine, W. V. O. (1968). Ontological relativity. *Journal of Philosophy*, *65*(7), 185–212.

Quine, W. V. O. (1969). *Ontological Relativity and Other Essays*. New York: Columbia University Press.

Radcliffe-Richards, J., Daar, A. S., Guttmann, R. D., Hoffenberg, R., Kennedy, I., Lock, M., Sells, R. A., & Tinley, N. (1998). The case for allowing kidney sales. *The Lancet, 351*, 1950–1951.

Radin, M. J. (1996). *Contested Commodities*. Cambridge, MA: Harvard University Press.

Rapaport, F. (1986). The case for a living emotionally related international kidney donor exchange registry. *Transplantation Proceedings, 18*(3), 2–9.

Regnault, J. (1863). *Calcul des chances et philosophie de la bourse*. Paris: Mallet-Bachelier et Castel.

Ricardo, D. (1809). The high price of bullion. In P. Sraffa (Ed.), *The Works and Correspondence of David Ricardo*, Vol. III (pp. 47–127). Cambridge: Cambridge University Press.

Robbins, L. (1932). *An Essay on the Nature and Significance of Economic Science*. London: Macmillan.

Roberts, H. V. (1959). Stock-market "patterns" and financial analysis: methodological suggestions. *Journal of Finance, 14*(1), 1–10.

Roberts, J. (2012). Poststructuralism against poststructuralism: actor-network theory, organizations and economic markets. *European Journal of Social Theory, 15*(1), 35–53.

Roscoe, P. (2016). Performativity matters: economic description as moral problem. In I. Boldyrev & E. Svetlova (Eds), *Enacting the Dismal Science: New Perspectives on the Performativity of Economics* (pp. 131–150). New York: Palgrave Macmillan.

Roscoe, P. (2013). On the possibility of organ markets and the performativity of economics. *Journal of Cultural Economy, 6*(4), 386–401.

Rosenthal, R., & Jacobson, L. (1968). *Pygmalion in the Classroom: Teacher Expectations and Students Intellectual Development*. New York: Holt, Rinehart & Winston.

Rosser, B. (2004). Epistemological implications of economic complexity. *Annals of the Japan Association for the Philosophy of Science, 13*, 45–57.

Roth, A. (2002). The economist as engineer: game theory, experimentation, and computation as tool for design economics. *Econometrica, 70*(4), 1341–1378.

Roth, A. (2007). Repugnance as a constraint on markets. *Journal of Economic Perspectives, 21*(3), 37–58.

Roth, A., & Peranson, E. (1999). The redesign of the matching market for American physicians: some engineering aspects of economic design. *American Economic Review, 89*(4), 748–780.

Roth, A., Sönmez, T., & Ünver, U. (2004). Kidney exchange. *Quarterly Journal of Economics, 119*(2), 457–488.

Roth, A., Sönmez, T., & Ünver, U. (2005). A kidney exchange clearinghouse in New England. *American Economic Review, 95*(2), 376–380.

Roth, A., Sönmez, T., Ünver, U., Delmonico, F. L., & Saidman, S. L. (2008). Utilizing list exchange and nondirected donation through "chain" paired kidney donations. *American Journal of Transplantation, 6*, 2694–2705.

Rubinstein, A. (1982). Perfect equilibrium in a bargaining model. *Econometrica, 50*(1), 97–109.

Rubinstein, M. (1985). Nonparametric tests of alternative option pricing models using all reported trades and quotes on the 30 most active CBOE option classes from August 23, 1976 through August 31, 1978. *Journal of Finance, 40*(2), 455–480.

Russell, B. (1943 [2009]). An outline of intellectual rubbish. In R. E. Egner & L. E. Denonn (Eds), *The Basic Writings of Bertrand Russell* (pp. 45–71). London: Routledge.

Sachs, J. (2005). *The End of Poverty: Economic Possibilities for Our Time*. New York: Penguin Press.

Saidman, S., Roth, A., Sönmez, T., Ünver, U., & Delmonico, F. (2006). Increasing the opportunity of live kidney donation by matching for two- and three-way exchanges. *Transplantation, 81*(5), 773–782.

Saldanha, A. (2003). Actor-network theory and critical sociology. *Critical Sociology, 29*(3), 419–432.

Sambuc, C. (2012). L'efficacité du marché des organes. *Revue Économique, 63*(1), 51–67.

Sambuc, C. (2013). Les relations familiales, apports à l'analyse économique des transplantations d'organes. *Revue française de socio-économie, 11*, 181–200.

Samuelson, P. (1938). A note on the pure theory of consumers' behaviour. *Economica, 6*, 344–356.

Samuelson, P. (1948). *Economics: An Introductory Analysis*. New York: McGraw-Hill.

Samuelson, P. (1952). Probability, utility, and the independence axiom. *Econometrica, 20*, 670–678.

Samuelson, P. (1954). The Transfer problem and transport costs, II: analysis of effects of trade impediments. *Economic Journal, 64*(254), 264–289.

Samuelson, P. (1965a). A rational theory of warrant pricing. *Industrial Management Review, 6*, 13–39.

Samuelson, P. (1965b). Proof that properly anticipated prices fluctuate randomly. *Industrial Management Review, 6*, 41–49.

Samuelson, P. (1973). Proof that properly discounted present value of assets vibrate randomly. *Bell Journal of Economics, 4*, 369–374.

Samuelson, P. (1977). St Petersburg paradoxes defanged dissected and historically described. *Journal of Economic Literature, 15*, 24–55.

Santos, A. C., & Rodrigues, J. (2009). Economics as social engineering? Questioning the performativity thesis. *Cambridge Journal of Economics, 33*(5), 985–1000.

Sargent, T. J. (1993). *Bounded Rationality in Macroeconomics*. Oxford: Clarendon Press.

Satz, D. (2008). The moral limits of markets: the case of human kidneys. *Proceedings of the Aristotelian Society, 108*(3), 269–288.

Satz, D. (2012). *Why Some Things Should Not Be for Sale*. New York: Oxford University Press.

Savage, L. (1954). *The Foundations of Statistics*. New York: Dover Publications.

Schabacker, R. W. (1930). *Stock Market Theory and Practice*. New York: B. C. Forbes.

Schelling, T. (1960). *The Strategy of Conflict*. Cambridge, MA: Harvard University Press.

Schelling, T. (1971). Dynamic models of segregation. *Journal of Mathematical Sociology, 1*(2), 143–186.

Schotter, A. (Ed.). (1976). *Selected Economic Writings of Oskar Morgenstern*. New York: New York University Press.

Schütz, A. (1954). Concept and theory formation in the social sciences. *Journal of Philosophy, 51*(9), 257–273.

Schwering, K.-L. (1998). *Don et incorporation. Les enjeux psychiques de la transplantation*. Louvain: Université catholique de Louvain.

Searle, J. R. (1969). *Speech Acts*. Cambridge University Press.

Searle, J. R. (1995). *The Construction of Social Reality*. New York: Free Press.

Searle, J. R. (2010). *Making the Social World*. New York: Oxford University Press.

Sen, A. (1993). Internal consistency of choice. *Econometrica, 61*(3), 495–521.

Sent, E.-M. (1998). Sargent and the unbearable lightness of symmetry. *Journal of Economic Methodology, 5*(1), 93–114.

Sent, E.-M. (1999). The randomness of rational expectations: a perspective on Sargent's early incentives. *European Journal of the History of Economic Thought, 6*(3), 439–471.

Sent, E.-M. (2001). Sargent's symmetry saga: ontological versus technical constraints. In U. Mäki (Ed.), *The Economic World View* (pp. 335–358). Cambridge: Cambridge University Press.

Sent, E.-M. (2002). How (not) to influence people: the contrary tale of John F. Muth. *History of Political Economy, 34*(2), 291–319.

Shapley, L., & Scarf, H. (1974). On cores and indivisibility. *Journal of Mathematical Economics, 1*(1), 23–28.

Sharpe, W. (1963). A simplified model for portfolio analysis. *Management Science, 9*(2), 277–293.

Sharpe, W. (1964). Capital asset prices: a theory of market equilibrium under conditions of risk. *Journal of Finance, 19*(3), 425–442.

Shiller, R. (2000). *Irrational Exuberance.* Princeton, NJ: Princeton University Press.

Simon, H. A. (1954). Bandwagon and underdog effects and the possibility of election prediction. *Public Opinion Quarterly, 18*(3), 245–253.

Simon, H. A. (1962). The architecture of complexity. *Proceedings of the American Philosophical Society, 106*(6), 467–482.

Simon, H. A. (1982). "Accurate predictions and fixed point theorems": comments. *Social Science Information, 21*, 605–626.

Simon, H. A. (1996). *The Science of the Artificial.* Cambridge, MA: MIT Press.

Singer, P. (1973). Altruism and commerce: a defence of Titmuss against Arrow. *Philosophy and Public Affairs, 2*(3), 312–320.

Skinner, Q. (1970). Conventions and the understanding of speech acts. *Philosophical Quarterly, 20*(79), 118–138.

Skinner, Q. (2002). *Visions of Politics, Volume I: Regarding Method.* Cambridge: Cambridge University Press.

Smart, J. J. C. (1959). Sensations and brain processes. *Philosophical Review, 68*(2), 141–156.

Smelers, N. J., & Swedberg, R. (Eds). (2005). *The Handbook of Economic Sociology.* Princeton, NJ: Princeton University Press.

Smit, J. P., Buekens, F., & Plessis, S. du. (2011). What is money? An alternative to Searle's institutional facts. *Economics and Philosophy, 27*, 1–22.

Solow, R. M. (1971). Blood and thunder. *Yale Law Journal, 80*(8), 1696–1711.

Stabile, D. R. (2005). *Forerunners of Modern Financial Economics: A Random Walk in the History of Economic Thought.* Cheltenham: Edward Elgar.

Staszak, J.-F. (2000). Prophéties autoréalisatrices et géographie. *Espace géographique, 29*(2), 105–119.

Steiner, P. (2001a). Don de sang et don d'organes: Le marché et les marchandises "fictives". *Revue française de sociologie, 42*(2), 357–374.

Steiner, P. (2001b). The sociology of economic knowledge. *European Journal of Social Theory, 4*(4), 443–458.

Steiner, P. (2005a). *La sociologie de Durkheim.* Paris: La Découverte.

Steiner, P. (2005b). Le marché selon la sociologie économique. *Revue européenne des sciences sociales, 43*(132), 31–64.

Steiner, P. (2005c). Pourquoi la sociologie économique est-elle si développée en France? *L'année sociologique, 55*(2), 391–415.

Steiner, P. (2007). Karl Polanyi, Viviana Zelizer et la relation marché–société. *Revue du Mauss, 29*, 197–220.

Steiner, P. (2010a). Gift-giving or market? *Journal of Cultural Economy, 3*(2), 243–259.

Steiner, P. (2010b). *La transplantation d'organes. Un commerce nouveau entre les êtres humains*. Paris: Gallimard.

Steiner, P. (2012). Religion et économie chez Durkheim. *Archives des sciences sociales des religions, 159*, 247–263.

Steiner, P. (2016). *Donner . . . une histoire de l'altruisme*. Paris: Presses Universitaires de France.

Steiner, P., & Vatin, F. (Eds). (2009). *Traité de sociologie économique*. Paris: Presses Universitaires de France.

Stephan, A. (2002). Emergentism, irreducibility, and downward causation. *Grazer Philosophische Studien, 65*, 77–93.

Stigler, S. M. (1990). *The History of Statistics: The Measurement of Uncertainty before 1900*. Cambridge, MA: Harvard University Press.

Strawson, P. F. (1954). Critical notice of Wittgenstein's philosophical investigations, *63*(249), 70–99.

Strawson, P. F. (1966). *The Bounds of Sense*. London: Methuen.

Sugden, R. (1986). *The Economics of Rights, Co-operation and Welfare*. Oxford: Basil Blackwell.

Sugden, R. (2000a). Credible worlds: the status of theoretical models in economics. *Journal of Economic Methodology*, 7(1), 1–31.

Sugden, R. (2000b). Team preferences. *Economics and Philosophy, 16*, 175–204.

Sugden, R. (2005). Why rationality is not a consequence of Hume theory of choice. *European Journal of the History of Economic Thought, 12*(1), 113–118.

Sunstein, C. R., & Thaler, R. H. (2003). Libertarian paternalism is not an oxymoron. *University of Chicago Law Review, 70*(4), 1159–1202.

Sunstein, C. R., & Thaler, R. H. (2008). *Nudge: Improving Decisions about Health, Wealth and Happiness*. New York: Penguin Books.

Svetlova, E. (2012). On the performative power of financial models. *Economy and Society, 41*(3), 418–434.

Svetlova, E. (2016). Performativity and emergence of institutions. In I. Boldyrev & E. Svetlova (Eds), *Enacting the Dismal Science: New Perspectives on the Performativity of Economics* (pp. 183–200). New York: Palgrave Macmillan.

Swedberg, R. (1994). Markets as social structure. In N. J. Smelers & R. Swedberg (Eds), *The Handbook of Economic Sociology*, 2nd ed. (pp. 85–97). Princeton, NJ: Princeton University Press.

Swedberg, R. (1998). *Max Weber and the Idea of Economic Sociology*. Princeton, NJ: Princeton University Press.

Swedberg, R. (2005). Markets in society. In N. J. Smelers & R. Swedberg (Eds), *The Handbook of Economic Sociology*, 2nd ed. (pp. 233–253). Princeton, NJ: Princeton University Press.

Teichmoeller, J. (1971). A note on the distribution of stock price changes. *Journal of the American Statistical Association, 66*(334), 282–284.

Telser, L. G. (1955). Safety first and hedging. *Review of Economic Studies, 23*(1), 1–16.

Thaler, R. H., & Benartzi, S. (2004). Save more tomorrow: using behavioral economics to increase employee saving. *Journal of Political Economy, 112*(S1), 164–187.

This, I. (1994). La construction d'un concept, des prophéties autoréalisatrices de R. K. Merton. *Économie et société, Série PE, 19*(4), 161–199.

This, I. (1996). Problèmes épistémologiques liés à l'autoréalisation des théories et des prévisions économiques. *Revue économiques, 47*(3), 555–565.

This, I. (1998). Le concept d'autoréalisation: de la sociologie à l'économie. *Social Science Information, 37*(2), 255–273.

This, I. (2006). Autoréalisation et communication en économie. *Revue Hermès, 44*, 191–197.

Thompson, E. (1993). *Customs in Common: Studies in Traditional Popular Culture*. New York: The New Press.

Titmuss, R. (1970). *The Gift Relationship: From Human Blood to Social Policy*. London: Allen and Unwin.

Tobin, J. (1958). Liquidity preference as behavior toward risk. *Review of Economic Studies, 67*, 65–86.

Tönnies, F. (1912 [2001]). *Community and Civil Society*, Ed. Jose Harris. Cambridge: Cambridge University Press.

Treynor, J. L. (1962). Toward a theory of market value of risky assets. In R. A. Korajczyk (Ed.), *Asset Pricing and Portfolio Performance: Models, Strategy and Performance Metrics* (pp. 15–22). London: Risk Books.

Treynor, J. L. (1965). How to rate management of investment funds. *Harvard Business Review, 43*, 63–75.

Treynor, J. L., & Black, F. (1973). How to use security analysis to improve portfolio selection. *Journal of Business, 46*(1), 66–86.

Treynor, J. L., & Mazuy, K. (1966). Can mutual funds outguess the market? *Harvard Business Review, 44*, 131–136.

Trigg, A. B. (2001). Veblen, Bourdieu, and conspicuous consumption. *Journal of Economic Issues, 35*(1), 99–115.

Trompette, P. (2008). *Le marché des défunts*. Paris: Presses de Science – Po.

Tversky, A., & Kahneman, D. (1974). Judgment under uncertainty: heuristics and biases. *Science, 185*(4157), 1124–1131.

Tversky, A., & Kahneman, D. (1981). The framing of decisions and the psychology of choice. *Science, 211*(4481), 453–458.

Tversky, A., & Kahneman, D. (1983). Choices, value, and frames. *American Psychologist, 39*(4), 341–350.

Tversky, A., & Kahneman, D. (1986). Rational choice and the framing of decisions. *Journal of Business, 59*(4), S251–S278.

Uzzi, B. (1996). The sources and consequences of embeddedness for the economic performance of organizations: the network effect. *American Sociological Review, 61*, 674–698.

Van de Vijver, G. (1997). Emergence et explication. *Intellectica, 25*(2), 7–23.

Vandenberghe, F. (2007). Une ontologie réaliste pour la sociologie: système, morphogenèse et collectifs. *Social Science Information, 46*(3), 487–542.

Vatin, F. (2008). L'esprit d'ingénieur: pensée calculatoire et éthique économique. *Revue de socio-économie, 1*(1), 131–152.

Veblen, T. (1899). *The Theory of the Leisure Class*. New York: Macmillan.

Veblen, T. (1914). *The Instinct of Workmanship, and the State of the Industrial Arts*. London: Macmillan.

Veblen, T. (2006). *The Place of Science in Modern Civilization*. New Brunswick, NJ: Transaction.

Venn, J. (1866). *Logic of Chance: An Essay on the Foundations and Province of the Theory of Probability, with Especial Reference to Its Application to Moral and Social Science*. London: Macmillan.

Von Neumann, J., & Morgenstern, O. (1944). *Theory of Games and Economic Behavior*. Princeton, NJ: Princeton University Press.

Von Neumann, J., & Morgenstern, O. (1947). *Theory of Games and Economic Behavior*, 2nd ed. Princeton, NJ: Princeton University Press.

Wallis, B., Samy, K., Roth, A., & Rees, M. (2011). Kidney paired donation. *Nephrology Dialysis Transplantation, 26*(7), 2091–3099.

Walliser, B. (2011). *Comment raisonnent les économistes. Les fonctions des modèles*. Paris: Odile Jacob.

Walter, C. (2010). Le phénomène leptokurtique. In C. Walter (Ed.), *Nouvelles normes financières* (pp. 59–77). Paris: Springer.

Walter, C. (2013). *Le modèle de marche au hasard en finance*. Paris: Economica.

Weber, M. (1904–1905 [2001]). *The Protestant Ethic and the Spirit of Capitalism*. London: Routledge.

Weber, M. (1921 [1978]). *Economy and Society: An Outline of Interpretative Sociology*. Berkeley, CA: University of California Press.

Whittle, A., & Spicer, A. (2008). Is actor network theory critique? *Organization Studies, 29*(4), 611–629.

Williams, B. (1985). *Ethics and the Limits of Philosophy*. London: Routledge.

Winner, L. (1993). Upon opening the black box and finding it empty: social constructivism and the philosophy of technology. *Science, Technology, and Human Values, 18*(3), 362–378.

Wittgenstein, L. (1953). *Philosophical Investigations*. Oxford: Basil Blackwell.

Wittgenstein, L. (1958). *Blue and Brown Books*. Oxford: Blackwell.

Working, H. (1934). A random-difference series for use in the analysis of time series. *Journal of the American Statistical Association, 29*, 11–24.

Working, H. (1956). New ideas and methods for prices research. *Journal of Farm Economics, 38*(5), 1427–1436.

Zelizer, V. (1979). *Morals and Markets: The Development of Life Insurance in the United States*. New Brunswick, NJ: Transaction.

Zelizer, V. (1985). *Pricing the Priceless Child: The Changing Social Value of Children*. New York: Basic Books.

Zelizer, V. (1997). *The Social Meaning of Money: Pin Money, Paychecks, Poor Relief, and Other Currencies*. Princeton, NJ: Princeton University Press.

Zelizer, V. (2005). *The Purchase of Intimacy*. Princeton, NJ: Princeton University Press.

Zelizer, V. (2011). *Economic Lives: How Culture Shapes the Economy*. Princeton, NJ: Princeton University Press.

Index

For Product Safety Concerns and Information please contact our EU representative GPSR@taylorandfrancis.com Taylor & Francis Verlag GmbH, Kaufingerstraße 24, 80331 München, Germany